Flickering of Light in the Midst of a Stormy Life

By
DeBorah Kithcart Washington
Marshall Barrow

Autobiography of an Ordinary Person
Who Is Surviving an Unusual Stormy Life

Copyright @ 2018 DeBorah Barrow

All rights reserved. No portion of this book may be reproduced in any form without permission from the author, except as permitted by U.S. copyright law or for the use of brief quotations in a book review. For permissions contact: DeBorah Barrow at www.kithcartllc@gmail.com

Based on my best recollections all the events, locales and conversations in this book are true. Although I did not represent conversations word-for-word, unless the text is italics, I have written the book in a way that recalls the feelings and meanings of what was said or done, and in all instances the essence of the situation is accurate. Some names have been omitted to protect the privacy of the people involved.

Scripture quotations marked (KJV) are taken from the King James Version of the Holy Bible.

Scripture quotations marked (AMP) are taken from the Amplified Bible, Copyright @ 1954, 1958, 1962, 1964, 1965, 1987 by The Lockman Foundation. Used by permission. (www.lockman.org)

Scripture quotations marked (AMPC) are taken from the (Amplified Bible, Classic Edition Copyright © 1954, 1958, 1962, 1964, 1965, 1987 by The Lockman Foundation. Used by permission. (www.lockman.org)

Scripture quotations marked (NIrV) are taken from the Holy Bible, New International Reader's Version®, NIrV® Copyright © 1995, 1996, 1998, 2014 by Biblica, Inc.™ Used by permission of Zondervan. All rights reserved worldwide. www.zondervan.com The "NIrV" and "New International Reader's Version" are trademarks registered in the United States Patent and Trademark Office by Biblica, Inc.™

Scripture quotations marked (NIV) are taken from the Holy Bible, New International Version®, NIV® Copyright ©1973, 1978, 1984, 2011 by Biblica, Inc.® Used by permission of Zondervan. All rights reserved worldwide. (www.zondervan.com)

Scripture quotations are from the ESV® Bible (The Holy Bible, English Standard Version®), copyright © 2001 by Crossway, a publishing ministry of Good News Publishers. Used by permission. All rights reserved.

Scripture quotations marked (NLT) are taken from the Holy Bible, New Living Translation, copyright ©1996, 2004, 2015 by Tyndale House Foundation. Used by permission of Tyndale House Publishers, Inc., Carol Stream, Illinois 60188. All rights reserved.

Scripture quotations marked (NKJV) are taken from the New King James Version®. Copyright © 1982 by Thomas Nelson. Used by permission. All rights reserved.

Printed in the United States of America By CreateSpace
First Printing, 2018
ISBN-13: 978-1718644366
ISBN-10: 1718644361
www.deborahstory.com

Dedication

This book is dedicated in remembrance of my beloved Momma, Ruth Naomi Kithcart, who gave me life and filled it with love, inspiration, and support until she took her last breath. My hope is my Momma is smiling down on me. To my beautiful daughters, Ivy and Sylvia, who are the loves and joys of my life, I thank both of you for loving me unconditionally through sunshine, and especially through the storms that at time also adversely affected your lives. I thank John Barnes, Maurie Nunn, Nicole Burton, and Elise Harrison for helping make this book a reality. Donna Davis, my God-given sister, who I have only known for three years, you will never realize how much our daily telephone conversations over the past two years helped me make it through many cloudy days as I strived to finish this book. Much appreciation to all my other family members and friends for loving, supporting and helping me throughout my journey through life. Lastly to anyone who is or have experienced a stormy life similar to mine, may you read something in this book that will encourage and motivate you to see a flicker of light in any life storm that comes your way.

Table of Contents

Chapter One -- Early Life 1
Chapter Two – Herman Washington..47
Chapter Three -- One Bad Decision Forever Altered My Life 126
Chapter Four -- Life Will Never Be the Same 149
Chapter Five -- Dark Storms Continue 164
Chapter Six -- Sylvester Marshall..183
Chapter Seven –1985 the Year of Unthinkable Storms 208
Chapter Eight – Incarceration 231
Chapter Nine – Home Sweet Home 260
Chapter Ten – Lots of Sunshine Then Abruptly a Storm......................277
Chapter Eleven – When Blessed Be a Blessing to Others 305
Chapter Twelve – Unexpected Healing and Adversity..........................334
Chapter Thirteen -- Blessed Despite it All..345
Chapter Fourteen – Pinnacles and Nadirs of Life 364
Chapter Fifteen – Went Too Far Stayed Too Long...............................385
Chapter Sixteen –Jerome Barrow..401
Chapter Seventeen -- Ivy and Aaron..474
Chapter Eighteen –Blended Families..485
Chapter Nineteen -- Accepting the Reality of My Third Marriage 499
Chapter Twenty -- Living on My Own 510
Chapter Twenty-One – Trying Again 528
Chapter Twenty-Two — Reliving a Previous Storms 553
Chapter Twenty-Three – In Need of Prayer and a Lot More Help 564
Chapter Twenty-Four – Life Changing Events......................................588
Chapter Twenty-Five -- Favor in the Middle of Thunderstorms 596
Chapter Twenty-Six – All the Time God Was Working It Out 604
Conclusion 622

"Flicker of Light in the Midst of My Stormy Life"
Chapter One -- Early Life

Beginning this transparent journey of my life story you can see from the book cover I am an ordinary person that has endured a life filled with inconceivable, unforeseen and life altering emotional storms. Having lived in Cleveland, Ohio my entire life, the weather is subject to abruptly change without any warning. Several times I would go out on a clear sunny day, only to be totally drenched from a thunderstorm that suddenly came from nowhere. If that was not strange enough, several times I would be driving on the southeast side of Cleveland on a clear winter day. Then by the time I reached the northeast side of town, I would be in the midst of a snow storm. The unpredictable changes in the weather in Cleveland always amazed me. Now over sixty years old I think how my journey in life is comparable to the weather in my hometown. One moment my life would be glowing in the sunshine. Seconds later without warning a dark storm would arise. The effects from both weather and personal storms can range from minor to colossal damage. The weather storms can result in damage to property, personal injuries or even loss of life. Although I have never personally faced a major storm, I have seen the after effects of two major storms. The first one happened on April 3, 1974, when my sister, Linda Faye was attending Wilberforce University and the city of Xenia, Ohio and its surrounding areas were hit by a devastating tornado that left over thirty-four people dead. My family was grateful that Linda Faye was blessed not to sustain any injuries. A few months later our Momma and I visited Linda Faye. When I saw the destruction caused by the tornado I knew it was a miracle that there were not more fatalities. Many years later in July 2005, I attended the Full Gospel Convention in New Orleans. I remember Bishop Morton preaching a sermon about *a storm is brewing*. Weeks later, New Orleans was hit by Katrina one of the deadliest and destructive hurricanes in the United States. One year later in 2006, when the Full Gospel Convention was held again in New Orleans, for the second time I saw the after math of a weather disaster as I rode through many of the areas affected by Katrina. To my surprise and disbelief, a year later the destruction remained very visible. I could only imagine how the areas looked immediately after the hurricane.

The personal storms in my life where similar to weather storms. These storms of my life ranged from mild to severe and caused some type of mental damage that left emotional scars. Depending on the intensity of my storm, the mental damage varied. During my mild storms, the mental damage would be minor to moderate, and the emotional scars usually were minimal which I could mend with prayer, self-motivation, and perseverance. During my more severe life storms, the mental damages were intensive and resulted in immeasurable painful emotional scars. These storms would cause my life to be drastically shattered with never-ending pain and sorrow and the emotional scars caused could only be temporarily eased with spiritual intervention. Different from the scars from my minor storms, the severe storms left permanent emotional scars that were constantly subject to being reopened.

Ringing absolutely true throughout each storm in my life was to forgive or seek forgiveness. Forgiving and seeking forgiveness was not a problem for me because I knew without forgiving, how could I expect to be forgiven. My problem was I could not forget the storms and the aftermath of the emotional scars. Because if I forgot what happened during the storm, I would not be able to learn and remember the life lessons the storm and emotional scars had taught me. My scars from self-inflicted storms that affected innocent people I could not forget because remembering those storms helped to prevent me from repeating the actions that started the storms. The storms and scars of my life caused by the actions of other people were unforgettable since each one taught me not to be vulnerable to the circumstances that allowed those storms and scars to occur. Therefore, forgetting the scars from my stormy life was not a choice for me.

Living a life filled with several terrifying unforeseen emotional storms, there were times when I was the harmed as the victim, and other times they were self-inflicted where I was the offender that caused detriment not only to myself but to the victims, loved ones, acquaintances, and innocent bystanders. At this stage in my life, I finally realize that regardless of the type of mental storm there were always flickers of light including grace, mercy, love, compassion, forgiveness, and many more from the Almighty to help me endure. It is my hope and prayer that by reading how my flickers of light from God brought me through horrific storms you will be encouraged to seek flickers of light throughout the storms of your life.

Conception. I was born on August 26, 1957 in Cleveland, Ohio. My birth certificate lists the name of mother, Ruth Naomi Kithcart.

The name of father states, *Unknown*. Eventually, I would learn why my father's name was not listed on my birth certificate. Throughout my life, Momma, together with other relatives, shared stories with me how she and Linda Faye moved from Gastonia, North Carolina to Cleveland, Ohio. Momma was about 25 years old and Linda Faye about five years old when they arrived in Cleveland. Momma and Linda Faye were living with friends of the Kithcart family, Bishop and Mrs. Williford. Bishop and Mrs. Williford were co-pastors of the St. James Righteous Church of God. Their son, Walter Timothy (Tim) Williford also lived with them. It was the intention of Momma to reside with the Willifords until she secured employment and a home for her and Linda Faye. During my childhood I remember Linda Faye and Momma's sister, Macel, who I called Auntie, would tease me saying Tim was my father. I was not sure why they would say this because except for a few occasions I never had any contact with Tim. He also had never treated me like his daughter. Then when I was fourteen years old, Momma abruptly told me how I was conceived. Unfortunately, that day I learned the beginning of my life started in turmoil in 1956 when Momma was impregnated after being raped by Tim. Momma told me the details of how one-night Tim returned to the house drunk and came into the bedroom she and Linda Faye shared and raped her. That was the night of my conception. Later Auntie, who had moved to Cleveland from Gastonia shortly after my birth, also gave me details about Momma being raped. When I asked Linda Faye if she knew about Tim raping Momma, to my surprise Linda Faye said she was laying in the bed right next to Momma the night

Tim came into the room and raped Momma. On top of being told how I was conceived, to add more dismay, I learned Linda Faye also was conceived by rape. Auntie and a few more family members also told me what happened to Momma when she was attending college in Winston-Salem, North Carolina. Momma went on a date with a man named Jimmy, a friend of her cousin, Hezekiah. After finding out what Jimmy had done to Momma, her father, Johnson Kithcart, uncle, and cousins went to the college to confront Jimmy and bring Momma back home. Hearing how my sister and I were conceived became a mental storm for me. Later in life I realized there definitely were flickers of light that helped not only me but my Momma with this mental storm. First the flicker of light was the mercy of God that eventually enabled Momma and me to forgive Tim for raping her. *For if you forgive other people when they sin against you, your heavenly Father will also forgive you,* Matthew 6:14 (NIV). Then despite of everything it was the flicker of light from God that strengthen Momma to be a strong woman who loved, cared for and supported Linda Faye and me in a single-parent household. *To You, O [God] my strength, I will sing praises; For God is my stronghold [my refuge, my protector, my high tower], the God who shows me [steadfast] lovingkindness,* Psalm 59:17 (AMP).

Shortly after my birth I was told, although Momma had secured employment, she was still looking for a place for us to live. During this time, I taken care of by a lady whose name is unknown to me, but I remember because there was an article in the *Cleveland Press* newspaper about how she offered babysitting services to young mothers. The article had a picture of me and another baby standing at the front door looking outside. I believe Linda Faye may still have a copy of that picture. As I understand, Momma never had a relationship with Tim after I was conceived. However, I was told Bishop Williford assured that Tim supported me. My earliest memory of Tim and Bishop Williford are when they drove Momma and me to my first day of school in the fall of 1962. The other memory is one Christmas when Tim gave me a *Cinderella* watch and Linda Faye a gold necklace watch. After Bishop Williford died, for years Tim no longer provided for, visited, or acknowledged me.

My Momma. A loving, beautiful, kind, soft-spoken, compassionate, hard-working, strong black woman that loved the Lord and Savior Jesus Christ is how I describe my Momma. As a child, I fondly remember the love, hugs, and kisses from Momma. My first memory of how Momma supported Linda Faye and me, was by diligently working as a housekeeper and babysitter for several Jewish families in a suburb of greater Cleveland. The first home I remember residing in was an apartment located upstairs from the Willifords church located on 72nd and Kinsman Avenue. There were five rooms including two bedrooms. Momma and I shared one of the bedrooms, while Linda Faye had her own room. Momma did her best to take care of us, and I have no memory of ever being homeless, without food, clothing, or utilities. I could not even tell we were poor. In fact, I would wonder why Momma would often get upset with me for inviting my friends to dinner or teachers to lunch. I now realize it was because she was barely feeding us. Living above the St. James church we regularly attended church services. Service was held on Sunday mornings and evenings as well as during the weekdays. Momma was an ordained minister and she preached every fifth Sunday. I remember people looking forward to Momma preaching because she was not long winded. My fondest memory of attending St. James was at the age of five when I learned and quoted the 23rd Psalm to the congregation.

Another childhood memory I was between the age of four and five years old when Momma needed to return to North Carolina because her father (my Grandfather Johnson) was gravely ill. I was told Bishop Williford, who was good friends with Grandfather Johnson, drove us to North Carolina to visit Grandfather Johnson. My recollections of being in North Carolina are being in a room banging on a piano while Grandfather Johnson laid in the bed, eventually one of the family members came in the room to take me out. The second memory was being too scared to use the outhouse that Momma had to place a tin can at the back door for me to use. I cherish those two memories, but often wonder why those are the only two memories from that trip.

In mid-1963, an unexpected storm began when Momma had a mental breakdown which affected our family. It started with Momma wandering around the house and neighborhood talking to herself and acting unusual. I can still remember the day Momma was taken away to the mental hospital. It began with Momma screaming out the windows and no one being able to get her to stop, then men in a large van took Momma away to the mental institution. I later learned that was the first time Momma underwent shock treatment. Exactly who took care of Linda Faye and me while Momma was in the institution the first time is unclear. But I do remember living a brief period of time with a nice couple, Mr. and Mrs. Panell who treated us good. Several weeks later Momma returned home in her typical loving, kind, and gentle nature. Following the initial nerve breakdown, like clockwork every five years Momma would have another breakdown. Each time Momma was admitted to the mental institution she received shock treatments and was prescribed various medications. During the breakdowns, not only was I very heartbroken to see Momma suffer, it hurt me to hear people talking about Momma. Even at such an early age I would cry because I could not make Momma feel better and stop people from laughing and making fun of her. The older I became the more difficult it was to see Momma have the breakdowns and be hospitalized. It was emotionally upsetting and draining to abruptly witness her behavior and personality change while I stood helplessly by unable to help Momma. I now realize even during those difficult storms there were flickers of light. First there was mercy from God that Momma was never permanently institutionalized. Typically, within a few weeks Momma would be back to herself and would not have another breakdown for several years. The other flicker of light was through the love of God, family members and friends, particularly the Panells and Auntie, made sure Linda Faye and I were never placed in foster homes while Momma was hospitalized. Later when Linda Faye was over eighteen, she would care for me with the help sometimes from Auntie and our neighbors, the Hodges and Thomas.

The most awesome flicker came many years later in 1984 when God answered our prayers with blessing Momma to be accurately diagnosed with, and treated for, schizophrenia.

Molestation. Although the initial molestation occurred when I was about five years old, it was not until around 16 years old that I realized I had been molested. At that time, the images came vividly back to me, of going to the house of our next-door neighbors, the Hamlets, to see if my friends could come outside to play. I knocked on the door. A few seconds later their teenage cousin opened the door. I asked him if my friends were home. He did not answer, but took my hand leading me inside the house. The house was quiet, and I did not see anyone but him. Still holding my hand, he led me to the bedroom of my friend's parents where he handed me a piece of candy. As I began to eat the candy, he laid me down on the bed. He pulled down my panties and began to rub something between my leg, which I realized at the age of sixteen it was his penis rubbing against my vagina. I just laid there, eating the candy until he stopped. My memories end there. I am unable to recall what happened after he stopped. I cannot even recall his name or if I ever saw him after that day. Only thing I can see is a silhouette of him and remember plainly what he did to me. I often wonder why this happened. Who was the boy? Where is he now? Does he remember what he did to me?

The second molestation occurred about three years later. We had moved into our second home on Kinsman Avenue. There were two children, Dolly and Kenney that lived downstairs. I was one year older than Dolly and Kenney was two years older than me. One day,

Kenney called me to the back stairway that connected our three-family home. I clearly remember Kenney pushing me against the wall. He pulled my panties down, took out something, what again I eventually realized was his penis, and began rubbing it against me. Soon I felt something wet running down my legs, then Kenney suddenly stopped and ran down the stairs to his house. Once more, not knowing what had happened to me, I simply went back into my home. I do not recall Kenney ever touching me again. Nor did either of us mention the incident. A few years later Kenney and his family moved to California. For a second time, I did not realize what really happened to me that day until the vision resurfaced when I turned sixteen years old. Like the first offender, I wondered if Kenney knew what he did to me and did either of them molest anyone else? When these two incidents were awakened in my mind, they immediately became a storm in my life. At that time, I wondered why this happened to me when I was only an innocent child. For many years as the memories steadily replayed in my mind, I did become depressed about me being molested. Then I had to concede although the offenders did abuse me, it was the grace of God that protected me from the molesters taking my virginity and that it only occurred the two times. So yes, today I gratefully realize during this storm there still were blessings and a flicker of light from God that He was my stronghold and refuge in the time of a distressful storm. *But as for me, I will sing of Your mighty strength and power; Yes, I will sing joyfully of Your lovingkindness in the morning; For You have been my stronghold and a refuge in the day of my distress*, Psalm 59:16 (AMP).

Over the years the more I became knowledgeable about molestation, I have continued to be unable to comprehend how a person can molest anyone, especially an innocent child. Some people who were not aware I had been molested have said to me if *a child is really molested why don't they say something when it happens*. My reply is, when I was molested, I had no idea what was being done to me because of not knowing about, and never having, sex. As they look at me in shock, I proceed to tell them that it was not until later in life when I became sexually active that it ignited a resounding visual memory of the two times I was molested. I usual end the conversation with I am thankfully that nowadays in most of our societies children and parents are more highly educated on how to detect, prevent, and understand the signs of a child that is a victim to sexual and other abuses. At the end of my conversation, these people usually have a better understanding of the plight of molested victims.

For my loved ones and the many victims of molestation, my heart breaks thinking of the pain you have endured, and I pray for your strength to live with the emotional scarring. To those that are being molested look for a flicker of light to give you grace, mercy, strength, and protection until you are delivered from your assailers.

The Move. In 1966, Momma rented a beautiful residence for us located across the street from a nice park at 9610 Kinsman Avenue. It was in a lovely neighborhood where people of different nationalities resided. It was a large three-family house. The first and second floor units had seven rooms. The third-floor unit was a smaller unit. We stayed in the second-floor unit. I was happy that there were no roaches or mice like our previous home. Kenney and Dolly family stayed in the first-floor unit. There was a Chinese couple staying in the third-floor unit. Linda Faye continued to have her own bedroom, while I still slept with Momma. As I grew older, Momma complained about me being a wild sleeper. When financially able, she bought a twin bed for me that was placed in her room next to the window. I was happy with sleeping right next to the window because I loved looking out the window, especially at night when I would look at the stars and moon. Initially when we moved, Momma had to wait until she got paid to pay the deposit needed for the gas to be connected. Always resourceful, Momma purchased a small charcoal grill to prepare our meals until we were able to use the gas stove. I remember the man living on the third floor looking out the window saying *that food really smells good*. Momma smiled. While I thought it was very funny.

I loved my new school, Boulevard Elementary School. My favorite teachers where Mr. Stewart and Ms. Jordan. Besides being friends with Dolly and Kenney, I became friends with several other children in the neighborhood. From the second through fourth grades one of my best friends was Vernice Randall. By the fifth grade, I met my soon to be best friend for years, Linda Childress (Linda C.). We regularly spent hours at each other's home and would talk on the phone for hours. Many weekends Linda's father would obtain free passes for us to see movies at the downtown Embassy and Hippodrome theaters. When her father could not take us to the theater, we would take the bus. If we were not downtown to see a movie, we would be shopping, eating at the Forum Cafeteria or simple window shop. When window shopping, we would pretend and dream of having the many beautiful items on display. We became inseparable. Many teased that if you saw Linda C., I was not far behind, and vice versa.

With Momma securing more housekeeping jobs she was able to do a few non-essential things for us. The one extra treat I enjoyed the most was going to the hairdresser every three weeks to have my hair washed, hot combed and curled. A lady named Lillian was Momma and my hairdresser, and Olivia was the hairdresser for Linda Faye hairdresser. Although Olivia was fifteen years older than Linda Faye, they became close. Olivia and her husband, James had been married for years, but did not have any children at the time. The closer Olivia and Linda became, she and James considered Linda Fay their god-daughter. Later Olivia introduced Linda Faye and me to her sister Hattie. Hattie had two sons, Jonathan, and Chad with her first husband. She later married James Howard (JD), and they had two sons, Desmond, and Jermaine. Over the years I became close to Hattie, she was like a big sister to me who was by my side through several of my roughest storms.

My Aunts. Momma's sisters begin to visit Cleveland in the mid-1960s. I would always look forward to the visits by Aunt Sue from Providence, Rhode Island, and Aunts Naomi, Elizabeth, and Sarah from North Carolina. Some of their children would often come with them. A few of my cousins that visited us were around my age. We would play all day and stay up late into the night talking. It was exciting for Momma, Linda Faye, and me to have our family members visit. To know I had other family members meant so much to me. In 1965, Momma planned a trip for us to visit Aunt Sue who lived in Providence, Rhode Island. Memories of the visit are vague, except for one. My cousin, Sheila and I went to the last floor of the apartment where we noticed stairs to the rooftop. We climbed up the stair and once on the flat rooftop I thought the hatch door looked like a sliding board. I said, lets slide down the slide. Once we tried to get on the hatch door, of course, it closed. Now we were stuck on the rooftop and afraid about how we were going to get down. I remember hoping we would not have to jump down from the three-story tall apartment building. Even in that moment when I did not know about the wonders of God, we received a flicker of light from God of deliverance when my cousin Kenny came walking towards the apartment. We screamed for him to help us. He said, okay as he ran into the building. Sheila and I was waiting for him to open the hatch door when the next thing we knew Momma and Aunt Sue were opening the hatch door. They snatched us both down from the roof. That day was the first time I remember Momma giving me a spanking. Days with my cousins will always be cherished and even to this day I remain in touch with a few of my cousins, in particularly Jennifer (Jay) Wright, who I am the closest to.

Recognition. Unlike many of my friends during my early childhood years Momma was not able to afford a television. Instead when not playing outside with my friends, I would enjoy my favorite pastime of reading. I loved to read. Books took me away from reality to many wonderful places where people had happy fun-filled lives. I would read while dreaming of one day living happily in one of those beautiful places. For many years Momma, Linda Faye, and I read and listened to the radio for our outlets to the world. The reading and the radio give us insight into other places, people, events of the world and entertainment. At least once or twice a week, I would go to the neighborhood library. Unbeknown to me, the librarian had taken notice of me. One day while at the library she approached me. The kind librarian let me know I had been selected by the librarians to represent the library in the city wide yearly book report contest. She explained contestants were to write a report about why they enjoyed reading books. The report was to also include the favorite author and book of the contestant. The librarian gave me an information packet with instructions for me to give the packet to my parents to complete. Excitedly I went home to tell Momma the good news. When I gave Momma the information, she was very overjoyed. It made me even happier to see Momma this proud of me. At that time, I was too young to realize how much my being selected meant to Momma. It was 1968 with us living in a neighborhood where black people were still the minority. To Momma it was a huge accomplishment to see her little daughter of color be selected to represent the library. When Momma reviewed the information packet it detailed how an awards banquet would be in the large banquet room of the prestigious Higbee's Department store in downtown. Prizes of $50 and $25 would be respectively awarded to 1st and 2nd place winners. Each other contestants would receive a Silver Dollar. The thought of receiving that much money was unbelievable. With the help of the librarian I prepared my report. The day of the awards ceremony, Momma and I dressed in our best clothes and took the bus downtown. Walking into the huge room with lots of tables decorated with beautiful linen, china, glassware, and silverware was like entering into a fairytale from one of my books. There were chandeliers, exquisite carpet, and drapery. Momma and I were in awe with the décor of the room. Then to my amazement there were servers dressed in white and black attire serving the tables. Even more surprising, besides Momma, me and about five other families of color, the other people were Caucasian. When my name was called, Momma was really proud as I walked on stage to receive my Silver Dollar. Arriving back at the table Momma had the biggest smile on her face. Later in life when I realized the social disparity of minorities in America at that time, I realized how much that day meant to Momma.

Earning Money at an Early Age. As a single parent with no financial support from our fathers, Momma was unable to provide Linda Faye and me with an allowance. Instead of complaining, Linda Faye and I found ways to earn money at an early age. On the weekends, Linda Faye babysat for the people Momma and Auntie worked for during the week. The first way I earned money as a child was working for our neighbor, Mrs. Hodges. She and her husband were well-respected in the neighborhood. Mrs. Hodges was a pastor of a small church, a notary public and tax preparer. Of course, at that time I had no idea what type of work a notary public or tax preparer performed. Mrs. Hodges would pay me ten cents to a quarter three times a week to pick up litter from the sidewalks of our street. My second childhood job was being known in the community for selling flower and vegetable seeds. I had read an advertisement in a magazine about how to earn money selling vegetable and flower seeds. Each year I would order and sell the seeds. Once I sold the seeds, I would mail the cost of the seeds to the company. I would use my earnings to buy personal items Momma was unable to afford or to buy small gifts for Christmas and birthdays for Momma and Linda Faye. By twelve, I occasionally babysat for Ms. Barbara who lived next door and one of my school teachers. Linda Faye had started to work in the corner store owned by Jim and Mary (MaeMae) Hamlin. Later I routinely babysat for Ronnie and Lois Hamlin, the son and daughter-in-law of Jim and MaeMae. New tenants, Jackie and Lawrence Johnson had moved into the third-floor unit of our home. When their baby Andre was born, they would periodically ask me to babysit him. Around thirteen years old, I sometimes helped MaeMae and Linda Faye in the corner store. When Linda Faye went to college in Wilberforce, Ohio, Linda C., and I worked in the store until MaeMae closed it in 1975 due to decline in sales. During my junior high school years, I worked through the City of Cleveland Summer Work Program. The program offered summer employment for students from low income families. By the tenth grade during the summer breaks I registered with Kelly Girls Temporary Agency and was assigned to work at various companies doing clerical work.

Holidays. Holidays were extra special occasions for us. Typically, each Memorial Day, Fourth of July and Labor Day, Momma would purchase me an outfit from one of the discount stores, either Jupiter or Woolworth. For Easter Sundays, Momma would dress us in matching mother daughter outfits that she usually purchased from the Aldens dream catalog. My favorite matching outfit was a light blue and yellow cape dress. When Linda Faye and I started complaining about being dressed alike, Momma stopped ordering the look-a-like outfits. Thanksgivings and Christmases were wonderful family times for us. Momma would prepare all the traditional dishes. Somehow, she always managed to have nice gifts for Linda Faye and me. The most unforgettable Christmas occurred when I was ten years old. Momma had been waiting all day for a delivery, but she needed to go grocery shopping before the store closed. During the 1960s grocery stores closed around 6:00 p.m. and where not opened on holidays and Sunday. After waiting long as she could, Momma told me she would be right back. Shortly after she left, the doorbell rang. The deliveryman said he had a delivery for Momma. I told him she was not home. He said he could not return and needed to leave the delivery. I said okay. He went to the truck bringing back a beautiful turquoise bike with a white banana seat and streamers coming from the handle. Walking up the stairs to place the bike on the stair landing the driver said he hoped this was not for me. Shrugging my shoulder in a I do not know motion, he said, okay. After he left, beaming with excitement I jumped on the bike pretending to ride. When Momma returned home she was disappointed to see the bike in the hallway. When she came into the house, Momma said to me, I should have known he would come as soon as I left. Looking at the disappointment on Momma's face, I said the driver told me to stay in the house while he left the delivery in the hallway. Momma glanced with a funny look on her face but did not say anything. I wondered if she believed me. That Christmas morning when I woke to see the bike under the tree, I was even more excited than the day the bike was delivered. How I still cherish the loving memories of my childhood holidays.

A Little Thief. Momma would often send me to Fisher Fazio grocery store to purchase a few items. I would wander through the aisles looking at the different items especially the toys in the little toy section. One day I notice a doll that I really wanted. I planned to save the money earned from picking up the litter to purchase the doll. A few weeks later Momma sent me to the store to buy a few items. For some reason I decided that day the doll was coming home with me even though I did not have any money. After filling the cart with the items Momma wanted, I went to the toy aisle where the doll was on the shelf. I picked up the doll and slid it inside my coat. Before I knew it, a security guard approached me saying, what did you put inside your coat. Scared I tried to run, but he grabbed my arm and took me to a room in the back of the store. A few moments later another man came in the room. It was the store manager, Earl Preston, who as fate would have it he would later in life became my choir director. The security guard told Mr. Preston how I tried to steal the doll. Mr. Preston told the security guard instead of calling the police, he was going to inform my parents I tried to steal the doll. Then he instructed the security guard to take me home and tell my parents how what I had been caught doing. Walking the few blocks to my house,

I was fearful of what Momma would do to me. When Momma opened the door, she was surprised to see me and the security guard. The security guard explained to Momma how I tried to steal the doll and how fortunate I was the store manager decided not to press charges. The security guard let Momma know I was no longer allowed in the store. Momma thanked the security guard for bringing me home and asked him to let the store manager know how much she appreciated him not pressing charges. When the security guard left, Momma scolded me about how wrong it was to steal and the consequences that could have resulted, including going to the detention home for bad girls, if Mr. Preston had not been nice enough to send me home with only a warning. Momma further told me how very disappointing she was in my behavior. I then received my second belt whipping. Although the whipping hurt, seeing the anguish on Momma's face was more painful. I had let Momma down. Later Momma asked me why I chose to steal the doll instead of asking her to buy it for me. Shrugging up my shoulder, I said I do not know. It was the truth, I really had no idea why I did not let Momma know I wanted the doll. In addition to letting Momma down that day, I did not get the items she needed and was no longer allowed in the store. Consequently, when Momma needed me to go to the store, she had to pay a higher cost for groceries from the small corner stores. Looking back on this incident years later, again I was thankful that even as a child God was blessing my life. There is no doubt it was only the intercession of the Holy Spirit through Mr. Preston, a man of God, that I was shown mercy by not being charged with stealing and potentially being sent to a detention home. Forever will I thank God for the flicker of light that day that enabled Mr. Preston to have mercy on me. *Be ye therefore merciful, as your Father also is merciful. Judge not, and ye shall not be judged: condemn not, and ye shall not be condemned: forgive, and ye shall be forgiven*, Luke 6:34-37 (KJV).

Puberty. The summer of 1968, I ran into the house to use the bathroom. I was in a hurry to finish and get back outside to play. Linda Faye walked into the bathroom. She looked at me, then hollered, *Momma, Debbie has started her period*. I did not know what she was talking about. All I knew was every once in a while, something red kept coming out of me. When it did, I would simply put tissue in my panties. That day Momma explained to me in the best way she knew about monthly menstrual cycles. Of course, Linda Faye offered more incite with emphases on now I could get pregnant and have a baby. They explained and showed me how to use *Kotex* pads. At this point in my life none of what they said registered with me. My only interest was going back outside to play and ride my bike.

Fatherless. Growing older I often felt a void and sad being around my friends who had fathers in their lives. They would ask me why my father did not live with me. I would reply, I did not know. Not hearing from Tim after the death of his father was disappointing. Then often Linda Faye and Auntie continued to tease me about Tim being my father and how I looked and acted like the Willifords. These comments always caused me to be upset and wonder why Tim never tried to contact me. Curious to know why Tim did not want to be in my life, I was determined to find him. I had overheard someone saying Tim hung out at the King Tutt Lodge located about 35 blocks from our home. One day when I was about eleven years old, I made up my mind to see if Tim was at the Lodge. I got on my bike and rode for about forty minutes until I arrived at the Lodge. I asked someone outside the door if Tim Williford was inside. The person called for Tim to come outside. When Tim came outside, he said what are you doing here girl. I asked him why he did not come to see me. He told me to get away from there. Then I said can you give me some money. He gave me a $1 and I rode off. When I returned home, to my surprise Tim's mother had phoned to let Momma know how I went looking for Tim at the club and begged him for money. She told Momma to keep me away from Tim because he now was married and had a child. That day learning for myself how Tim and his family thought about Momma and me, I swore to never again look for him. Being denied by the Willifords became part of my stormy life. As I grew older the flickers of light that got me through this storm was love, grace, comfort, and encouragement from God. With these flickers I eventually came to know how my heavenly Father and Lord and Savior would always love me unconditionally even when my earthly father did not. *Now may our Lord Jesus Christ Himself and God our Father, who has loved us and given us everlasting comfort and encouragement and the good [well-founded] hope [of salvation] by His grace, comfort and encourage and strengthen your hearts [keeping them steadfast and on course] in every good work and word,* 2 Thessalonians 2:16-17 (AMP). Later in life the song *Father in You* sung by Mary J. Blige became a reflection of my life with Tim.

A New Job for Momma. Momma was blessed to stop working domestic positions for individual families when she obtained employment with Ohio Bell in 1971. The new job answered the prayers of Momma to provide a better life for her daughters. Even though the position was in housekeeping, it meant a lot to Momma, especially since when she initially moved to Cleveland in the 1950s she was unable to obtain this same position due to her race. Momma told us how during that time and many years thereafter only white women were hired for housekeeping positions. She was glad things had finally changed to enable her to be hired. Linda Faye and I also were extremely happy for Momma as she excitedly let us know how with the new job she would have steady employment with good pay and even benefits, including medical and dental. Then when Momma said we no longer would have to be on public aid, we shouted for joy. Looking at Momma, I could see in her eyes and hear in her voice that being able to be self-supportive meant the world to her. Through sunshine, rain, sleet, or snow Momma would leave home at 4:30 a.m. to make it to work by 6:00 a.m. Once she arrived at work, she would call Linda Faye and me each morning to make sure we were up for school. A few months later, Momma began saying to us that her dream was one day Linda Faye and I would work at the desks in the offices she cleaned, and her future grandchildren someday would be managers in those offices. This dream of Momma became a goal for Linda Faye and me.

Church Life. After moving to our Kinsman Avenue home, we no longer attended St. James. We begin attending the church where

Rev. Woolworth, was the pastor. Rev. Woolworth was married to Aunt Sue's sister-in-law, Helen. Auntie who had married William Lewis and had three children, Michael, Karen, and David, also attended the church. A brief time later, Momma stopped attending church. Once Momma stopped attending, I began to attend the neighborhood Lutheran Church or went to church with Linda C. Around 1969, MaeMae invited me to attend Olivet Institutional Church, where Rev. Odie Hoover was the pastor. Momma and Linda Faye would sometimes attend church with MaeMae and me. One Sunday when Pastor Hoover extended an invitation for discipleship, I accepted Jesus Christ as my Lord and Savior and united with Olivet as a candidate for baptism. Pastor Hoover baptized me a week later. I joined the youth usher board and the youth choir that was directed by Earl Preston until he was called to preach the word of God. When the church travelled out of town, MaeMae would take me with her. I will always cherish the time, encouragement and integrity instilled in me by MaeMae and her sister Carol Howell.

Memories of Olivet remain with me today. Besides the general church services, there were programs held revolving around civil rights movements and election of political candidates. I remember these programs being attended by Jessie Jackson, elected officials, civil right leaders, and other political candidates, since this was a time-period when our nation was facing many social issues. One social issue Olivet addressed was justice for people of color. By the time I was fourteen years old, this became an important concern to me. My interest in this social issue was further intensified when Linda Faye became good friends with Juba, a member of the Black Panther party. I became intrigued with Juba stance on black power. Black power, Huey Newton, Angela Davis, and the red, black, and green flag became a part of my life. Although I truly did not know the exact views of the movement, what I did understand was a black little girl like me was not treated in the same as white girls. Even our neighborhood was changing. The white people were constantly moving out and only black people were moving in. Most of my classmates were now black students. It was the beginning of the 1970s not 1940s, so why were black people still fighting to be accepted by and treated the same as white people? This was very confusing to me.

Junior High School. In 1969, I graduated from elementary school and Linda Faye from high school. Momma was proud of us. Linda Faye continued to work in the corner store while attending Cuyahoga Community College. I excitedly prepared for seventh grade at the big junior high school. Even though my close friends and I were happy to graduate, we were concerned about the change from our small elementary school to the intimidating big junior high school. Siblings of my friends would tell us various aspects of junior high school. No longer would we have one teacher instructing on various subjects. Instead each course would be taught by a different teacher for a certain length of time. We would be required to quickly change classrooms at least five to seven times a day. They scared me when telling us how seventh graders would be hassled, teased, and called *flats* by upper class students. Hearing these types of stories, I became more nervous as the first day of school approached. Ever since they had told us about the upper classmates, I had worried about being humiliated by them. It had been only a few months ago that I had started dealing with the difficulties of becoming an adolescent. Now, I was contending with the potential challenges of attending junior high. I fretted if my friends and I did not have the same classes would my new classmates be friendly. Thoughts of being unaccepted and alone was frightening. Then I was nervous about being unattractive because of my physical appearance. I was a very awkward unattractive skinny girl with *bucky beaver teeth* and government issued eye glasses. My looks worsened the summer before school when puberty caused my face to break out with acne. Moreover, I agonized if kids from the neighborhood would keep on teasing me about not having a father and Momma's nervous breakdowns. Worried if they did continue to tease me, my new classmates would find out and join in on making fun of Momma and me. These thoughts made me feel timid and self-conscious as I started the seventh grade at Audubon Junior High School. With all my worrying about my seventh-grade year overall it turned out okay. For the first few weeks it was a big adjustment. Changing every forty minutes to another classroom with a different teacher, subject matter and classmates was very confusing. Eventually I learned my way around the big school building and adapted to the changing classrooms. I was also happy when I began new friends. I even started noticing boys. Although not a part of the hip crowd, I was happy to have several good friends. Besides Linda C. being my best friend, I became good friends with Carolyn Walker and Robin St. John. Robin lived in a nice house with a swimming pool which made me believe her family was rich. Carolyn had a handsome uncle who I secretly admired. Then there was my math teacher, Mr. Edward Young. I was infatuated with Mr. Young to the point I wrote him a few love letters. Years later I thought how most likely Mr. Young was thinking to himself I was a silly little girl. Today I look back wondering why even at such an early age I was attracted to a man much older than me. The most unusual occurrence for me during the seventh grade happened when I was sitting on the gym floor next to one of my classmates whose name was also Deborah. We were listening to the gym teacher give us instructions on how to climb the robes. Talking to Deborah, I could see she was sad with tears in her eyes. I asked her what was wrong. She replied, *I am pregnant.* At that point in life, I had no idea what pregnant really meant, still I told her everything would be alright. A few years later I learned the meaning of pregnant. Many years later I would see Deborah and she looked beautiful and had a successful career and life.

By the end of the school year I had survived the seventh grade and was promoted to the eighth grade. I was excited to be on summer break. That summer Momma's friend, Fannie Tucker and her children moved a few blocks from our house. Ms. Tucker was a nice lady who had eight children ranging in age from two to twenty-four years old. Each of her children's first names began with the letter *M*. I became good friends with Marsha, the middle daughter of Mrs. Fannie. That summer and for several years thereafter Marsha and I spent lots of time together. Meanwhile, Linda Faye became good friends with

Myra (Joyce), the oldest daughter of Mrs. Fannie. Linda Faye and Joyce would often go to the University of Toledo to watch her brother Melvin play football which I thought was cool. The summer of 1970 went by slowly. By September I was ready to start the eighth grade. Sadly, by the middle of the eighth grade, life just did not seem fair or worthwhile for me. Momma had recently suffered from another mental breakdown which required hospitalization. Linda Faye was caring for me and we often argued because she wanted to act like my Momma. This made me mad because she was not Momma. Moreover, this was the first time I missed Momma more than ever before. Why did the most important person in my life have to suffer? Thankfully several weeks later Momma returned home. Once again, she was her normal self. Even with Momma home, I frequently was unhappy and lonely. It became difficult to comprehend and accept being fatherless. I asked God why the man that was supposed to be father did not want to be in my life. Witnessing the recent reoccurrence of Momma's mental illness with no cure in sight was painful. Moreover, being an unattractive clumsy skinny girl, who boys called *Olive Oyl*, *Twiggy*, and sang Joe Tex 1967 song *Who'll Take the Woman with the Skinny Legs* made me feel ugly. With all those emotions and thoughts, together with my adolescent issues at times I wanted to run away from home. Then for some unexplainable reason for the first time I thought about committing suicide. Why this thought came to my mind is a mystery because I cannot even recall how I knew what committing suicide meant. One morning shortly thereafter while at school I took around thirty of the psychotic medicine prescribed to Momma. Once I had taken the pills exactly what happened is unclear until in a daze I began to gradually wake-up. My next clear memory was lying in a hospital bed. I saw Momma looking at me with a sigh of relief on her face while a nurse was asking how I felt because my stomach had been pumped. Momma later told me the nurse for the school had called to inform her I had overdosed on pills and the ambulance was taking me to St. Luke's Hospital. Momma had called Auntie to bring her to the hospital. The hospital social worker let Momma know if I ever again tried to commit suicide I would be reported to Juvenile Court for prosecution. As I was getting dressed to leave the emergency room, Momma tightly hugged me saying she loved me with all her heart and never wanted to lose me. Then in her low soft voice Momma said to me, she had endured a lot in her life. She went on to emotionally tell me *with everything she had went through in life never had she thought about taking her life*. Momma then affectionately said to me, *no matter what I should never want to take my life*. Even today I can see the mixed emotions of relief, fear, and disappointment in the eyes of Momma and hearing her kind, devoted and loving voice saying those words of encouragement to me. Trying to commit suicide that day ignited a storm that resulted in a permanent emotional scar that stayed camouflaged and suppressed for years. Without a doubt later in my life I knew on that day there was a flicker of life of the redeeming power of Jesus Christ and favor and mercy of God that kept me alive and did not put Momma through the grief and sorrow of losing her baby daughter. *Since all have sinned and are falling short of the honor and glory which God bestows and receives. [All] are justified and made upright and in right standing with God, freely and gratuitously by His grace (His unmerited favor and mercy), through the redemption which is [provided] in Christ Jesus*, Romans 3:23-24 (AMPC). Before being allowed to return to school, Momma and I had to meet with one of the administrators of the school to confirm I was okay to resume attending classes. I was grateful that upon returning to school, none of the students said anything about the incident. Friends only asked me if I was okay. The remainder of my eighth-grade school year was typical. Overall, I was a good student, even though I did have a couple of incidents of misbehaving in a few classes. Thank goodness these incidents never required disciplinary actions.

My summer of 1972 was mostly spent working summer jobs. Shortly after beginning the ninth grade, I received information from my counselor about Jane Addams Vocational High School, a vocational school for only girls. The school prepared students for vocations in the fields of legal or medical secretary, cosmetologist, fashion retail, and culinary services. My counselor explained the school did not offer college prep courses. At that point in my life this was okay with me because I had no intention to immediately attend college. Looking at how Linda Faye seemed to be struggling financially in college, my goals for life were different. I intended to graduate from high school. Following graduation, I would obtain a good paying full-time job. Then I planned to enroll in college part-time. One of the other reasons I wanted to attend Jane Addams it would boost my self-esteem because I would be away from silly boys that still thought it was funny to tease and make fun of me. My school counselor informed me to be accepted into Jane Addams, prospective students had to complete an admission application. Momma and I completed the application. I requested to be placed in the legal secretary program. My counselor submitted the application with the other required school documents. A letter from Jane Addams came while Momma was at work. Bursting with excitement I opened the letter. My heart dropped when I read not accepted. No Lord this could not be. Why wasn't I accepted? My grade point average met the requirement and the letters of recommendation had been submitted by my teachers and counselor. At that moment I thought my attempt to commit suicide had come to haunt me and this was the reason I was not accepted. Thoroughly disappointed at the thought of attending the co-ed school, John Adams, I felt let down. I began to pray to God to help me get enrolled in Jane Addams. Knowing the quiet modest-spirit of Momma, I was not sure she would pursue contacting the school to inquire why my application for admission was denied. With that in mind, I decided to pretend like I was Momma and call the school to find out why I was not accepted. When a lady answered the phone I changed my voice, saying I was Momma calling to ask why my daughter was not accepted into the school. The lady said, wait a moment I will check the records. When she returned to the phone, to my surprise the lady said, your daughter was accepted and soon will receive information in the mail. Wanting to shout hallelujah and thank you Jesus, I tried to calmly tell the lady thank you. Although I had lied to the lady about being Momma, it was a relief knowing I would not be attending John Adams. Later in life, I told Momma about impersonating her to be accepted in the school. She simply said, *girl you are a mess*. Attending Jane Addams shaped many of the outcomes of my future. At times I think what might have happened in my future if I had attended John Adams instead of Jane Addams. Would I have attended college or joined the armed services immediately after graduation? Or alternatively like some of my friends became pregnant before graduation.

High School Years. In the spring of 1972, Momma was once again proud of the educational achievements of her daughters. Linda Faye had graduated from Cuyahoga Community College with her associates degree and had been accepted to attend Wilberforce University in Wilberforce, Ohio. Weeks later I graduated from junior high and began preparing for high school. MaeMae and Olivia assisted Linda Faye in preparing to attend Wilberforce by purchasing items she and Momma were unable to afford. Cedric, a friend of Linda Faye drove her, Momma, and me to Wilberforce. Even though the college campus was nice, I still was not impressed enough to want to attend college after graduation. This was especially true since the college Linda Faye was attending was in a small country town. Once we had Linda Faye settled, we headed back to Cleveland. On the ride home Momma said I could stay in Linda Faye's room while she was away at college. Finally, I would have my own room. I kept the tradition of Linda Faye by hanging my favorite posters of singers, actors, Angela Davis, and Huey Newton sitting in the wicker chair on the walls. It felt great to sleep in my own room in a full-size bed where I could talk on the phone without disturbing Momma. A few weeks later, it was time for me to begin the tenth grade at Jane Addams. The school was several miles away requiring me to catch the city bus. This was a newly built school building with students attending from all areas of greater Cleveland. Attending a vocational high school was different from junior high school because instead of constantly changing classes, we were in our vocational training class for much of the day. I was glad to become friends with several of my classmates, including Lenora, Beverly, Brenda, Sybil, Natalie, Monica, and Tracey. I even became friends with Bridgett my first white girlfriend. Meeting new friends was good because my friends from junior high school were attending the high schools closest to their lived. Although we stayed connected for a while, eventually except for Linda C., we went our separate ways. Besides enjoying school, life was good at home. With Linda Faye at college, Momma and I became much closer. I was thankful and happy for the past three years Momma had been mentally stable. The only sad aspect of my family life was it had been five years since I had gone to the lodge to see Tim. Even though I was keeping my promise to never to contact him, the emotional scarring from him not being in my life was at times heartbreaking. At those times, I held on to the flicker that my heavenly Father loved me.

Hitchhiking. For years I had seen Linda Faye and her friends hitchhike to and from school and other places in the city and surrounding areas. When she hitchhiked to stores, sometimes she would take me. Wanting to be like my big sister, of course I thought it was alright for me to hitchhike to and from high school. This was despite the fact Momma would give me money for bus fare. Linda C. and I would also hitchhike to go shopping downtown and a few other places in the greater Cleveland area. The difference was Linda Faye began hitchhiking in the mid-1960s when it was a little safer. In 1974, Linda C. and I realized hitchhiking was becoming more dangerous. This was especially true when one Sunday we had hitched a ride with a man who was going to take us downtown. Instead he kept talking while driving to the other side of town which was completely opposite of downtown. Linda C. and I both became concerned and afraid thinking he was going to harm us. After telling him several times that was okay we did not need a ride, he finally stopped the car to let us out. Thankfully we were close to a bus stop and had enough money to ride the bus downtown and back home. Today I can testify that the flicker of light was the mercy of God that kept me, Linda C., Linda Faye, and her friends safe from harm during the years we hitchhiked. *The Lord takes care of those who are not aware of danger. When I was in great need, he saved me*, Psalm 116:6 (NIrV).

Loss of My Virginity. In late 1972, I would often go skating at the local rink with my friends. One day in December I fell hard to the floor and a very handsome skating guard came to assist me. Helping me to the bench, he asked if I was okay. I said, yes. About ten minutes later, the guard came by the bench to check on me. I let him know my head was still hurting, but otherwise I was okay. He told me his name was Bobby Cordell and asked me my name. I said, DeBorah. Then he told me to let him know if I needed anything. Once I felt better, I went home. A few weeks later, I went skating. When Bobby spotted me, he came over to say hello. We talked sporadically throughout the evening. Before I left, he asked for my phone number. That night he called, and we talked for hours. Thereafter we talked every day. He was four years older than me and worked at a factory and part-time at the skating rink. Each day I eagerly looked forward to talking to Bobby since this was the first time I had talked this much to a boy. After about a week of talking on the phone, when I would go skating Bobby began taking me to the back room of the skating rink where we would kiss. Shortly thereafter he began driving me home, where we would sit in his car kissing. Before long he was not only kissing me but caressing my body. When he drove me home, after we finished kissing, I would only let him walk me to the door because I did not want Momma to know I was seriously talking to a boy. Within a month of passionate kissing and caressing, Bobby wanted to have sex. I thought why not. Many of my friends had already lost their virginity. The sexual revolution was in full bloom. *Let's Get It On* sung by Marvin Gaye was playing on the radio. I said to myself why keep on waiting and be considered a square and old-fashion by my friends. I decided the next time Bobby asked, my answer would be *yes*. What should have been one of the most important decisions of my life, I made it very nonchalantly without a second thought. When Bobby asked again, I simply said, *yes*. He looked a little shocked, as we began to discuss the when and where. I told him at my house after Momma left for work. We planned for him to come to the house before I went to school. Linda Faye had a red negligee in her dresser drawer that I put on then waited for Bobby to arrive. When he arrived, I let him in the house. We started kissing and went into the bedroom. That day I lost my virginity to Bobby. I distinctly remember it was very painful and was over quickly. When he got off me, I immediately jumped out of the bed. Bobby had a complexed look on his face as he said to me, *we ain't finished yet*. Embarrassed, unemotionally I said, *I have to get to school*. With a concerned look on his face, Bobby said, *why didn't you tell me you were a virgin?* With a stunned look on my face and feeling stupid, I simply did not reply. We dressed in silence. As we left the house, Bobby asked when I planned to continue what we started. I replied, I did not know, while fully aware I did not want to have sex with him again. Bobby and I talked for a few more weeks before gradually we stopped calling each other. Several years later while in line at a neighborhood ice cream stand, I heard someone call my name. When I looked around it was Bobby. I said, *oh, hi*. Very arrogantly Bobby said, *do not act like you do not know me, you should never forget who I am*. Feeling embarrassed, I did not respond, but merely walked away. That moment felt exactly the same as the day I did not say anything when Bobby asked me why I did not tell him I was a virgin. More importantly what Bobby had just said was absolutely true. Never would I forget him because I had casually and hastily given him my precious virginity. For the rest of my life he would be embedded in my mind, body, and soul. This was the first of several times in my life the sayings *if only I had known then what I know now* and *if I could take that day back* were truly my sentiments. The nonchalant way I gave my virginity to Bobby I have yet to understand. I can only think it was my curiosity. The sexually explicit books one of my friends had given me to read might have caused it. It might even have been because I did not want to be the oddball because many of my close friends were already having sex. It also could have been because I had always tried to mimic my sister, and over the years, I had saw her passionately kissing her boyfriends, so I wanted to do the same. Then when I found her foam spermicide birth control. At first, I did not know what is was and thought Linda Faye was a junkie because foolishly I thought the applicator was a needle and the can was drugs. When Linda Faye explained it was a form of birth control, then I also wanted a reason to use birth control. Regardless of the reasons, with the passing of time the emotional aftermath of how I lost my virginity became a stormy part of my life that mentally haunted me. Memories of the decisions made the day I lost my virginity made me whole-heartedly regret it and yearn to turn the clock back. This self-inflicted storm of how easily I gave away my virginity eventually contributed to other storms. Years later I was thankful when the Holy Spirit revealed to me even during this self-inflicted storm there was a flicker of light of the forgiving mercy from God that brought me out of the bondage of guilt and enabled me to walk with my head held high. *I am the Lord your God, who brought you out of Egypt so that you would no longer be slaves to the Egyptians; I broke the bars of your yoke and enabled you to walk with heads held high,* Leviticus 26:13 (NIV).

Promiscuous. After breaking up with Bobby, I did not talk to any young men for months. Then for some unknown reason, I begin to talk to different men that were ten to fifteen years older than me. I typically met these men while hitchhiking or simply walking down the street. From mid-1973 to early 1974, I had sex with several men. Fortunately, after the talk with Linda Faye about birth control, I was smart enough to go to Planned Parenthood for birth control. A couple of the men I had monogamous relationships. These men showed they cared about me and treated me very well with or without sex. The few others were non-monogamous one or two-nights stands. They would jive talk me with sweet enticing words and deeds to lure me in bed. Being young, silly, and foolish, I thought this meant they cared about me. As soon as I agreed to have sex, they would disappear coming back weeks later to try to run the same game. When this happened at least then I was wise enough to tell them to take a hike. Comparable to losing my virginity, each face and name of the men I was promiscuous with are forever embedded in my memory and body. I have never been able to give a logical reason I was sexually promiscuous during this time. I would ask myself over and over why was I allowing my body to be violated without a firm commitment from a man? I did not have a reason then nor do I have one now. I have no clue why I behaved in this manner. Over the years I asked myself was it like some people would say, I was looking for a father figure for the love I did not receive from Tim, or was I merely a fast girl gone wild? Only thing I knew for sure after losing my virginity is I wanted to be in love. Looking at the romance displayed in the movies and television shows, heard in the lyrics of love songs, and read about in romance books, I wanted to feel loved, cared for, and respected like those women. When I now reflect over my life, this behavior in my teen years eats at my conscious and soul. This self-inflicted storm eventually became another painful layer to the emotional scarring previously caused by the nonchalant manner I lost my virginity. Yet again it was only the mercy of God that enabled me to weather through this self-inflicted gloomy storm. Today I truly acknowledge and appreciate the flicker of light from God of shielding me when I was promiscuous. *But thou, O Lord, art a shield for me; my glory, and the lifter up of mine head*, Psalm 3:3 (KJV). For it was only God who shielded me from all hurt, harm and dangers that could have resulted from my being promiscuous. Hallelujah, my awesome God kept His naïve promiscuous child from contacting any sexually transmitted diseases, no child was conceived out of lust, and Momma's heart was not broken by finding out that often I had sex with much older men in her home while she was at work. I will always regret my periods of promiscuity. If I could do it over again only one man would have known my body intimately.

Trying to Drive. One of my monogamous relationship was with Ted who was eight years older than me. He worked for the Cleveland Illuminating Company and was helping in directing plays at a small local theater that my friend, Brenda and I had joined. One day Ted asked me if I could drive. I said, yes, even though I had never drove a car in my life, because I thought it would be easy to drive. Ted would let me drive a few times while he was in the car. Each time I drove, I did better. One day, he told me I could go home and then come back to get him later. Foolishly I said, okay. I was driving down the street when suddenly I was in the middle of heavy traffic. The traffic impeded me from turning on the correct street to get to my house. When I finally was able to get in the turning lane to turn off the main street onto a side street, I lost control of the car and ran up on the curb. I was able to get the car off the curb. But then lost further control when I tried to turn but ended up hitting a tree. The crash caused me to hit my head and face quite hard. A lady came out of her house to see if I was okay. I said, yes, then asked if I could use her phone. She said, yes. I called Ted and explained what happened. He calmly said okay, and he was on his way. Ted arrived within ten minutes. Once he arrived, Ted made sure I was okay. He told me not to worry about the car because he had insurance. Ted then called the police. When the police arrived, Ted said he was driving. The police could not understand how he parked the car between two trees. I was sorry for wreaking his car. He again assured me it would be okay the insurance would repair the car. Several weeks later Ted asked me to help him pay his deductible of $500. Sixteen years old without a job, I was unable to pay him any money. He then came to the house to ask Momma for money. She told him I was a child, so why would you let her drive your car? My actions that day could have been detrimental for others as well as myself. After that accident, I never got behind the wheel of another car until I completed my driver's education classes. Again, another flicker of light of how Jesus Christ sustained me by the mercy and grace of God throughout my teenage years. Even in my foolish ways God miraculously saved innocent people and me from injury or even death.

Marvin Scott. While hitch-hiking, in 1973, I met Marvin Scott. When hitch-hiking I often used the fictitious name of *Tommie*. This is what happened when I hitched a ride with Marvin. Although I eventually told Marvin my real name, he still always called me Tommie. When meeting people with him, he even would introduce me as Tommie. Marvin who was eleven years older than me was a genuinely nice, caring man. He became an extremely reliable platonic friend to me, he was like the big brother I never had. When I needed a ride somewhere, I could depend on Marvin to be there for me. He would sometimes take me to the movies or out to eat. During the twelfth grade, the counselors at the school selected me and several other students to attend a five-day leadership conference at Athens University in Ada, Ohio. Marvin was kind enough to drive Momma and me to the University. He then returned five days later to pick me up. I deeply appreciated Marvin. One day when Marvin and I stopped at his apartment, I met his cousin, Herman, who had recently begun to stay with him. Immediately upon meeting Herman, I thought he was a handsome man that resembled Smokey Robinson and appeared to have a funny personality. Marvin and I remained friends for several more months, but when he started to seriously date, he stopped contacting me.

Prom Date. One day while visiting Linda C. we were looking through Clifton, her older brother, senior high school yearbook. There was a boy named Michael Glover whose picture caught my eye. Showing the picture to Linda C., I said, he is handsome. The yearbook included the phone numbers of the graduates, so I decided to call him.

When he answered the phone, I said, I saw your picture in the yearbook and thought you were cute. He could not believe that is why I called him. That day we talked for a little bit. Before hanging up, he asked for my phone number. The next day he called me. We again talked for a while. Over the following few days, we talked several times. Michael was only two years older than me and was employed at a factory. He lived with his parents and sisters. Within a week we met in person, and were mutually impressed with, and attracted to, each other. Over the next several weeks we spent time together in person and talked on the phone for hours. Michael had come to visit me a few times. The first time he visited, he met Momma. Michael was one of three male friends that Momma met who she allowed to visit me when she was at home. How thankful I am that Momma never knew how I had men in her house when she was at work. Michael also took me to meet his family. They were a close-knit family who were very protective of Michael. I was glad they were cordial and seemed to like me. Before talking to Michael, I had decided any future relationships would be different from previous ones. No longer would I rush into having sex. I had committed to sexual abstinence until dating for at least six months to a year. When I told Michael about my commitment, I was happy he agreed to honor it. The most we did was passionate kissing and a little fondling. This was honestly my first true romantic relationship. During the weekdays Michael and I would spend hours talking on the phone. We would talk about what we did that day and make plans for being together over the weekend. Our weekends were spent going out to eat or the movies, parks, or shopping. Sometimes we would stay at my house watching television and listening to music. Each holiday we spent together. On Valentine Day, Michael gave me the biggest stuff animal I had ever seen. Michael even assisted me with my driving lessons. Once I completed my driving course, he took Momma and me to take my driving test. That was an exciting day when I passed the test and received my driver's license. The beginning of 1975, Michael and I began making plans for my prom. Since Michael drove a light green Camaro, we decided to wear lime and black. The day of the prom, when Michael came to the house, Momma took pictures of us and told us how nice we looked and to have fun. When we walked out the door the neighbors wished us well. We then went to the house of Jackie and Lawrence, the couple I babysat for who had moved into their own home. Jackie took pictures and told us to have a wonderful time. Once we left Jackie's house, we stopped by Michael's house for his family to take pictures. When we arrived at the prom venue, I was amazed by the beautiful the atmosphere. I felt all grown-up as Michael and I sat as a couple at the table with the beautiful décor and table settings. The DJ played good music while we danced the night away and had a fun time. After the prom Michael took me home because we had not planned to attend the after prom. Once I was home, my friend, Monica called and talked me into attending the after prom. I called Michael to see if he wanted to go. Michael said, no, he was too tired and had to go to work in the morning, but for me to enjoy myself. The after prom also was a lot of fun. I was glad I had decided to attend. Following my graduation ceremony, Michael and I dated for a few more months. Eventually we were intimate a few times. Although having waited past the abstinence timeframe, Michael and I still slowly began to drift away from each other. By September 1975, we were no longer dating, but I have always considered Michael my first real boyfriend.

Dysplasia. At the age of 17, I had my first pap smear that showed dysplasia. My doctor informed me it would be necessary for the dysplasia to be checked closely to assure it did not progress into carcinoma. Because of the abnormalities, over the years I had several cone biopsies that removed the dysplasia cells. My pap smears would be normal for twelve to eighteen months. Then unfortunately, the dysplasia cells would gradually return. The flicker of light was by the grace of God the dysplasia was diagnosed at an early age.

Graduation and Employment. Linda Faye graduated from Wilberforce in May 1975. Momma, MaeMae, her nephew Tony and I attended the graduation. It was remarkable to attend a college graduation. That year Isaac Hayes was the special guest. Momma was truly pleased to see her oldest child graduate from a four-year college. Even before Linda Faye had graduated she had obtained employment in Columbus, Ohio. A month later, I graduated from high school. Again, Momma was extremely proud of me as she, Lois and Jackie watched me received my diploma. Linda Faye was unable to attend because she had just started her new job. Graduating from high school signified to me the end of my childhood and teenage years and the beginning of my journey into adulthood. Days after graduating I looked back over my first eighteen years, and thought of a few things I definitely would've done or handled differently, including: each moment spent with Momma would've been cherished and appreciated more; my body would've been valued for the temple it is instead of easily giving up my virginity; I wouldn't have been promiscuous; I would've taken my education more seriously and stayed more active in church. These regrets caused me to pray that the mistakes and regrets from my youth would give me wisdom to live a more diligent life in the upcoming years.

Like Linda Faye, I had been blessed to obtain employment prior to graduating. Initially, I applied for and was hired at the John H. Bustamante Law Firm. I also had applied for a position with Cleveland Clinic. I received a call to be interviewed for a position with the Clinic. After the interview with the Clinic, I was offered a position. Upon considering the variance in pay and benefits between the Clinic and the law firm, I decided it was in my best interest to accept the position with the Clinic. I was hired to be a clerk in the registration and routing department responsible for inputting certain patient information into the computer database. Determined to make a good impression on my supervisor, each day I eagerly looked forward to going to work where I put forth my best efforts to promptly and accurately complete each assignment. I was pleased that my efforts were quickly recognized by my supervisors.

Because the Clinic was several miles away from our home, unless one of my friends gave me a ride, I caught the bus to and from work. Although I had my driver's license, I had not thought about purchasing a car. After working a few months, Momma began to discuss with me how she would help me buy a car. In October 1975, Ramaro one of my co-workers at the Clinic offered to help me in selecting the right a car. He took Momma and me to the dealership where he had recently bought a car to he help us negotiate the purchase of my first car. I selected a 1975 Ford Granda. Several days later Momma obtained a loan to buy the car from her credit union. Under the loan I would be the primary borrower and Momma the co-signer. It was an exciting day when I drove my brand-new car off the auto parking lot. Forever will I remember and be thankful for Momma helping me buy the car.

Chapter Two – Herman Washington

Shortly after beginning to work at the Clinic, I met Dana Coleman. One day we decided to go to lunch together. That day we discovered we shared an important date, our birth date. August 26, 1957. Dana and I would often have lunch together and quickly became close friends. Besides having lunch together, Dana and I started talking on the phone in the evenings. We even went to various places together from shopping to social and family events and outings. During one of our conversations, Dana mentioned her boyfriend Herbert (Hubby) who soon would be leaving for the armed services. She showed me pictures of Herbert. I was stunned and could not believe it, Herman, Marvin's cousin, was in one of the pictures. What a pleasant surprise. Dana told me that Herbert and Herman were brothers. Looking at the picture, I thought how handsome Herman looked. Really wanting to talk to him, I asked Dana if she would give Herman my phone number. She said, yes. A few weeks later Hubby left for basic training.

By early 1976, I received a call from Herman. He told me he was surprised to get my message from his brother. After talking for a few moments Herman explained his concerned about calling me because of my relationship with Marvin. I let him know Marvin and I had a brother-sister relationship. Herman told me that was good to hear. He talked to me for a little while longer before telling me he would call me again soon. A few days later, Herman called. He let me know Marvin had confirmed our relationship had not been a girlfriend/boyfriend relationship but a brotherly-sisterly friendship. After that day Herman and I talked daily. When he asked my age, I said eighteen. Herman said, *wow, I'm eleven years older than you.* He asked, is that a problem? I said, no. I asked him if he was dating. He told me, he was single and not dating. Then he told me he was married once and had two sons. Herman Leavitt (Vet), age 8 from his first marriage to Christina, and Dion age 3 with a former girlfriend, Diane. Eventually Herman asked me out for dinner. The day he arrived at the house I opened the front door to see Herman standing there looking more handsome than I remembered. He was light-skinned, medium height with a thin physique. He smiled saying, hello and handed me a small bouquet of flowers. His voice, demeanor, good looks with those beautiful dimples and light brown eyes gave me goose bumps. I was totally mesmerized by him. Inviting him inside, I was apprehensive as we walked upstairs for him to meet Momma. A few days before I had told Momma about my date with Herman. I let Momma know Herman was eleven years older than me and had two young sons. Momma did not think I should go out with Herman because she thought he was too old and was concerned about me talking to a man with children. Finally, I convinced Momma to at least meet Herman. Now with Herman walking up the stair, I was worried Momma would let Herman know her personal disapproval of us talking. Instead Herman won Momma over with his charming smile, friendly mannerism, and witty personality. It was a relief to know I no longer had to worry about Momma not approving me going on a date with Herman. Our date was extremely nice. Herman was a total gentleman at dinner and the movies. Even when took me back home and walked me to the door, he did not even try to kiss me goodnight. He simply held my hand while telling me he would talk to me tomorrow. The next morning, I told Momma how nice my date went. Momma told me of the guys she had met, Herman seemed to be one of the good ones, but she still let me know Michael was the one young man she liked the best.

Over the next several weeks, Herman and I spent a significant amount of time together. Herman was very funny and lovable and could always made me laugh. He enjoyed the outdoors, including fishing, hunting, and going to picnics in the park. At least five times a month he would go to the Thistledown Race Track to bet on the horses. On our second date and many thereafter we went to the Shaker Lakes parks where we would have romantic picnics and Herman began to teach me how to play chess. It took me weeks to get down the concept of chess, but Herman was very patient with me. Once I memorized the moves for the pieces and a few strategies, we could play a game for at least thirty minutes instead of five before Herman had me in checkmate. Besides going on picnics, to dinners and movie dates, we went on an overnight fishing trip. The trip was enjoyable even though I was too afraid to touch the bait and fish. My only dislike was no readily available public restrooms. He was such a gentleman who treated me like I was a princess. I really appreciated that he was not pressuring me to have sex. After dating for about two months, he asked me to be his girlfriend. I gladly said, yes. After that day, we were inseparable. The first time we were intimate was the most romantic I had ever experienced. It began with a lovely dinner. Then a room with rose petals, wine, bubble bath, and soothing music. The next morning, we had breakfast in bed. It was a dream come true. My prince had finally come into my life.

In the spring Momma and I were planning to visit Linda Faye. She was now living with her boyfriend, Darrell Buford in Xenia. Because I never liked driving on the freeway I asked Momma if Herman could go with us. Momma said, yes. I then asked Linda Faye if it was okay for Herman to come, she said yes. Herman drove us to Xenia. When we arrived at their home, Linda Faye and Darrell were glad to finally meet Herman. Linda Faye thought he was a nice guy. The plan was for Momma to stay at the house with Linda Faye and Darrell, while Herman and I stayed at a motel. The next morning, we all went to Kings Island Amusement Park where everyone had a fun time together. The next day Herman drove us back to Cleveland. He had made me incredibly happy that weekend, I was truly beginning to believe he was my dream come true. The only issue I noticed was he sometimes drank too much. On a dinner date at the Brown Derby he went to sleep while eating at the table. It took me over ten minutes to wake him up. When he did wake up, he stated he had drank homemade wine and taken some cough syrup. He told me this was not his typical behavior. For this reason, I chalked it up as a one-time occurrence.

Momma had decided she wanted us to move into an apartment. Months later Momma had located and leased a two-bedroom apartment in Warrensville Hts. She was glad the apartment was on the main bus line which allowed her to easily take the bus to work. The apartment was much smaller than our previous house, but big enough for the two of us. The way Herman and I were growing closer, I hoped one day we would be totally in love and get married.

    Meanwhile Dana and I remained close friends, and she let me know that Hubby would be returning to Cleveland soon because he had received an early medical discharge. When I saw Hubby, he was happy to know Herman and I were dating. One day Hubby and I were talking when he shared some information with me about one of Herman's former girlfriends. In turn I told Hubby something Dana had entrusted to me, which he promptly told Dana. Of course, even though I apologized, Dana was furious and disappointed with me. Although we remained cordial, unfortunately my gossiping negatively affected our friendship and it was never the same. My betraying Dana was a terrible mistake that I would forever regret. It also taught me the hard way how this type of behavior can permanently damage a relationship beyond repair. I know now that there even were flickers of light from this self-inflicted storm. First, it became one of my defining moments in life when I promised never again to partake in ruthless gossiping. Secondly, I quickly realized this experience was a lifelong lesson that by divulging secrets or gossiping it can negatively and detrimentally affect the lives of others. To this day, this situation stops me from gossiping. In addition, it helps me to expose others that gossip in order to stop the spreading of gossip that might be detriment to someone like it was to Dana. For without a doubt *once words are spoken, they can never be taken back even after an apology.*

Now You Return. Out of the blue in the spring of 1976, Tim had contacted Momma saying he was in Cleveland with his mother. He asked Momma if they could see us. The nerve of this man to call us. He had abandon, betrayed, and neglected Momma and me. Now he just shows up and wants to see us. My sweet darling Momma asked me to be kind and respectful. I asked her why? Then angerly said, *he hasn't done anything for us but abandon us*. My loving Momma said, *he is still your father*. I told Momma, *I did not care who he was, I had nothing to say to him or his family*. Momma insisted I forgive and go to see them. Hesitantly but obedient to Momma, I said, okay. The next day we went to the house of Mary McDonald, Tim's sister. This was the first time I had seen Tim since the day at the Lodge. Tim together with his mother, Mother Williford; brother, Andrew; sister, Mary; her husband, Rev. McDonald; and a few more people were at the house, and from what I am able to recall, we had a cordial visit. After that visit, I did not see or hear from Tim for several more years. Of course, this brief visit reopened the emotional scars from the effects of the storm of being deserted by my father. The flicker of light from Jesus Christ was knowing true love bears all. *Love bears all things [regardless of what comes], believes all things [looking for the best in each one], hopes all things [remaining steadfast during difficult times], endures all things [without weakening]*, 1 Corinthians 13:7 (AMP). Many years later, Gregory, Mary's son, told me he had a homemade movie that was filmed that day. Gregory converted the movie into a video. I was thankful to see the video because I had little memory of that day. It was astonishing to see Momma and me happily interacting with the Willifords that day.

Dreams of a Blissful Life Takes an Unexpected Turn. By the fall of 1976, Herman and I began to discuss living together. I talked to Momma about getting an apartment. I did not tell her that Herman was planning to move in with me. Momma said, aw, that she did not really want me to move, but if I could afford to live on my own it would teach me how to be a responsible adult. Several months later, I leased an apartment in the Bear Creek apartment complex the city of Bedford Hts. This was the beginning of Herman and me living together, that I believed would be the start of a blissful life with the man I dreamed of marrying. About six weeks into living together we were eating dinner talking and joking around. Suddenly for no reason Herman jumped up and slapped me in the face. Shocked and afraid he would hit me again, I quickly jumped up from the table. Beginning to cry I ran into the bathroom and locked the door. Within a few seconds Herman came to the bathroom door saying he was sorry as he told me he had drank too much beer. Upset, crying, and still scared he would hit me again, I just wanted him to stay away from me, so I told him to leave me alone. Herman kept on saying how sorry he was for hitting me. He asked me to forgive him while repeatedly saying it was because he had drunk too much. He pleaded with me to open the door. Eventually I came out of the bathroom. Herman quickly began to hug me while asking if I was okay. I said, yes. Gently kissing my forehead, Herman promised to never again hit me.

Although our lives went back to normal, I prayed Herman's hitting me was a once in a lifetime incident. Then for some unexplainable reason two events that were clearly imbedded in my few childhood memories ran through my mind. Both incidents happened when I was around five or six years old. The first occurred when I was watching with a crowd of other people a woman on the ground crying and bleeding from the head. People around me were saying she had been beaten by her boyfriend. The next incident was when I heard Momma talking to someone about how her hairdresser dead at home when her husband shot her then killed himself. Although I did not know the causes and ramifications of the two tragic events, now all these years it baffled that after Herman had hit me thoughts of those two incidents resurfaced in my memory. Were these incidents simply coincidental or some type of foresight into my future? At that time, it was a hypothetical question, but eventually in my life it would become perfectly clear to me why I thought about those two incidents.

In December 1976, Herman and I attended a party at the Camelot Party Center with friends I worked with at the Clinic. Having an enjoyable time dancing, talking, eating food, and drinking we were enjoying the party. Herman and I had danced several times. A popular disco song was playing when one of my co-workers asked Herman if it was okay for him to dance with me. Herman nodded, yes. After a few moments on the dance floor, I felt a tap on my shoulder. When I turned around, Herman punched me in the face knocking me to the floor. By being semi-unconscious, I vaguely what all happened next, but I do remember my nose bleeding while Herman dragged me like a rag doll off the dance floor. Faintly I heard voices asking Herman to stop. There were blurry imagines of people attempting to help me. I could vaguely see their efforts being hampered by Herman hollering at them. Once outside, although Herman was fussing, I could not understand exact what he was saying as he yanked me towards the car. He opened the car door and threw me into the passenger seat, he got into the driver's seat and then drove off headed towards our apartment. I do not remember how, but somehow during the commotion Herman had gotten our coats and my purse. Still in a state of bewilderment, I sat quietly trying to stop my nose from bleeding. The entire drive Herman hollered and screamed. Repeatedly accusing me that I made him hit me and insisting it was my fault. He asked me why I made him act that way. When Herman pulled into the parking lot of the apartment, he did not get out the car but sat there saying over repeatedly why did you make me hit you while he hit the stirring wheel. Still too frightened to say anything, I sat quietly continuing to try to keep my noise from bleeding. Finally, he got out of the car. I sat there for a moment wondering what to do. Do I stay in the car? Should I try to run away from him? Herman turned around looking at me with rage in his eyes yelling for me to get out of the car. I got out of the car. When I stood up the pain in my head intensified. Feeling lethargic I slowly walked behind Herman. Shaking and too afraid to say anything, I kept quiet with my head down holding the paper to my nose. When we entered the apartment, I went directly to the bathroom. Attempting to close the door, Herman pushed it back open. He restarted to persist on blaming me for causing him to hit me. Not wanting to fuel his anger, I remained quiet while holding back my tears. I took a wash cloth off the towel rack, ran some water on it and held it to my nose as I made sure the bleeding was under control. Once the bleeding had totally subsided, I began to wash the blood from my face, neck, and hands. Herman was intensively staring at me. Suddenly his voice changed to a calmer tone as he began saying he was sorry for hitting you. Then he said he was just upset when I danced with my co-worker. Although in my mind thinking, he is the one that said it was okay to dance with my co-worker, I simply kept my head down and did not say anything to him. Suddenly Herman came towards me, I jumped in fear he was going to hit me. He said, I am not going to hurt you. Pulling me into his arm, he told me he was sorry for hitting me. He took the wash cloth from my hand then started to wipe the blood off me. He started to help me take off my dirty, bloody, torn clothes. I needed to take a shower but was too tired. I only wanted to get in the bed and bury my head in the pillow and go to sleep in hopes I would wake up to find out what happened this evening was only a dream. Laying in the bed, Herman soon got in the bed with me and pulled me into his arm. Holding me he repetitively asked me to forgive him. Saying many times, he was sorry and how he loved and needed me. He went on to promise he never would hit me again. I remained silent and did not move. Several times Herman said, please tell me you love and forgive me. With tears in my eyes I finally mumbled, I love you and accepted your apology. He then started to make love to me. Lying there numb with my mind a million miles away, I prayed to God for understanding why this was happening to me. In the morning, Herman woke up like nothing bad had happened. Not wanting to get him upset, I said nothing. Picking up my dress, coat, and hat off the floor I painfully looked at the blood stains. I thought, *was this normal? Do all men hit their women?* The remainder of the day Herman acted like his normal self. Desperate to keep the peace, I followed his lead. When he wanted to talk, I talked. If he wanted me to do something, I did it. The next day at work my co-workers asked if I was okay and expressed their concern for my safety. I let them know their support was appreciated and assured them things were better with Herman and me. After the first time Herman hit me at the apartment, I was too embarrassed to tell anyone. Now even though my co-workers had witnessed him hit me, I had no intention of letting anyone else know he had hit me. I did not want Momma and Linda Faye to know what was going on. Believing Herman loved me the same way I loved him, I trusted him to keep his promise not to hit me.

Prior to dating me, Herman dated Laurice Price who was the woman Hubby had told me about. I had wondered if Laurice was the lady with Herman the day Marvin introduced me to Herman. In January 1977, Herman had not come home for several days. None of his family members had seen him. Initially I was worried something had happened to him, then I would think he was with another woman. My thoughts switched from worried to pissed-off. Five days later Herman returned to the apartment. Furious, I immediately begin to ask him why he had not been home for four days. Sarcastically I said, you must have been with another woman. He refused to answer or say anything to me. Becoming upset and crying I told him how wrong he was to treat me this way. He told me to grow up. I told him to get out and go back wherever he had been. Herman said he was not leaving. We began to argue. Sensing the argument escalating out of control, I left the living room to go into the bedroom. Before I reached the bedroom, a punch hit me hard on the side of my side of my head causing me to stumble to the floor. Laying curled up on the floor holding my head, Herman bent over hollering at me that he was not going anywhere. He hit me several more times on my head as I cried and screamed for him to stop. Finally, I managed to turn on my back and I started swinging my arms and kicking my feet. One of my kicks hit him in the groan. Herman rolled over onto the floor holding his groan. I knew this was my opportunity to get away from him. Staggering to get up, I made it to the door. Hollering for help, I ran out the door headed towards one of the neighbor's apartment. Banging on their door, I cried and screamed, *please help me*. The couple opened the door saying what is wrong. By this time Herman was in the hallway. He grabbed and drugged me back into the apartment. The neighbors hopelessly tried to help me. Herman told the neighbors to mind their business while he pulled me in the apartment and slammed the door close. He then punched me in the stomach. I felled to the floor. The neighbors were knocking on the door. He hollered, get away from my door. Straddling me he put his hands around my neck choking me while simultaneously beating my head against the floor. Losing my breath and everything becoming fuzzy, I faintly heard Herman shouting, *I'm going to kill you*. Pinned to the floor with his hands around my neck it was becoming more difficult to breathe. No longer could raise my hands or legs to try to fight him off. Unable to move I laid motionless. Finally, Herman let go of my neck. I turned on my side coughing as I tried to catch my breath. All the time Herman was standing over me, saying you better not move. He then hollered, why you make me do this. There was suddenly hard rapid knocking on the door. Herman told me to be quiet. A man said, *police* is everything alright? Herman was now straddled back on top of me telling me not to move. I started screaming out, *help me*. He covered my mouth. The police shouted, *open the door*. Herman tried covering my mouth while I attempted to scream. Once more the police shouted, *open the door before we knock it down*. Herman yelled, everything is okay officer. Within a second the police officers busted through the door. They pulled Herman off me and subdued him. I tried to sit up but could not. Herman was trying to tell them everything was alright. One of the police officers asked Herman what was going on. He said, *we just had a disagreement*. The other police officer came towards me asking what happened. I tried to explain how he jumped on me but was in too much pain and emotional distress. The police officers observing my physical and mental condition called for an ambulance. One of the police officers then told Herman he was under arrest and took he out of the apartment. The other police officer stayed with me until the ambulance arrived. During that time the police officer told me typically they will only talk to both parties. However, in this case observing how severely beaten I was, they had no choice than to arrest Herman. At the emergency room I was tested and evaluated for head trauma. Thankfully I was diagnosed with only a mild concussion. My face, neck, hands, and arms abrasions were treated. Prior to my release the police officer took my statement and pictures of the injuries. The medical staff gave me a prescription for pain medicine and discharge instructions. Too embarrassed to let anyone know what had happened, I asked the nurse to call a cab to take me home. I later found out Herman was charged and released on bond. I was unaware where he went once he was released.

Although, I was I trying to get accustom to living without Herman in my life, I spent hours trying to figure out why he had those violent outbursts. His split personality of going from being loving to hostile was confusing and weighting heavily on my heart. Given that I had only lived with Momma and Linda Faye with no male figure in our home, I questioned was Herman's demeanor normal. Did all men beat on their woman? Was it something I was doing wrong that caused Herman to hit me? All this resulted in me feeling at fault, depressed and insecure with very low-self-esteem. Those feelings coupled with being too ashamed to tell anyone what was going on, I would sit in the apartment in tears trying to figure out what was wrong with me. Each evening when I came home from work, I would look out the apartment window, crying and listening non-stop to the album *The Best of Deniece Williams*, especially the songs *If You Don't Believe*, *It's Gonna Take a Miracle*, *Silly*, and *Waiting*. For several weeks I had not heard from Herman when unexpectedly one evening he called from all places the city jail. He said, please do not hang up. I asked him what he wanted. He explained Laurice had him arrested for nothing. I asked him what he had done. Herman claimed nothing, that she just had him arrested. He let me know if he did not get out of jail soon he would lose his job. He asked me to please post bond for him before he was fired. Hesitantly my response was I would let him know. After I talked to Herman, I wanted to know the real reason he had been arrested. I called Laurice after locating her phone number in the phone book. When she answered the phone, I let her know who I was, and that Herman had called me from jail. She informed me Herman had jumped on her and cut up some of her furniture. I shared with her how recently he also had been arrested for beating me. We agreed it was best for us to leave him alone. Once we hung up, I was upset and humiliated. How could Herman do this to Laurice and me? What kind of man does this to women? I was done with Herman and never again wanted to see his face or hear his voice. Not wanting any memory of him in my sight, I looked at his clothing and belongings as I thought about how he had hurt me and torn up Laurice furniture. Suddenly, I piled all his belongings by the door of the apartment. Then I made several trips to the garbage chute where I threw his things down the chute, all the while swearing how dare he do this to Laurice and me.

  The next day Herman called. Immediately I told him I knew what he had did to Laurice, and adamantly told him to stop calling me because I was done with him. I let him know just like he hurt me and torn up Laurice furniture, I had thrown all his belongings away then I hung up the phone. Herman called me non-stop at work and home pleading for me to help him not lose his job by bailing him out. He apologized for everything he had done to me. To my surprise he admitted needing help with his temper and promised to get professional help. I told him to call his family members or friends to post bail. He said he did not have anyone that would help him. The next time he called, he said how he would understand if I would not be with him anymore, but if I ever loved him could I please bail him out. He began to constantly say how sorry he was for hurting me and promising to get help for his temper. About the fourth day, Herman asked me to please come to visit him. Beginning to feel sorry he had no one to help him, I agreed to visit him. Because of never visiting anyone in jail I was a bit nervous. This city jail was on 18th and Payne Avenue. When I walked in I was horrified. The conditions were deplorable. The guard instructed me to go stand by a door with a window. As Herman walked towards the door I could see he looked weary and frightened. Once he was at the door, he began to talk through a narrow window saying how sorry he was and that he missed and love me. Within the few minutes we spoke, Herman begged me to please bail him out because he could not lose his job, plus the conditions and treatment in the jail were horrible. He compassionately told me several more times how much he loved me. Then remorsefully saying repeating how he was sorry for ever hitting me and promising to get help. It was disheartening to see him through the window in such a humiliating and humbling demeanor. Then listening to him pour out his heart rekindled my feeling for him. Looking and hearing him I knew deep down inside my heart I loved him despite the hurt and pain he had caused me. Before leaving

Herman had my assurance to think about posting the bond. Once I walked out the door of the building, I already had made up my mind to bail Herman out of jail. When I talked to him the next day, I let him know my intention to post the bail. With relief in his voice, he honestly expressed how much he loved and appreciated me. He let me know I would not regret it because he planned to make everything up to me. The next day, I bailed Herman out.

When I picked Herman up from the jail, he was extremely grateful to be released. He kept telling me how much he loved and appreciated me, and that he only wanted to hold me in his arms forever. Laughing he said, of course after a long hot shower to get the dirt and grime off. As I drove to the apartment, Herman said several times how he thanked God for blessing him with me to be in his life. He let me know how sorry he was for hurting me and asked me to forgive him, as he promised to prove to me how much he loved me. Once at the apartment, Herman took a long shower. Because I had thrown his clothes away, I washed and dried the clothes he was wearing when he was arrested and let him know we could go shopping in the morning for some clothes. Afraid he would lose his job, Herman asked if I could prepare a letter to his job using letterhead from the Clinic saying he had missed work due to being sick. Not wanting him to be fired, I warily agreed to prepare the letter. Although the letter allowed him to keep his job, this was a decision that would later affect my future. Herman was doing as he promised by going to work, paying his share of the household expenses, and being the loving, supportive, and devoted man that I had fell in love. Our lives were filled with more joy, laughter, and fun times than ever before. My dreams of being the ideal loving couple was back on track.

A few months later, Herman came home from work later than normal. Through I believed he had not been drinking in months, that night when he walked through the door I could tell he had been drinking. He immediately started complaining about and questioning why Laurice and I were trying to send him back to jail. Standing in the kitchen trying to finish warming up his dinner, I tried to change the subject. Herman would go right back to fussing about how we were trying to ruin his life. He said, *why you woman always doing this to me*. I did not answer. Before I knew it, he came over to the kitchen counter where I was standing and slapped me in the head. When I tried to go around him to leave the room, Herman punched me in the face knocking me backwards into the wall. Trying to protect my head and face with my arms and hand, I said, *Herman, you promised not to hit me*. Grabbing the broom from the corner, he began poking me with the broom stick. Begging him to stop while again trying to leave the room, Herman grabbed and pushed me to the floor and told me to sit there. Doing as he told me, I sat on the floor with my head down as Herman continued to fuss about how Laurice and I had hurt him and was trying to send him back to jail. Herman had picked the broom back up and was intermittently poking me in the side with the broom stick. When I tried to grab the broom stick while crying out for him to stop, Herman snatched the broom stick and began hitting me several times on my head and over my body with the broom. Raising the broom stick in the air he began threatening to split my head open. Trying to bury my face in the floor to shield my head and face, I cried out, please do not hit me. It was a blessing from God that Herman did not carry out his threats. I was laying on the floor while Herman sat in front of me with his back against the wall. Periodically he would nod off, then suddenly he would wake up and again start to fuss and poke me. This went on for more than an hour. Finally, when I was certain he was asleep, quietly I got up from the floor. Quickly and silently, I grabbed my coat and purse and left the apartment. I drove to Momma's apartment. Opening the door to the apartment with my key, I called out to Momma that it was me. She was startled to see me. Momma asked what was wrong. Then she saw the bruises on my face and tears in my eyes. That night, tearfully and ashamed, I finally let Momma know that Herman had been beating me. Momma could not believe what Herman had did to me and told me I had to stay away from him. After telling Momma, I called Linda Faye to let her know what had happened. She too was shocked and agreed with Momma that I could not keep seeing him. I agreed with Momma and Linda Faye to no longer see Herman. The next morning, I contacted the leasing office to request the door locks on my apartment be changed. Once I thought Herman had left the apartment, I drove back to the apartment and checked the parking lot to make sure his car was gone. When I was sure he had left, I went to the leasing office to ask the maintenance personnel to go with me to the apartment to change the locks. I called Momma to let her know the locks were being changed. She was relieved Herman was not at the apartment when I got there and that the locks had been changed.

Momma encouraged me to be strong and stay away from Herman. That night Herman began to call me non-stop. When I heard his voice, I would hang-up the phone. Eventually I stopped answering the phone. I let Momma and Linda Faye know because Herman kept calling me, if they needed to call me to let the phone ring once, then call me back. Determined to get my life back on the right track without Herman, a few weeks later, I asked Momma if I could move back in with her. She said, of course, I could always live there because my name was still on the lease. I contacted the apartment manager to request an early termination of my lease. It was another blessing that the owner agreed to my early termination of the lease without any penalty. A month later, I prepared to move back in with Momma. I contacted Marvin to ask him to have Herman arrange to move out his bedroom set and personal belongings. Working with Marvin, we arranged an amicable time when I was not at the apartment for Herman to move the items. At that time as far as I knew, Herman moved back in with Marvin.

Not as Smart as I Thought. Heartbroken, confused and needing to get away from all the bad memories in Cleveland, I decided to join the armed services. When I met with the recruiting officer, I let him know my goal was to become a surgical nurse. He said, that would be an excellent career and scheduled a date for me to take the entrance exam. I spoke with my manager and others at the Clinic concerning a military leave of absence. My supervisors and other appropriate managers approved the request for leave. Many of my co-workers were excited for me. To make sure I had the fortitude to be a surgical nurse a few doctors arranged for me to be in the operating room for several surgeries, including an open-heart surgery. A few weeks later I took the military entrance test. My recruiting officer called me to schedule a meeting to discuss my career options. Upon meeting with him, he nicely informed me because of my low test score the only position I could be offered was in the bakery, not in the medical field, as I wished, or even a clerical position. Although disappointed in the position offered by the air force, I told my recruiting officer to let me know when the swearing in ceremony would be held. Leaving the recruiting office, I could not understand how my test score was so low when I had graduated from high school in the upper part of my class and had been employed since I was 14 years old. Yet my test score indicated my writing, spelling, interpretation, and mathematical skills were far below average. Unfortunately, I did not realize at that time the low score was an indication that I needed a significant amount of further education. Nor did I comprehend how I was not nearly as smart as I thought. Not realizing and comprehending how uneducated I was would end up being another big mistake in my life.

Another Chance. Herman had called nonstop the first few weeks after I had changed the locks on the apartment, but I refused to talk to him. It had been over two months since I had seen or talk to Herman when one day at work he was able to get through to me on the phone. When I heard his voice say hello, can we talk, instantly it was a challenge not to talk to him. Yet, I did not relinquish, as I told him I could not talk and hung up. Just hearing the sound of his voice had stirred up emotional confusion within me. I went from having a desire to be with Herman, to feeling disgusted at the thought of him. For weeks I had been working hard not to think about Herman. If only my heart would obey my mind. I would be good. The problem was my heart was still in love with him. My mind was telling me there was no way he loves you because of the way he treats and hurts you. A few days later Herman called me at work. This time I talked to him and the first thing I told him was my decision to join the air force. Herman asked why I was leaving everyone that loved me. I let him know I needed to get away to change my surroundings and improve my life. He asked if I even thought about him when I made that decision. Beginning to feel emotional I told Herman, *if I did think about him it would not make a difference because he had no intention of changing the way he treated me.* Herman told me, I was wrong because *he did love me and did not mean to hurt me.* He went on to say that he had a problem with his temper and needed me to help him get professional treatment. He pleaded if I gave him one more chance, I could personally make the doctor appointments for him to get treatment. Then he said words I was not prepared to hear. In the sincerest voice I had ever heard Herman speak, he said to me, *please do not leave me, I love and want to marry you.* Listening to him express his love and desire to marry me melted my heart. However, thoughts came to my mind if he would really stop hitting me. Knowing he would be getting professional help did give me hope that he would be able to stop hitting me. Trusting in my heart I begin to believe with Herman getting professional help we could have a loving beautiful life together. By the end of the conversation, I had agreed to marry Herman. Even though Herman knew I loved him and wanted to get married, he knew our future was contingent on him getting professional help. I made it perfectly clear, unless an appointment with a professional to address his angry outbursts was scheduled and attended there would be no marriage. The next week we made the appointments at the Clinic for Herman to see a psychologist. A week later Herman began his counseling sessions. I contacted my recruiting officer to let him know I would not be sworn in because I had decided to get married. He congratulated me and wished me the best in my future.

Herman and I had agreed once he started meeting with the psychologist, I would move into the apartment with him and Marvin. Momma and Linda Faye vehemently let me know how much they did not think it was a good ideal for me to again live with Herman. I explained to Momma and Linda Faye how Herman was being treated by a doctor at the Clinic for his anger issues. They let me know I should wait until he finished the counseling session before moving backing, but I let them know with prayer, our love for each other, and the counseling sessions I believed there would be no more hitting incidents. A month later, Herman and I went to Saint Phillips Lutheran Church, were several members of his family attended, to meet with Pastor McAdoo for a pre-marital counseling session and to set our wedding date. During the session neither of Herman or I mentioned his violent outbursts. We only discussed our love and commitment to each other and decided our wedding date would be July 7, 1977. In happy anticipation of getting married, our love and support for each other was steadily growing. On several weekends, Herman even went to get Vet and Dion to spend the weekend with us. Those weekends were fun filled with wonderful family time together. It was always great to see Herman interact with his sons. Looking at Herman with Vet and Dion made me excited about planning to have our baby. Herman was being a good fiancé by going to work regularly, not drinking and attending his counseling sessions. Our life was finally on the right track.

Once Herman and I were engaged, I soon experienced the phrase *it is a small world*, when Jackie, our family friend I had babysat for as a teen, worked at Ohio Bell with Herman's first wife, Christina. Somehow Christina knew Jackie was a close friend of my family. One day Jackie called me to ask if I could stop by her house. I said, yes. When I arrived, Jackie informed me Christina had asked her to let me know Herman was not the man I thought he was. She told Jackie to encourage me not to marry him. Of course, I thought it was because she was jealous that we were getting married. Jackie like other family members and friends had no clue about Herman beating me. Only Momma, Linda Faye, Darrell, Linda C. and the few co-workers that were at the cabaret, knew about the violent outburst. I asked Jackie did she give a reason for me not to marry him. Jackie answered, no, only that he was not the man he appears to be. I told Jackie thank you. Leaving her house, I still believed my first inclination that Christina was jealous we were getting married.

Marriages. In May 1977, Linda Faye and Darrell were married in Xenia. Momma, Herman, and I drove down from Cleveland. It was a lovely outdoor ceremony held in the backyard of the home of Darrell's sister and brother-in-law. Several family members and friends attended. Looking at Momma's face I could see it was one of the happiest days of her life as she watched her oldest daughter get married.

On July 1, 1977, Pastor McAdoo called me to confirm Hernan and I still planned to get married on Saturday, July 7th. Except for selecting and depositing a small payment towards my wedding dress, we had not made any other wedding plans. For this reason, I asked Pastor McAdoo if I could call him back. He said, of course. I spoke with Herman who said, of course we were getting married. I called Pastor McAdoo to let him know we would be there on the 7th to get married. Herman and I called our mothers to ask them to attend. The next day we went to the jewelry store to buy our rings. Linda C. and I then went to the wedding gowns store. I explained to the manager that I was getting married on Saturday and need a less expensive dress. The manager of the store was nice enough to allowed me to use my deposit towards the purchase of a less expensive dress. Although it was not the beautiful wedding dress I had selected, it was a charming laced beige dress. That Saturday we picked up Momma and Mrs. Ethel, Herman's mother. With our parents and Linda C. as witnesses, Pastor McAdoo married Herman and me. Although it was not the large fairytale wedding with all the bells and whistle I had dreamed of since a child, I was happy that day when I said, *I do*, to the love of my life. As I glanced at Momma smiling at me, I knew that day brought joy to her knowing that both of her daughters were married to the men they loved. Even though it was our special day and I could tell how happy Momma was for us, thoughts came to my mind of how much I wanted Momma to find true love and get married. I promised to continue praying she too would one day find her true love. After we took a few pictures, we went to dinner to celebrate.

Broken Promise. Although we did not go on an actual honeymoon, over the next few weeks it seemed like each day we were beginning our honeymoon all over again. Every day I was glad to be called, Mrs. DeBorah Washington. A few months later in mid-September, Herman had not given me his part of the bill money. Because we had been getting along so well, I was hesitant to rock the boat by asking him about the money. In the past when he had lost the bill money at the race track, he would get irritated. That day I believed that with his counseling sessions and now being married, Herman would not get upset when I asked about the money. When he came home, I pleasantly asked him about the money for the bills. Immediately I knew I was wrong about Herman staying calm. Herman immediately became argumentative. I tried to defuse the situation, but it was too late. Before I knew it, Herman walked over to the bed where I was sitting and slapped me in the head and face several times. He hollered at me for a short while about how he was tired of me nagging him. I sat quietly on the bed while he ranted and rave. He eventually went into the living room. I stayed in the bedroom, until I heard the door open and close. When I was sure he had drove off, I got off the bed, completely dumbfounded that he had broken his promise. However, I was glad this time he did not restrain me or hit me with the same intensity he had used in the past. Still sad and disappointed, I cried wondering why he continued to be unable to control his temper. Feeling defeated, I sobbed until I went to sleep.

When I woke up the next morning, Herman had not returned home. I began to feel very stupid for trusting Herman. Negative emotions of abandonment, worthlessness, and hopeless began to make me feel there was no use of living. For the first time since junior high school, I wanted to die. Initially I attempted to cut my wrist but was unable to withstand the pain. Then finding all the pills in the apartment I took them and went to bed. My next memory was waking up in the hospital. Later Momma told me she had tried calling me throughout the day. By late that evening when she was unable to contact me, she called the police to request they check on me. Momma told me how she explained to the police officer that Herman often beat on me and this made her worry he had seriously hurt me. When I did not respond to knocks on the door, the police had the building superintendent open the door. I was found in the bedroom unconscious. Momma said it was like déjà vu when the police officer called informing her of my condition and that the ambulance was taking me to the emergency room. Momma called Auntie and they both came to the hospital. Just like when I was in junior high school, my next memory was waking up groggy, hearing Momma voice and seeing a blurred vision of her face. Even though not fully conscious, I could see Momma looking nervous and worried as she walked towards me in the bed. With a sigh of relief in her voice, Momma said, *thank you Jesus for saving my daughter*. Holding my hand tightly,

Momma painfully asked, *why DeBorah Gail, why did you do this?* She went on to say, *the doctors had to pump your stomach to save you, please promise me you would not do this again.* Regretting disappointing my Momma this way again, tearfully I said how I was and terribly sorry. Momma let me know not to worry. Saying how overjoyed she was God had answered her prayers to let me be okay. Momma stayed with me until visiting hours were over. Throughout the night I thought how worried Momma looked and I felt horrible for letting her down. I humbly prayed to God for forgiveness and healing from trying to take my life. *Bless (affectionately, gratefully praise) the Lord, O my soul, and forget not [one of] all His benefits—who forgives [every one of] all your iniquities, who heals [each one of] all your diseases*, Psalm 103:2-3 (AMPC). I also prayed to God to deliver Herman from his violent outbursts and restore us to a healthy happy relationship. *Restore us again, O God of hosts; and cause Your face to shine [upon us with favor as of old], and we shall be saved*, Psalm 80:7 (AMPC). The next morning, I was stable enough to be discharged. I was questioned by doctors concerning my mental stability. After assurance from Momma that I would follow-up with a doctor at the Clinic, I was discharged. Auntie came to take us to Momma's apartment. Momma had called Linda Faye to let her know what happened. The next day Linda Faye and Darrell arrived in Cleveland. Linda Faye contacted Kathy, my supervisor, to informed her I tried to commit suicide over the weekend and per my discharge instructions I needed to have a follow-up psychiatric examination. After Linda Faye spoke with Kathy, arrangements were made to admit me for a psychiatric treatment. I remember little about the psychiatric treatment received, except talking to doctors about my suicidal attempt and attending group meetings. I later learned that Herman had not been to the apartment for two days. When he did return to find me not there, he called my job and was told I would not be in that day. He then called Momma's house. Linda Faye answered, and when Herman asked her if I was there, she let him know I tried to kill myself and was in the hospital. The next day Herman visited me at the hospital. He appeared earnestly concerned I had tried to take my life. Once more he swore the same typical things: never again going to hit me; would attend more appointments for counseling; and professed how much he loved me and wanted our marriage to work. Too mentally exhausted to dispute with Herman, I agreed to whatever he said. Momma and Linda Faye once more urged me not to go back with Herman. To the opposition of Momma, Linda Faye and my own mind telling me to stay away from Herman, when I was discharged from the hospital, I returned to the apartment with him. Although I went back to Herman, I did wonder why I persistently allowed the love in my heart to overrule my mind and the pleas of my loved ones to stay away from Herman. Was I insane to listen to Herman promises instead of Momma and Linda Faye urges? How could I keep on forgiving Herman for his violent outbursts? The only answer I had at that time, was I believed he would one change.

Once more, we appeared to be on the right track. Herman daily told me how thankful he was I did not die. More than ever before, he affectionately and compassionately expressed his love for me. He was going to work and being more financially responsible. The drinking and gambling had also subsided. He let me know appointments had been made to resume his sessions with the psychiatrist. Then in November 1977, the turbulent behavior resurfaced when Herman came home drunk and came into the bedroom and woke me up. He had decided that night he wanted to question me about my relationship with Marvin. When I asked Herman what he was talking about, it made him angrier. Attempting to avoid him getting more upset, I tried to leave the room. Herman pulled me down pinning me to the bed. He was hollering at me to answer his question. Before I could respond, he slapped me in the face. When I tried to squirm away, he pinned me down to the point I could not move. To my disbelief, for the first time Herman ripped off my clothes, pulled me to the bed, pinned me down and uncompassionately had sex with me. Afterwards he started dozing off while still on top of me. When I thought he was sleep, I would try to get up, but each time he would awake to stop me. He restrained me so long, I tried to tell him I needed to use the bathroom. He refused to let me up. This made me go to a new low when because I could no longer hold it and ended up urinating on myself. Despite being soaking wet, I could not get Herman off me. Finally, when I attempted to get from under him, he rolled off me and did not wake up. Quietly slipping out of the bed, I went into the bathroom. Scared and a nervous wreck I hurriedly wiped myself off. Tiptoeing back into the room, silently as possible I got dressed, grabbed a few clothes, and left the apartment. It was after midnight, when I arrived at Momma's apartment. Opening the door, I called out to Momma to let her know it was me. Momma woke up immediately asking if I was okay. Sitting on her bed I told her bits and pieces of what happened, except I was too embarrassed to tell her what he did to me sexually and how I urinated on myself. Momma firmly told me I had to stop going back to him. I let Momma know my plans to ask Linda Faye if I could come stay with her and Darrell for a few days. Momma agreed that was best for me. After Momma and I finished talking, I called Linda Faye. The first thing she said was are you okay. I told her yes and asked if I could come to their house for a few days. She said of course and told me to be careful. I let Linda Faye know I would be careful and would let her know what time the Greyhound bus would arrive in Xenia. Linda Faye said, okay, and that Darrell would pick me up from the bus station. I called my supervisor, Kathy to let her know my need to take a few vacation days. She said, okay. Although Kathy did not ask me, from the tone in her voice, she knew it had something to do with Herman. A few hours later I was on a Greyhound bus headed to Xenia. Upon my arrival, Darrell picked me up from the bus station. The entire time I was there, Linda Faye and Darrell were incredibly supportive and encouraging. I stayed with them for five days without any communication with Herman. My time was spent earnestly crying out to God for guidance for my life and marriage. From the day Herman first hit me, I had prayed to God for understanding why he hit me and to deliver him from his violent temperament. At this point in my life I was at my wits end and could only cry out to God for strength, help and understanding. I would sit for hours wondering how my relationship with Herman started loving and caring with such a great deal of potential only to turn abusive and cruel. In less than three years Herman had hit me several times causing physical injuries. How could he abruptly hurt me then moments later say he loved me. Why couldn't he always be the lovable, funny, supportive man I knew existed underneath the violent rage? How could my dream to be happily married long enough to celebrate fifty years of marriage become a reality if he would not stop hitting me. Lately I had even began to wonder if I would live long enough to celebrate my first anniversary yet alone fifty? My thoughts were filled with many mixed emotions. One moment I would be feeling full of peace as I spent time quietly studying the Bible, reading inspirational books, meditating, and seeking the will of God. Then the next minute adverse notions would overtake my mind triggering feelings of despondency, anxiety, loneliness, and indecisiveness. Thankfully this was another time when unaware to me there was a flicker of light being the mercy and grace of God sustaining me. *Behold, God is my helper and ally; The Lord is the sustainer of my soul [my upholder]*, Psalm 54:4 (AMP). With a fresh anointing of the Holy Spirit together with the love, support and encouragement received from Linda Faye and Darrell my soul was spiritually revived. It was soon time for me to return to Cleveland. I wished Momma and I could move to Xenia, but that was only wishful hoping. Reluctantly I returned to Cleveland with plans to live with Momma.

    I had not spoken with Herman since leaving the apartment. When I returned to work my co-workers told me Herman had called several times a day. The day of my return Herman reached me on the phone.

My heart sank at the sound of his voice, I said, hello. Without saying a word, I listened to Herman repeat the identical rendition of how much he loved me, and he was sorry. He assured me he was willing to get more professional help and was not drinking or going to the race track. It was mind-boggling how a week ago when jumping on me his voice was full of anger and hate. Now his voice sounded kind and loving. It was like he had two personalities. He was a mean violent man when attacking me. Then when he was not having a violent outrage, he was an affectionate, caring, and supportive husband whom I believed loved me. It was only when his other side of uncontrollable aggression roared up that troubled and scared me. I had no doubt if only he could control his temper we would be a happy couple, and the fairytale marriages I had watched on television and read about in books growing up would be attainable. This is what made it difficult for me to give up on Herman. Plus, I longed for our marriage to work, and I really wanted to believe Herman would not hit me anymore. Holding me back were the thoughts in my mind urging me to realize Herman had not changed, that he was not going to stop beating me, and would not attend the counseling sessions. On top of those, when Herman called me at Momma's apartment, after I hung up the phone, Linda Faye and Momma repeatedly told me they did not want me to go back to Herman because they were afraid he would seriously or permanently hurt me. Weeks went by with Herman calling several times a day asking me to give him another chance. Repeatedly he promised not to lose his temper. Slowly the love in my heart over ruled the thoughts in my mind and the desires of Momma and Linda

Faye. Yet again I forgave Herman and began to go out on dates with him. For several weeks it was like the days we dated. We went out to eat, movies, parks, and long drives. Although I had not moved back into the apartment, we spent lots of time there bonding by talking, playing games, and holding each other. Spending increasingly time at the apartment without any signs of violent behavior, eventually I moved completely back in with Herman. Momma and Linda Faye fervently questioned my decision. Despite their thoughts, I did not listen. With a hardhead and bleeding heart I refused to give up on Herman and our marriage.

As usual for about two months, our marriage was going smoothly. Herman was working hard and keeping his promise not to physically hurt me. Then unexpectedly Herman did not come home for several days. I checked with his family members and friends. No one had heard from Herman. On Friday it had been four days since he had been home. Several weeks before I had made plans for that night to take Kim M., one of my co-workers that had recently began to work at the Clinic, out to dinner to celebrate her birthday. Kim M. picked me up and we went to the restaurant. Although we often talked at work and lunch, this was our first time socializing outside of the Clinic. We had a nice dinner and enjoyable time becoming more acquainted with each other. Talking and laughing we discussed our job, family, teenage years and hopes for our future. In my typical manner I was too embarrassed to discuss my marital problems. Unless a co-worker at the Clinic had told Kim M., she had no idea of how Herman had knocked me out in front of several co-workers.

Throughout the dinner my women's intuition had silently been kicking into high gear. On our way back to her car, I asked Kim M. if we could make one stop before going home. She said, of course. Although Kim M. had no idea where we were going, I knew. I planned to ride by Laurice house to see if Herman's car was there. When Kim M. pulled down the street, right away I spotted his car. My intuition was right. His car was parked in front of her house. I had thought on the way over what I would do if his car was there. My intention was to knock on the door and ask for him. When Herman came to the door, I planned to tell him to leave me alone and stay with Laurice. Pointing to the house I told Kim M., I needed to stop at that house for a moment. She said, okay. I did not tell her why. Getting out the car, I said, I will be right back. I walked up the stairs, rang the doorbell and knocked on the door. A few moments later a voice asked, who is it? I said, tell Herman his wife is outside. It took Herman over five minutes to come outside. By the time Herman came out I was standing on the side walk. As he walked towards me, I threw my wedding ring towards him while yelling, stay with Laurice because I am done with you. Turning to head back to the car, I suddenly felt the pain for being hit on in my head that caused my knees to buckle and I fall down to the ground. Before I could get up, Herman was bent over swinging punches to my head and upper body, shouting, *I'm going to kill you.* Attempting to get away from him, I was screaming, flinging my arms, and wildly kicking my feet. I finally managed to scoot a few inches away from Herman as I tried to get on my feet. Herman grabbed the back of my coat pulling me back down. I could hear Kim

M. screaming, leave her alone. Trying desperately to get away, I persistently kicked and used my hands and arms to shield the blows to my head. Eventually one of my kicks hit Herman, and he bent over, and I was able to stumble to my feet. Unfortunately, he was still able to grab me again by the back of my coat. The collar and arm of the coat ripped and was hanging off me. Then Herman grabbed me by my dress and it tore. Struggling I finally bit his hand and was able to break away from his grip. Staggering to run, I spotted a garbage can on the curb. I grabbed the lid of the trash can throwing it towards him. By this time my entire dress was hanging around my ankles. I had no idea where my shoes were. To run, I stepped out of my dress. Running towards the car Kim M. opened the passenger door. She was yelling for me to hurry up and get in the car. Herman was behind me, but instead of chasing me he headed for his car where he was opening the trunk of his car. I had made it to the car and Kim M. was driving off. When Kim M. looked out the rear-view mirror, she yelled, *he has a shotgun*. I turned looking out the back window, where I saw Herman with the shotgun in his hand trying to chase after the car. Kim M. floored the gas pedal. Shaking and nervous we felt relieved when Herman was out of our sight, and we sighed a breath of relief. We were both shouting thank you Jesus he did not get to the gun before I got into the car.

My eyes were swollen and practically shut closed. Blood was flowing from my nose and lips. Mostly every inch of my body was aching. With nothing but my slip and underwear on I was cold and shivering. Kim M. stopped the car to get a blanket out of her trunk.

Thanking her I wrapped the blanket around me. Kim M. said, you're welcome, and said she was still in shock. She went on to say, I cannot believe what just happened. Then Kim M. said, please do not tell me that was Herman your husband. I said, yes. Trying to drive she looked over at me startled and said with earnest concern, *you must leave and divorce him before he kills you.* I nodded my head in agreement.

Driving towards Warrensville Hts., Kim M. asked if I was okay to make it to Suburban Hospital emergency room. I answered, yes. When we arrived at the emergency room, I received medical attention for black eyes, cuts, abrasions, and bruises. X-rays were taken to confirm no head trauma or upper body internal injuries. The Warrensville Hts. police department were called. A police report was made, and photos taken of my face, head, and body. I was diagnosed with mild to moderate contusions on my face and over my lower and upper body. I also had a slight concussion. Following treatment and finalizing the report with the police officer I was discharged. The nurse had given me prescriptions, together with directions to follow at home. She explained how to watch for complications and instructed me to schedule a follow-up appointment with my doctor. Kim M. then took me to the apartment. I was glad Marvin was not there as I put some clothes on and grabbed as many clothes as possible. When left the apartment, Kim M. asked if I was able to drive my car. I answered, yes. She told me she would follow me to my mother's apartment. Once I was parked in Momma's parking space, I went to Kim M.'s car and gave her a big hug and told her how sorry I was for spoiling her birthday celebration and thanked her for everything. Kim M. said, it was no problem, but she only wanted me to promise to stay away from Herman. I said, okay. Opening the door to the apartment, I called out, Momma. Hearing her say, *are you okay*, I could sense the concern in her voice. I said, yes, I'm okay, and went directly into my old bedroom. Momma came into the room. When she saw the bruises over my face and the exposed parts of my neck, arms, and hands the expression of anxiety on her face broke my heart. I told Momma what happened. Momma let me know how it was breaking her heart to see me abused by Herman. She begged me to leave him before he completely maimed or killed me. I said, okay, Momma. She then told me to try to get some sleep. In the morning, my body ached all over. Kim M. called to check on me and was kind enough to get my prescriptions filled for me. In pain, but mostly because I did not want anyone to see my bruises, I stayed off work for several days until my body wasn't as sore and the exposed bruises weren't very visible.

After returning to work I received many messages that Herman had called. That day and each day thereafter he called. For several days I ignored his calls. One day I broke down and answered his phone call. This time not only was he apologizing for hitting me and insisting he wanted our marriage to work, Herman vowed never again to see Laurice. Momma and Linda Faye were pleading with me to stay away from Herman. Kim M. was also constantly telling me not to talk or see him. Thinking I knew better than them I refused to listen to their pleas for me to leave him alone. Instead for weeks I secretly kept it from Momma and Linda Faye that I was talking to Herman. Regardless of what they said about the manner in which Herman treated me was not true love, but I was sure he loved me. They also did not understand I needed my marriage to work. As in the past, within a couple of weeks, I had forgiven Herman and moved back into the apartment. Yet again, we started working towards reconciling our marriage.

    One day I was cooking while Herman was laying on the couch watching television. I opened the door to the electric stove. Suddenly there was a loud booming sound with a bright spark of light. It caused me to be thrown back. I heard Herman scream my name. He then appeared in the kitchen, grabbed, and hugged me tightly. He asked if I was okay. I replied, yes. When he was sure I was okay, Herman called the janitor to let him know what happened with the oven and asked him to come check it out. That day two things happened in those few seconds for which I gave thanks to God. First the janitor informed us the boom was caused by an electrical short in the oven. He told us without the oven mitten I could have been electrocuted. I now can appreciate even on that day there was a flicker of light from God of mercy that did not allow an unexpected electric short in the stove to physically harm me. *The Lord will keep you from all harm— he will watch over your life,* Psalm 121:7 (NIV). Second when Herman screamed out my name, I heard the love and concern in his voice because he thought something terrible had happened to me. In addition, when he grabbed and held me tightly asking if I was okay, it reminded me of the beautiful days we shared when he was not having violent outbursts. That day I saw how much Herman did love and care about me. Seeing that side of him always made it hard to understand why he was unable to control his outbursts of rage. It made me begin to wonder if Herman had a mental disorder like Momma. With Momma, her mental breakdowns were triggered every five years like clockwork. Was there something within Herman's mind that triggered his rages? I began to pray more fervently for Herman to be healed from his outbursts. My prayer also was that he would adhere to his promises to be faithful, continue the sessions with the psychologist and that the sessions would give a solution to deter the violent outbreaks.

Our Own Home. For more than four months, Herman had kept his promise of being a good husband. He had not hit me, come home drunk, or stayed out all night. We were doing much better. In early March, I begin to feel sick and thought it was a virus. Suddenly I realized I did not have my monthly cycle. When I went to the doctor, I was given a pregnancy test. The next day the doctor told me I was pregnant. Herman was extremely excited stating he wanted it to be a girl. It was one of the happiest days for us. Starting a new family, we knew residing at the apartment with Marvin was not going to work. We agreed it was time to start looking for a house to buy. In April 1978, with the financial help of Momma, we purchased a colonial style home on Glendale Avenue in Cleveland. In our own home, Herman was like a new man and truly contented as a husband and soon to be father again. Because Herman loved building, painting, and fixing things, he did a lot of interior and exterior work on the house. A few months later, Herman let me know his mother needed a place to stay. Of course, I agreed to her moving in because I adored

Mrs. Ethel and we had a good relationship. Our lives once again seemed on the right track.

But, oh no, the *honeymoon period* always ended without any warning. In June, I was about five months pregnant, it was a Friday and pay day for Herman. We were discussing the bills to be paid when he told me he was going out and would give me his portion of the bill money when he returned. In the past, Herman would sometimes tell me same story on his pay days, only to go out and return home broke. This would leave it up to me to make up the difference. That day I decided to ask him not to take all the money because he might spend more than he should. This made him mad. Before I knew it, Herman began slapping my face and head as he hollered saying do not tell me what to do with my money. I ducked under one of his swings and ran down the stairs crying and screaming for him to stop. I went into Mrs. Ethel's room, jumped into her bed, and I tried to get her to shield me from Herman who had followed me down the stairs. Mrs. Ethel told Herman to stop, while I hide behind her back holding onto her arms. Not listening to his mother, Herman grabbed my feet and pulled me out of her bed, up the stairs that lead to her room into the living room where he hit me several more times. Mrs. Ethel came out of her room shouting for Herman to stop. He yelled at both of us to shut up. Finally, he stopped. Herman grabbed his car keys and left out the house. A few seconds later, I heard his car zoom away.

Suddenly I began to feel like I really needed to use the bathroom. I went up the stairs to the bathroom. Sitting on the toilet pushing as it seemed like I was constipated. Within few minutes, I felt something coming out of my vagina, it was the baby. Oh, no my baby had come out. I hollered out to Mrs. Ethel to please come help me. When she came into the bathroom, I told her the baby had come out. Not knowing what to do, I asked her to bring me scissors to cut the cord. She said, no, you cannot cut the cord, we need to call the ambulance. Mrs. Ethel called the emergency operator for an ambulance. When the paramedics arrived, the cord was removed from the baby and I was taken to the hospital. Laying on the gurney in the emergency room, I saw Herman come rushing into the doors of the emergency room. He was rushing towards me. I held out my arms for his embrace believing we were about to console each other for the loss of our child. Beyond my wildest beliefs, when Herman reached the gurney he started to jump on me. When the emergency room employees and security guards noticed what he was doing to me they ran to help me. Everyone tried to calm Herman down, but he would not stop trying to attack me. He was repeatedly saying, *you killed my baby*. The hospital employees pushed my bed into an area away from Herman. One of the nurses later told me the Warrensville Hts. police had arrested Herman and taken him to the police station. Momma arrived at the hospital upset and worried about my welfare. She was even more upset when told why Herman was arrested. The medical staff assured Momma I would be okay. Laying in the bed, I could see the disappointed and upset look on the face of Momma and the disbelief on faces of the medical staff. I also heard a few people whispering about the way Herman behaved. Seeing the expressions on their faces and hearing the whispering, I knew there was no way I could tell them

Herman had jumped on me shortly before I lost the baby. It was a blessing the bruises on my face was not too evident. Once Herman calmed down, he was released and allowed to come back to the hospital. He returned in a calmer demeanor. He apologized to me, Momma, and the hospital staff. We then mourned the loss of our baby boy. I was admitted to the hospital and a dilation and curettage (D&C) procedure was scheduled for the next day. The day after the D&C, Herman came to pick me up after I was discharged from the hospital. Herman and I never discussed the fact his hitting me prior to the miscarriage could have contributed to the miscarriage.

The grief from losing our baby boy was emotionally difficult for me. Thankfully Herman was more affectionate and support of me during this time. It seemed like the tragic loss of our unborn child was helping bonding us closer together. Disappointedly it was another façade. After several months of living a normal life, we prepared to attend the birthday party for Mary, one of my co-workers and friends from the Clinic. Mary was one of my co-workers that had witnessed Herman knock me out at the Camelot. I was getting dressed and Herman was fussing at me about something that I cannot even remember. Suddenly Herman hit me in the back of my head, he then spun me around and hit me on my face and head several times. He then began to choke me. As I began to fall to my knees, Herman let go of my throat. Coughing I crawled to a corner of the room where I curled up as I continued to cough and started crying. Seeing Herman coming toward me, I wished I could call out to Mrs. Ethel for help, but she was not home. When Herman reached me, he hit me a few more times before he stormed out of the room. I stayed curled up in the corner until I heard his car pull out the driveway. Emotions of hurt and emptiness from the miscarriage, coupled with hopelessness of Herman ever changing the way he beat me, I did not want to live. For the third time in my life, I attempted suicide. I took a variety of pills. Herman returned home and woke me up. Due to the pills I was in a semi-unconscious state. It was like I was sleep walking. I remember almost nothing about that evening. I do not recall getting dressed or going to the birthday. The only way I realized that I attended the party is Mary told me. She let me know how Herman and I arrived and I talked and ate. She knew something was wrong with me, but with Herman with me she did not want to ask too many questions that would cause him to get upset. Without Mary letting me know I was there, I would have thought it was a dream. I never told Herman about taking the pills. Mentally to myself I questioned why I did not die while also trying to figure out what caused Herman to return home. Today I know it was another flicker of light from God that saved me when I was too weak to stand for myself. *My flesh and my heart faileth: but God is the strength of my heart, and my portion for ever.* Psalm 73:26 (KJV). It was a two-fold blessing that day, Herman returned home and woke me up which kept me from dying that night.

Visits from Tim. Mid-September 1978, Tim contacted Momma asking for my phone number because he wanted to visit me. Initially I was hesitant for Momma to give him my phone number. Momma encouraged me to be nice to Tim and allow him to visit. She reinstated to me that I had to be nice regardless of circumstances because he was my father. Shortly thereafter, I called Tim to arrange the visit. Given that Tim had never met Herman, this would be a good opportunity for them to meet. Surprisingly when Tim arrived he had a little girl with him. He came into the house and introduced the little girl, she was his daughter, my little sister, Kimberly (Kim) Ann Williford. I said hello and asked her how old she was. She told me twelve years old. We sat on the couch with Kim sitting quietly next to Tim while Tim and I talked. We had a cordial visit. Herman did not come home before Tim had to leave, so I told him they would meet the next time he visited. Over the next few months Tim visited several times. Tim and Herman met on one of those visits. Since they both were born in December, Herman and Tim felt they had a lot in common and enjoyed talking and joking together. During one of his visits, Tim let Herman know that his brother Philip had several small business ventures. One of the business was selling socks and pantyhose. Tim asked Herman to sell the items in the Cleveland area. Even though Herman knew nothing about sales, he agreed to try to sell the items. This was a short-lived agreement because Herman did sell the items. The problem was Herman spent not only his profit, but the money he was supposed to give to Tim and Philip. After many unsuccessful attempts to get their money from Herman, they gave up. Shortly thereafter, Tim disappeared from my life until the late 1990s.

Unexpected Disgrace. A few weeks later Herman let me know his mother would be moving in with one of her daughters. It was bitter-sweet for me because I enjoyed her company but would have thought her living with us would have stopped Herman from hitting me. Sadly, it had not. After Mrs. Ethel moved, Hubby would occasional stay with Herman and me. In October 1978, Herman, and I together with Hubby and other family members attended a birthday party for one of his cousins in Cleveland Hts. After the party, Herman was driving home with Hubby and me in the car. His nephew, Leo was following behind us with family members in his car. Herman abruptly started to hassle me. Knowing he had drank at the party, I sat quietly trying not to agitate him. Herman said to me, *don't you hear me talking to you*? Next thing I knew Herman reached over and backhanded slapped me in the face several times and I could feel my lips bleeding. When he stopped at a red light, I jumped out of the car. Herman got out the car hollering at me while chasing me down the street. When Herman caught me, he yanked me around and began punching me in the face and head, while saying where you think you going. I stumbled backwards to the ground as I tried to protect my head and face from his blows. Leo, Hubby and a few other family members had gotten out of their cars. They ran towards us trying to stop Herman from beating me. Herman started hitting and screaming at them. Eventually they were able to stop Herman from hitting me. Everyone went back to their cars as Herman pulled me back into the car, pushed me inside and drove off. All the way home and after we were in the house, he yelled about why I always made him hit me. I said, what did I do? This only made him more furious resulting in more hits. Although Hubby was downstairs, he did not come to help me. Eventually Herman stopped screaming and hitting me and went to sleep. The next morning Herman looked at the bruises over my body. He then apologized for hitting me. Followed by assuring me he would stop hitting me. I sat quietly listening. Months ago, I had to finally concede that Herman would never keep his promises not to hurt and hit me. Feeling hopeless, tired, and weary I decided in the future to simply succumb to his yelling and hitting me.

In October 1978, I woke up feeling sickly. I made an appointment with my doctor. He asked me when I had my last menstruation. I could not remember so the doctor ordered a pregnancy test. The next day the doctor informed me I was pregnant. Once again Herman was excited hoping it would be a girl. I began to pray that God I would be blessed to carry the baby to full term. That by His grace the baby would be healthy. Through the mercy of Jesus Christ my pregnancy would not be filled with violent outbursts from Herman. I further prayed for a miraculous intervention from the Holy Spirit upon Herman for him to become a non-violent husband and excellent father. Paraphrasing 2 Corinthians 9:14, *And [I] yearn for [us] while [I] pray for [us], because of the surpassing measure of God's grace (His favor and mercy and spiritual blessing which is shown forth) in [us]*. Gratefully after being told I was pregnant the hope of a bundle of joy coming into our lives brought a renewed positive outlook into our marriage. Praise be to God that answers to prayers were being revealed with the disposition of Herman gradually improving. With Thanksgiving Day approaching, I was thankful to God that I was pregnant again, and I prayed that our baby would be born into a loving family, and that Herman would no longer have his violent outbursts towards me.

Unforeseen Disastrous Storm. I often heard the sayings *you never know what tomorrow will bring* and *just when you think things are getting better they turn for the worse.* True to those statements an unexpected ravaging storm that would hit me like a ton of bricks was on the horizon. My work schedule had always included working every other weekend. November of 1978, I was scheduled to work the weekend after Thanksgiving Day. While placing documents on the desk of my supervisor, Kathy, I noticed my name on her calendar for a meeting with the director of our department. For a few passing moments I wondered why my name was on the calendar, but soon forgot about it as I began to complete my work assignments. On Monday when I arrived at work, I had forgotten about the note on the calendar until Kathy called me to her desk stating the director needed to meet with me. I said, okay. Going to get my coat to walk to the other building where the meeting was being held, I thought to myself it had to be something positive because I was a superb worker that received excellent reviews and was highly regarded by my supervisors, co-workers, and patients. The director might need to see me because he had received another letter or gift from one of my patients in appreciation of the services I rendered to them. Even better yet it could be a promotion. Excited at the thought of meeting with the director, I hurried to office where Kathy told me the meeting was being held. When I arrived at the office, I knocked on the door. A man's voice said, come in. When I entered the office, the director was sitting in a chair and a security officer behind the desk. They told me to come in, close the door and have a seat. After I sat down, the security guard behind the desk told me that I was being fired from the Clinic for using the letterhead of the Clinic to falsify correspondences to the employer of Herman Washington that said he had appointments at the Clinic. In total shock my mind reflected on the last letter I had given Herman for missing work. Terrified I began to nervously shake and with tears filling my eyes, I tried to explain why I had written the letters. While talking, my mind wandered back to the first time Herman had asked me to write a letter to his job using the letterhead. It was when Laurice had him arrested. After writing the first letter, Herman would get drunk and be unable to wake up for work the next day. Each time this happened he would insist I write a letter to excuse him from work. Writing the letters, I was too imprudent to realize my grammar and spelling had not improve since taking the military exam. When Herman's employer received several letters with spelling and grammar errors, his supervisor contacted the Clinic. The management of the Clinic reviewed the information from the supervisor and knew without a doubt I prepared the fraudulent letters. Not only did the Clinic decide to fire me, the director intended to file charges against me for forging the name of the doctor. The security officer behind the desk asked how I knew not to use the actual name of the doctor. Holding my head down in shame with tears running down my face I answered, I did not know. Looking at me with skepticism and condescension he told me, *I must really know about forgery because I did not use the actual name of the doctor*. I replied, *no I knew nothing about forgery*. Unbeknown to me I could only be charged with forgery if I had used the actual name of the doctor. Thankfully the Clinic was unable to press charges against me for forgery because I never used the actual name of any doctor. As I was escorted to get my personal items then off the premises, my heart sank, and fear consumed me. Looking back on that day there is no doubt that in the midst of that self-inflicted heavy storm bearing down and exploding into one of the traumatic times of life there were flickers of light from Jesus Christ of forgiveness and being blessed. *And their sins and their lawless acts I will remember no more [no longer holding their sins against them]. Now where there is [absolute] forgiveness and complete cancellation of the penalty of these things, there is no longer any offering [to be made to atone] for sin*, Hebrews 10:17-19 (AMP). That day because of my self-inflicted sin, I could have been charged with forgery, instead Jesus Christ blessed me to only lose my job. Often throughout various times of my life I think back pondering two things about being fired from the Clinic. First, I knew nothing about not using the actual name of the doctor would prevent a forgery charge. The reason I did not use the first name of the doctor was because I did not know if or how to correctly spell it. Second if I would have been charged with forgery how what would be the difference in the future? Unfortunately, both are hypothetical questions, that praise be to God I no longer ponder why.

Shortly after I arrived home, Herman came home. He also had been terminated from his job. Waking up the next morning to the reality of being several weeks pregnant with both of us unemployed, I knew wallowing in sadness and pity was not an option. Too embarrassed to let Momma, Linda Faye, or anyone else know that we both were fired and why, I pretended life was good. With little savings meant we had to quickly obtain employment. A few days after my termination I re-registered with Kelly Girl Temporary Agency. The manager was glad to have me available to again work again for the agency. Within a day the agency referred me to CT Corp, a statutory agent company for corporations. Fortunately, I was immediately hired by CT as a secretary. It was a small office located in downtown Cleveland. The employees consisted of three lawyers, two agents, and three secretaries, including me, and I was the only minority. Needing to have enough income until Herman obtained employment, I also obtained a part-time job as a server at Red Lobster in Beachwood. I worked at Red Lobster during the evenings and weekends. In the meantime, Herman had applied for and was approved for unemployment that he would receive until he secured employment. To enable Herman to seek employment, I would take the train downtown to my daytime job. After getting off my daytime job, I would take the train to the stop closest to my second job where Herman would pick me up and drop me off at Red Lobster. He would pick me at the end of my shift.

Even with the termination of our jobs, we were both trying to maintain our lifestyle and prepare for the birth of our baby. Christmas of 1978, Momma, Linda Faye, and Darrell came to our house for dinner and to exchange Christmas gifts. When Herman gave me my gift, it was a big box that I quickly opened. To my surprise inside the big box was a shoe box. When I opened the shoe box it was only one of my old tennis shoes. Disappointed I threw the shoe at Herman. He began to laugh. Linda Faye said you should look inside the shoe. Still laughing Herman said, no, she does not want what is inside. I said, *yes, I do, please give it back.* After fondly teasing me for a moment, Herman handed me the shoe. Looking inside the shoe there was a small jewelry box tucked inside. When I opened it, inside there was a wedding ring. Herman had bought me another ring to replace the one I threw at him in front of Laurice's house. We then hugged each other tightly. That day was one of the most memorable days of our marriage. I prayed that each day in our future would be that loving.

A few weeks later it was a very wintry night in January 1979, I was very tired from working both of my jobs. Anxious to get home to go to bed, I waited for Herman to pick me up. My shift had ended at 9:30 p.m. After waiting for twenty minutes, I called the house to see if Herman had overslept. There was no answer. I had waited so long for Herman the restaurant had closed. All the employees had left, except the manager who reluctantly stayed with me. Around 11:30 p.m., two hours after the time I had told Herman I would get off, he zoomed into the empty parking lot. I thanked the manager for waiting with me. When I got into the car, Herman had a beer in his hand and appeared to be drunk. He had the audacity to be laughing at the situation thinking it was funny. He repeatedly said I should not be upset. Exhausted and disappointed he had made me wait so long, I begin to cry telling him how wrong it was to leave me waiting that long. I asked him how he could do this to me when I am three months pregnant and had worked my day and evening jobs. I also let him know that getting home this late I would not get much sleep before I had to get up to go back to work. Noticing Herman was getting irritated from me complaining, I sat quietly the remainder of the ride home. He pulled into the driveway of the house. Before I could get the door of the car opened, Herman punched me in the head. Jumping out the car Herman came around the car opened my car door. He snatched me out of the car by the hood of my coat. Holding onto me by the hood, Herman was trying to open the door of the house. I tried to run away, he caught me by the collar of my coat. Opening the door to the house he dragged me into the eating area of the kitchen, tossed me against the wall and began hitting. Instead of trying to shield my head, I bent over to protect my stomach. He punched each side of my head several more times. He then grabbed the broom from the corner of the room. He swung the handle hitting my legs and back. Staying crouched down frantically I tried to keep my stomach shield. With the broom in one hand Herman grasped and pulled me to the kitchen table where he made me sit. He began to lecture me on why I made him hit me. How I always made him get upset by talking too much and it was my fault he was upset. Herman asked me did I understand what he was saying. When I did not reply, he swung the broom so hard it was a blessing I had moved my hand, because the broom handle hit the table so hard that it put a dent in the wooden table. Years later that dent reminded me of that terrifying night. Learning from previous attacks it was best for me to be submissive and quiet until he went to sleep. That night when Herman went to sleep, with as little noise as possible, I put clothing and personal items in a bag. Quietly I took the keys to my car and left out the house. Pulling out the driveway I wondered where to go because I was not ready to tell Momma and Linda Faye that Herman again had jumped on me. I knew if Momma and Linda Faye found out Herman had hit me this early in my pregnancy it was only going to make them be even more worried and afraid about the well-being of me, and now, the baby, as well. The only other place I could go was to Linda C.'s apartment. While I drove to her apartment with tears in my eyes I was distraught and beyond understanding the reason Herman would try to hurt our unborn baby and me. Crying out to God, I prayed please shield and protect our unborn child from harm, together with guide and strengthen me. All the while my mind was going haywire trying to comprehend how could Herman hit me again while I was pregnant? Didn't he remember what happened before when I lost our other baby. How was I going to bring a baby into a home with such a volatile environment? If I could not keep myself safe, how would I be able to protect my baby?

It was around 1:30 a.m. when I arrived at the apartment. Knowing Linda C. worked the second shift, I was not for sure if she would be home yet because she usually arrived home a little after 2:00 a.m. After ringing her doorbell with no answer, like I anticipated she was not home yet. Eventually someone came out the lobby door and I was able to enter the building. I went to the apartment door of Linda C. where I sat on the floor to wait for her. Sitting there I silently cried and prayed because I had no idea what I was going to do. When Linda C. turned the corner to see me sitting on the floor, she was shocked. Beginning to hurry down the hall she said, *what is wrong*? One look at me told the reason I was waiting for her to come home. Tears still in my eyes, I asked if I could please stay with her for a little while. In a concerned tone Linda C. said, of course. She gladly welcomed me into her apartment. I was very thankfully to God for blessing me to still have my childhood best friend in my life here to support me in this urgent time of need. The next morning, I let Momma and Linda Faye know I was staying with Linda C. I did not let them know that Herman had jumped on me and what caused him to lose his temper. A few days later, I met with Attorney Ed Wade for legal advice about getting a divorce. Once Mr. Wade informed me about the procedures for filing a complaint for divorce and what to expect, I let Mr. Wade know my intentions and that I would follow-up with him.

In early February during my routine examination my obstetrician, Dr. Kelly, informed me due to my previous miscarriage and the weakness of my uterus, a suture known as a cervical cerclage might would be required for me to carry the baby to full term. Because Dr. Kelly did not perform this type of procedure or treat high-risk pregnancy cases, he referred me to a high-risk pregnancy doctor, Dr. Michael Gyves. I made an appointment with Dr. Gyves and at my first appointment, he explained the suture procedure to me. Although I called Herman to let him know about the procedure and when it was scheduled, the day of the procedure Herman did not come to the hospital. Linda C. took me to the hospital where Dr. Gyves successfully performed the procedure. Once I was discharged, Linda C. took me back to her apartment. Following the procedure, a few days later I returned to work and continued living with Linda C.

without any communication with Herman. Like previous times when separated from Herman there would be times I thought about and missed him. The difference this time was my primary focus was on the future of our baby that I was fighting to bring to full term instead of worrying about Herman. For the first time I was positively adjusting to living without Herman. By the beginning of March, I decided to quit my part-time job at Red Lobster because I was becoming too exhausted trying to work both jobs.

Uneducated and Embarrassed. One day in April 1979 when I arrived at work I was informed by the office manager that the general manager was taking me to lunch. Surprised, I wondered why he wanted to have lunch with me. I prayed it would be a positive luncheon. Sitting down for lunch our conversation was pleasant small talk. Initially he asked how I was feeling, which was probably because in mid-February I had told my co-workers I was pregnant. Of course, they had no idea of my marital problems. The manager asked me a few more non-invasive personal questions about my past educational and employment background. I was beginning to believe this was simply a casual luncheon. This thought quickly faded when suddenly the conversation changed when the manager told me he and the office manager had been contacted by a few clients about correspondences from Anthony (Tony), the agent I worked for, complaining the documents had several typographical errors. The manager pulled for his suit jacket pocket several correspondences. He pointed out to me spelling and grammar errors in the correspondences. Stating he understood Tony dictates the correspondences then I listen to the tape transcribing it to a typed document that I give to Tony to sign. The manager went on to say Tony is signing the documents I type without reading them. Memories of being fired from the Clinic rushed throughout my mind. The only difference was instead of the employer of Herman, clients had called the manager. This time the problem was not forged documents, but many typographical errors in several correspondences I had typed. The manager with sincere concern stated, usually this situation would result in termination. The manager then told me he had decided not to fire me under certain conditions: I would have to work on thoroughly proofreading the documents I typed; and until I proved my ability to efficiently proofread the office manager would review my correspondences. I expressed to the manager my heartfelt appreciation for giving me a second chance. Promising him I would work hard to improve my writing and spelling skills. Walking back to the office although very thankful to still have my job, I felt humiliated. This was the third time my inability to proficiently read and write had negatively affected my life. Why hadn't I taken the incentive to improve my ability to read and write when I scored extremely low on the military entrance test or when writing fraudulent letters having typos caused my termination from the Clinic? That day, I pledged to constantly read books to improve my vocabulary and writing skills together with learning the spelling and meaning of unfamiliar words. Each day I tried to learn how to spell an unfamiliar word. My goal became to know the spelling of each word I spoke. Gradually my ability to write, proofread and speak started to improve. Lunch that day with the manger resulted in several blessings. I was blessed to maintain my job which was a miracle for me being that I was six months pregnant. Then definitely I finally realized the need to improve my spelling and grammar skills. It also made me recognize the importance of a good education. At that point I vowed one of my top priorities for my unborn child would be to assure a thorough education by enrollment in the best possible schools. Reflecting on the day I had lunch with the manager there was truly a flicker of light from God of immeasurable grace and blessings. *And He raised us up together with Him [when we believed], and seated us with Him in the heavenly places, [because we are] in Christ Jesus, [and He did this] so that in the ages to come He might [clearly] show the immeasurable and unsurpassed riches of His grace in [His] kindness toward us in Christ Jesus [by providing for our redemption]. For it is by grace [God's remarkable compassion and favor drawing you to Christ] that you have been saved [actually delivered from judgment and given eternal life] through faith. And this [salvation] is not of yourselves [not through your own effort], but it is the [undeserved, gracious] gift of God,* Ephesians 2:6-8 (AMP).

My Reason to Live. My pregnancy was going well. Living with Linda C. was working good for both of us. Linda C. was the epitome of a loyal friend. She was very caring, giving and loving to me and her soon to be niece or nephew. Momma, Linda Faye, and Linda C. were happy and proud of me for staying away from Herman. Mentally I struggled with how being a single parent I was going to take care of my baby. I knew first-hand how being raised in a single-family home with no father affected me psychologically with feelings of being abandoned and discarded. Thoughts of my baby experiencing those feelings were daunting. My other concern was Herman had no problem hitting me with our baby in my stomach. This made me wonder if after the birth he would harm our baby. Because to my knowledge Herman never hurt Vet or Dion, it was my prayer he would not mistreat our child. With the passing of each day emotionally it was a mental battle within me if I could provide for my baby as a single parent like Momma did for Linda Faye and me. I began to question what type of life would my baby have with only me? Could I be a good mother and provider like Momma? Consuming my mind was uncertainty and doubt. Could I be a good mother when I was unable to be a good wife? I began to doubt my ability to give my baby a stable loving home when I could not make a happy loving household for Herman and me. My baby deserved a nurturing home with two good parents that loved, cherished, and supported each other and their baby. Could I provide that life for my baby? Consuming my mind was would I even make it to full-term with my pregnancy. Entering my eighth month of pregnancy I hid from everyone not only my thoughts of suicide but how emotionally exhausted and worried I was about caring for my baby. I knew my baby deserved a stable home, not one filled with arguments, fighting, drinking, depression, and my reoccurring thoughts of suicide. Alone with my thoughts I begin to contemplate if adoption for my baby would offer a much better life.

A few days later in June 1979, I begin to see spots of blood in my underwear. I called Dr. Gyves, his answering service answered, I let the lady know why I was calling. She said, Dr. Gyves would be paged. A few moments later, Dr. Gyves returned my call and told me to go to the emergency room. Once examined at the emergency room, I was admitted for further evaluation. When Dr. Gyves came to examine me, he noticed I was not my usual self. Somehow, he detected my state of depression. Of course, nowadays I know it was the grace of God that Dr. Gyves recognized my mental state. Dr. Gyves suggested I talk with a counselor. Upon speaking with the counselor, I shared my concerns about being a good mother to my baby and thoughts of adoption. As usual, I did not mention the violence in my marriage, only that we had problems and were separated. Afraid of being required to see a psychiatrist, I did not say anything about my thoughts of suicide. The counsel suggested I keep thinking about my choices and let her know my decision. Tearfully I said ok, that I would. In spite of calling Herman to let him know I was in the hospital, he never came to visit. Thankfully I had Momma, Auntie and Linda C. came to visit me. A few days later I was discharged with instructions to stay off my feet as much as possible.

Although Herman and Hubby were living at the house, they were not paying the mortgage. On July 16, 1979, I called Herman to ask if I could get a few items from the house. He said, yes. Upon arriving at the house, I knocked on the door. Hubby opened the door, smiled saying, hi Tommie. Herman was sitting on the couch. I spoke, then asked if I could get the items. Herman said, okay. This was the second time I had been in the house since leaving in January. The other time had been to get my clothes when no one was home. It took me a few moments to gather the items. Once I had everything, walking towards the front door I said, thanks, bye. I heard Herman say, you think you are going to take stuff out this house, you ain't going nowhere. The next thing I knew he hit me in the back of my head. Losing my balance, I extended my arms towards the floor trying not to fall on my stomach. Hitting the floor on my side, I was trying to get up and could not. Herman was bending over me and he hit me several more time in my head on backside. I screamed, *stop Herman, please stop.* Suddenly he stood upright lifted his leg to kick me in my stomach. Swiftly turning to my right side, I prevented him from kicking my stomach. Instead he stomped my hand. It was a blessing for God that Hubby was there because he finally intervened and stopped Herman from beating me. Once Hubby pulled Herman away from me, I struggled to get to my feet. Once up, I grabbed my purse and ran out the door. Crying and trembling, I got into my car and drove away. Tears streaming down my face it was unbelievable Herman had tried to kick my stomach and hurt our unborn baby. Did he hate me that much? What had I done for him to be this mean to me? Had I been this stupid all this time to believe he really loved me? At this point what was I supposed to do? What was going to happen to our baby? When I arrived at the apartment, I did not tell Linda C. what happened at the house with Herman. Though I am sure when she looked at me, she knew what had occurred.

Two days later in the early morning, my water broke. Linda C. and I prepared for her to take me to the hospital. She called Momma and Herman to let them know my water had broken and we were leaving to go to the hospital. Once we arrived at the hospital, I was admitted and taken to the maternity ward. Herman arrived a few moments later. When Linda C. figured out Herman was not going to be hostile towards me, she left to get some rest before going to work. Herman sat in the chair acting like the proud father to be, constantly saying he hoped the baby was a girl. When Dr. Gyves came in the room to examine me, the first thing he said was, *what happened to you, where did all those bruises, cuts and scratches on my face, neck and hands come from?* With Herman sitting in a chair only a few feet away from me, I looked at my husband staring at me with a what you going to say expression on his face. I then held my head down and replied, from falling down the front porch stairs into the bushes. Even today I can still picture the look of disbelief in Dr. Gyves eyes. Before the labor pains became too intense, throughout the day I called Momma, Linda Faye, and Linda C. After twelve hours of labor our beautiful daughter was born later that evening. My heart melted and bubbled over with love and joy when she began to cry. She was the tiniest perfectly gorgeous baby I had ever seen. I could not believe we made this lovely little baby girl. She had beautiful skin, a head full of black hair, a little round face, with beautiful slanted eyes. This became the happiest day of my life. Herman seemed as elated as me, and said he was naming her *Ivy, a name of a character in a book he had read.* I gave our daughter the middle name *Kristolynn*. I had decided on *Kristol* because one of the times when I had left Herman and went to stay with Linda Faye and Darrell for a few days, Linda Faye had taken me to see a performance by the *Alvin Ailey American*

Dance Theater. Looking through the program one of the names of the dancers caught my attention, it was *Kristol*, I thought it was a beautiful name and uniquely spelled. At that moment, I said to myself if I ever have a daughter, the name *Kristol* was going to be part of her name. Then of course, my daughter's name had to a *Lynn* for Linda Faye and Linda C.

After I was settled my postpartum room, I called Momma, she excitedly answered the phone saying, *is my grandbaby here yet*. When I said, *you have a healthy beautiful granddaughter*, I could hear the joy in her voice as she said, *I cannot wait to see my grandbaby*. The day Ivy Kristolynn was born was truly a God given blessing for our family. Herman also called several of his family members and then he told me he was leaving and would be back later on. I said, okay and thanked him for being there for the birth of our daughter. Herman replied, he *would not miss it for the world.* Early the next morning while breast feeding my beautiful baby girl, the hospital social worker came to ask if I was still considering adoption for Ivy. With my face beaming with joy and heart overflowing with love, without any hesitation or doubt I said, *no way, my baby is the love of my life and there is no way I would ever give her up.* As the social worker smiled at me holding Ivy, she said, I can see you are incredibly happy. I replied, yes, I am, God has blessed me with a miracle that I will never let leave my arms. Patting me on my shoulder, she told me, good for you, I wish the best for you and your baby.

After the social worker left the room, I kissed and whispered to my baby that she was my reason to survive and live in this world.

Tightly cuddling Ivy in my arms close to my heart, I prayed a prayer of gratitude to God for the blessing us with a perfectly healthy baby girl and expressed how much I appreciated being able to touch her tiny hands and feet. I acknowledged what a blessing it was to kiss Ivy lightly on her forehead. I praised God for being able to whisper in my tiny daughter's little ears that for as long as I lived I promised to always love, protect, and support her. That day and many days thereafter, I the sang to my baby *You Are My Sunshine, My Only Sunshine* as written by Jimmie Davis and Charles Mitchell, that I would at times adlib by saying her name and things specific to her. Later that day Momma, Auntie and Linda C. came to visit. Although they could only see Ivy through the glass window of the nursery, they were overjoyed to see the new addition to our family.

Even though Herman was there for the birth of Ivy, it was my intention to continue living with Linda C. So, the day Ivy and I were discharged, Linda C. came to take us home. Linda Faye and Darrell came to visit the following weekend. Linda Faye adored her little niece. Ivy was our bundle of joy that we immensely loved. Momma was so fussy about her grandbaby that even before Ivy left the hospital, she let us know there was no way her beautiful granddaughter was wearing the paper disposable diapers that were becoming extremely popular. Momma insisted Ivy only wear only cloth diapers to the point she ordered and paid for diaper services for Ivy until she was potty trained. It became a family joke that Momma thought her grandbaby was too good for paper diapers. It was another blessing to have Momma, Linda Faye and Linda C. help me provide and care for Ivy.

A Leopard Cannot Change Its Spots. Shortly after the birth of Ivy, Herman called to let me know he had moved into the third-floor unit of the house of Annie, his sister. He told me the bank had filed a foreclosure complaint because he had not paid the mortgage in eight months and the utilities were or shortly would be disconnected. Disappointed to know the house would be taken by the bank. I said, okay. If only he had let me have the house months ago, Momma would have helped me save the house. The second week in August, Herman called to let me know Vet would be visiting with him on Friday. He told me Vet really wanted to meet his sister, then Herman asked if Ivy and I could come over on Friday. Although I hesitated for a moment, I agreed to visit knowing Herman had not seen Ivy since she was born. More importantly I wanted Vet to meet and get to know his little sister. That Friday Ivy and I went to Annie's house. It was good to see Herman, Vet, Annie and her children, Nettie, and Robert. We had a great visit filled with eating, talking, joking, laughing, and bonding. Around 9:00 p.m. Herman asked to use my car to go to the store. A little apprehensive but believing with Vet and Ivy visiting there would not be any problems, I said, yes. Once more I was wrong. Hours went by without Herman coming home. A little after midnight everyone in the house was sleep, except for me as I was trying to stay woke so I could leave when Herman came back. At some point, I must have dozed off because around 6:00 a.m., I was woken by Ivy crying. Looking around the room there was no sign Herman had returned. True to form Herman did not return to the house until around 9:00 a.m. He came into the house in a happy-go-lucky attitude like nothing was wrong. I was prepared to leave with Ivy and told Herman we were getting ready to leave. Looking at me with a fiercest look in his eyes, Herman told me, *y'all are not leaving*. Not wanting to enrage him, I said, Ivy does not have any clean diapers. With an expression on his face of who cares, Herman began to insist that we were not leaving the house. Attempting to prevent further intensification of the situation, I said, okay. When Herman went into the bathroom and closed the door, I picked up Ivy and her diaper bag. I ran down the stairs to Annie house for help to leave. Immediately Herman came downstairs busting through the door. The door swung opened almost hitting Ivy in the head. Herman yelled I told you to stay upstairs. Vet who was in the kitchen ran pass Herman down the stair towards the basement. Within seconds Herman slapped me in the face. With Ivy in my arms Herman grabbed my left arm and started yanking me through the house while I screamed for him to stop. Ivy was now crying. Annie came towards me and was able to get Ivy out of my arms as she, Robert, and Nettie, were pleading with Herman to stop. Ignoring their and my pleas, Herman shouted for us to shut up as he continued to pull me towards the living room. He stopped pulling me and hit me several times upside my head. I stumbled to the floor where I cuddled up with my hand between my legs. Herman was standing over me hitting me across my head several times. I tried to use my hands and arms to shield my head while crying and screaming for him to stop. I could hear Annie also asking him to stop. Finally, Herman quit hitting me and went to sit on the couch.

He told me to stay on the floor and I better not move. After he made me sit on the floor for over ten minutes, Annie began to repeatedly ask him to let me get up. Herman refused. I sat quietly because I had learned from the past to patiently sit motionlessly until Herman went to sleep. Since he had been out all night, I was sure he had been drinking, so I was praying he would quickly go to sleep. When Herman finally dozed off to sleep, Annie, Robert and Nettie hurried to help me get Ivy and our belongings into the car. I was relieved to pull out the driveway. When I stopped at the stop light, I realized the milk and cereal vouchers Ivy received through the Women, Infants, and Children Food and Nutrition Service Program were not in my purse. I called Annie from the phone booth asking her to please have Nettie bring the coupon book to me at the corner store. Annie said, of course. As Nettie handed the coupon book to me, she asked if I was okay. I told her, yes. We hugged and said we talk to each other soon. On the way to the apartment, I was completely demoralized. I would have never in a million years thought Herman would jumped on me with our little baby in my arms and in the presence of Vet, Annie, Robert, and Nettie. There was no doubt something was wrong with him. He really needed psychiatric help.

Ivy and I returned to the apartment. Linda C. was in her room getting ready for work. I simply hollered out, hey. She replied, hey, how are you and my baby niece doing. I said, fine. Immediately I gave Ivy a bath and put her on clean clothes. Then I sat cuddling and hugging her in my arms while thanking God she had not been hurt by her father. Simply too embarrassed to tell Momma, Linda C., or anyone else what had occurred, I could only pray that God would give me guidance on my future and how to take care of Ivy. Once Linda C. went to work, I cried out like I never had before pleading to God for strength and help. Throughout all I had endured with Herman this was the worse day. No matter how hard I tried to understanding Herman, I could not comprehend how cruel he was today. Beating and subduing me always had been wrong, but tragically today Herman had taken his anger to another level. His attacking me weeks after giving birth to our daughter was frightening and inconceivable. Then for Herman to jump on me in front of our baby, his son and family members made this the bleakest day of our relationship. At this point knowing only God could help me, I began to pray for continued direction and wisdom. Looking down at Ivy innocently sleeping next to me, I restated my promise to always love, support and protect my beloved baby. Snuggling Ivy close to me my mind began to mull over many different thoughts. I knew God had entrusted me with Ivy's well-being and that my life was no longer only about me. Thus, no matter what happens my problems could no longer take precedence over the needs of my baby. Kissing my baby, I thought how grateful I was that from the moment I laid eyes on her my negative thoughts of giving up on my life and committing suicide had ceased. Now after the outburst of Herman today, it confirmed without a doubt I had to live to take care of Ivy. His actions today proved if something happened to me he would not take proper care of our baby. I would never understand how he could think it was okay to hit me when our baby was still in my stomach and today as I held Ivy in my arms.

Rubbing the tiny hands of Ivy, I praised God for blessing us today to escape the violent outburst of Herman. Picking up Ivy and holding her to my shoulder, I patted her softly on her back when thoughts of how she also needed her father ran across my mind. Earnestly I would love for Herman to be a good father to Ivy, especially since it was disheartening to think of Ivy growing up like me in a single-parent home without her father. Even before what happened a few hours ago, I had daily prayed for Herman to become a good, hard-working, non-violent husband and father; if not for my sake, for the sake of our daughter. After what happened today I began to pray that one day soon a doctor would figure out why Herman had these violent outbursts. With the advancements in medical and mental treatments, there had to be a cure or remedy to prevent his outbursts.

The six weeks maternity leave I had taken was ending in two weeks. I tried to set aside my marital problems and concerns about my future to concentrate on preparing to return to work, including arranging for the care of Ivy. With the help of Linda Faye, arrangements were made for Hattie to care for Ivy. Even though I knew Hattie would take care of my baby, it was extremely difficult to leave Ivy. Each day for several weeks I cried when I dropped off Ivy while wishing I was in a financial position to take more time off from work to be with Ivy. Unfortunately, that was impossible, I had to work. Taking into consideration Herman and I had not spoken since I left Annie's house, I did not expect any financial help from him for Ivy. Although Momma, Linda Faye and Linda C. assisted me as much as possible, I could not forever rely on them to support us. With determination to keep my promise of being the best mother possible to Ivy, I prayed for strength as I returned to work to support our financial needs.

Try and Try Again. It was the end of September, when Herman called to ask if he could see Ivy. We had not talked or seen each other since the incident in August. The first thing he told me is he was attending counseling sessions. I explained to Herman how the last violent attack had caused me to be more fearful of him than ever before. I told him the thought of Ivy seeing his violence outbursts were a major concern to me. I let him know that both of us needed to be physically and mentally okay to raise Ivy. Herman agreed with my concerns and reassured me he would no longer hurt me. Although extremely fretful about seeing him, I knew Herman needed to be in Ivy's life. Besides during my meeting with Mr. Wade, he had told me even if I did not let Herman see our daughter now, the court would eventually grant him visitation rights. Regardless of everything that had occurred between Herman and me and as hard as I tried, I could not stop loving the non-violent side of Herman. Longing for us to one day have a normal family life, I continued to pray for spiritual intervention to put an end to the violent outbursts of Herman, heal our marriage, and allow us to be excellent parents to our daughter. After talking several times to Herman, I agreed to bring Ivy to see him. The visit went very well. Annie, Robert, and Nettie were glad to see us. Over the next several weeks we visited more, even going out for walks, to the park and dinner. Eventually Ivy and I began to stay overnight with Herman.

When Ivy turned three months Momma and I wanted her to be Christened. I talked to Herman about the Christening. We decided to ask Pastor McAdoo to officiate the Christening of Ivy. He said, of course and scheduled the Christening for the third Sunday in October. Momma purchased the loveliest white Christening dress for Ivy. That Sunday with Ivy looking like a beautiful doll baby, Herman, Momma, Linda C., I, and several members of the Washington family attended church for her Christening ceremony that would be held prior to the end of the morning service. When Pastor McAdoo called us to the front of the church, he began officiating the spiritual dedication and blessing of Ivy, which included administering oaths to Herman, Momma, Linda C., and me to do our individual parts to raise Ivy in a loving, nurturing, supportive Christian home. I thanked God for the special occasion shared in harmony with our family members. After the service, we went to Momma's apartment for Sunday dinner. It was an enjoyable time as we talked, laughed, and took pictures together. That day the family bonding time was much needed and appreciated by everyone. A few weeks later, I took Ivy to have professional pictures taken in her Christening dress.

Herman would periodically check on the house and retrieve the mail. He called to let me know the bank that held the mortgage for the house had sent a letter. The letter proposed the foreclosure proceedings would be dismissed if we agreed to the terms of a modification and reinstatement of our loan. We would be required to pay $2,000 of the delinquent amount and the balance of $1,500 would be rolled into the modified loan. After he received the letter, Herman let me know how much he wanted us to be together as a family. He told me how hard he was working to prove he would be a good husband and father. I knew Herman had been work temporary jobs, was regularly attending his counseling meetings, and had only drank an occasional beer in the past two months. He suggested asking Pastor McAdoo for marital counseling. My concern was it had only been three months since the last act of violence. How could I trust he would not become violent once we were back together? It was no longer only my well-being to consider but our darling Ivy. One day Herman caught me off guard when he asked that we start praying together as a family. He had never said anything about praying. With this new willingness to seek God to heal him and our marriage, I began to think my prayers had been answered and that Herman would stop his violent outbursts and be a good husband and father. The change in his demeanor was incredibly significant to me because I knew Ivy needed to grow up in a loving home with both parents.

By early November, I reconciled with Herman. When I told Momma everything about how we reconciled and how Herman wanted us to be a praying family, Momma let me know she still was worried about his violent tendencies. She went on to tell me how she hoped and prayed that God had delivered Herman from the outbursts and would bless our marriage. We then discussed the reinstatement of the loan for the house, and I let Momma know we were $800 short. Without hesitation Momma let me know she would give us the money. Giving Momma a big hug, I let her know how much I appreciated everything she did for Ivy, me and even Herman. With the financial help of Momma, we were able to meet the terms of the loan modification. When I returned to the apartment, I let Linda C. know how much I appreciated what she had done for Ivy and me over the past ten months, and how Herman and I had reconciled and would be moving back into the house in several weeks. Sighing Linda C. said, oh no, I am going to miss you and Ivy. She went on to say how much joy it had brought her with us living with her, especially Ivy, who she lovingly called, *her little darling niece*. Linda C. shared how each day when she walked through the door of the apartment she looked forward to holding Ivy and seeing her smiling face. With Linda C. knowing the difficulties of my life with Herman, she said with loving concern how she hoped this time everything would work out for us and that Herman would no longer mistreat me. I explained to her how for the first time we were going to get spiritual counseling and pray together as a family. She then assured me regardless of what happens in the future, I should never forget she would always be there if Ivy and I needed anything. Hugging Linda C., I let her know how much I loved and cherished her for always being there to support and help me. Linda C. was truly a God-given blessing to me that I was thankful to have as my best childhood friend that I now considered my beloved sister.

Within a few days the loan modification documents were finalized. By mid-November we had moved back in our home. Happy to be reunited in the home as a family, we eagerly cleaned and revamped the house. I was most excited about decorating Ivy's room. From the day we purchased the house I had anticipated decorating the room for our child. Ecstatically I brought many lovely pink décors for Ivy's room. A few days later to my surprise I came home to see a tow truck in our driveway. Herman enthusiastically told me he had purchased the truck to start his own towing business. He explained his plans to make extra money working in the towing business. Seeing Herman this eager about starting his own business, I let him know how proud I was of him and that he had my full support. A couple of weeks later I asked Herman to see if Vet and Dion could spend the weekend with us. Christina and Diane both said, yes. That Friday evening Herman picked up the boys. The moment they walked through the door we began to have a delightful time. They were both excited to hold and play with their baby sister. I cooked, and we sat around the table eating and joking with each other. After dinner we talked and played games. That Saturday I had made an appointment for Ivy, Dion, Vet and Momma to take professional pictures. After taking the picture we went to Pizza Hut for lunch. Saturday evening was filled with more fun time bonding together. Before Vet and Dion went home I took pictures of my husband with his three children. It was a picture-perfect weekend. Vet and Dion enjoyed spending time with their dad and playing with Ivy, while Herman had an awesome time with his children. Seeing Herman being the father I knew he could be was an answer to my prayers. I praised God for blessing us with a beautiful weekend together.

With Christmas approaching, Linda Faye let us know Darrell and she would be unable to spend Christmas day in Cleveland due to their work schedule. Momma and I decided to visit Linda Faye and Darrell a few days before Christmas. Herman would stay at home to work his temporary job and towing business. Momma, Ivy, and I had a wonderful pre-Christmas celebration with Linda Faye and Darrell. On December 24th Momma, Ivy and I were returning home, when suddenly I became extremely dizzy to the point it impeded my ability to drive. I stopped at a rest area to take a little break. After sitting for a moment, I became dizzier. I called Linda Faye letting her know I was not feeling good and was not able to drive. Linda Faye let me know she and Darrell were on their way to get us. When they arrived, Linda Faye said she was going to drive my car to Cleveland while Darrell followed in their car. Once we arrived in Cleveland, Linda Faye made sure Momma and I were settled. After Linda Faye was satisfied we were okay, they headed back to Xenia, so Darrell could get to work on time. Thankfully Linda Faye and Darrell returned safely in time for Darrell to get to work. The next day even though I still was not feeling well we had a blessed Christmas day. Herman picked up Momma to bring over the dinner she had prepared for us. We had a joyful time celebrating the birth of Jesus Christ and Ivy's first Christmas. A few days later I went to the doctor. I was diagnosed with anemia and prescribed iron supplements.

In January 1980, laying in the bed watching television I heard sounds coming from the kitchen that made me cringe. Herman had come into the house and was in the kitchen. From the noise he was making I knew he was drunk. It had been five months ago when he had the last violent outburst. I begin to pray that tonight he would not become violent. When Herman came into the bedroom, I pretended to be sleep. That did not work. He immediately started to shake me. Opening my eyes, he began badgering me. Trying not to provoke him, I did not say a word. When I thought he was finish fussing, I begin to get out of the bed to go to the bathroom. Herman jumped out the bed hitting me with his typically one-two punches to my head that threw me off balance and made me stumble forward. I hit my face and head hard against the solid wood dresser. Trying to open my eyes, my vision was blurry, and I felt something wet running down my forehead. I faintly heard Herman repeatedly calling out my name and saying are you okay, I am so sorry. I was trying to get up. but my head was hurting too much. My vision was getting slightly clearer as I looked up at Herman. He was now telling me that he was taking me to the hospital, as he grabbed a piece of clothing by the bed and put it on my head trying to stop the bleeding. I murmured, let me sit up for a moment, thinking I could get my eyesight focused and contend with the bleeding and throbbing headache better sitting up. When I tried to sit up, I slump back down onto the floor. Herman told me, you are going to the hospital. I told him to wait a minute, but when I could not sit up, let alone stand up, without being woozy, I agreed to go to the hospital. Herman hurried to put clothes on me and Ivy and carried us one at a time to the car. When we arrived at the emergency room the receptionist asked us what happened. Looking at Herman from the gurney began to say some, I quickly said mumbled, *from falling down the stairs*. Each time I examined by a different hospital employee, I had to repeat this lie. Fortunately, the test confirmed the head trauma did not result in a concussion. However, three stitches were required for the gash in my head. Treatment was also required for the bruises to the side of my face. A prescription was written for pain and instructions on how to reduce the swelling. I also was instructed to follow-up with my medical doctor for the removal of the stitches. As Herman drove us back to the house, he said his normal apologetic speech. I was too exhausted to respond. My only concern was if Ivy was okay. I thought as we drove home the only difference from all the other violent outbursts, it seemed because this was the first time Herman had to personally contend with the injuries his hitting caused me, together with being the one to take me to the emergency room, he might earnestly have some remorse for causing these injuries. For several days each time he looked at my injuries he vowed to never again put his hands on me. Over the next weeks, once more I wondered if Herman would ever change stop hitting me. Of course, not wanting Momma and Linda C. to see the bruises, I avoided seeing them in person for several days, keeping our communication via phone. There was no way I could let my loved ones know the violence had once more resurfaced. When my co-workers saw my face and asked me what happened, I told them the same lie as I had told the hospital's employees. More than ever, I meditated and prayed for guidance concerning our future. I reiterated to myself that Ivy deserved a loving, happy, and safe home with both parents, but given the unpredictable violent outbursts from Herman, I questioned if we ever could give her that type of normal stable life.

Although CT Corp had been really good to me, I needed to earn more money. Herman was working his tow truck business and a few other temporary jobs. The problem was his income fluctuated from week to week. With his unpredictable income and my income, we were paying our bills, but only able to save a small amount money. In April 1980, I decided to seek a higher paying position. Within days I sought and obtained employment with the Cleveland Board of Education. I was hired as a clerk to Eddie Wycoff, the program manager at the Woodland Job Center (WJC), an adult training center. My pay increased by thirty percent and the benefits were much better. My last days at CT, I expressed my heartfelt appreciation for the opportunities the management had extended to me. I especially thanked the manager for pointing out my shortcomings that enabled me to improve my writing, spelling, and proofreading skills. I thanked God for blessing me with my former employment and the new opportunity and financial blessings. The end of April I began my new position at WJC.

In May 1980, Herman came home after midnight drunk. He woke me up wanting to tell me he was upset about an incident between him and one of his brothers. I was sitting up in the bed with my head propped up with a pillow listening to him rant and rave for about an hour. I must have dozed off because the next thing I remember is feeling the pain of a punch to my face and my nose profusely bleeding. Trying to get up, I fell back on the bed. Herman had run to get a towel. We tried to stop the bleeding. When we were unable to stop it. once again Herman had to take me to the emergency room. I was very thankful Ivy was too little to comprehend what was happening between her parents. This time when asked what happened by the hospital employees, with Herman by my side, I lied saying while going to the bathroom, I did not cut on the light in the bedroom and accidently walked into the door. My nose had to be packed to stop the bleeding. Once the examination determined my nose was not broken, I was released. This time on the way back home Herman blamed me for causing him to hit me. There were no apologies. Only ranting about what his brother did to him earlier that day and how I did not respect him when he came home. I said nothing, sitting silently knowing Ivy and I could not live in this hostile environment. A few days later, I called Rev. Sanders who was the pastor of Lee Road Baptist Church. This was the neighborhood church Ivy and I had been visiting. I asked Pastor Sanders if he could provide spiritual guidance regarding marital problems. He said, yes and scheduled an appointment. When I met with Rev. Sanders, I mentioned in a roundabout way the violent outbursts of Herman that was causing our marital problems. Rev. Sanders strongly suggested I seek legal advice. Following my meeting with Rev. Sanders, I knew a divorce was the only way to get away from the violent outbursts of Herman. I undoubtedly knew Ivy did not deserve to live in an unsafe home filled with negativity and violence. Months ago, I had promised my baby to put her first. Her well-being and future had to take priority, not mine.

Chapter Three -- One Bad Decision Forever Altered My Life

Living in your own home in fear is a dreadful feeling. Over the years my close family members and friends became aware of how Herman beat and intimidated me. However, none of them knew about the most recent two incidents because I was too ashamed to let them know that even after Ivy's birth, Herman never stopped hitting me. After speaking with Pastor Sanders, I decided to talk to Linda C. about my discussion with him and the most recent violent outbursts from Herman, and how I was seriously contemplating getting a divorce. Linda C. said Ivy and I could always count on her for her love and support. She let me know we were always welcome to live with her again. Even though Linda C. was glad I had finally decided to consider divorcing Herman, she earnestly expressed her concerned that if I tried to divorce Herman, he would attempt to seriously harm me. She said I really needed to consider protecting myself. She said I should consider purchasing a gun. At that moment what Linda C. said could happen to me, hit cords of fear throughout my entire mind and soul. It was the first time anyone had truthfully spoken the reality of what could happen to me in my volatile life with Herman. It made me worry more than ever about what would happen to Ivy. If I was seriously hurt or died who would care for Ivy? As I thought about all the times Herman had hit me from the first slap at the dinner table to the most recent punch in the face a few weeks ago, I wondered how he would react to my filing for a divorce. Could I honestly believe Herman would accept the divorce and let me live in peace without fear of his wrath? Would he finally adhere to his many promises never to hit me again once we were divorced? My mind began to think nonstop about the violent tendencies of Herman. From the numerous times Herman simply slapped my face or head to the many violent outbursts that resulted in injuries. These thoughts made me become more fearful for Ivy and my future if I filed for a divorce. Especially thinking about the last two times while Ivy slept in the other room. Thinking Linda C. was correct I needed something to help me scare Herman and protect Ivy and me from being violently harmed. A few days later I had made up my mind to purchase a gun. After work I drove to a gun store on Northfield Road to purchase a gun. Knowing I only wanted to scare Herman into not hitting me anymore I did not want a big gun. So, looking at the many types of guns, I asked the clerk to show me the smallest gun. Even though I had no knowledge about guns for some unknown reason I believed the smaller the gun the less harm it would cause. The store clerk told me the 22-caliber gun was the smallest gun. I decided to purchase the gun. The clerk gave me a general demonstration on how to load and unload the gun. I asked the clerk, *this will not kill anyone will it*? The clerk told me *it depends because any gunshot can be fatal.* Soon I would learn my thoughts to buy a small gun was another wrong decision in my life. After completing the paperwork, I left the store with the gun in my purse with no intention of telling anyone I had bought a gun.

A few days later, a friend of Linda C., Ernest, referred me to Joseph Blackwell of the law firm Willis & Blackwell. I called Mr. Blackwell to schedule a meeting with him the first week of June 1980 to discuss a filing for a divorce. At our initial meeting I informed and discussed with Mr. Blackwell all the good and more difficult aspects of my pre and post-marriage life with Herman. He listened with a look of disbelief on his face when I talked about the most traumatic beatings. I let him know because Herman was not keeping his promises to stop beating me, I had to get a divorce for the safety of Ivy and my sanity. Mr. Blackwell with expressions of concern assured me he would be able to help me. He told me not only did I need a divorce, but a temporary restraining order (TRO) was an absolutely must. He explained the TRO would keep Herman from within a certain distance from me. I informed Mr. Blackwell to proceed with preparing the divorce and TRO paperwork. Several days later I returned to Mr. Blackwell office to review the divorce complaint and TRO. Mr. Blackwell told me he wanted to introduce me to Mr. Willis, his partner. Mr. Blackwell gave Mr. Willis a brief rundown why I needed a divorce. Mr. Willis told me he had handled cases with these types of volatile circumstances. He told me I needed to be extraordinarily careful until the divorce was granted. At that time, I informed Mr. Blackwell and Mr. Willis that I had purchased a gun. They looked at each other, then Mr. Willis said to me, *do not pull the gun unless I was ready to us it, otherwise I could end up the one the opposite side of the gun and get seriously hurt or dead.* His statement sent chills down my spine and resonated in my mind. The next day the complaint for divorce and TRO were filed.

On June 12, 1980, I attended the graduation ceremony for Robert, with Annie and Nettie. Herman stayed home with Ivy. Following the ceremony Robert asked me if he could use my car. I said, yes. When Robert dropped me at the house, I let him know I would be ready around 7:30 a.m. in the morning to leave for work. He said, okay. Upon entering the house, I saw Herman knocked out sleep on the couch with several empty beer bottles on the floor. It broke my heart to then notice laying on the floor next to the couch was our innocent baby. I picked up Ivy, her diaper and clothes were soaking wet. I went upstairs to get us ready for bed. Once I had bathed Ivy, I put on her night clothes and laid her in her crib. I then got ready for bed. I had been keeping the gun in the car. But, since I had let Robert use the car, I had put the gun in my purse. Before I went to bed, I took the gun out of my purse placing it under some clothes on the side of the bed.

    The next morning when I woke up in my typical routine I got dressed for work then prepared Ivy for us to leave. When I was almost ready, I called Robert to bring me the car. In about fifteen minutes, I heard Robert pull into the driveway and Hubby open the door. With Ivy in my arms, I prepared to leave the house. I left out of the bedroom and was walking down the stairs and Herman was coming up the stairs. We did not say a word to each other. As I headed for the door to leave, I realized I had forgotten Ivy's diaper bag upstairs. With Ivy in my arms, I went back upstairs into the bedroom. Herman was laying across the bed on his stomach with his arms stretched across the bed. Immediately the thought he had found the gun ran through my mind. Before I could reach Ivy's diaper bag that was laying at the foot of the bed, Herman abruptly jumped out of the bed. He came towards me yelling you going to get the money out the bank today since you filed for a divorce. I was trying to be calm in order not to further agitate him. I reached for the diaper bag, while saying to Herman that I would go to the bank after work. In my mind knowing it was a Friday the bank would be open late. Herman said, no, you are going now. Then with Ivy in my arms Herman hit me in the face. I fell back on the bed. Beginning to cry I told Herman not to hit me at the same time trying to get up with Ivy and reach for the diaper bag. Herman hit me again. This time, the force of the hit made me fall completely back onto the bed and caused Ivy to roll out of my arm onto the bed. Herman was standing at the edge of the bed hollering at me. I managed to reach on the side of the bed and felt the gun. Herman had not found the gun. By this time Herman was reaching for me on the bed, I turned over onto my left side to avoid him grabbing me. With my right hand I pulled the gun out, flipped on my back and started screaming while shooting the gun. Herman had a startled look on his face as he turned and ran down the stairs. I followed behind him. He ran to the left into Mrs. Ethel's old bedroom. I ran to the right out the front door. Still with the gun in my hand, I continued running and screaming into the street. There was a car coming down the street. I ran towards the front of the car yelling please help me. Hysterically yelling for help the gentleman stopped the car. Opening the door of his car I told him my husband was jumping on me and I needed to call the police. The gentleman looked stunned but drove down the street to the phone booth. Unable to recall our complete conversation during the few seconds drive to the phone booth, I do remember him asking me if I was okay. Once at the phone booth I dialed the operator and asked to be connected to the police. When connected with the police, a woman's voice said, *dispatcher, what is the nature of your emergency*. Hysterically crying, I said, *my husband was jumping on me and I shot at him*. The dispatcher asked where I was located. I said at the phone booth on the corner of Lee Road and Glendale. She asked where the shooting took place. I gave her the address to the house. The dispatcher told me the police were on the way and to stay where I was. She then asked where the gun was. I told her in my hand. She instructed me to put the gun down and make sure my hands were visible when the police arrived. I did as she told me. At the end of the call with the dispatcher, I dialed the operator and requested to be connected to Hattie's phone number. When Hattie accepted the call, I asked her to please get Ivy from the house because I had shot at Herman. She said, oh no, I am on my way. Within the next few minutes a police car arrived at the corner. The police officer shouted, *put your hands up; where is the gun*? I pointed to the gun on the ledge of the phone booth. One police officer retrieved the gun, while the other police officer placed me in the police car. The gentleman that drove me to the phone booth was talking to another police officer.

 Upon returning to the house as I sat in the back of the police car, a woman police officer can to the car and told me the unthinkable. *Herman was dead*. My world stopped as my heart sank, and mind went haywire. I could not breathe. Nothing was audible. Everything was blurry. What I was just told was not true. No way. It could not be true. I do not believe it. How was he dead? A few minutes ago, we both were running down the stairs. Herman ran to the left and I ran to the right. He is not dead. Oh God, what have I done, what have I done? Trying to breath, I looked around me coherent enough to realize this was not a dream. This was reality. Slowly I became aware of several people and police officers outside the house. Mrs. Dorothy Pound, the lady that lived next door who I had attended church with on occasions, was standing close to the police car talking to the woman police officer. I could finally comprehend what the woman police officer was asking me. She wanted to know if I had any injuries. Franticly, I asked where is Ivy? Where is my baby? The woman police officer pointed to Hattie holding Ivy in front of the house. Hattie began to walk towards the car with Ivy. My baby had tears in her eyes with a frightened look on her little face. I wanted to grab my baby and disappear into thin air. Hattie's voice snapped me back into reality. Hattie was saying she was sorry for what happened and for me not to worry about Ivy because she would take care of her. Then she asked if I wanted Ivy to stay there with everything that was happening. I shook my head, no. There was no way I wanted Ivy to be around this dreadful scene. I asked Hattie to please take Ivy home with her and to call my Momma. Although Ivy was only eleven months old, I did not want to take a chance of her remembering this horrible day. Once Hattie and Ivy left, the woman police officer asked me again if I was injured. I answered, no that Herman had only hit me in my face a couple of times. I then said, I really had to use the bathroom. Mrs. Dorothy having heard me tell the woman police officer I had to use the bathroom, let the woman police officer know I could use her bathroom. The woman police officer took me into Mrs. Dorothy's house. The woman police officer said it was necessary for her to wait outside the door with it cracked while I used the bathroom. Mrs. Dorothy stood nearby talking to the woman police officer. To my embarrassment, that day the saying *scared the mess out of me* happened to me. After using the bathroom, I apologized to the woman police officer and Mrs. Dorothy for the stinky scent in the bathroom. They both said they understood. As the woman police officer and I were leaving Mrs. Dorothy said to me, *I wish you would have stayed away because he was never going to stop beating you.* Until that day, I never knew Mrs. Dorothy was aware of what was going on behind our closed doors. I thought for a moment how many other people knew Herman was beating me, a secret I thought I had kept camouflaged from the world.

    The woman police officer placed me back in the police car. Sitting in the car I became overwhelmed with feeling guilty of being a terrible wife and mother that had purchased a gun and shot and caused the death of my husband. Silently crying out I pleaded and begged God for forgiveness for causing the death of Herman. Within a matter of seconds at the age of twenty-two years old my life together with the lives of my baby girl and many other people had drastically changed forever by the sudden death of Herman. I would have never thought when I woke up only a few hours ago that my husband would be dead. Ivy, Vet and Dion fatherless. The Washington family without a son, brother, uncle, and cousin. None of our lives would ever be the same. My soul was screaming out in pain Lord I did not want my husband to die. Why Lord, why. Then suddenly memories came to my mind of the two violence incidents I witnessed as a child when the lady was bleeding on the sidewalk and the hairdresser of Momma was killed by her husband. This caused me to instantly regret not figuring out why thoughts about those incidents came to me when Herman first hit me. Now I was sitting in the back of the police car and Herman in our house dead. How I truly regretted ignoring the visions about those two ladies after the first time Herman hit me. Why didn't it knock some sense into me the first day Herman hit me, and then those two tragic visions reemerged into my thoughts? Only if I would have left Herman after the first or even second time he hit me instead of believing it would not happen repeatedly, he would not be dead, and I would not be sitting in this police car. Regrettably, that did not happen. I had lived in a fantasy world that my love would stop the beatings. Oh, how wrong I was, I was so wrong. Why didn't I heed the warning signs of the devastation the violent outbursts from Herman could cause me as the victim, him as the assaulter, and the many innocent family members and friends? Why didn't I listen to the pleas of Momma, Linda Faye, Linda C., Kim M., and others to stop forgiving and going back to Herman over and over again. Why did I go buy a gun, which was the most fatal life decision I ever made that has caused the death of my husband? With thoughts in my mind spiraling out of control, I closed my eyes to the image of Hattie holding Ivy. Imagines of my innocent sweet Ivy crying and looking confused and scared by everything going on around her now flooded my mind. I was visually seeing how Hattie walked towards the police car with Ivy reaching out to me for comfort, but I could not. My baby needed me, but I was unable to help her. At that moment, my baby became my flicker of light. The image of my baby reaching for me suddenly gave me a surge of hope in an extremely sorrowful and dreadful life-changing day. I know it was God who used my little baby daughter to keep me sane even during this dreariest day. There was a flicker of light from God that gave me strength was realizing and accepting that Ivy could not lose both of her parents on June 13, 1980. With the Holy Spirit descending upon me, I was given incentive to be strong and hopeful for my daughter. Knowing I had to survive for Ivy, I began to pray to God for forgiveness, mercy, and compassion for my sins. *I have sinned greatly because I have done this thing. But now, I beseech You, take away the hateful wickedness of Your servant; for I have done very foolishly*, 1 Chronicles 21:8 (AMPC). The flicker of light on that grave day was the mercy of God that blessed me with forgiveness and strength to endure the regret and pain from causing the death of my husband. *Incline Your ear, O Lord, and answer me, For I am distressed and needy [I long for Your help]. Protect my life (soul), for I am godly and faithful; O You my God, save Your servant, who trusts in You [believing in You and relying on You, confidently committing everything to You]. Be gracious and merciful to me, O Lord, For to You I cry out all the day long. Make Your servant rejoice, For to You, O Lord, I lift up my soul [all that I am—in prayer]. For You, O Lord, are good, and ready to forgive [our sins, sending them away, completely letting them go forever and ever]; And abundant in lovingkindness and overflowing in mercy to all those who call upon You. Hear, O Lord, my prayer; And listen attentively to the voice of my supplications (specific requests)! In the day of my trouble I will call upon You, For You will answer me*, Psalm 86:1-7 (AMP).

After a while, the police officers officially arrested me and took me to the county jail. I was placed in the suicidal prevention unit. Once allowed to make phone calls, I called Mr. Blackwell to inform him what happened. He stated he would contact Mr. Willis because he was the criminal attorney. I then called Momma. She was a nervous wreck saying over and over she thought they were going to tell her I was dead. Momma told me Auntie was helping her until Linda Faye and Darrell arrived. I told Momma not to worry I was okay and loved her very much. Next, I called Hattie. She said Ivy was fine and not to worry about anything. I thanked her for all her help. My last call was to Jackie. Jackie and I were talking when the local evening news reported a man had been shot and died on the eastside of Cleveland. The reporter did not mention any names and no pictures were aired. A short article about the shooting was published in the evening newspaper, *The Cleveland Press*. The article stated a man had been shot by his wife while arguing over money. Herman's name was listed, but not mine, and there were no pictures published. Later that evening I was taken to a room where a man was sitting, he introduced himself as a detective and he asked if I wanted to give a statement. With no idea of how the legal system worked, but having nothing to hide, I agreed to give a statement. Honestly knowing I did not intend to kill Herman, I told the detective a summarized version of exactly what happened over the years between Herman and me. The detective persona was straightforward with an unrelenting stare as I talked. He asked a few questions, that I answered. When he finished to my surprise he shook my hand. The guard then escorted me back to the holding area. Early the next morning, Auntie brought Momma downtown to meet with the bail bondsman. When the bond was issued, the guards escorted me to the release area. When I saw Momma and Auntie, I ran to them tightly hugging them. I was very thankful and happy to see them. As we walked to the car, Momma told me I had been charged with manslaughter and my bond was $5,000. Hearing those words once again my heart sank into disbelief, disheartened at the thought the legal system had believed I meant to kill Herman. Momma and Auntie both said how sorry they were Herman had died but wanted me to be encourage and stay strong for Ivy. I promised them I would. Momma nervously said several times she thought they were going to say it was me dead. Auntie and Momma where still talking when my mind drifted away. Once again, I was reflecting on why the legal system believed I intentionally killed my husband whom I dearly loved and was the father of my child. When I purchased the gun and shot it, the thought of Herman dying never entered my mind. My only intention was to scare him in hopes he would keep his promises to not hit me. The thought of never seeing, touching, holding, or talking to Herman had never entered my mind. Yesterday morning when I woke up, it was inconceivable to me that this tragedy would occur. Now a day later, I am looking out a car window, struggling to accept the fact my husband was dead. To add on top of grieving his death and the horrible repercussions, I was now facing the fact the legal system and other people were thinking I intentionally killed Herman. All of these thoughts made my heart heavy and spirit weak. Closing my eyes and holding my head down, I thought didn't everyone know for the rest of my life I would wake up each day knowing I caused the death of my husband and father of our daughter? I would have to look forever at my daughter knowing I shot her father. Perpetually his death would be on my mind, in my soul and a part of my life. Looking back out the window I wondered how God would keep me strong enough to endure the emotional scarring from this storm.

Nearing Hattie's house, I silently cried out to God to anoint me with a double-portion of strength to endure this tragic self-inflicted storm. I then prayed for the divine intervention of the Holy Spirit to direct my path on how to let people know I never intended for my husband to die. When we pulled in the driveway Hattie brought Ivy out to me. I took my baby in my arms and held her tightly. I hugged and thanked Hattie. We both said we would call each other later. I got back into the car still cuddling Ivy close to me. While Momma and Auntie talked, I sat quietly trying to once again accept this was not a dream. It was true. Herman was dead. Ivy's daddy and my husband was gone forever. Ivy would now be raised without her father in her life, precisely what I had tried so hard to prevent and never wanted for my baby. In a split second I caused a permanent void and a lifetime of grief not only for my baby and me, but to everyone that loved Herman. What do I do now? Thinking why did

I have to be the one to shoot him? What had I done to deserve this tragedy? Why did I buy the gun? Why was I still alive? The fact that the legal system already thought I intentionally meant to kill Herman, I began to believe people would despise and not forgive me for shooting my husband.

Upon arriving at Momma's house, I thanked Auntie for always being there to help Momma and me. Momma and I tried to get through the remainder of the day the best we could. Herman's sister, Doris, called me to let me know she would not rest until I was punished for killing her brother. Shocked at how hateful she talked to me, I tried to explain what happened, but she did not want to hear it. The only thing she knew was her brother was died and it was my fault. Once she hung up on me, I thought of all of Herman's family members, I had thought Doris would in some ways understand the dilemma I was in with Herman beating me. This was because when I first met Doris, Herman told me she would call him when her husband was hitting her. Herman said he would make sure her husband knew what would happen to him if he hit his sister again. Doris did not realize, and I did not bother to tell her that Herman had told me she also was hit by her husband. After that call, I knew although I had been close to several of his family members and some were even aware and had witnessed his violent outbursts, I had to come to the realization that blood is always thicker than water. I had to accept that Herman's family members and friends wanted me to be punished for causing his death. Truthfully, I knew my family would have felt the same if Herman would have killed me. Nonetheless, hate Herman's family had towards me became another painful part of this grievous storm.

Linda Faye and Darrell arrived in Cleveland on Sunday. I was so thankful to have them there to support Momma and me. Linda Faye was always stronger than Momma and me. Darrell as the only positive male role model for us was always supportive. Later that day Christina called to extend her sympathy and support. She even shared with me how on many occasions Herman had violently beaten her, as well. This was the reason she tried to tell me not to marry him. However, at that time, she had not mentioned the beatings she endured. Even if I had known how Herman had beaten Christina, would it have stopped me from marrying him? In all likelihood, it would not have deterred me. I was blindly in love with him. That day the phone call from Christina turned out to be a flicker of light when she offered to testify in support of me about the violent outbursts she endured from Herman. I let her know how much I appreciated her support. After feeling horrible after the call from Doris, God gave me a flicker of light of encouragement with the call from Christina. Her parents, Mr. and Mrs. Corbitt also offered to pray with me over the phone. Before ending the call, they extended an invitation for me to attend church with them on Wednesday. Christina and her parents will never know how much that call meant to me. After talking to Christina, I do not know who suffered the most her or me from the violent outbursts from Herman. Unfortunately, why he had the outbursts now would never be known. That Wednesday, I went to Christ Temple Apostolic Faith Church where Mr. & Mrs. Corbitt were faithful members. They introduced me to the Bishop who briefly spoke with me. He did not want to know all the details of my need for prayer. He only asked if I believed in the Lord and that the blood of Jesus Christ would save me. I said, yes. The Bishop told me to confess to the Lord and ask for forgiveness. Although I had asked God for forgiveness in the police car, passionately I again confessed and asked God for forgiveness. After meeting with the Bishop, he and several members of the church prayed with me in the Holy Spirit. I will always cherish the thoughtfulness of Mr. and Mrs. Corbitt during this time of despair by inviting me to attend their church, as well as their praying for me and consoling and encouraging me.

A few days later Doris called again, this time telling me it was my responsibility to pay for the funeral. Without hesitation, I told her okay, even though she made it clear I would not be welcome at the funeral. After paying the bill for the funeral, I asked the director of the Wills Funeral Home if I could have a private viewing. The funeral director told me since I had paid the bill, I could make whatever decisions I wanted for the funeral. I let him know the private viewing was all I wanted. Once Herman's body was ready for viewing, the funeral director called me to let me know I could come to view Herman. He let me know he would send a car to bring me to the funeral home. When the car arrived Linda Faye, Darrell and I went to the private viewing. Momma stayed home with Ivy. Walking into the room once more the truth hit me sending jolts of pain throughout my body. Herman was really gone. In disbelief as if in a dream I looked at my husband in the casket, saying over and over in my mine, Herman was not dead. This was a delusion. He was going to get up. But, no matter how much I cried, prayed, and hoped, my husband was not getting up. Linda Faye and Darrell prayed as I mourned the death of the love of my life, my husband and father of my child. While we were there Linda Faye shared with me the last time she saw Herman. She said it was when Herman was running across the street to the race track. Linda Faye then recalled another time when Herman said to her, *you don't like me do you.* She told us she replied to him, *I like you, but not the way you treat my sister.* Before leaving I caressed his hands, kissed my husband for the last time and prayed to God for forgiveness for causing his death. When I finished praying, Linda Faye and Darrell again prayed, then the driver drove us back to the apartment.

A few days after the funeral, Doris called me to ask if Ivy was okay and to tell me to make sure I went to social security to get death benefits for her. When I hung up from the conversation with Doris, I begin to mull over when Herman told me how he went to help Doris when her husband would mistreat her, and it put an end to her being mistreated. This made me wonder if someone would have confronted Herman after he had beaten me could it have made a difference in our lives. I thought perhaps if someone would have intervened for me it might have stopped Herman from beating me. In turn, I would not have bought the gun and Herman would still be alive. Several days of being depressed over the *could have, should have, and would have* thoughts I had try to accept that nothing was going to change the fact that Herman was no longer with us. Difficult as it was I had to accept life as it had unfolded for me. I had to face the facts and truth there was nothing that could change the reality of the death of Herman.

The call from Doris after the funeral was the last time I heard from the Washington family. This was not by my choice because I had hoped they would have stayed in contact with Ivy, because regardless of the circumstances she was still Herman's daughter. This began another storm because due to my actions Ivy, who was a Washington, would not have the chance to get to know the Washington side of her family. It was another heartbreaking reality to know our daughter was being punished for both of her parents' sins – Herman's sins of beating me and my sin of shooting the gun that killed him. I know Herman would not have wanted his death to separate Ivy from his family. But it did. For many years, no one related to Herman tried to contact Ivy, except for Christina and Vet. Shortly after the death of Herman, Christina would allow Vet to visit Ivy. The three of us went on outings to the zoo, amusement parks, and the circus. Later in life, I was grateful that Vet continued to stay in contact with Ivy.

What Happens to Us Now? The police had given me the approval to reenter the house. Not yet wanting to return to the house, I asked Linda Faye and Darrell to get the items Ivy and I needed to live with Momma. A few days later they returned to Xenia with the promise to return for the court proceedings. My boss, Eddie was extremely supportive and told me not to worry about my job. Linda C., Jackie, and Hattie continued to be there for Ivy and me. Jackie had introduced me to her neighbors, the Morrows. They were a nice family that became another vital part of Ivy and my life.

After a few weeks, I knew I had to get back to work in order to support Ivy. The four thousand dollars that Herman and I had in our savings was used to pay for his funeral and my legal fees. I called Eddie to ask when I could return to work. He told me whenever I decided. Since it was already Thursday, I let him know Monday. Upon returning to work my co-workers appeared to be understanding and supportive, especially Eddie and Della Hameen, who both became good friends. If there was any negative talk or gossip about what happened with my husband, I never heard it. The only situation that was unusual was when Mr. Wright, the plumbing instructor, hurriedly came into my office. Without saying a word to me, he handed me two dollars he had borrowed weeks ago. Then he quickly turned, walking out the office. I tried to say something to him, but he simply raised his hands and kept walking. To this day, I figure he must have he read the news article that stated Herman and I were arguing about money, and thought I shot my husband because of money. If only I could get him and the world to understand the death of my husband was never my intent. I would give anything, including my own life to retract the day I purchased the gun and the day I shot it.

Soon it was clear without any income from Herman, I could barely pay my expenses. Living with Momma and returning to work enabled me to pay most of my expenses but it was becoming more a struggle to make ends meet. Within a few months I was financially insolvent. Paying for the funeral and legal fees, our other debts, and relinquishing the house to the bank depleted our savings and ruined my credit worthiness. I knew the mortgage company would soon refile its foreclosure complaint and try to recoup any losses and fees. Taking all my financial woes into consideration, I decided to contact Mr. Blackwell to discuss filing bankruptcy. He reviewed my finances and agreed filing bankruptcy was my best option. He prepared the paperwork and filed a chapter 7 bankruptcy case. During the preparation of the bankruptcy case, it was discovered Herman had obtained the loan for the tow truck with me as the co-signer without my knowledge. Mr. Blackwell discovered Herman had taken another lady who represented she was me to the dealership. On my behalf, Mr. Blackwell contacted the bank regarding the fraudulently obtained loan. Without court intervention, the bank settled for two thousand dollars and withdrew the debt from my credit report. This was really an unexpected financial blessing for Ivy and me. Then a few weeks I received a letter from social security stating Ivy would receive survivor benefits from her father's social security benefits. Once more a financial blessing that would be used for Ivy's education. These were more flickers of light from God that by His glory my needs were supplied to help me get back on my feet financially. *But my God shall supply all your need according to his riches in glory by Christ Jesus*, Philippians 4:19 (KJV).

Ivy and I had been staying with Momma for about six weeks when Ernest told me about a duplex his friend Earl Hawkins had for rent. After looking at the house, I decided to rent it. Because Ernest and Earl knew my husband had died in our home, they were kind enough to arrange to move the furniture from the house to the new house. Even though Earl was twenty years older than me we became good friends. Besides his help with moving me, he was a reliable and supportive friend to me, especially when my car would breakdown and I needed to locate reliable mechanics. He even understood the few times when I had to pay my rent late. Over the years, I would help Earl with certain business matters relating to his nightclubs and rental property.

During this time the relationship Ivy and I had with the Morrows: Andrew and Willtha and their two beautiful daughters, Andrea, and Jan, were becoming remarkably close and they soon became a very intricate part of our lives. When Momma and Hattie were unable to babysit Ivy, Mama Willtha, as I called her, or Jan would babysit for me. I was grateful that even with my stormy life the Morrows were exceedingly kind to both of us. Right away the Morrows loved, and adored Ivy and she loved them. They called her their *Moocha*. Each time Ivy walked into their house they would look forward to her running in calling out for Papa Andrew and Mama Willtha with her arms open ready to give them a big hug and kiss. Within a few months it was like we had been family for years who loved each other unconditionally. Even though Jan was a teenager about to graduate from high school she stole my heart with her beautiful, bubbly smile and personality and became like a little sister to me. One of my most memorable times with Jan was when she went with Momma, Ivy, and me to visit Linda Faye and Darrell. Jan had recently obtained her driver's license and was excited about helping me drive. On the way back, I let her drive. It was an experience I never forgot. When Jan got behind the wheel she put the pedal to the metal flying down I-71. She would pull close behind vehicles. If the driver did not move to the other lane, Jan would flash the hi-beam lights until the driver moved over. I was on pins and needles the entire ride while Jan laughed at me for being nervous. Arriving in Cleveland, I blew a sigh of relief. The Morrows were very inspiring to me, especially Mama Willtha. Early in the beginning of our relationship, she shared how she endured some abuse from Papa Andrew. Thank God things worked out for them. Years later they would be blessed to be married for over fifty years. Husband and wife until Papa Andrew died. Even today when thinking of their marriage, I wish I could have endured the violent outbursts of my husband instead of causing his tragic death. Then perhaps my teenage dream of celebrating fifty years of marriage could have materialized. The Morrows and I shared many good times together. The wedding of Andrea was one of those good times. It was also the first time Ivy was a flower girl. Then when tough times came, we were there to encourage and support one another. Sorrowfully later in life those tough times included the passing of Andrea from a brief battle with cancer. I will always cherish and appreciate the Morrows. At a time when I needed it the most they became a God-given family that unconditionally loves and support us and vice versa.

A few months after Herman passed, Linda C. introduced me to her co-worker and friend, Arthur Gholson. Arthur became a good friend who helped me like a big brother. He reminded me of my relationship with Marvin. Like Jan one of my fondest memories of

Arthur was driving Momma, Ivy, and me to visit Linda Faye and Darrell in his classic lime green Thunderbird. Another time was when Ivy was three years old, and I asked Jan to take Ivy to the circus with Arthur and his son. Jan was not a happy camper because she thought Arthur was too old. Several years later, Jan was proven to be irrefutably wrong about how she initially felt about Arthur. This is because several years later Jan and Arthur were united in holy matrimony and to this day remain married. They were blessed with two sons, Lawrence, and Michael. It was an honor when Jan and Arthur asked me to be the god-mother of Michael. Like Jan babysat Ivy, Ivy would often babysit Lawrence and Michael. From birth Michael suffered with a heart disease, which sadly, resulted in his passing at the early age of seven. Even to this day the Gholsons and Mama Willtha remain an important part of our lives.

Chapter Four -- Life Will Never Be the Same

One day while Ivy and I were shopping at the grocery store, I ran into the mother of Lenora, one of my high school friends. We greeted each other and started talking about how each other was doing. She then asked if I knew *one of our classmates killed her husband*. Ashamedly I said, *yes, that it was me*. She looked shocked and said, oh. We then talked a few more moments before saying our goodbyes. Following that encounter, I knew without a doubt people were forever going to talk about me killing my husband. Even if people did not say it directly to me, they most likely would be thinking and talking about what happened to my husband. This made me aware that in the future anyone that became close to me I had to tell them what happened to Herman before someone else that knew me told them. That day made me feel completely alienated by the world knowing for the rest of my life I would be labelled a *killer*. Once more I wondered why me? Why did I survive all the beatings only to be labeled a *killer*?

The Trial. In September 1980, the grand jury indicted me for murder instead of manslaughter. Numb and afraid I would spend the rest of my life in prison, I inwardly became severely depressed. Not wanting to worry Momma, my other family members, and friends, I did not tell anyone about the indictment. Instead I turned totally to God praying for strength and mercy. Later that day I contacted Mr. Willis about the indictment. He told me not to worry that it was typical for the grand jury to indict on the higher offense. I said okay, even though mentally, I was a wreck. Aware I was in desperate need of spiritual strengthening and guidance; Ivy and I visited several churches in the neighborhood. Although my world was whirling out of control and filled with heartache, I hid my true feelings within not letting anyone know what I was enduring. The trial was scheduled to begin the second week of November. Mr. Willis began to prepare for the trial. He scheduled appointments to interview potential witnesses, including: Christina; several policemen from the cities of Bedford and Warrensville Hts.; medical professionals from the Clinic, Bedford Hts., Suburban and Brentwood hospitals; Pastor Sanders from Lee Road Baptist Church; the initial divorce lawyer, Ed Wade; the lawyer that represented Herman in the Bedford Hts. court for the case when he assaulted me at the apartment in Bedford; co-workers and friends who had witnessed the violent outbursts; and my family members that observed injuries and bruises caused by the violent outbursts. The first day of the trial Momma, Auntie, Linda Faye, and Darrell went with me. Waiting in the lobby of the courtroom looking at Momma I could tell the trial was going to be mentally too much for Momma to bear. Already feeling terrible, it made me feel even worse to see Momma anxious and nervous as she tried to endure this heartbreaking day with me. Even before they called me into the courtroom, I let Momma know with Linda Faye and Darrell attending the trial each day, she did not have to attend. The reaction from Momma let me know she was relieved not to have to attend. I asked Auntie to take Momma home, which she did. Over the course of the trial besides Linda Faye and Darrell attending daily, Auntie, Linda C., Jan, and Ernest attended a few days. Several members of Herman's family also attended. Before the trial began, my charge was reduced to manslaughter. Then the prosecutor asked to speak with Mr. Willis and me. He offered a plea bargain for me to plead guilty to manslaughter and receive one-year probation with no jail time. In my heart and soul, I knew without a doubt I did not intentionally kill Herman. Together with my attorney telling me he was confident that with the evidence and testimonies from the witnesses would prove I did not intend to kill Herman, I declined the plea bargain offer. Later, in hindsight, I should have taken the probation. Or better yet chose to have the case heard and decided by a panel of judges instead of my peers.

The first day of trial involved the selection of the jury. The next day the prosecutor for the State of Ohio and my attorney made their opening statements. Followed by the prosecutor calling the witnesses for the State. The two main witnesses for the State that I remember, were Robert and the gentleman that drove me to the phone booth. To my dismay was the testimony of Robert who said the night of his graduation I told him, *one day his uncle was not going to wake up*. When asked if he ever witnessed Herman abusing me. He stated, no. Both answers were untrue. Nonetheless I understood and forgave Robert for not testifying truthfully. I had to accept the fact the Washington family wanted me to be held accountable for causing the death of Herman. The gentleman that took me to the phone booth was called to testify. That day and even to this day, I cannot remember what he looked like or the type of car he drove. He testified while in the car I said, *Herman will not hit me anymore*. This statement I do not remember saying. Unsuccessfully I have tried during the trial and over the years to recall the entire time in his car. The only thing I can remember saying is, *my husband was jumping on me and I needed to call the police.* Regardless if his or my recollection is correct, I have always been thankful he stopped to help me that day. The only other witnesses for the State I can recall were the arresting police officers, the detective that interviewed me at the city jail, a doctor that performed the autopsy and a few expert witnesses. When one of the expert witnesses testified, I learned my ignorance had caused me to make another terrible mistake when purchasing the gun. One of the expert witnesses testified I had bought a 22-caliber gun, which he said was considered the most dangerous gun because the small bullet ricochets throughout the body with no clear exit. This is exactly what happened to Herman. The bullet entered his left side ricocheting through his body. This immediately began to mentally plague me. Oh, how I regretted ever purchasing a gun. After the prosecutor presented the case for the State, Judge Roman stated the trial would resume the next morning. The next day Mr. Willis began presenting my case. He called one of the police officers that kicked in the door of the apartment in Bedford Hts. and arrested Herman. The officer gave details of that evening. Mr. Willis then called the attorney that represented Herman in the Bedford Hts. case. The attorney gave testimony concerning my contacting him to represent Herman when he was arrested for assaulting me at the apartment and his representation of Herman in the Bedford Hts. court case. My friend, Kim M., was called to give testimony about the night Herman jumped on me at Laurice's house. Pastor Sanders testified about my counseling sessions with him. Attorney Ed Wade offered testified concerning my meeting to discuss his being my attorney in a divorce case. Linda Faye attested to seeing the after effects from the violent outbursts of Herman that caused mental and physical damages and seeing my emotional breakdown related to the attempts to commit suicide. Medical professionals from the Clinic, Bedford Hts., Suburban, and Brentwood hospitals presented medical documentation in support of emergency room treatments for injuries and psychiatric reports from my attempts to commit suicide. The prosecutor objected to certain aspects of each of these witnesses' testimonies. Judge Roman sustained some of the objections while overruling others. This resulted in certain crucial testimony, evidence and reports being inadmissible. Then came one of the most disappointing aspect of the trial. The testimony of the psychiatrist together with the related medical records from the therapy sessions she had with Herman for his violent outbursts were objected to by the prosecutor. The court sustained the objection resulting in the imperative testimony and medical records of Herman being inadmissible. When Christina was called to testify, the prosecutor objected. Once more, Judge Roman sustained the objection. To my dismay, the testimony of the violent outbursts afflicted upon Christina by Herman were precluded. This decision troubled me because the jury would not hear about the pattern of violent outbursts Herman inflicted not only us, but other women. Christina knew a lot more about those incidents than me, because she was aware of Herman being stabbed and shot at by women he had beaten. I only knew bits and pieces of what Laurice told me over the phone the night Herman had the violent outburst at her home. While Mr. Willis was stating his arguments against the testimony of Christina not being allowed, I sat wondering how he had survived the stabbing and shots being fired by other people. If he survived those incidents, why didn't he survive when I shot the gun? Why was it my destiny that Herman would die by my hands? That day and for the rest of my life I constantly try to understand why Herman died when I shot that gun. Once I started writing this book, I began to realize that God wanted me to eventually bear witness to others how He gave me strength to live with the permanent emotional scars from this awful tragic storm in my life. Christina later told me with family members of Herman present in the courtroom, she had become concerned about testifying. Consequently, God worked this out for her best interest. There was no need for the Washington family to despise Christina for trying to help me. My actions could not be the reason for strife between the Washington family and Christina. After Christina's testimony was disallowed, I was called to the stand. Mr. Willis begin to question me about my relationship with Herman. Starting from the moment Marvin introduced me to Herman, I began to tell everyone in the courtroom the unadulterated account of my life with Herman. Around 5:00 p.m., I began to testify about when we were married on July 7, 1977 when Judge Roman interrupted my testimony. He stated due to the late hour he was adjourning the trial to the next day. As Linda Faye drove us home, I felt disheartened with the amount of testimonies and evidence not being admitted. Not allowing such imperative information during the trial bother me for years, until 1984 when I watched the movie the *Burning Bed* which helped me become aware of domestic violence. It also made me realize I was not the only woman that had been beaten. Similar to me there were many other women whose mates abused them. Sadly, like me at times those abusive relationships ended tragically for one or both persons. In addition, the movie helped me think certain evidence from my trial was not allowed because at the time Herman was beating me and during my trial, society did not consider beating a woman a serious offense. It seemed to me once the movie was aired domestic violence started to gain more nationwide attention.

The next day the trial reconvened with Mr. Willis examination of my life with Herman after our marriage to the day of his death. Once Mr. Willis finished with his questions, the prosecutor began his cross-examination. Although most of the questions by the prosecutor are vague, there are several I remember without any doubt. He asked me to look at the picture taken at the time of my arrest. After I looked at the picture, he asked me to point to the side of my face that Herman hit me. I pointed to my left side. Then he asked why I did not go to my family or friends like I had previously. I answered with our baby it was no longer easy to simply pack a bag and leave because I now had to think about the well-being of Ivy. He asked if I considered myself abused. I answered, I do not know because I really did not understand what abused entailed. I went on to say I believed my husband had violent outbursts towards me when he was upset that usually occurred when he had been drinking or was angry about something or with someone. But, I was unsure if this type of behavior was considered abuse. Mr. Willis had a few redirect questions. Once I answered his questions, Judge Roman adjourned the trial until the next morning, and instructed unless there were more witnesses, closing arguments would be heard the next morning.

That day Ernest had attended the trial. He offered to buy me dinner before taking me home. During dinner, Ernest said during my testimony I did not come across strong and convincing enough. I did not respond to his comment, though it did concern me because I had honestly testified exactly what occurred in my life with Herman. For many years his statement mentally haunted me. Over thirty-five years later, I shared with a psychiatrist what Ernest told me that day and the affect it had on me. The psychiatrist let me know unless you have studied the characteristics of domestic violence and victims of abuse, you will not understand their demeanor. She explained to me in today's society court cases involving domestic violence typically call an expert witness to explain the demeanor of victims of domestic violence. During the years of violent outbursts from Herman support of this nature was not available. I am tremendously glad that in society nowadays, the resources for victims of domestic violence has improved. It is my prayer that this book will bring further attention to the plight of people that are abused.

The next day during the closing arguments, the prosecutor stated why I should be found guilty. Followed by Mr. Willis stating why I should be found innocent. The prosecutor made two statements that are forever imbedded in my mind and heart. The first, was *why didn't*

I run as I had previously. The second, was *what will I tell my daughter happened to her father*. As hard as those statements were to accept, I had to accept the fact they were true. The accuracy of those two statements, became another heavy emotional storm in my life. In retrospect, it was true, I should have just run like I had previously. If I had ran, Herman would be alive. Then the prosecutor was absolutely correct about what would I tell Ivy. Causing my daughter to become fatherless is what I regret most from the death of Herman. Knowing causing my daughter's father death would cause her to forever suffer the painful agony of being denied the chance to get to know and have memories of Herman became a perpetual sentence of damnation for me. How would Ivy even be able to love me, the woman that caused her to be fatherless? It was entirely inconceivable to comprehend the pain Ivy would endure with never getting to know or have any memory of Herman. I lived for years with the emptiness and pain of Tim not being in my life. Ivy would have to live for a lifetime with only pictures and memories of others about her father. Over the years each time I have seen the void in the eyes of my child when she is thinking about not having any memories or knowledge of her dad, I recall the words of the prosecutor and regret the day I purchased the gun. I can never forgive myself for what I took away from my beautiful daughter. So yes, the prosecutor was right. *What will I tell my daughter happened to her father* brought unending grief to both my child and me. The little glimpse of light from God in this painful situation are the few pictures of Herman especially the ones holding Ivy. The other spark of light occurred when Ivy was in her twenties and she found in a file cabinet a copy of my appeal transcript. The transcript detailed some of the violent outbursts I endured. It was my prayer and hope that reading the transcript Ivy found at least a little peace knowing I had been truthful about the difficulties Herman and I sometimes faced. Even with Ivy knowing about our marital problems, nothing can remove the pain I see in Ivy's eyes about never knowing who her father really was and having no memory of him. If only I had done what the prosecutor said, *run as I had previously*.

Subsequent to the closing arguments, Judge Roman read to the jury the instructions to decide the disposition of the case. The jury requested several times to have the instructions re-read pertaining to if I became the aggressor at any time. After two days of deliberation, the jury had reached a verdict. Standing with Mr. Willis and Mr. Blackwell beside me, Judge Roman said, *has the jury reached a verdict*. The foreman of the jury said, *we have*. The next think I heard was, *we find the defendant guilty*. I felt nothing. Completely numb from head to toe. Then a tear formed in my eye. I fought back the tears. Coming back to my senses, my heart was racing. My mind was shouting *you are guilty*. Motionlessly, I looked at Judge Roman. He was talking but I was not comprehending a word. I only knew twelve people believed I intentionally killed my husband. He was the love of my life. Why couldn't they see I never wanted to hurt him? I just needed Herman to stop hitting me. Later I was told the jury found me guilty because the jury instructions stated if at any time I became the aggressor I must be found guilty. The jury believed I became the aggressor when I pulled out the gun. Another very horribly dark stormy day of my life by a split-second decision that had taken the life of my husband, and by twelve people deciding I was going to prison for a long time to pay for my sinful decision. Now our innocent baby was losing both of her parents. What will happen to Ivy? How did my life come to this? All these bad decisions. Should I have given Ivy up for adoption? Had it been wrong for me to bring Ivy into a home where her parents had an unstable violent marriage? Was I the horrible killer the jury thought I was? Why wasn't I killed? How would I survive in prison? What reason do I have to live? When court was adjourned, Mr. Willis explained to me Judge Roman would set a date for my sentencing hearing in a few weeks. Mr. Willis stated he would be filing an appeal of the case. Finally, I was able to look around the room. Several members of Herman family were talking. They appeared very satisfied with the guilty verdict. My family of course was looking devastated. I nor my family and friends knew anyone who had been convicted of a crime, let alone been found guilty and sent to prison. The only person, prior to myself that I knew had been in the Cuyahoga County jail was Herman. Thoughts of the unknown of what would happen to me in jail was frightening to me and my loved ones.

Being found guilty of manslaughter by a jury of peers completely shattered me to the core. Knowing that others believed I shot the gun with intent to kill Herman was heartbreaking. After the verdict I had to accept the reality that regardless of the circumstances of physical and mental abuse, I had caused the death of Herman. For the rest of my life, I would have to live with the hand that held and shot a gun that took the life of my beloved husband. My split-second decision resulted in never-ending suffering not only for myself, but Ivy and Herman's many loved ones. Waiting for the sentencing hearing, I survived by hugging Ivy close to me exactly like I had when Herman had beaten me once she was born, and after he passed away. The unconditional love, forgiveness and support from loved ones, friends and coworkers also helped sustain me. Thankfully when the jury of peers did not understand my true intention was not to kill Herman, the Holy Spirit had imparted into my soul that God forgave me of this grievous crime. The flicker of light from God was forgiveness through the blood of Jesus who died for my sins, which encompassed shooting the gun that took the life of my husband. *He touched my mouth with it and said, "Listen carefully, this has touched your lips; your wickedness [your sin, your injustice, your wrongdoing] is taken away and your sin atoned for and forgiven,* Isaiah 6:7 (AMP).

Over the next several days, I spent time with Ivy, Momma, Linda Faye, Darrell, Linda C., Jan, and a few other close friends. Linda Faye and Darrell had to leave before the sentencing hearing to return to work. I thanked them for all their love and support. They prayed with me before leaving assuring me that they would be there to support Ivy and me. In my time alone with Ivy, I prayed for God to intervene. My main prayer was seeking mercy if not for me, for Ivy. I did not want my baby to loss both of her parents at sixteen months of age. That Sunday I attended Assembly Baptist Church where I had been attending for the past several weeks. The pastor and members had no idea of my situation. The pastor said for anyone in need of prayer to come kneel at alter. Holding Ivy, I humbly went praying again for forgiveness and grace and mercy for Ivy. I enjoyed attending this church. The pastor reminded me of Bishop Williford. Once I returned home, I spent time with Momma and Ivy. I wanted to spend as much time with them as possible. Over the next few days, I began to make preparation for going to prison. Hattie had agreed to take care of Ivy for me. I prepared the necessary paperwork for her to have guardianship of Ivy.

A few days later, Mr. Willis called to let me know the sentencing hearing had been scheduled. After that call, I had no incentive to do anything. It was like I was in a trance and was just going through the motions of life emotionlessly and hopelessly. My state of mind was to accept the fact my way of life as I knew it to be for the past twenty-two years was swiftly coming to an end. I would soon be a prisoner of the State of Ohio. The day of the sentencing hearing, Linda C. came to get me and Ivy to take us to the courthouse. I was taking Ivy because I needed her to be with me until they carried me away to prison. That day only Doris attended on behalf of the Washington family. Mr. Wills met me in the lobby of the courtroom. He explained that first he and the prosecutor would meet with Judge Roman in his chambers. Afterwards I would be called into the courtroom. The bailiff called us into the courtroom and instructed me to take a seat at the table with Mr. Wills. When Judge Roman entered the courtroom, everyone stood. Judge Roman asked me before rendering my sentence if I had anything to say. Although I do not recall every word I said, what I do remember saying is how much I regretted shooting and causing the death of my husband. I extended my sincere apology for the pain I had caused the Washington family and anyone else affected by my actions. Judge Roman asked if anyone else had any statements to render. Even though I expected Doris to say something, she did not. Judge Roman then sentenced me to 4 to 25 years. As tears begin to fill my eyes to my amazement, Judge Roman then said my requests for an appeal and an appeal bond were granted. Mr. Willis had told me that morning if the Judge granted the appeal bond, I would be released pending the decision of the court of appeals. The Judge went on to say that my appeal bond was to continue in the same amount of $5,000 as my earlier bond. He further told his bailiff to let me stay in the courtroom waiting area pending the processing of the paperwork instead of in the jail holding area. Judge Roman then instructed the paperwork be processed as soon as possible because I had my baby with me and needed to get her back home. Instantly, standing in front of Judge Roman my tears of sorrow turned into tears of thankfulness and joy. I had to suppress the desire to holler thank you Jesus and run to give Judge Roman the biggest hug of appreciation. Instead, I simply expressed on my face the joy in my heart. I stood there in total awe of the grace and mercy of God. As we went outside the courtroom to the lobby area, I immediately went to the phone to call Momma with the wonderful news that for now I was not being sent to prison. I quickly explained to Momma the appeal was another chance to prove I did not intentionally kill Herman. Momma was elated with thanksgiving to God. Within an hour I was released on the appeal bond. As we left the courthouse, I was exceedingly grateful to God for blessing me not to be sent to jail that day. Mr. Wills told me he would be in contact with me throughout the appeal process. He assured me not to worry that everything would work out for me. In the car as Linda C. drove Ivy and me home, I was bursting with thanksgiving for I knew it was only by the grace of God that I was spared to be riding in the car instead of behind bars. Although still unsure about my future with the pending appeal, I knew that for now I would be able to care for Ivy and work on spiritually and mentally healing myself from my life with Herman and being found guilty. The bright flicker of light that day was God had undeniably kept His promise to never forsake me and answered my prayer to not have to leave my baby parentless. *Be strong and of a good courage, fear not, nor be afraid of them: for the Lord thy God, he it is that doth go with thee; he will not fail thee, nor forsake thee,* Deuteronomy 31:6 (KJV).

Chapter Five -- Dark Storms Continue

Awaiting the decision on the appeal, I worked diligently at WJC where I was receiving excellent performance evaluations. The Sunday after the sentencing hearing, I joined Assembly where Rev. Willie Judie was the Pastor. Within the next few months, I became a member of the choir. Before joining the choir, I talked to Pastor Judie about my life with Herman and the pending appeal case. It was a relief when Pastor Judie told me he was not concerned about my past for God loves and forgives us all. He stated unless I wanted the members to know there was no need to let anyone else know what had occurred in my life. Another ray of light during this unpredictable tedious journey in my stormy life.

Devastated Again. In January 1981, while shopping at Randall Park Mall, I ran into a teenage friend, Dwight. We talked briefly before he asked if I would go to the movies and dinner with him. I thought about the last time I went on a date was with Herman. The past four years of my life had resolved totally around Herman. Now at twenty-three years old I was a widow and single mom who was being asked on a date. I told him I would think about it. We exchanged phone numbers before saying goodbye. That evening Dwight called. We had a good discussion about our teenage years and what we had been doing over the past years. He knew I had been married, but I was unsure if he knew that I had caused the death of Herman. Either he knew but decided not to mention it or had not heard how my marriage ended. We talked on the phone for several days.

By the second week, I agreed to go to dinner and a movie with him. We made a date for Saturday at 4:00 p.m. The day of the date Momma had asked for Ivy to spend the night. I let Momma know that would be good because I had a date with an old friend from junior high school. Momma was happy for me. Dwight picked me up and we went to dinner at Ponderosa Restaurant. After dinner we went to see the movie *Stir Crazy*. For the first time since the death of Herman and the trial, I was not in my usual gloomy state of mind. I was enjoying myself. This was mainly because Dwight had always had a good sense of humor. He could make people laugh even when they were sad. A few times throughout the date there were things said or seen that caused me to think of a happy memory with Herman. Those incidents caused me to mentally digress for a few moments. A few times suddenly I would hear Dwight talking and I would say huh. He would say, did you hear me, are you listening. I would say, yeah. That night I knew whether good or bad memories my life with Herman would always be a part of my heart, mind, and soul. When we returned to my house, Dwight said it is still early, you want company for a little while. Thinking it was only about 9:30 p.m., I said, okay. We had been watching a movie for about thirty minutes when Dwight unexpectedly tried to kiss me. I turned to let his lips kiss my cheek instead of lips. He again tried to kiss me. I told him, no, I do not want to kiss. Dwight did not listen. He kept trying to kiss me. I thought first he was playing and joking around. Then he would not stop. He was more aggressively forcing himself on me. Getting upset I keep saying, *no, stop*, while pushing him away. He began saying, *you know you want it.* Beginning to panic and scared, I franticly shouted, *no, it is time for you to leave, please leave.* Pulling away from him, I trying to get up from the couch. I managed to get half-way up, but Dwight forcefully grabbed me back onto the couch. Screaming at Dwight, *stop, do not do this to me, get off me,* I continued to struggle to get away from him, but slid off the couch onto the floor. Trying to off the floor, Dwight stood up and pushed me until I was laying on my back on the floor. He climbed on top of me. I kept on screaming at him and swinging my arms and kicking, but he forcefully pinned me to the floor by placing his arm under my chin. This made it difficult for me to breathe and move. I looked at him with tears in my eyes and tried to scream, *please stop,* but could only whisper because of his arm pressing hard again my neck. Seeing the look of rage in his eyes and his voice eerily saying, *do not make me hurt you.* I closed my eyes, froze in a state of shock, and regressed to thoughts of the violent outbursts from Herman. With his arm still wedged under my chin, I began to feel his other hand snatching and tugging my skirt off. Even though my eyes were still closed, tears were running down the side of my face. Although I had my legs crossed tightly together, I could feel Dwight yanking at my pantyhose and underwear until he ripped them off enough to get his fingers inside of me. With his every move I was clenching my eyes shut, laying almost motionless under the pressure of his arm under the chin and weight on my body. He took his finger out of me and began to force my legs apart. I tried as hard as I could to hold my legs tightly together, but he had taken his arm from under my chin, so he could pry my legs apart. With his arm no longer under my chin, I franticly wiggled and twisted in an attempt to get him off of me, but I could not. Dwight was just too strong and was able to pull my legs apart enough to forcefully enter my body. I unrelenting tried to hit, scratch and even bit him, but he grabbed my arms and pinned them down as he kept viciously violating my body. With no more energy to fight, I laid there lifeless as my mind flashed back to being molested. I also wonder if Dwight had planned to do this to me because he knew what happened to me in my marriage to Herman and the outcome of my trial. Although it was only minutes, it seemed like it was hours before he finally got off me. Dwight was saying something while extending his hand to help me up from the floor. I refused to take his hand, as I struggled to get on my feet. When I got up, I could see Dwight was laughing while fixing his clothes. I turned and ran into the bathroom and locked the door. Dwight came to the bathroom and tried opening the door. When he could not he started banging on the door saying, *open the door, it wasn't that bad was it girl.* Laughing he said, *you know you wanted it as much as I did.* Crying and shaking, I told him to please leave. Banging harder on the door he said, you thought I was only going to be teased? Nervously I said, please leave. Several times while banging on the door he said, you are a black bitch and slut. Thinking back on when Herman was enraged, I knew it was best not to say anything else. Sitting quietly, I prayed he would not knock the door down. A few moments later I heard the front door open and close. Then I could hear his car start and drive off. Unlocking the door, I came out of the bathroom. I went to the front door to lock it. Crying and shivering, I got into the shower where I stayed for a long time washing my body over and over while I constantly cried out, why me, why me. Slowly I made it to my bed. In shock and mentally drained, I could not understand how I was generating this much devastation in my life. Was I such a bad person that these terrible things were occurring in my life? Were there dark clouds lingering all around me resulting in terrible things happening in my life? I cried out to God, why me, Lord, what am I supposed to do now? Then I thought with my uncertain future, there was no way I could report what Dwight had did to me. It would be too embarrassing to let everyone know that I had already let another man take advantage of me. Besides, he would deny what he did to me. Being free on bond I had to think about how this could affect the appeal bond. Knowledge of the rape could negatively affect the appeal. Feeling alone and defeated I began to argue with God, why am I going through all this? What is even my purpose for living? After crying and arguing with God until I was too weak to do anything else, I humbly began to pray. In silence my mind, heart and spirit prayed to God to strengthen and anoint me with His grace and mercy to accept what had happened to me that night. I asked that God enable me to bury this vicious rape far within the depths of my soul, because as far as I was concerned only God, Dwight and I would know what happened that dreadful night. For several years I kept the clothes skirt, pantyhose, and panties that Dwight ripped off me as a reminder of what he did to me. Frequently I wondered if Dwight realized the mental damage he caused me that night. This became a miserably dark stormy part of my life. Yet even in this appallingly time of my life, I can now say there were flickers of light from God of being my refuge and stronghold that gave me strength to endure the ruthlessness from Dwight. *In you, O Lord, I have put my trust and confidently taken refuge; Let me never be [a]put to shame. In Your righteousness deliver me and rescue me; Incline Your ear to me and save me. Be to me a rock of refuge and a sheltering stronghold to which I may continually come; You have given the commandment to save me, For You are my rock and my fortress. Rescue me, O my God, from the hand of the wicked (godless), From the grasp of the unrighteous and ruthless man*, Psalm 71:1-4 (AMP). That night Dwight could have permanently harmed me physically, but God was my refuge that kept me from being severally beaten or worse killed. God also shield me from the shame of contacting any sexually transmitted diseases. On top of those blessings, the next month I had my menstruation cycle. I had prayed the entire month not to be pregnant because I was not on birth control when Dwight raped me. Even though I had no intentions of being sexually active, a few days later I began to take my birth control pills.

The morning after Dwight raped me, I went to pick up Ivy. The moment I laid my eyes on Ivy, I picked her up, held her tightly to me never wanting to let her go. Momma asked me about my date. I told her I did not have a date after all that I had been stood up. Momma said, aw, no. After that day I threw all my time and energy into raising Ivy. On Sundays and Wednesdays Ivy and I attended services at Assembly, and on Fridays I went to choir rehearsal. I worked extra hours at WJC in the evening program that had recently been added to the curriculum. Any spare time was spent with Ivy, Momma, Linda C., or the Morrows. My marital life had already dimmed my hopes for a healthy relationship with a man. What Dwight did to me further marred those hopes.

Another Unthinkable Decision. In April 1981 I was working the evening program and was in my office talking to the evening program administer Mr. Black. Suddenly I started bleeding profusely from my vagina. Mr. Black not knowing what to do, called Dellar into the office. Due to the large clots and the amount of blood I was losing, the ambulance was called. Once the paramedics examined me, they said I needed to be examined at the hospital. I asked to be taken to University Hospital where Dr. Gyves was on staff. Before leaving, I asked Dellar to call Momma and Hattie to inform them I was going to the hospital. My thought was the bleeding was because my pap smears had remained abnormal. Upon arrival at the emergency room, I was examined and asked if I could be pregnant. I said, no while thinking about the night Dwight raped me. I let the nurse know I had not had sex in over four months, not mentioning it was when I was raped, that my menstruation cycles had been normal, and I was on birth control pills. Several tests were administered. The doctor came into the room informing me of the results of the test. To my disbelief, the doctor said I was several months pregnant. No, this could not be true. How could I be pregnant? Not only had I not been sexually active after the date rape, I had restarted taking my birth control pills and was having my monthly menstrual cycle. Plus, there had been no notable change in my weight. Always weighing between 90 to 105 pounds, I had no noticeable weight gain. The doctor ordered a sonogram that confirmed I was indeed pregnant. Unsure of why I was heavily bleeding and to confirm the bleeding had not adversely affected the baby, the doctor admitted me to the hospital for further testing. In total panic, what do I do now? I have been convicted and did not know if I would be sent to jail. How could I have a baby while in prison? I called Momma and Hattie letting them know I was admitted for abnormal vaginal bleeding. Momma said, *oh no, are you okay*. I told her *yes*, not to worry everything would be okay. Before hanging, up I let Momma know how much I loved and appreciated her, she told me she loved me too. When I spoke with Hattie, she said not to worry about Ivy because she would take care of her for as long as needed. After talking to Momma and Hattie I thanked God for blessing me to have them in my life. The next morning Dr. Gyves came to examine me. When he asked about Ivy and Herman, I told him Ivy was doing fine. I then let him know Herman had passed but did not tell him I was responsible for his death. Dr. Gyves did not ask me if Herman was the father, and of course, I didn't tell him the circumstances of how I became pregnant. After he examined me, Dr. Gyves stated it was a possibility the baby might not go to term even with the suture. He further explained although the baby could be born healthy, there was a possibility for problems, including birth defects, due to my taking the birth control pills and the amount of blood I had loss. Nervous, depressed, and scared, I needed intercessory prayer. I found the phone number for Pastor Judie in the phone book. When I called the number, it was the home of his ex-wife, Willie Mae Judie.

I asked her to please let Pastor Judie know I was in the hospital and requested that he pray for me. She was kind and agreed to let him know. That night until I went to sleep, I prayed to God without ceasing for understanding and guidance. The next morning to my surprise, I looked up to see Pastor Judie and another pastor walking into the room. It uplifted my spirit so much to see them. Pastor Judie hugged me, and I told him how much their visiting me meant to me. Pastor Judie introduced me to Pastor Randle and told him that Ivy and I recently joining the church and what nice young lady I was. Although I did not tell them what was happening medically with me and they did not ask me, they encouraged me to depend on God for healing and deliverance. Before they left, they prayed for my strength and healing. Later that day I received a beautiful bouquet of flowers from Assembly. Later I received floral arrangements from my co-workers, Earl, and even one of the students that attended WJC. The floral arrangements really uplifted my spirits because I had never received floral arrangements. Pastor Judie taking the time to visit me, and the receipt of the floral arrangement fortified my dedication to him and Assembly. The flowers from my co-workers, Earl, and the student was also greatly appreciated. Momma and Auntie came to visit that evening. Momma let me know Ivy was doing fine with Hattie caring for her and Jan had offering to help. Momma and Auntie looked concerned knowing my pap smears were abnormal and because several family members had cervical cancer. Hiding my problem behind a fake smile I assured Momma things would work out. I thanked Auntie for bringing Momma to visit. Linda Faye, Jan,

Dellar, several other family members, friends, co-workers, and members of Assembly called me to wish me a speedy recovery. Feeling tremendously ashamed of how I had allowed myself to get into this unthinkable situation, I did not tell anyone what really was happening with me medically. However, holding everything within was causing me to drift into an emotional state of hopelessness and perplexity.

The tests and examinations ordered by Dr. Gyves were completed by the third day. Dr. Gyves told me the test were inconclusive as to the health of the baby. He explained despite the fact the bleeding had subsided, he was not sure the bleeding would not restart; and if it did restart, I might be ordered to be on full bed rest for the next five months. Dr. Gyves said even with the suture and bedrest it was a possibility the pregnancy would not go full term. He asked me if I wanted him to schedule to have the suture inserted. I asked him if I could let him know tomorrow. He replied, yes. Throughout the night I thought about what Dr. Gyves said about the pregnancy. Wrestling with how could I bring another baby into this world with all the potential uncertainties? How could I give birth to an innocent baby in prison knowing the baby would be taken right away from me to an indecisive future. The pressure of what would happen to Ivy if the appeal was denied already was extremely disheartening. I would be depending on Momma, Linda Faye, Linda C. Hattie, and the Morrows to help take care of her if I had to go to jail. How could I expect them to take on the care of another baby without help from the father? Thoughts that both Ivy and the unborn baby eventually might end up in an orphanage terrified me. Would a family adopt the child whose mother caused the death of her father? Would anyone want to adopt my unborn child knowing the baby had been conceived by the vicious act of rape and the mother had killed her first husband? I had been born from an act of violent rape and look at how my life was spiraling out of control. Would it be the right thing to repeat the cycle that Momma faced with me for this innocent baby? How could I face people who already thought I was an awful person who intentionally killed her husband? What type of woman would I be to have a baby this soon after the death of Herman? How would I explain how I got pregnant? What would I say about the father? Did I have the courage to tell the dark secret of being raped? Praying to God for mercy, grace, and forgiveness in the name of Jesus Christ, the next morning I made another extremely difficult, life changing, self-inflicted decision. With my mind in total chaos, remorsefully I informed Dr. Gyves my decision to have an abortion. Dr. Gyves looked at me disappointedly stating he did not perform abortions. He then said he would refer me to one of his colleagues that would perform the abortion at this late stage of pregnancy. Later that day a female gynecologist came to talk to me about the procedures for an abortion. She scheduled the procedure for the next day. The remainder of the day was spent with my mind seesawing from seeking forgiveness from Jesus Christ for my sins to feelings of condemnation for my sins. My soul cried out, why me? Early the next morning began another one of my most dreadfully stormy days of my life. Never will I forget taking the medicine to induce labor. Shortly thereafter I began to feel groggy followed by the pressure of feeling like I needed to use the bathroom. Wobbly, I went into the bathroom and sat on the toilet. With the pain of the pressure increasing, I pushed the call button for the nurse. I could feel the head of the baby coming out. By the time the nurse arrived the baby was out with the umbilical cord connected to me. Although feeling woozy my mind had flashed back to when I miscarried Herman and my baby boy. The thoughts diminished by hearing the nurse calling for help. The next thing I remember is waking up in the recovery room. The doctor had previously informed me after the baby came I would be taken for a D&C procedure. When I later returned to my room on the unit, the nice nurse told me the baby boy was stillborn and had been blessed. As I thanked her, I felt like the worse sinner in the world.

    The abortion resulted in a self-inflicted, intensive storm of inconceivable mental disgrace in my life. I felt like a truly horrible person not worthy of living. For I now had caused the death of Herman and taken the life of my unborn baby boy. Continually I begged God to forgive me for not having the strength and faith to have my baby. Repeatedly I asked God what the purpose of my birth was when I was only bringing grief in the world. Spiritually this was another sinful dreadful day of shame and guilt that nothing could heal. Yet my heart was saying to me remember you serve a forgiving God who will forgive you no matter what. But, regardless of how my mind and heart felt, my soul was being tormented by the purchase of the gun that killed Herman and the abortion. I knew even though I made two life changing decisions under difficult circumstances, I still had to pay for what I did, including living forever with the agonizing emotional scars from these self-inflict sins. Though today I believe that a decision to have an abortion is a choice that should be made by the woman, each woman must fully comprehend the after effects. Never have I forgotten about aborting my baby boy. Often around the time my baby boy would have been celebrating his birthday, thoughts of how old he would be come to my mind. I think of what the baby boy could have achieved in his life. The abortion forever stained my mind, soul, and heart. Throughout the years I shared with a few people that were deciding whether to have an abortion my emotional after effects with the hope that by sharing my experience it would help them make the correct decision. Personally, I suggest anyone contemplating an abortion to consider the emotional scars you may contend with for the rest of your life.

After being discharged from the hospital I felt so unworthy and confused about my purpose in this world. Once I arrived at home the depression became worse. I did not want to go on another second. Thankfully the Holy Spirit swiftly would bring to my remembrance of my promise to always love and support my beautiful baby, Ivy Kristolynn. Giving up and falling apart was not an option. There was no choice, I had to get it together and focus all my attention on providing for Ivy. The pity parties and wallowing in misery had to stop. I had to learn to survive regardless what came my way in this world, if not for myself, for Ivy. The only means of survival was to turn everything over to God. There was a song the choir sang at Assembly that said *turn it over to Jesus and He will make everything all right.* At that point that is what I had to do, I had to trust and believe that Jesus would see me through this tough time of my stormy life. Still to this day having an abortion bothers haunts me. Gratefully even after the arduous decision to abort my baby boy, there was the flicker of light that by the infinite power of God all my sins had fallen on Jesus Christ. *All of us like sheep have gone astray, we have turned, each one, to his own way; But the Lord has caused the wickedness of us all [our sin, our injustice, our wrongdoing] To fall on Him [instead of us]*, Isaiah 53:6.

Loved in Spite of My Faults. As the months passed by in 1981, I focused all my energy on Ivy, working on my job and at Assembly. I survived one day at a time with prayer, the grace of God, and the love and support of my family members and friends. Ivy and I were surrounded by the unconditional love and support of Momma, Linda Faye, Darrell, Linda C., Eddie, Dellar, the Morrows, and Hattie. Even Earl had become a faithful friend. Ivy and my circle of special friends was growing with Pastor Judie and several members of Assembly especially the Williams and Taylor families becoming significant people in our lives. I also became close friends with two other ladies I worked with at WJC: Ruth Antwine, who I affectionately called *Antwine* and she called me *Reynolds* after Debbie Reynolds, worked with me during the evening programs; and Molly Wilson who worked for Mr. Black. Like Pastor Judie, Antwine and Molly befriended me despite knowing about the death of Herman. All these people became an integral part of my life, loving me unconditionally.

In late 1981 Momma had a slight battle with her mental illness.

Thankfully it did not require hospitalization. Praise be to God with her medication she quickly bounced back. Her next obstacle came when she was diagnosed with diabetes. Momma was prescribed the oral pills but would later have to take insulin intravenously. Throughout all Momma endured, she always wanted to make sure Ivy and I were okay emotionally and financially. Each morning her voice continued to be the first voice I heard at the beginning of my day. I remember the day my phone was disconnected because I was unable to pay the bill on time. Momma called me on my office phone highly upset that she was unable to contact Ivy and me that morning. Scolding me, Momma told me to never to let any necessary utility be disconnected. Momma then told me to come to her house to get the money to pay the bill because she wanted the service to be immediately reconnected. This is one example of the love and support Momma always gave Ivy and me. To this day, I have never allowed my utilities to be disrupted.

Momma had been coming to Assembly with us for several weeks and she eventually became a member. Later Auntie and her children David and Karen became members. Shortly thereafter Linda C. became a member. Linda Faye and Darrell would visit Assembly when they were in Cleveland. Everyone enjoyed the worship services and the jovial personality of Pastor Judie.

It was nearing Ivy's second birthday. Antwine had a beautiful backyard and extended the use of the yard for Ivy's birthday party. It was a joyous occasion, especially since her first birthday was weeks after the death of Herman when life was chaotic. Many family members and friends attended. Ivy had a beautiful day with the children that came to celebrate her special day. It was a start of having many special birthday parties for Ivy with *Disney*, *Barbie* dolls or other popular party themes. Later in life I would be teased about the three different cakes she had for each birthday party. There would be an ice cream, cassata, and party theme cake. Some people considered the materialistic things I gave Ivy too excessive. In my mind, Ivy, although she did not know it yet, would had the void of never knowing or having Herman in her life. Because I could not give her the fatherly love and support Herman would have given her, what I could do was let Ivy know how much she was loved in every aspect of her life. In addition, I did not know if at any moment I would be sent to jail, so I wanted to shower Ivy with all the love, affection, attention, and support, as well as provide her with many materialistic needs and desires as long as I could. I constantly prayed that God would watch over and keep Ivy in His loving grace and mercy and bless her with a joyful happy life despite of the void from not ever knowing her father and what potentially could happen to me.

Although my life was getting better being alone at home at times was mentally challenging. Once Ivy went to sleep my mind would drift to many thoughts. I would relive the death of Herman. Wonder why the jury found me guilty? Think about if I would have to go to jail? Question why did the rape by Dwight cause me to get pregnant? What would be my punishment for having the abortion? The flicker of light from God was strength to endure those nights. Each day the grace and mercy of God enabled me to wake up without allowing negative thoughts to consume me. When I got to weak, the Holy Spirit constantly reminded me the promises I made to Ivy and that she was depending on me.

The closer I became to Antwine who was several years older, she would insist I realize how beautiful I was inside and out and stop wallowing in self-pity. She would invite me to several social events, but I would say, no, next time. Eventually she persuaded me to go out. At one event she introduced me to Dr. William (Billy) Walker. That evening the three of us talked and laughed. As we were leaving Billy asked if he could take me to lunch or dinner. Before I could answer, Antwine said, yes, you most certainly can because she needs to get out of the house. I simply smiled at Antwine. Billy asked for my phone number. Thinking in my mind this man looks old as Momma while Antwine was nudging me to saying give him your number before I do. Several days later, Billy called to invite me to lunch which I accepted. He was a perfect gentleman. Over the next couple of weeks, he took me out to eat several times. One day to my surprise he invited me to attend a golf outing in Toronto, Canada. Not knowing how to respond, I said, I will let you know. As soon as I got home, I called to tell Antwine. She of course encouraged me to go. A few days later, I let Billy know I would go with him. He said, great. Antwine helped get me select what to wear and even let me borrow her luggage. When Billy told me when he would be leaving, I let him know I had a mandatory meeting for work on that day. He asked me when I could leave. I told him the next day. He said, okay, I will buy you a plane ticket for that day. I said to myself, *fly*, I had never flown or even thought about flying, nor had anyone close to me flown. Again, Antwine insisted it was nothing to fly and I could do it. When I told Momma about the trip, leaving out the fact Billy was her age, she was happy for me. I let her know Antwine would keep Ivy, and Momma said, good. Momma had first met Antwine at Ivy's second birthday party and seen her several times thereafter and she thought Antwine was a nice woman. A few days later, Antwine and Ivy took me to the airport. I was excited about my first flight to another country. As the plane took off and flew up into the clouds, I thought of the wonderful world that God created. It became overwhelming thinking that a little over a year ago I did not know this type of world existed. I began to ask God could I possible still have a happy life. Upon arriving in Toronto, Billy picked me up at the airport. As usual, he was a perfect gentleman those four days. He showed me another lifestyle with superb accommodations at a gorgeous condo overlooking the golf course, eating at five-star restaurants and shopping at stores that advertised in the high fashion magazines. One evening for the first time I ate escargot and drank champagne at a restaurant that revolved around the top floor of a building. When he and his friends were golfing, he gave me money to go shopping with the other ladies that were there. Downtown Toronto was beautiful. I had an exciting time shopping and having lunch with the ladies. The next day everyone rode the ferry to the Toronto islands. It was breathtaking. Those few days took me to a world far away that I never knew existed. When I returned to Cleveland excitingly telling Antwine about the trip, she said, I told you there was another world waiting for you to discover. She was happy that even though it was only for a little while I had gotten away from all the troubles in my life. At that moment I knew Antwine was an imperative part of my emotional healing. After a few more golf trips, one to scenic Seven Springs, Pennsylvania, and a few other locations in Ohio, I knew there was no true future with Billy. This was mainly because I remembered how the ten-year age difference between Herman and me was of concern to Momma, I knew without a doubt Billy being close to her age would totally be unacceptable. After a few more date, I let Billy know how much I appreciated him, but that I had to stop going out with him. He understood. Occasionally he would call to make sure I was okay, which I appreciated. I was unsure if his kindness was because he knew of my past and felt sorry for me or simply was a nice man. Looking back over my life, I thought Billy could have been a flicker of light to encourage and show me there was more to relationships than the chaotic life I had with Herman and horrible night with Dwight. In any event, he showed me a side of life that I appreciated and cherished.

Chapter Six -- Sylvester Marshall

In September 1981, Assembly had a banquet in honor of the anniversary of the organization of the church. The banquet was being held on a Saturday evening at the Cathedral of Tomorrow. Momma, Ivy, Earl, and I bought tickets to attend. When I arrived, I distributed to the attendees the programs I had prepared – shortly after I had joined Assembly, I began preparing the programs for the church services. This was the first time we had attended a church banquet. It was refreshing to be a part of gathering together to dine with our fellow church members. Following dinner there was an uplifting spiritual program with musical selections from the choir and a sermon by a guest speaker. The next day Momma, Ivy and I attended morning worship. Several months prior Pastor Judie had appointed me the church's assistant financial secretary, to help in keeping the financial records and counting the offerings with the other financial officers, including Adrene Taylor who was the financial secretary. Adrene was a beautiful woman whose appearance was always immaculately stylish. The first time Ivy and I visited Assembly, she was the first member who spoke and extended kindness to us. Often, she would share the snacks she had for her daughter, Kelly with Ivy. Kelly was about a year older than Ivy. Usually while counting the offering, Adrene with her funny happy go lucky personality would keep everyone laughing. I enjoyed talking to her before and after service. That day when we were in the office counting the offering, Adrene in front of the other three members in the office said to me, her nephew,

Sylvester (Syl) Marshall, saw me at the banquet last night and thought I was cute. She went on to say he asked her to see if I would give him my phone number. A little embarrassed that she said this in front of the others in the office together with being shocked that someone noticed me at the banquet, blushing I told her it was okay to give him my number. That evening Adrene called me to let me know she had given my number to her nephew so to expect his call. I laughed, okay. We then talked and laughed about several topics before saying goodnight.

Several days later, Syl called and we had a brief conversation. I learned that he was eleven years older than me and was a bus driver for the Regional Transit Authority. He let me know he did not really go out to bars, clubs, or parties, preferring instead to attend concerts, plays, movies and going out to eat. I was glad when he said he did not smoke or drink alcohol or beer. This was because I believed drinking had contributed to the violent outbursts of Herman, and I had vowed to avoid talking to men that drank excessively. After a few more phone conversations, I was startled when Syl informed me he was married. He stated he was considering getting a divorce due to marital problems. I told him I understood. He asked if we could continue to talk. Seeing there was no harm in being platonic friends, I said, yes. Over the course of other conversations, Syl told me although he and his wife did not have children, he had two children with two former girlfriends. A son, Mark with Barbara, and a daughter, Zelina, with Christina. One day Syl asked me if I wanted to go to lunch. I said, yes. He suggested we go to Adrene's house for because she cook great pancakes. He suggested lunch at Adrene's house because I had told him how I loved pancakes and could eat them anytime of the day. Adrene later called me jokingly saying, so you are coming to lunch for pancakes. I said, yeah, as we laughed and then talked for a while. When Syl picked me up from the job, it was good to finally see him again. Each time we had talked on the phone, I was trying to remember what he looked like, now I could finally put a face with a voice. He was a handsome, tall, slender brown-skinned man, with big dreamy eyes and was wearing a good smelling cologne. Like on the phone, his voice was soft-spoken with a slight stutter. He had a bashful well-mannered personality. Lunch at Adrene's home was filled with laughter and joking and her pancakes were delicious. I also had the pleasure of meeting a few of her other children. She had told me her eight children that ranged from 3 to 24 years of age. Following having lunch together, every few days Syl and I would have friendly phone conversations. Even though I enjoyed talking to him, I knew with him being married we could only be friends. Unexpectedly his marital problems met its final straw when Syl returned home to find his wife with another man in their home. Syl called me furious telling me what had happened and asked me if I knew any divorce attorneys. I recommended him to the only one I knew, Mr. Blackwell. He met with and retained Mr. Blackwell to file for a divorce. Once he had filed for a divorce we began to see each other on a regular basis. He also formally met Ivy when he took us to breakfast one Saturday morning. The first time they met he smiled and tried to play with her, but Ivy cried and clung onto me. The more

Syl came around, Ivy would sometimes play with him, while other times she would cry and cling to me. When Momma met Syl, she said, her first impression was he was a nice man and hoped her inclination was not wrong this time as it had been with Herman. With our relationship growing closer, I told Syl about my marriage to Herman, how it tragically ended and my pending appeal. His reaction was that of bewilderment as well as concern and support for Ivy and me. Thank goodness my past stormy life with Herman did not deter him from wanting to be in my life.

Although his mother, grandmother and aunts and other family members, attended Assembly, he had never attended regularly. His family was now happy he had begun to regularly attend Assembly. By early 1982, Syl and I were together practically every day and he had joined Assembly. We however did not think it feasible with his divorce not yet finalized for the entire membership of Assembly to know we were talking. The only members that knew were Momma, his family members, and Pastor Judie. We had discussed our relationship with Pastor Judie after Syl filed for a divorce. Pastor Judie was happy for us and shared how he emotionally and spiritually handled his recent divorce after many years of marriage. Syl and I believed once his divorce became final our relationship would flourish because we had a lot in common. Not only were we both growing spiritually, we were homebodies. Both of us enjoyed staying in the house watching television shows. Our most popular show was *All My Children* that we both would VHS record to watch later. Besides attending church services, we enjoyed going out to eat and to the movies. On most Saturdays Syl would take Ivy and me to breakfast. I was thankful to God to have someone to talk to and spend time with that was likeminded.

Earl had always been a good friend and supportive part of my life after the death of Herman. Disappointingly Earl had begun to neglect the upkeep of the house by not performing maintenance work on the interior and exterior of the house. Mice were getting inside the house, and I always had been afraid of mice and rats. The day I saw the first mouse in the house, I ran with Ivy into the bedroom and jumped on the bed. I called Earl, but he did not answer. Then I called Arthur. When he answered, I begged him to please come over and get the mouse out of the house. Arthur lived on the other side of town, but he came and caught the mouse. Arthur still teases me about coming to catch the mouse. In December 1981, Earl had not done anything to take care of the house and more importantly the mice problem. I talked to Syl about the problems. He told me his Aunt Rose and Uncle Richard owned the apartment building where his grandmother, Mama Lula Sisson lived. One of the units in the apartment building was available to rent. I contacted his aunt and uncle to arrange to see the apartment. After looking at the apartment, I informed them I would like to rent it. We reached an agreement to the terms of the lease of the apartment. By early 1982, Syl, a few of his family members and friends moved Ivy and me into our new apartment.

Around March 1982, I had not been feeling well. Then my menstrual cycle was irregular with only spotting. I became worried knowing I had been intimate with Syl before I started retaking my birth control pills. Once the spotting stopped, I made an appointment with Dr. Gyves. My appointment was scheduled for Tuesday morning. At the appointment Dr. Gyves asked if I could be pregnant. I let him know it was possible. He ordered a pregnancy text. The next day Dr. Gyves informed me I was indeed pregnant. The news was with bitter sweet. Bitter because I still did not know the status of the appeal and I was not married. Sweet because seeing how ecstatic Syl was about the pregnancy made me happy and we even started talking about plans for our future. That Friday night Momma wanted Ivy to spend the night. Once Syl and I dropped off Ivy to Momma, we went to dinner and to the movies to see *Ragtime*. Syl then took me home. He stayed for a little while before going home. Even though Syl had filed for a divorce in January, he intended to stay at his house until the divorce was finalized. Once he left, I went to bed. Around 4:00 a.m. I woke up with sharp pain in my pelvic area. The pain became intensely worse to the point I could barely move. I called Adrene to ask her to call Syl. She was unable to reach him. In unbearable pain, I called Gary Harris my friend who was like a brother to me and whose mother worked with me at WJC. Letting Gary know how much pain I was in, I asked him to please get me from my house and take me to the hospital. He said, of course. By the time he arrived, I was laying on the floor next to the door. The pain was to the point it was making me delirious. Gary picked me up and carried me to his pickup truck. He drove as fast as possible to University Hospital. When we arrived at the emergency room, I informed the receptionist I was pregnant. Immediately I was taken to the examining room. It was a blessing Dr.

Gyves was the OB GYN doctor on duty that weekend. He examined and informed me it was a tubular pregnancy and the fetus had erupted inside my fallopian tube causing internal bleeding. Dr. Gyves told me immediate emergency surgery was necessary to stop the internal bleeding because not stopping it could be fatal. While Dr. Gyves made preparation for the surgery, I called Momma to let her know Gary had brought me to the hospital emergency room because I was having abdominal pain. I explained to Momma it was a tubular pregnancy that required immediate surgery. Sounding worried Momma said, *okay, I will be there as soon as possible*. I assured her everything would be alright, that she did not have to try to get there since she had Ivy. Nervously Momma said, alright, but to keep her informed of my progress and not to worry about Ivy. Next, I called Adrene to ask her to let Syl and Pastor Judie know I was in the hospital and going up for emergency surgery. She told me she would let them know. The surgery was performed successfully but one of my fallopian tubes and ovaries had to be removed. When I woke up in the recovery room, Syl and Pastor Judie were there. Syl was upset that he had not been there for me and disappointed about the tubular pregnancy. I assured him everything would be okay. Pastor Judie encouraged us to be strong because Syl and my lives would get better if we trusted in God to be the head of our lives. Lying in bed that night, I felt disappointed about losing another baby, but prayed to God giving thanks for bringing me safely through the surgery. I offered prayers of appreciation for allowing Gary to get me to the hospital in time and for Dr. Gyves being on call. I knew from Gary to Dr. Gyves being there for me that day was not coincidently but was the goodness of God. Without a doubt that day the flickers of light from God was being blessed that Gary and Dr. Gyves were there for me, I had a successful surgery and lived to see another day. Spiritually and mentally I thought to myself God must not be ready for me to leave this earth. I had to remain in the hospital for five days after the surgery, during which time Momma, Hattie, Jan, Moms Willtha and even Syl worked together to care for Ivy. Linda Faye was unable to come to Cleveland because of her work schedule but she frequently called and wrote me letters of encouragement.

Once discharged from the hospital, Dr. Gyves placed me on six weeks medical leave. During those six weeks, I received tremendous support not only from my core support group, but also from Syl's family members, members of Assembly, and co-workers. Syl would come each day to prepare or bring Ivy and me food. Until I was able to go outside, he took care of Ivy and my needs. One of the special moments was Easter Sunday when I woke up to the smell of delicious food. I got out of the bed and went into the kitchen, and to my surprise, Syl was preparing a full Easter dinner with ham, greens, fresh sweet potatoes, and a cake. This was a first for me to have a man cook dinner for me. I felt special to have him be very thoughtful and caring. Syl and I were growing closer each day. Knowing we wanted to be together, we were considering living together. With the hearing for his divorce only a few weeks away, we decided he would move in with Ivy and me following the divorce. Again, the drawback was our church family. How could we attend and serve at Assembly while living together? As Pastor Judie had mentioned to Syl and I, shortly before I joined Assembly, he had divorced his wife of many years, and I had been told by Adrene and other members this caused a major division among the members of Assembly. I surely did not want our living together to negatively affect Assembly. For the second time we discussed our concerns with Pastor Judie, he told us, he without sin throw the first stone. He encouraged us if we were living together to make sure our plans included uniting in holy matrimony. In the meantime, he asked for us to stay faithful members, continue to serve at Assembly and to pray for guidance and growth in Christ. Following many years of unpredictable tribulations my life appeared to be on the right path. I was taking care of Ivy, being spiritually feed, and had been blessed to have a good man in my life. Yet lurching in the back of my mind was the status of the appeal.

Sylvia Marshall. The first week of April, I had my six-week follow-up examination with Dr. Gyves. He cleared me to return to work and gave me my prescription for birth control pills with instructions to start taking the pills following my mensural cycle. The following Monday I returned to work. The next month Syl divorce was granted and he moved in with Ivy and me. It had been two years with only Ivy and me. Consequently, for the first couple of days it took some readjusting to get accustomed to living with Syl. In no time we were a perfectly blended family. It was approaching a little over three weeks since my follow-up examination with Dr. Gyves. I became alarmed because I had not started my mensural cycle. I called Dr. Gyves office for advice. The nurse suggested I make an appointment, which I did. A few days later Dr. Gyves examined me and suggested I take a pregnancy test. I said to myself, no way. The next day I called the nurse who informed me that I was indeed pregnant. I could not believe it. Once I told Syl, he was again happy. I also was happy, but worried if the pregnancy would come to term. Knowing Momma would be upset with me being pregnant this soon after the tubular pregnancy, I asked Syl not to let anyone know until I was in the second trimester.

Momma always had wanted to attend the renowned World's Fair. When Linda Faye and I realized the fair would be held during the summer of 1982 in Knoxville, Tennessee during the same time we were planning on being in Knoxville to support Darrell and the group he sung in, the *Ralene Gospel Singers*, we made plans for us to also attend the fair. That July, Syl drove Ivy, Momma, his son, Mark and me to Linda Faye and Darrell's house. The next day we all left for Knoxville. Although it was extremely hot weather, the fair was amazing with great exhibits from around the world, amusement rides and tasty food. The second day at the fair the hot weather and morning sickness made me ill. Determined not to let Momma or Linda Faye know I was pregnant, I said my stomach was upset from something I ate. Syl said he would take me back to the hotel, while everyone else stayed at the fair. The next day I waited until later in the evening to attend the fair. That Saturday evening and Sunday afternoon, we attended services at local churches where the *Ralene Gospel Singers* were the featured in concert. Monday morning, we headed back to Ohio. It was a good vacation that allowed Ivy and me to bond with

Mark. When we returned from the trip, I informed Momma and Linda Faye I was pregnant. Both were happy for Syl and me. Momma, Linda Faye, and I believed Syl was a God-fearing, loving, responsible and hardworking man. Each of us remained uneasy about how the members of Assembly would view my pregnancy given that Syl and I were not married. Once again, we talked to Pastor Judie. He assured us everything would work out. He stated I was not the first to get pregnant out of wedlock and neither would I be the last. Pastor Judie shared how he had been born out of wedlock. His words of encouragement eased my fear. Once the members of Assembly knew I was pregnant, most of them appeared to be happy for us. Even though Syl and I were talking about getting married, to know our relationship and my pregnancy would not adversely affect our membership with Assembly meant a lot to both of us. Outwardly I was ecstatically happy with my life. Inwardly no one knew I was mentally coping with my uncertain future. What was the status of the appeal? Would our baby be born in prison? Would I be able to get married before going to prison? Would Syl still marry me if I went to prison? When would the appeal court decide? Each day I woke up wondering if I would be told the appeal was either granted or denied. I had been sentenced two years ago, why hadn't there been any word from Mr. Willis or the court. Even with my unforeseen future I moved forward with my life praying to God that the appeal would be granted. With faith in God, I believed everything would work out.

A few weeks later, Dr. Gyves successfully inserted the suture. The pregnancy was going well, except for a hernia developing below my stomach. Life with Syl was great. Ivy was excited about being a big sister and adored Syl. Fall was fast approaching, and we were making arrangments for the holidays. On Thanksgiving Day Momma, Linda Faye, Darrell, Syl, Ivy and I had dinner with Auntie and her family. We had fun playing games and eating all the delicious food Auntie prepared. Christmas morning was spent watching Ivy open and play with her gifts. Later we had dinner with Momma. I returned to work on the 27th of 'December. I was feeling extremely tired. By the end of the work day, I let Eddie know it I might need to take my maternity leave early. He said to let him know whatever I needed. Early the next morning, my water broke before Syl left for work. He called his brother, James to take Ivy to Momma house. Once James had left with Ivy, Syl took me to the hospital. After being examined it was determined I was in labor. The decision whether it was best to induce my labor had to be made. My concern was our baby was not due until February 14th it was only December 28th. After several consultations and examinations, it was decided by inducing my labor it would be less stressful on our baby. Following hours of labor, late that evening I gave birth to our premature baby girl. My second daughter was born on December 28, 1982 weighing only 3 pounds and 11 ounces. Although I had hoped for a boy, the moment I heard her cry, I fall in love with my gorgeous baby. She was very tiny, barely the size of our hands. With a head full of hair, I could tell she had huge round eyes like Syl. Holding her tightly I adorned our innocent bundle of joy. I called Momma to tell her it was a girl. She said, aw, because both of us had been hoping for a boy. Linda Faye told me when Momma called she reluctantly said, *it is another girl*. Momma wanting a boy changed the moment she saw her new granddaughter. Smiling and cooing at her second granddaughter melted her heart. We had not selected a name because of the premature birth and we were certain it would be a boy. We finally settled on *Sylvia*, which of course was for Sylvester. I had wanted to name her Sylver, the name of a character on the soap opera, *All My Children*, but no one agreed with me. To this day, I sometimes call my beautiful baby *Sylver*.

Because Sylvia weighed less than four pounds and had a slight level of jaundice she required natal care. To my dismay I had to stay on the maternity ward. This required me to walk every two hours to the natal care unit to see and feed Sylvia. During one of the feeding times, Sylvia refused to drink the formula. The nurse told me if she did not drink all the formula, a feeding tube would be inserted. Prior to the next feeding I prayed my baby would not require a feeding tube. I tried to get Sylvia to drink the formula. Sylvia drank a little but refused to drink the remainder of the formula. It was evident she was not hungry. In faith I poured the rest of the formula down the sink drain. When the nurse returned she looked at the bottle and said, *good she drank it all*. I simply smiled. Nowadays, as I look at my healthy daughter, I often share when I stepped out on faith by pouring the formula down the drain. Syl would visit each day. On a few days family members and friends visited. New Year's Eve 1983 was spent with me holding Sylvia. Syl, Momma and Ivy spent the evening at Assembly for watchnight service.

I was discharged on January 3rd. To our dismay Sylvia was unable to be discharged because her bilirubin levels were not yet high enough. Each day I would go to visit and feed Sylvia. Praise God I finally received a call that Sylvia could be discharged. To excited to wait hours for Syl to get off work, I called Antwine and asked her to take me to get my baby. She said, of course. Antwine drove me to the hospital to bring my second bundle of joy home. Riding back to the house with my second little baby daughter, I rejoiced in another miracle the Almighty had brought me through. When we arrived home, Mama Lula came downstairs to meet her new great-grandchild. I told Mama Lula how worried I was about Sylvia because she was so very tiny. Mama Lula told me that each year when their pig had its litter, she would always get the runt pig of the bunch. By the end of the year her pig would always be the biggest pig of the litter. She then said that Sylvia would be a fine and healthy baby. I thought to myself that Mama Lula did not know what she was talking about by comparing my baby to a pig. Quite the opposite, I soon learned Mama Lula was absolutely right, Sylvia became a healthy baby. Later that week I was happy to receive gifts from co-workers. A few weeks later I had a small baby shower at the home of Bessie, Syl's mother. Sylvia Williams Bailey Anderson (Big Sylvia), a member of Assembly who later in life became like a sister to me, visited and brought a nice baby book gift. I was blessed to take a two months maternity leave. It was a terrific time for our family to bond. When I returned to work, Hattie babysat Sylvia and Ivy started preschool at Kidd's Pre-School.

The year of 1983 went quickly. Syl and I worked diligently at

Assembly and on our jobs. Syl had always desired to get a Mercedes. In the spring with Momma helping pay the down payment that dream came true. Later that summer, we drove Momma and the girls to Linda Faye and Darrell house to spend the week. While they stayed in Xenia, Syl and I drove to Norristown, Pennsylvania to visit his Aunt Gussie, his mother's sister, and her family. We then went to Atlantic City before returning to Xenia. It was a wonderful time during which we discussed getting married. During the year we also had happy times celebrating birthdays and holidays. Ivy's third birthday was celebrated with a party in the backyard attended by family members, Dellar and her daughter, Eddie's two daughters, friends, and children from Assembly. Thanksgiving and Christmas days were spent between both of our families. Over all it was a blessed year filled with plenty of love and cherished memories. As the year ended, we celebrated the New Year at watchnight service held at Assembly. While kneeling in prayer with the New Year ranging in, I gave thanks for the many blessings bestowed upon me in 1983. I prayed for all my loved ones, my home, job, and Assembly. I ended my prayer asking for continued grace regarding the appeal. It was now over three years without any word from anyone. I began to believe no news was good news.

A Second Chance. At the beginning of 1984, Syl and I decided we would get married on the 14th of January. Although I had always wanted a big church wedding and reception, Syl wanted a simple ceremony at the altar of Assembly. Syl asked that we only invite my Momma and Mama Lula. I agreed. On the 14th, Pastor Judie married

Syl and me at Assembly with Ivy, Sylvia, Momma and Mama Lula in attendance. Even though it was a chilly winter day, to us it was a beautiful day. I thanked God for blessing me with another chance of a happily ever after marriage. Shortly after our marriage Syl wanted to legally adopt Ivy. I prepared the paperwork. However, after much prayer, I decided Ivy should keep her father's last name. Remembering what the prosecutor had stated in his closing arguments, I knew one day I would have to tell Ivy what happened to her father. It was important to me for Ivy to know about her birth father and that she had two brothers and other family members. My aspiration was for the Washington family to never think I tried to erase the memory of Herman as Ivy's father. For these reasons instead of the legal adoption, we started using Ivy Marshall. Later in life, she would use Ivy Washington-Marshall.

When Syl and I were married in January, we were unable to go on a honeymoon. It was not until several months later when we were able to plan a romantic getaway to the Paradise Stream Resort in Mt. Pocono, Pennsylvania. The resort was known as a couples-only resort with themed suites. Willard, Syl's uncle, and his girlfriend, Linda decided to go with us. It was a beautiful time of bonding for Syl and me. We had a spectacular time in our cove fantasy suite. The suite was like nothing I had seen before with a private indoor heated pool, heart-shaped whirlpool bath tub, and round king size bed with mirrored headboard and celestial ceiling. Uncle Willard and Linda had the champagne room with a giant whirlpool in the shape of a champagne glass. We enjoyed horseback and bike riding, dining, dancing, and the entertainment. I truly was thankful for the many blessings God was bestowing upon me.

Soon thereafter to my surprise, I found out that Momma and Pastor Judie were talking, going out to dinner, and he was taking her to and from work. I was overjoyed with happiness for Momma to have a male friend. When I called Linda Faye with the news that they were talking and going places together, she was also happy for our Momma. The relationship between Pastor Judie and Momma, resulted in Linda Faye and me becoming even closer with him. Pastor Judie began to proclaim to everyone that Linda Fay and I were his daughters. He celebrated holidays and special occasions with us. It was truly a prayer answered for Momma to have Pastor Judie in her life. Momma had dated a few men when I was growing up. However, for the past several years she had not dated. Far back as I could remember, Momma rarely went out socially to nightclubs or parties. Occasionally family members and friends introduced Momma to someone that she would date for a while. I remember Auntie and their friend Mrs. Virginia, introduced Momma to Mr. Al Dixon, who she dated for about a year. They later introduced Momma to a musician, Mr. Eddie and they went on several dates with Mr. Eddie. Later Mrs. Fannie Tucker had introduced Momma to Mr. Ruffin, and they dated for a few years. All three of the men were nice to Momma, Linda Faye, and me. I would often hope they would marry Momma and become my father. Unfortunately, those hopes did not come true. In the late 1960s Linda Faye and I keep hearing about matchmaking companies that used new computer programs to match people. We talked Momma into calling the company. Momma was told she would receive a questionnaire to complete and return to the company. The company would input the information into the computer then a compatible person would be selected. Of course, there was a fee for service. When Momma received the questionnaire, Linda Faye and I helped her complete and return it to the company. Momma received a call from the man the computer had selected. They set a time for him to come meet Momma. When he came to visit Momma, to our surprise he was a very thin and about 4'11" feet, while Momma was 5'4". However, his height was not what was most notable about him. What was more obvious he was Caucasian. As they sat on the couch in the living room, Linda Faye and I were in the other room laughing until our stomachs hurt. Once he left, we teased Momma. She said, *I told you girls that was a waste of money and time*. He called Momma a few days later and they talked, but she never heard from him after that call. The computer company never matched Momma with another date. As I grew older, I wondered if Momma's relationships only lasted a few years because of the reoccurrence of her mental breakdowns. As time went on I thought the men like many other people in our lives simply did not understand the occasional changes in the behavior of Momma. It was my prayer with Pastor Judie finally Momma had found someone to love her unconditionally that would understand her battles with the nervous breakdowns.

Our family were steadily growing spiritually, mentally, and financially. We diligently worked on various ministries at Assembly. Having a compassion to work with children and youth, I served as the director of the junior and young adult choirs. Over the years the membership voted me to the positions of correspondence secretary, financial secretary, and church clerk. In addition, I organized several fundraisers and out-of-town trips to Niagara Falls and Chicago. Syl and I would escort the children and youths to various outings. We took them tobogganing and skating, and on trips to amusement parks, camping and to haunted houses. On any given weekend you could find one or more of the youths spending the night at our house. Next to my immediate family, the members of Assembly had become my second family.

During this time, I became close to several of the youth members. Two of the youths April (Trina) Williams-Daniels and Keiasha Williams-Thomas became and remain to this day a special part of my life. In 1980 when I met them, Trina was twelve years old and Keiasha eleven years old. I soon considered Trina my god-daughter and Keiasha my little sister. From teenage years to womanhood I have been blessed to be a part of their lives. Trina and Keiasha both were members of the youth choir, junior usher boards and candy stripers at Assembly. Immediately, when Trina began to sing in the youth choir, the members knew she had the gift to sing like her mother, Willie Mae Williams, who was the music director for Assembly. When Trina sang in church it caused people to stand to their feet, shouting hallelujah, and crying tears of joy. To this day Trina continues to spiritually blesses people through songs of praise. In their teen years, Trina, Keiasha and I shared many good times. I was blessed to celebrate with them their graduations, proms, weddings, and births of children and grandchildren. Likewise, in times of bereavement, sickness, and despair we loyally supported one another.

The older Trina became she matured from my little god-daughter to my dearest adult god-daughter. Our relationship changed from me taking Trina shopping, out for dinner, and other outings to her either taking or going with me to many outings and events. We begin to travel out-of-town to conventions and other getaways. We went on trips to Las Vegas, cruises, and out-of-town shopping trips. The most memorable trip with Trina was in the early 1990s when she performed on the Amateur Night at the Apollo Theater in New York City. She won third place out of fifteen contestants. That night I was proud of her. Even though April did not make worldwide stardom in New York, in the greater Cleveland area she became a prominent well-known singer. She is frequently called upon to sing in church programs, concerts, plays and at funerals. What is amazing about our relationship is in several ways our lives mirror each other. We both were raised by single mothers that loved the Lord. Both of our mothers had two daughters that they worked hard to support. Our mothers always sacrificed their needs and happiness to raise their daughters in a nurturing home full of love, support, and encouragement. Although both of our mothers desired and deserved to be happily married, neither of them ever married. Sadly, both of our mothers were diagnosed with diabetes, which in time would abruptly affect their lives. As the years have gone by, just as our mothers did for us, Trina and I have loved, cared for and support our children. Trina and I truly have a special God given bond. I will always be thankful how Trina has supported me wholeheartedly throughout many of my darkest storms. For many years we have talked on the phone several times a day and saw each other a least once a week. Even now we still talk several times a month. God blessed me with Trina and the entire Williams family to be in my life not for a season but for a lifetime.

More Blessing for My Family. Needing more living space, Syl and I begin to look for a larger place to live. In the fall of 1983, we leased a house on East 142nd Street off of Kinsman Avenue. It was the second-floor unit of a two-family home with seven room. From his divorce Syl had been awarded most of the marital furniture. Uncle Richard had allowed him to store the furniture in the large storage room in front of the apartment building. We were glad finally to have enough space to use the furniture. The girls would have nice size bedroom and a playroom. I was excited about the separate living and dining rooms which I let everyone know, were decorated to be kept nice and neat for special occasions. The girls would later in life tease me how they were not allowed to play in those two rooms. The unit even had an in-law room with its own separate entrance.

Syl and I were truly being blessed. We had a loving happy marriage with two adorable daughters. Spiritually we were constantly growing. Because our employment enabled us to be financially stable, it seemed my childhood dreams of summer vacations were now possible. During my childhood we did not have yearly vacation trips. However, Momma was blessed to take Linda Faye and me one summer to Providence, Rhode Island, and another summer to Niagara

Falls and Toronto, Canada. During our summers Momma would try to make sure we would at least go to the local parks, beaches, or amusements parks. Beginning with the trip to the World's Fair, Syl and I began to think about yearly vacation trips. Initially we took small trips to Earl, Arkansas where Syl lived and went to school, and Memphis, Tennessee where he was born. We later travelled to Chicago, Illinois to visit his family members. Several times we visited Niagara Falls, including twice with Assembly. The summer of 1984, Syl and I were blessed to take Mark, Ivy and Sylvia to Disney World and the Epcot Center in Orlando, Florida. It was our first long road trip. The first day Syl drove to Atlanta, Georgia where we stayed overnight. The next day he drove to Kissimmee, Florida where we had made hotel reservations. The hotel was nice with a few amenities but was several miles away from the theme parks. The first day we went to the Disney theme park, we parked in the general parking area. To enter the theme park, we had to take the monorail. As we rode on the monorail it passed through the Disney World property hotels. Impressed with the beautiful hotels and the direct access to Disney and Epcot, I talked to Syl about staying at the Contemporary Hotel. He agreed. When we went back to our hotel, I called to see if rooms were available at the Contemporary. There were rooms available. Excitedly we packed up, checked out, and headed to the Contemporary. When we pulled up to the door, the man came to open the car doors to valet park the car. He welcomed us then ask what luggage he should get out of the car. Mark happily shouted, *yes, no more carrying luggage*. We were all thrilled about staying at the

Contemporary. Not only did we no longer have to carry our luggage to the room, we did not have to drive to the general parking lot. We simply walked out of the hotel lobby to the monorail. The hotel room was gorgeously decorated and very modern. Throughout the hotel were several swimming pools, game rooms, Disney character restaurants and shops. After we returned from the parks, Mark would play in the game room for hours. Several evenings he stayed in the game room so long, Syl had to go tell him it was bedtime. Syl and I realized that this was the first time we had stayed in a five-star hotel. Syl would say how far he had come from the cotton fields of Arkansas. We thanked God for all our blessings. This also made me think that regardless of how well life was going for me, always lingering in the back of my mind was the appeal. Had it been granted or denied. I began to say and believe no news was good news.

Another blessing was Momma was still doing well. She even had taken a train trip by herself to Providence to visit Aunt Sue and cousin Frances. Regrettable Momma still suffered from mental breakdowns. Like clockwork she had a breakdown in September 1984. Praise be to God she was admitted into the Clinic where a doctor finally diagnosed her correctly with schizophrenia. The doctor started Momma on the correct medical treatment and medicine. Finally, our prayers had been answered, Momma would now receive the correct medical treatment. We were all grateful to our Lord and Savior for enabling the doctor to give Momma the correct diagnosis and treatment.

Shortly after Syl and I began dating, he asked me to ride with him to pick up his cousin from Ohio State University in Columbus, Ohio where she was a student. That day I met Andrea (Cha) Taylor a beautiful, witty young lady, who was one of the daughters of Adrene and Ulysses (Bro). Over the next two years I would often talked to Cha when I visited Adrene or at family gatherings. At some point she began dating Donald (Don-Don) Lamb. Sometime after that she became pregnant, and a few months later Syl and I were among many other family members and friends that attended their wedding at Assembly. I thought they were one of the cutest couples. A few weeks after their wedding, Cha called me to say she was in the hospital due to complications with the pregnancy. Sadly, their baby was still born. Soon thereafter, unfortunately, in the spring of 1984, the police arrested Don-Don. Cha not knowing what the disposition would be with Don Don's case and not wanting to continue to live were they were living, asked Syl and me if she could live with us for a little while. Aware of what Cha had recently been through, we gladly said, yes. This was the beginning of an unconditional loving relationship between Cha and me. Later that year Don-Don had his trial, the jury found him guilty, and sentenced him to prison.

The winter of 1984, the family in the first-floor unit moved. Adrene and Bro were interested in moving into the unit. Syl and I talked to the landlord, and she approved Adrene and Bro leasing the unit. A few days later Adrene, Bro, their adult daughters Doris and Terri, adult sons, Donald and Rodney, minor son, Cedric, minor daughter, Kelly, and grandsons, David and Terrell moved in the downstairs from us. It was a flicker of light when Adrene moved in because shortly thereafter Hattie decided to get a full-time job and stopped babysitting. Thankfully Adrene, and Cha, when she was not working, agreed to babysit Sylvia.

Chapter Seven – 1985 the Year of Unthinkable Storms

Carcinoma. My pap smears were continuously showing dysplasia cells. In March 1985 my pap smear shown the cells had elevated from dysplasia to stage four carcinoma. Dr. Gyves informed me if I did not have a hysterectomy as soon as possible, it could rapidly elevate to stage five carcinoma. I asked Dr. Gyves if I could wait for at least a year because I wanted to try to have a baby boy. He strongly disagreed with that idea. Dr. Gyves insisted on having a meeting with Syl and me to explain the dangers of waiting to have the surgery. A few days later, Dr. Gyves met with Syl, Momma and me. He explained in detail the need for me to have the surgery. After the meeting, I agreed to have the surgery. It was scheduled for the next week. Thankfully only my uterus had to be removed. Glory be to God I was able to keep my cervix and one ovary. Dr. Gyves also removed the hernia that had developed when I was pregnant with Sylvia. Following the surgery my pap tests have been clear with no evidence of any abnormal cells. Once again in the midst of a heavy storm, I received a flicker of grace from God of healing power. *O Lord my God, I cried to You and You have healed me*, Psalm 30:2 (KJV).

In June, Momma, Syl, Sylvia and I attended the kindergarten graduation program for Ivy from Kidd's Preschool. We all were overjoyed to see our bubbling beautiful Ivy get ready for first grade. Momma had always wanted Linda Faye and me to attend private schools but was unable to afford the tuition. Momma was hoping her granddaughters would be able to attend private schools. I begin to look for a private elementary school for Ivy and a preschool for Sylvia.

The Most Unbearable Day. At the end of June, Momma was waiting at the bus stop to go to work when she suddenly passed out. She was taken to Brentwood Hospital emergency room that was coincidentally next door to her apartment. When I received the call that she was at the emergency room, hysterically I drove to the hospital. Rushing in the emergency room, I prayed that Momma was okay. Entering the room, I was filled with relief and thankfulness that although Momma still weak, she was feeling a little better. The doctor informed me that Momma was experiencing complications from her diabetes that caused her to faint. Momma would be admitted for further treatment and observation. Each day I would visit Momma. Auntie, Pastor Judie, and other members of Assembly also visited her. I called Linda Faye to let her know Momma was in the hospital. At that time, she and Darrell were unable to come to Cleveland. We stayed in touch by phone on how Momma was doing. On Saturday, July 6th, Ivy, and I visited Momma. That day Momma was a little irritated about not being discharged. She had been in the hospital for eight days and wanted to go home. I suggested to Momma talking to the doctor the next day about plans for her discharge. This made her feel better. The remainder of our visit was good. When Ivy and I prepared to leave, Momma said she would walk us to the elevator to get some exercise. By the elevator there was a floor to ceil window that overlooked the parking lot. Ivy said, Grandma our car is down there, are you going with us. Momma said, not today, but hopefully tomorrow. When the elevator door opened, we gave each other hugs and kisses. I told Momma I would be there tomorrow after church. She said okay. Momma stayed by the window to watch me and Ivy walk to the car. Walking towards the car we looked up at the window waving while Ivy shouted, bye Grandma.

The next day during church service, the usher came in the choir stand to let me know I had a phone call. I went to the phone said, hello. It was Auntie. She was fussing at me saying Momma needed to be picked up because she was being discharged. Auntie then said instead of me being at that church I should be getting my mother. I tried to explain to Auntie I did not know Momma was being discharged today. That I had visited her yesterday and none of the medical staff had stated she would be discharged. I assured Auntie I was on my way to pick up my Momma. Immediately I went into the choir stand to get my purse while motioning Syl to meet me in the hallway. Once in the hallway, I let him know Momma was being discharge and I was leaving to take her home. He could expect me home after I had Momma settled in her apartment. When I walked into Momma's hospital room, her face lit up with excitement when she saw me. Momma was very relieved to have been discharged. Even though Momma appeared to be a little weak because her blood sugar levels were normal, the doctor stated she could be discharged with instructions to follow-up with her medical doctor. When Momma sat down in the car she jokingly said, let me get ready for this long ride home. It was funny because it would take us all of a minute to drive next door to her apartment. Momma opened the door to the apartment and said, *thank God, I am so glad to be home.* I helped Momma get settled in by getting her mail from the mailbox and throwing out old food. Momma made a list of the few items she wanted from the store when I picked up her prescriptions. Momma said she would go to her favorite grocery store, *Heinen*, later in the week to get more items. When I returned from the store, I prepared the weekly insulin needles for Momma, while she began to cook something to eat with the items from the store. We talked about the girls and trying to find good schools for them to attend. Momma let me know she had called Auntie and Linda Faye while I was at the store. We discussed her not rushing to return to work. After she had everything she needed, I prepared to go home. Before I left we gave each other our usual hugs and kisses. Walking out the door I said, I will call you when I get home. Momma said, okay. Once home, I called Momma to let her know I was home safely. I asked her how she was feeling. She said, I am good. As we did each night we both said to each other, *goodnight, talk to you in the morning and love you.* I thanked God for letting Momma feel better and being able to come home. In the morning as she normally did, Momma called to wake me up. We talked for a few moments. I asked her how she was feeling. Momma replied, fairly good. Then she talked about working on alterations to her clothes because she did not believe she would regain the weight she had lost. Teasing her I said you can buy new clothes. We laughed. I let Momma know I would call her later from work. She said, okay. Then we said our usual, *I love you.* While preparing for work, I again was grateful Momma sounded happy and was looking forward to getting on with her life. After I was dressed, I woke up Ivy and Sylvia to prepare them to go over Grandma Bessie's house, because she was keeping the girls for the summer months. I dropped the girls off, then went to work.

Once I had a few free moments at work, I called Cedar Hill Christian school requesting information about the school and if they were still accepting applications for employment in the first grade for the upcoming school year. They replied, yes and that the application and related paperwork would be mailed to me. Next, I called La Petite Nursery School regarding enrollment for Sylvia. After talking to the owner, I scheduled a time for Syl and me to tour the school. Around 9:30 a.m., I called Momma to let her know I thought I had found a Christian school for Ivy to begin first grade, and a preschool for Sylvia to attend. Momma did not answer the phone. After trying several more times to reach Momma, I begin to worry knowing Momma would never leave the house without calling me. I tried to call a few more times, still no answer. Too worried about Momma, I let Eddie know I had to go check on my Momma. Driving to the apartment, I prayed Momma had not passed out. When I opened the door to Momma's apartment, I called out, Momma. She did not answer. Walking towards her bedroom I kept calling out, Momma. Reaching the doorway to her bedroom I could see my Momma laid back on the bed with her mouth open. She was not moving. I vaguely remember screaming and running into the kitchen to the phone. Nervously dialing the operator when I heard a voice, I cried out my Momma is not moving please help me. The voice said an ambulance is on the way. Looking at my Momma it seemed like she was sitting on the foot of her bed then fell back because her feet were still on the floor. I kept saying, Momma, Momma, Momma. Hearing the sirens, I went to open the door. Showing the paramedics where Momma was in the apartment they asked me to stay back while they worked on Momma. The paramedics said they were taking her to the emergency room. As they prepared to take Momma to the ambulance, I called Eddie to let him know I was on the way to the emergency room with Momma. Then I called Adrene letting her know about Momma and asking her to call Syl job, so they could contact him. Driving next door to the emergency room, with tears streaming down my face, I cried out to God to please let Momma be okay. Sitting in the waiting area, I anxiously waited for the doctors to come let me know how Momma was doing. A few moments later Eddie walked through the doors of the emergency room. Seconds later a staff member came into the waiting area asking me to come with her. She escorted me and Eddie to an empty room within the emergency room area. A doctor came in saying he was sorry to say Momma had passed. I painfully remember crying out. My heart sinking while my legs going limp as I began to fall to the ground. I faintly remember Eddie catching me. My head was spinning. My heart was breaking into pieces. While my entire soul cried out. In the background I could hear the doctor asking Eddie if he could please calm and quiet me down. I could not stop. The pain was too much to bear. I could only cry out, *Momma, Momma, not Momma, not my Momma, no God, why my Momma.* Syl arrived a few moments later. He took me into his arms saying words to try to console me. I could not stop crying out in pain. The initial shock was slowly turning to a state of silent disbelief. The doctor came back into the room to request approval for an autopsy given that Momma had died less than 24 hours of discharge. I gave my approval. In a daze and thoroughly weary I signed the necessary documents required by the hospital. Then I became aware there was no longer a need for me to stay here. They were not going to call me back when they had Momma stabled. Instantly without any warning, just like Herman, my Momma was gone. How could this be true, Momma and I talked only a few hours earlier. Syl took me into his arms holding me tightly while we walked to the car. Eddie walked with us to the car where he gave me a hug. I told him thanks for being there for me. He said he would call me later. I sat down in the car while Eddie and Syl talked for a moment then shook hands. When Syl got into the car, he said we would get my car later. Tears began to again run down my eyes. As he drove out the parking lot, I looked up at the windows of the hospital and thoughts of how Ivy and I had less than two days ago waved bye to Momma as she stood in one of those windows waving bye to us. I again became overwhelmed with grief as my heart broke into thousands of fragments of pain. Even today I can clearly see Momma standing in the window waving at us and it makes my heart aches; and each time I go to that hospital, I look up at that window visualizing Momma standing there waving and I want to turn back the hands of time to wave back at my Momma.

I sat in the car while Syl went inside to get the girls. Mrs. Bessie came out to the car giving me a hug saying how sorry she was to hear about Momma. I said, thanks. Watching Ivy and Sylvia run down the steps towards the car brought a ray of light into a very dark moment. Seeing the girls relieved some of the heavy burden my heart was feeling. Sitting down in the car they happily said, *hi Mommy*. I said hello my babies. The girls talked and played as Syl drove with one hand on top of mine, I looked out the window trying to wake up from this nightmare. Adrene met me at the door hugging me saying words of consolation. Once in the house, I begin to make the dreadful calls to Linda Faye, Auntie, and Pastor Judie to let them know my beloved Momma had went to her eternal rest. Linda Faye could not believe our Momma was gone. She let me know her and Darrell would leave for Cleveland as soon as possible. Auntie in shock, told me she would call the other family members. Except for letting family members and friends know Momma had passed, I decided to wait for Linda Faye to arrive before making any decisions. Eddie stopped by on his way home to make sure I was doing better. Later that evening Linda Faye and Darrell arrived. Hugging my sister, we grieved the loss of our Momma and prayed together for guidance and strength from God. Except for Herman, neither Linda Faye nor I had anyone close to us die. When Herman died, I only paid for the funeral while his family made the arrangements. We decided to ask Pastor Judie to help us with the arrangments. He said, of course and recommended the Martin Funeral Home.

On Tuesday afternoon after meeting with the funeral director, Linda Faye and I agreed to have Martin Funeral Home handle the arrangements for Momma. We stayed in contact with Auntie regarding the arrangments. While we waited for the coroner to release Momma's body, Linda Faye and I worked on the obituary. We also discussed the clothes Momma would wear and ordering floral arrangements. Tuesday evening, the funeral home had received Momma body and began preparing her for burial. On Wednesday evening the funeral director called to let us know we could come to view Momma. Linda Faye, Darrell, Syl, the girls, Pastor Judie and I went to the funeral home. Entering the room my heart was heavy. Then I looked at Momma laying in the casket as if she was simply sleeping. The mortician had done an excellent job. The weight of my heart lifted a little to see the beautiful peaceful look on Momma's face. To touch and kiss her made me feel even better. Ivy said, *is Grandma sleeping?* While holding Sylvia, I told her, *yes, Grandma is sleeping.* Due to the late hour, we could only stay for a little while. Linda Faye took a few pictures of Momma. We then prayed. Before leaving we let the funeral employee know we were satisfied with the appearance of Momma. The funeral would be held Saturday morning. The next few days Linda Faye and I finalized the other details for the service. On Thursday and Friday, I went to the funeral home to sit with Momma for as long as I could. Being able to see and touch her helped ease the pain of my broken heart. On Thursday evening Momma's sisters, Naomi, Sue, Sarah, and Elizabeth had arrived from out of town. They were staying with Auntie. When we arrived at the funeral home on Friday to our surprise the room was filled with many beautiful floral arrangements that had been sent by family members, friends, members from Assembly, and co-workers of Momma, Linda

Faye, and me. We were happy and thankful to see the thoughtfulness of others. Our aunts came to view Momma later that day. Linda Faye and I were glad to have a chance to spend time with them. Linda Faye took more pictures that day with our aunts. Even though it was a grim time of bereavement, it was good to see them.

Saturday came quicker than I wanted. Linda Faye and I was unsure what to expect as far as who would attend the home going service for Momma. When the car pulled up to the church, we were greeted by Assembly's nurses' guild board in their white uniforms standing on each side of the pathway leading to the doors. From there we were escorted into the sanctuary where there were many family members, friends, members of Assembly and co-workers. To see all the people, I could feel how much my Momma was loved. Not only were all her sisters there, several of her cousins, nieces, and nephews from the Cleveland area and out of town attended. During the wake hour, it was good to be greeted by everyone. Linda Faye took more pictures of Momma and the congregation during the wake. Even though some people questioned and looked at her strangely, I will forever be grateful for Linda Faye taking pictures. Over the years looking at the pictures have brought much comfort to me during many lonely hours when the void of not having the physical presence of Momma weighs very heavy on my soul. When the home going service began it was truly a celebration of the life of Momma. Many family members and friends spoke of Momma in such high regards. They described Momma as a Christian woman that was a loving, beautiful, generous, thoughtful, gentle, and kind who dearly loved her daughters and granddaughters. Jan gracefully read the obituary. The Assembly Mass Choir sang uplifting songs. Pastors and ministers spoke of how Momma was dedicated to preaching the word of God when she was young and loved working with the church's missionary society. Pastor Judie delivered a heart filled eulogy about how Momma inspired the lives of him and many others. How dedicated she was to Assembly, especially as the President of the Missionary Society. That Momma's presence would be missed by many including himself, her daughters and granddaughters, other family members, friends, and co-workers. All memories of Momma that were shared and the thoughtful and encouraging words meant so much to me, if only it did not have to end. When the final words were spoken followed by the closing of the casket, my soul cried out. Syl held on to me while he and Jan whispered words of encouragement. The past few days while I could see Momma's body in the casket had been as if she was sleeping. The casket was closed, which meant it was final. Never again would I see her face with that lovely smile and sparkling eyes. I would not be able to feel her warm tender touch hugging and holding me. The sounds of the way she talked, laughed, and sung where gone forever from my ears. With Syl holding me tightly in his arms, the funeral directors escorted us to the family car. Sitting in the car waiting to leave for the cemetery, several people came to the car to express their condolences. It was at that time I regretted listening to Adrene when she said the weather was too hot to have a repass at Assembly. In hindsight, I would have loved to return to Assembly to spend time with the many family members, friends, and co-workers some that I had never met. Later as I looked back on that day, I also regretted not agreeing for Linda Faye to have an opportunity to speak during the home going service. Instead I had listened to other people tell me she would be too emotional. From the home going service for Momma I learned that people must grieve in their own personal manner not the way that is convenient for others.

On July 8, 1985, I lost my heart. Momma left me forever. She was my number one person. Momma was always there for me through my sunny and stormy days. Unconditionally loving me. Always supporting and encouraging me whether I was right or wrong. When Momma departed from this earth, I was only 26 and she 54. It was simply not enough time together. The Sunday following the home going service for Momma, while at Assembly, Mother Ida Williams, said words of encouragement. She said to count myself blessed because my mother was with me longer than her mother was with her. Mother Ida let me know when she was only 13 years old her mother died, while I was blessed to have had my mother for 26 years. Still today I often remember what Mother Ida said to me that day. God used Mother Ida to give me a flicker of light during the most heart wrenching times of my life. Her words helped me realize even though Momma left me too soon, I was blessed to have Momma with me for 26 years while some people had many less years with their mother. Days after the funeral many other family members and friends continued to express their condolence and support that I appreciated. Even with all the love from everyone, still the tears came, and my heart ached for Momma. From the moment the doctor told me

Momma had passed away, mentally I was never the same. It was hard to understand why after her mental health problems finally had been correctly diagnosed, Momma did not live to enjoy life without suffering from the breakdowns. Before Momma passed it seemed like the latter years for Momma would be better than her past, that she would have a life full of joy and happiness. Instead she entered her eternal rest with her Lord and Savior Jesus Christ.

As the days passed, I knew Ivy and Sylvia were depending on both of their parents to take care of them. Once more mentally I had to get myself together. More importantly, I knew Momma would expect me to go on with my life. Often Momma had talked about when she was a teenager her mother passed. She had to grieve while immediately taking on the duties of helping her father care for her younger sisters, especially Auntie. Exactly like Momma, I had to return to work and take care of my husband and children. The first day I was returning to work, I laid in bed in disbelief that I would never receive those calls from Momma each morning saying *it was time to get up*. Adjusting to life without Momma was not easy. How do I adjust to life when the most important person in my life is gone forever? My Momma who in the face of suffering a tragedy to conceive me, carried me for nine months in her body and went through labor to birth me. From the moment I was born she loved me unconditionally, and always took care of me and supported me through each stage and storm of my life. First when I could not do anything, but cry, Momma loved, feed, and took complete care of me. Then holding my hand, she took me to my first day of school assuring me all the way everything would be okay. Momma encouraged and helped me to learn as much as I could to achieve my dreams in life and support myself. She dealt with my thinking I knew everything attitude and shenanigans during adolescences. My Momma was always there to share the joys and pains of my womanhood. When she was no longer able to kiss away and put a bandage on my aches, pains, disappointments, mistakes, and heartbreaks of life, she prayed that God would watch over me. Regardless of how old I was, Momma would always say I was her baby. Now my life would have an emptiness that would never be filled again. Since July 8, 1985, so many times I have cried and hollered out for Momma, *because there is no one that loved me like she did.* She was my heart and I was her baby daughter. My true love. My one and only Momma. On July 8th, God said come home Ruth Naomi Kithcart, your work on this side is done. With this extremely heavy storm added to my life, I sought the guidance of God for wisdom, understanding and strength. The little flicker of light was God easing the pain my broken heart. *The righteous cry out, and the Lord hears them; he delivers them from all their troubles. The Lord is close to the brokenhearted and saves those who are crushed in spirit. The righteous person may have many troubles, but the Lord delivers him from them all,* Psalm 34:17-19 (NIV).

Weeks following the passing of Momma, Linda Faye and I learned that the funeral cost would be totally covered by the life insurance from her job and an insurance policy Momma had purchased. After the funeral expenses were paid, Linda Faye and I each received close to $20,000. We later learned the autopsy report revealed that Momma had died from a blood clot to her lungs. Initially I sought legal advice to determine if the hospital had been negligent by not detecting the blood clot. With the uncertainty of the outcome of the lawsuit, I decided not to pursue any actions. A few months later when my life continued to unfold, I gained full understanding and wisdom from God concerning why He called Momma to her eternal rest.

The Third Heavy Blow in Eleven Months. In August, Ivy began first grade at Cedar Hill Christian School while Sylvia was enrolled at La Petite Preschool. I was very thankful we were able to fulfill one of the dreams of Momma that Ivy attend a Christian school. Each morning I would drop the girls off at school and Syl would pick them up after school. Several years earlier at WJC, I had met Jessie Larkins who worked for the City of Cleveland. Jessie and I became good friends. Shortly after we met, we realized she knew Syl through her sister who worked with him at RTA. Through our friendship, Jessie and her son, Nathan became members at Assembly. She also enrolled Nathan at Cedar Hill. Once Nathan began attending Cedar Hill, we often coordinated with each other to drop off and pick-up the kids from school. Sometimes Jessie's mother would assist in transporting the kids to and from school.

Subsequently to the passing of Momma several people stated, and sympathy cards recited the familiar quote *time heals all wounds*. Losing Momma felt like no amount of time would ever ease the pain in my heart. Not wanting to be a burden or get on the nerves of family members and friends by constantly talking about Momma or wallowing in grief, I did my typical pretending like life was great, while silently within I was living with a grieving heart. This storm had ripped through my life causing colossal emotional damage to my heart and soul. Once more, I unrelentingly prayed to God for the strength and guidance to be a good wife, mother, sister, and friend despite my internal pain. I knew that through all the stormy weather, God had truly blessed me with my loving family, spiritual growth at Assembly and gainful employment. Without the grace and mercy of God there was no way I could have made it through the storms of my life. At times albeit not as often as previously, I wondered what happened with my appeal. Then I would believe no news was good news and that evidently things went in my favor.

The second week of November 1985, feeling ill I did not go to work. Sylvia was sleeping in the bed with me. Around 10:00 a.m. Adrene called upstairs saying police were surrounding the house asking for Deborah Washington. I called Eddie to ask him if the police had been at the job. He said, yes, they had been there looking for me. The police told him not to call me because he would be intervening with official police business. Within seconds of hanging up the phone, the phone rang. The voice of a man said he was a police officer. He went on to say there was a warrant for my arrest. Then he asked if I had any weapons in the house. I answered no. After that moment, I must have gone into shock because I have never been able to recall exactly what happened for at least the next hour. Even writing this book I attempted to recall what occurred when the police entered the house but was unsuccessful. What I know had to happen was the police came inside the house. At some point I had to be allowed to put on clothes because I had my night gown on when the police called. I do not know who came to get Sylvia. But for family to be home to get my baby was the favor of God and the first flicker of light in the beginning of this grave storm. If no family member had been there, Sylvia would have been taken by social services until Syl could get her. Walking out of the house to the police car and the ride to the jail is a total blank. Any discussions during this time I am unable to recollect. The one thing I remember is it was a cloudy and frigid day. The first memory is being at an area with a glass window with my hands in handcuffs. The next recollection is waking up in a bed. When I looked around the room what had happened the past few hours still were unclear, but I did know I had been arrested. In complete shock and disbelief of being in jail, I wondered how and why it took five years to deny my appeal. If I did not know before, I knew it now everyone believed I intentionally killed Herman. Why did not anyone believe me that I never intended for Herman to die. Still in a trance I heard a female voice asking if I was okay. I looked up to see a woman correction officer that I replied, yes, I am okay. The officer said I fainted at the intake window after being arrested. She informed I was arrested because my appeal bond issued in 1980 had been revoked and suggested I contact my lawyer for further information. Following a physical and mental examination, I was placed on suicidal watch. This meant I would be placed in the psych unit which mandated suicidal checks every 15 minutes by the guards. This turned out to be a second blessing from God. The flicker of light was not being in the general population unit. In the psych unit inmates were assigned an individual room. Meals would be eaten in a small communal area outside the sleeping areas. Later that afternoon I could make phone calls. I called Syl. He was so devastated. Barely able to talk without crying, he asked me what had happened. He wanted to know why I was arrested. I let him know the officer told me the appeal bond had been revoked. That I had to contact my lawyer to find out the details. After Syl and I talked, I called Mr. Willis office. His secretary said he was in court. I informed her about my arrest. She assured me as soon as he returned she would let him know about my arrest. Early that evening I was able to again call Syl. He sounded a little better. He had talked to Mr. Willis who told him appeals had been filed and both were denied years ago. He told Syl my appeal bond should have been revoked several years ago. Syl then put Ivy and Sylvia on the phone. I remember Ivy asking me when I was coming home. Holding back my emotions, I told my baby soon. Hearing their voices brought joy and pain. Appreciative and overjoyed to hear their voices. Then feeling the ache throughout my soul of not knowing when I would be able to again touch, hold and kiss my baby girls. Hanging up the phone I wanted to holler out, why Lord? Why must my innocent babies feel the wrath from my sins? How could I survive? Less than four months ago my heart had been ripped to pieces when my beloved Momma was abruptly taken to her eternal rest. Suddenly without any warning today I had been torn away from the loves of my life Syl, Ivy and Sylvia. My darling husband was now without his wife. Our beautiful daughters were without their mother. At that point I hated more than ever the day I was born and prayed to God to please let me die that night. I condemned myself for the sins that landed me in this predicament. For buying the gun. Shooting Herman instead of running. Not taking the plea bargain with parole. Not checking on the status of the appeal. Involving innocent people in the mess and sins of my past. Throughout all my miserable storms God had given me the strength to conceal my fears deep within the depths of my soul. Once more that day and throughout the night I know it was only God that kept me because I was at the end of my rope. The African American song, *Jesus Lifted Me* inspired me throughout the night. The next morning, when I talked to Syl he told me how many of my family members and friends could not understand how I was never arrested when the appeals were denied over four years ago. He let me know he was doing all he could to find out how this happened, including seeking help from everyone he or I thought could help us and contacting the media. One local television station responded and interviewed him about the case lingering for five years without being arrested. Syl emotionally told the news reporter about how I restarted my life, had lived as a good citizen, the affect my arrest was having on him and our daughters, and how I was doing since the arrest. The broadcast was very moving. Syl and others I was able to call let me know that after the broadcast many friends and strangers questioned the delay of my arrest and offered words of encouragement and support. Syl then spoke to several attorneys and politicians who were surprised and sympathetic, but unfortunately, there was nothing they could do. Syl even organized a small protest outside the Justice Center where I was being held attempting to bring attention to why the court neglected to timely inform me of the denial of the appeal. Once again, more people had compassion for our circumstances with some even extending offers to help, only to learn there was nothing anyone could do. After Syl and I had both talked to various attorneys, judges and Mr. Willis, the fact was Mr. Willis had neglected his duty to inform me the appeals were denied. As my attorney he was responsible to either personally escort me to the police station or instruct me how to turn myself into the proper authorities. The court not issuing a warrant for my arrest within the past five years was merely an oversight. Although I am not sure if it was true, Mr. Willis told me that Judge Roman never thought the jury was going to find me guilty, and when they did, he released me on the appeal bond, thinking my appeal would be granted. After the appeals were denied, Judge Roman never issued a warrant for my arrest. In 1985 Judge Roman died, and after his death, Judge Ann Dykes was assigned his caseload. Judge Dykes discovered my outstanding case and executed the warrant for my arrest. Thus, regardless of the reasons why Mr. Willis or Judge Roman did not tell me the appeals were denied, I was at the end of this battle with no one else to argue with or blame. It was time to accept the fact that my appeals were denied, and the appeal bond revoked. No ifs, ands or doubts about it, I had to prepare to serve my sentence.

Once more an unexpected life changing storm had erupted in my life within a matter of seconds. I began to repeatedly ask God the why and what questions. Why again was my life unexpectedly shattered. What sense was it to start my life over only to be knocked back down? Why did the sins I committed have to affect and cause pain to my loved ones and others? What would happen to Ivy and Sylvia? Why didn't I die years ago to prevent all the misery my living was bringing to the people that loved me? Knowing without a doubt shortly I would be incarcerated, the only flicker of light in this dark moment was the peace of knowing that Momma was not here to see me go to jail. I never intended for my sins to cause Momma or anyone else that loved me to suffer from the trickle-down effect of my being found guilty and incarcerated. I knew putting Momma through this humiliation would have caused her too much agony. Even now knowing the grief of my being in jail was causing Syl and my other loved ones was already too discouraging for me. So, I could only imagine the pain and disappointment my incarceration would have inflicted on Momma. Her anxiety would have been too much for either one of us to withstand. Hence, yes, the flicker of light that Momma did not have to endure this hardship was a true blessing.

With the storm raging in many other areas of my mind, my thought was all over the place. Should I have known the appeal was denied? Had I foolishly taken it for granted the appeal bond had been granted? The first few years after being found guilty, I would constantly think about the appeal. Each decision was made thinking any day I could be in jail. As time went on, I thought less about the status of the appeal. I began to believe by submersing in serving God in the church and helping others my prayers for the appeal to be granted would be answered. This helped me not have to deal with the thoughts of what if the appeal was denied. I was wrong. This horrific storm in my life that had been lingering dormant for five years was now front and center in my world. It was time to be accountable for the consequences of my sins. Sadly, it was to the detriment of my girls, Syl and other loved ones. If only this massive storm did not have to affect others.

While Satan negatively attacked my spirit, God intervened with flickers of light to remind me how blessed I had been over the past five years. I had married a loving devoted man. Given birth to another beautiful daughter. Had rededicated my life to Jesus Christ followed by serving diligently at Assembly. Was blessed with the love and support of many family members, old and new friends, the members of Assembly, and co-workers. Been gainfully employed with stellar reviews and promotions. Had taken great family vacations. Most importantly was being able to be with my beloved Momma until she was called to eternal rest with the Lord. Knowing how God had blessed me, not only over the past five years but throughout my life, I had to realize this massive storm was causing negative feelings of fear and anxiety in an attempt to waiver my faith. But, praise God I knew if I did not allow this storm to overwhelm me with doubt by fixating on my unforeseen future God would see me through as He had throughout my stormy life. Then the Holy Spirit gave me another flicker of light to know my faith and trust in God was one hundred times stronger than five years ago. My life was now enriched with a body of spiritual believers that knew the power of prayer. I began singing to myself the song by James Cleveland *I Don't Feel No Ways Tired* and prepared to believe God would see me through whatever the future held. Even though I still had a heavy heart; my eyes were filled with tears; there were troubling thoughts in my mind; and I was hurting to the core of my soul, I knew my Lord and Savior was instantaneously providing flickers of light filled with mercy, grace, strength, and hope. I began to think of the blessings that were already raining down on my loved ones and me. Since the day of my arrest, Syl, Ivy and Sylvia there were many family members, friends, members of Assembly, and our co-workers that embraced them with love, support and offers to help. They were assisting with the care of Ivy and Sylvia. Preparing meals. Helping with the housekeeping. Extending emotional, spiritual, and financial assistance. Jessie and her mother stepped right in to help with transporting Ivy to school with Nathan. The owner of La Petite gave support to Syl for Sylvia attendance at the school. Although later, Adrene began babysitting Sylvia in order for Syl not to worry about getting her to and from school. Each kind deed was truly a blessing when our family was in a time of crisis and a gloomy point in our lives. We were extremely thankful for every kind deed that was rendered to us.

Chapter Eight – Incarceration

While in the county jail, I continuously prayed for a miracle or to wake up from this nightmare. Linda Faye and Darrell had come to Cleveland the day after my arrest. She and Syl visited me during the visiting hours. I spoke with the clergy which helped. The psychiatrist also met with me for a second time and kept me on suicidal watch status. The second night before going to sleep I turned off the small light embedded into the wall. Within seconds the guard opened the door to the room entering with her flashlight. In a calm tone she told me the light must always be on. I turned the light back on while saying I was sorry, I was unaware the light had to stay on. The guard told me turning off the light could result in receiving disciplinary actions. I replied okay, thanks for letting me know. The kindness of the guard that night will always be appreciated. Another flicker of the grace of God through a total stranger. Inmates were required to maintain their sleeping and communal areas. During the day and evening there sometimes were religious services and activities. I remember attending one religious service where I spotted from a distance Sarah the neighbor that lived next door on 72nd and Kinsman Avenue. Her cousin was the boy that first molested me. We waved but were unable to talk because she was in general populations. The third evening I attended one of the daily activities. We were taken to an area where inmates were able to play basketball. Besides these memory, my imprisonment at the county jail was spent praying and hoping that God would grant me a miracle of being released from prison.

The fifth day at the Cuyahoga County jail, I was abruptly awakened around 4:00 a.m. by the guard. The guard instructed me to get up, dressed and to place my few personal items in a paper bag. Within the next minutes I figured out it was my day to be transferred to the State of Ohio Reformatory for Women in Marysville, Ohio. Several other women and I were escorted to a van. My heart was racing in fear of the unknown, while my mind was whirling in disbelief thinking how I did not have a chance to say goodbye to Syl or my babies. Walking towards a van we were told to take a seat. I cannot remember if my hands were handcuffed, but I clearly remember the van driving into the early morning traffic. At that moment it became apparent nothing miraculous was going to happen. It was yet another reality check, I was going to prison. Looking up at the newly constructed BP Building and other buildings that made up the Cleveland skyline, I wondered if I would ever again see those buildings. Trying to prepare for my next years in prison, I prayed that God would give Syl, Linda Faye and other loved ones the strength to take care of my little girls. Once Syl and I were married, I stopped worrying about who would take care of my girls if I was taken away. In the back of my mind I had always assumed Momma and Syl with the help of both of our family members would care for my babies. With Momma dead who would help Syl take care of Ivy and Sylvia? Hattie and I did not talk as often as previously. Linda Faye and Darrell lived out of town and I knew Syl would not want the girls to be away from him. Linda C. was now married with her own family. Jan would help as much as possible when she was not working or attending college. Lord, what about my girls? Would they be okay? The van was now on the highway as I began to wonder once again why my two innocent girls must suffer because of me. Often, Although I have been unable to find it in the scriptures, I had heard in sermons, *you do not question God*. But at that point I needed to know why I did not die instead of Herman? Because as hard as I tried to come to grip that with all I went through with Herman, the rape, abortion and within the past nine months, the hysterectomy, the death of my Momma, being torn away from my family, and now on my way to jail, I could not understand how God expected me to want to wake up or try to survive in this world? I truly desired to trade places with Herman. Thinking of facing my babies, husband, and many others after letting them down made me feel like the scum of the earth. Once again taking over my thoughts were the *whys*. Why did I buy that gun? Why did I pull that trigger that took Herman's life? Why did he die instead of me? He had always survived when other people had stabbed and shot at him. Why not when I shot at him? Why was it my destiny that Herman would die by my hand? Over and over, I tried to understand. Until the day I die my mind will wonder why Herman died when I shot that gun. No matter how I tried to conceive the answers to my *whys*, the only answer was I made the wrong decisions to purchase the gun and shoot it at Herman. Now it was time to pay the consequences of my self-inflicted sins of serving 4 to 25 years of imprisonment.

<u>Prison Orientation.</u> Within a few hours we pulled up to the reformatory. To my surprise it was not a single big dark ugly scary building with bob-wire fences and bars on the windows. Instead there were several brick buildings separated by well-kept landscaped areas. There were no fences with bob-wire. I saw women walking from and to different buildings. The van stopped on the side of one of the larger buildings. The guard instructed us to form a line and go inside of the building and told this was the primary area for new inmates to receive orientation on the rules and regulations for life at the reformatory before going into the general population areas. The area was comprised of three huge rooms consisting of the day room, sleeping room and the bathroom area. Once more to my surprise there were no jail cells. It did not look anything like what I had seen on television or in movies. Instead, there were ladies sitting at tables throughout the day room reading, writing, talking, or playing games. We were instructed to leave our personal belongings with a guard. Then we were directed to an area where we were assigned clothing and sleeping area. We were told we could take a shower before changing into our assigned uniforms and that lunch would be in the day room, but for dinner we would go to the main reformatory dining area that was in another building. After the first day and night not only did the prison not appear as I had pictured, the environment was nothing what I expected. There were no fights with knives and blades. No one was getting raped and abused in the showers. Each day my fears and thoughts of being in a dangerous scary jail filled with physical violence, sexual abusive, drug infested, and communal restrooms and showers were proven to be untrue. This relieved a little of the fear from my mind. The mental struggle to accept my fate was a different story. During the day I went through the motions like a zombie, quietly humming, *soon I will be done with the trouble of this world, goin' home to be with God,* from one of my favorite songs *Troubles of This World* written by William L. Dawson as sung by Mahalia Jackson. With every inch of my body numb, my mind blank, and my body aching in sorrow, I could feel my heart breaking into a million pieces. Tears were constantly filling my eyes. I felt like an empty vessel. At night I silently cried out to God to deliver me into my eternal rest or wake me from this nightmare. Then each morning when I heard the alarm for inmates to get up, the realization came rushing back to me – no DeBorah, you are not dead nor at home, you are property of the State of Ohio. By my third day, while seated at a table reading, an inmate asked me if I signed up to go to the chapel for service. I said, no. She asked me if I wanted to go with her. There it came again. A tiny flicker of light from God to encourage me to go listen to the word of God. I told her, yes. That afternoon I went to my first church service in prison. It was the beginning of my frequent attendance at worship services. Although that day the worship service did not relieve a lot of my depression, it gave enough flicker of the Holy Spirit to ignite a tiny spark within my heart. With each passing day that tiny flicker became brighter and brighter.

New inmates remained in orientation for three to four weeks. Numerous documents were required to be completed. Physical and mental examinations were given. Group meetings with the warden, chaplain and other personnel had to be attended. Discussions were held with personnel to determine assignments for school or work details. Sessions on the rules and regulations of the reformatory were conducted. It was emphasized that this was no country club, and we were prisoners of the State of Ohio with nominal freedoms and rights. They told us as inmates, the State would provide us with basic necessities. Outside of basic necessities, everything else was considered privileges that would be taken away when rules and regulations were violated. Inmates that violated any of the rules and regulations would be given a violation ticket. A few of the most common violations were: being in a location without permission (known as being out of bounds); not attending a roll call; having contraband items; disruptive behavior; fighting; stealing; showing affection or being intimate with another inmate. A violation ticket could result in the loss of a range of privileges, including, among other things: weekly phone calls could be suspended; visitation rights revoked; unable to wear street clothing; suspension of commissary privileges; being placed in solitary confinement. Each inmate was assigned a State of Ohio Inmate identification number. That day I was assigned my State inmate number, 180396. Any information relating to me must include my name, DeBorah Washington, followed by my State inmate number. This include any outside correspondences or packages we received. While in orientation I could only wear the uniforms issued by the State. There were also more rigid schedules of when to get up, shower, eat, and clean the facility than the general population. Inmates during their orientation period were escorted to the general population dining area where we ate in a specific area away from the general population. After meeting with the psychiatrist, it was determined I was still severely depressed. For this reason, I was assigned to dine in the exceptional circumstances dining area that was in a different building than the general dining area. Another flicker of light since there were only a few women that were assigned to eat in the exceptional circumstances dining area.

In my state of mental depression, it was uplifting that the conditions of the prison were not bad as I had pictured. The guards were even as cordial as possible under the circumstances. Nonetheless it was still prison with an extremely rigid controlled environment. Each day I worked towards pulling myself together, adjusting to life as a prisoner, and learning to adhere to the mandatory rules, regulations, and schedule. Eventually I began talking to a few more inmates. Each person I talked to was nice and helpful especially the inmates that had been previously incarcerated, which I learned were referred to as repeat offenders. When I began to share the events that resulted in my incarceration many of them could not believe I was found guilty and how five years had passed without me being notified of the denial of the appeal. Some suggested suing my lawyer for malpractice on the grounds of gross neglect. Others encouraged me with this being my first offense to file for shock parole. When I researched shock parole, I learned it was a request by a first-time offender to the parole board to obtain an early release after serving six months. If granted I could be released and placed on probation for a certain period of time. Knowing about this possibility gave me hope. I went from hopelessness to thank you Jesus for this flicker of hope.

With each passing day I became more familiar with the reformatory. There were women incarcerated from all parts of Ohio.

Each week new inmates arrived from various counties. I met several ladies while incarcerated from many diverse backgrounds, ethnicities, and races serving sentences for various crimes. Ladies were incarcerated for many reasons including: assault, manslaughter, and murder from crimes of passion; self-preservation or premeditated against other people; damage or theft of property; or drug abuse, addiction, and trafficking. Many like me were victims of abuse that never meant for their actions to end tragically with a fatality. To my astonishment, I was not the only abused women who had killed her husband. Most of the women I spoke with had earnest remorse for their crimes regardless of the type of crime. During my incarceration I made several acquaintances. I became closest to: Helen, was Caucasian and about 65 years old, who had killed her husband over 40 years ago; Barbara and Joyce who were both ten years older than me and had a drug addiction problem that were serving time for grand theft; and Geneva who came a few weeks after me was several years younger than me who had caught her boyfriend cheating and set him on fire while he was sleeping; and Sara, who was Caucasian and the same age as me, who was in for fraud and cashing fraudulent check.

Grateful to be Loved. Visiting privileges could not begin until my list of visitors was approved. Waiting for the approval of my visitation list, I cherished the letters I began to immediately receive from Syl, my girls, Linda Faye, and many other family members and friends. Receiving the letters together with pictures helped eased the emotional pain and loneliness. Syl told our daughters that I was at a special place until I got better. This caused Ivy to assume I was sick, because later in life she asked me if I was in the special place because I ate the hamburger with bugs in it. She had remembered few months before my arrest, I had bought a hamburger that when I unwrapped the paper had tiny bugs crawling on and around it. Ivy obviously was listening when Syl and I were discussing the bugs and how it made me sick because I almost ate it. Another appreciated flicker of light was my babies at their young ages did not realize what was really occurring. My incarceration and the death of Herman was something that I wanted to tell Ivy and Sylvia when they were old enough to more fully understand. The more letters I received my worrying about Ivy and Sylvia being loved and cared for was short lived. Syl wrote me how he was receiving a lot of help from Adrene, Cha, Pastor Judie, Jessie, Linda Fay, Linda C., the Morrows, many of the members from Assembly and co-workers. Vet even had contacted and visited Ivy. He brought her several toys that she cherished.

    Within a couple of weeks, the visitation list was approved. Many family members were approved to visit me. Minors under the age of 18 could also visit with an adult. Glory be to God I received my first visit with Syl, Pastor Judie and the girls within three weeks of arriving at the reformatory. The moment I walked through the door to see their faces put a huge smile on my face and lifted a great deal of grief from my weary spirit. Hastily I walked to the table where they were sitting with my arms stretched out eagerly ready to hug and kiss my daughters. Once they were in my arms I held them tightly to me not wanting to let them go. Finally, when I stopped loving on my daughters, Syl and I affectionately embraced each other per the regulations of the reformatory. Then Pastor Judie and I gave each other a big hug as he said, I am so glad to see you daughter. Hearing those words meant a lot to me. What a thankful day it was for us. Once again, a flicker of grace from God to finally be able to see my loved ones. Those weeks of not being with my babies, husband and other loved ones had seemed like years. But, from the second I looked at their faces and embraced them in my arms wiped away the feelings of loneliness and agony I had endured since last seeing them. Ivy and Sylvia sitting on my lap or right next to me filled my heart with joy. Then holding the hands of Syl and Pastor Judie gave me strength. After our heartwarming greetings, when I finally looked around the room, once again to my surprise the visiting area was nothing like I had imaged. I had envisioned a glass window separating us or a small dingy room. Instead the visiting room was a large area with many long tables where you visited with your family. Vending machines were available for visitors to buy foods, snacks, and beverages. There was an area where pictures could be taken. Following the first visit, it became a routine for each visitor to bring a camera to take pictures with me. Syl or Linda Faye would later include copies of the pictures we took in the letters they wrote. For the children there was an outdoor visiting area with a play area and swing set to use when weather permitted. That day Syl and Pastor Judie bought a lot of snacks and beverages for us. This was really a treat because I had only had the institution food. We talked non-stop trying to catch up on everything going on since we had last seen each other. Playing and laughing with the girls was like medicine to my soul. Even through the visiting period was for a couple of hours, it seemed like it ended too soon. Tearfully we said our goodbyes with Syl promising to bring the girls back next week to visit. He let me know money had been deposited on my account, which would allow me to shop at the commissary. Another flicker of light from God was after the first visit, except for two weeks, I was blessed and grateful to have a visit each weekend. A vital part of my sanity during this challenging time was the many visits. Ivy and Sylvia visited each weekend with either Syl, Pastor Judie, Mrs. Bessie, and her husband Robert (Bo), my sister-in-law, Barbara, and brother in laws, James, and Ray. When Ivy and Sylvia were staying with Linda Faye and Darrell, they would visit with them. Mark and Adrene son, Cedric and grandson David visited on several occasions. Auntie, Karen, and David visited one weekend. Auntie had cooked all my favorite foods but was disappointed when she was told outside food was not allowed in the visiting area. I received visits from the youth of Assembly, including Trina, Keiasha, Stacy, and Pam. Once a month Syl visited by himself for us to have alone time. Every visit was filled with love and good times. It was a time for much needed hugs and kisses while we talked, laughed, took pictures, and ate snacks from the vending machines. To add even more glory to this stormy time of my life, I continued to receive lots of mail from loved ones that could not visit. My aunts that lived out of town, Linda C., Hattie, Eddie, Dellar, Adrene, Cha, Ruth, Molly, Jessie, the Morrows, and many others wrote letters or sent cards. Each visit, letter and card gave me strength to stay strong while separated from my loved ones. Every person that took the time to visit or write me will forever be appreciated. It was truly awesome to have such a huge amount of moral support from my loved ones during that daunting and uncertain time of my life. My fellow inmates would often tease me about how I received a letter each day and a visit every weekend. They would tell me your family loves you, to which I agreed without question that yes, they do, and I love them more than they will ever know.

Inmates could receive boxes from their families four times a year. Syl and Linda Faye prepared and sent my first box in late December. It included the permitted items of Momma's Bible, clothes, shoes, television, radio, and food. Thereafter, each time a box could be sent, I received a box full of many thoughtful items. My loved ones always would generously make sure money was on my account to purchase items from the commissary. Visitors would typically deposit twenty dollars on my books each week. I again rejoiced and praised God for the flickers of light of blessing me with loved ones that sacrificed their time and money to make my sentence as comfortable as possible. With all my sins, my loved ones still were standing with and providing for me. Without the love and support from my family only God knows if I would have survived. Even in one of my most turbulent storms, the love of God was abounding throughout my life.

Prison General Population. After orientation, it was time to transition into the general population. I was assigned to Elizabeth Cottage, a huge three-story brick building. The first floor consisted of three principal areas. There was a large communal area used for roll calls and for inmates to watch television and communicate with each other. The other two areas consisted of the phone and laundry areas. The second floor consisted of single occupancy rooms. These rooms had a twin bed, toilet, sink, built in shelving area, a window with a heavy metal screen, and door with a peephole which the guards used to check on inmates. On the third floor there were three open styled dorm rooms, a full bathroom, and half bathroom. Each of the rooms housed from three to six inmates. Initially I was assigned to the third floor in the room that housed six women. My roommates were friendly. Because each of them was repeat offenders they were able to help me understand and acclimate to prison life. They had or were incarcerated for either theft or drug related offences. None of their charges were as detrimental as my crime. They like others were surprised I was found guilty and that it took five years for my arrest. In general population I was amazingly relieved there were no signs of how television shows and movies portrayed life in prison. Similar to the time I spent in orientation, none of those horrible preconceived thoughts I had been afraid of occurring in prison was happening in general population.

Living with roommates at times was mentally healthy, but on the other hand at times it was difficult because I was still very depressed and grieving. Abruptly I would become emotionally overburdened with thoughts of my stormy life, in particular thoughts of how my actions caused the death of Herman, having the abortion, and the unexpected death of Momma. On top of those thoughts, I was persistently confronting the heartbreaking fact that my self-inflicted storms were negatively affecting my innocent loved ones. Trying to cope with my emotions while always in the presence of my roommates was difficult. Without any privacy I was unable to openly release my sorrow through praying, mediating, crying, and singing. It was like living in my constant fake mode all day and night. This became too difficult for me to handle. I needed a quiet place to mediate, pray and study the word of God. A few weeks later, I completed the paperwork for a single room. Shortly thereafter, I was thankful to be assigned to a single room. Before moving, I expressed my gratitude to my roommates for their advice and support. We remained friends, often meeting in the communal area to talk, have Bible study or play games. Once in my own room in the evenings I could meditate and pray without any interruptions. With my own television I watched my favorite Christian television broadcasts and other shows. Writing letters was even easier to do. Having my own room was another flicker of light.

In general population there were three roll call periods, morning, afternoon, and evening. Inmates were mandated to attend each roll call, unless you signed the required paperwork that you were staying in your room for a particular roll call. During the week inmates were mandated to attend two daily roll calls, and on the weekend, one roll call each day. The days I was not scheduled to work my assignment in the special dining room, I would request permission to stay in my room during the morning roll call. My typical weekday consisted of attending the morning roll call, followed by going to breakfast before the start of my work assignment. Lunch would be around noon afterwards I returned to my work assignments. At the end of my work assignment, I went to dinner. When I did not go to dinner, I had to inform the cottage guard when I returned to the cottage that I did not go to dinner. This was because at all time my whereabouts had to be known. When I would return to the cottage, I would stay in the communal area room talking with fellow inmates until evening roll call or went directly to my room for the evening. Saturdays I usually stayed in my room until my visitors arrived. After my visitation time was over, I would reserve time in the laundry room to wash my personal clothes. On Sundays I would attend worship service. Upon returning to the cottage sometimes I stayed in the communal area to talk or play games with fellow inmates or return to my room.

Amazing Grace in the Midst of a Raging Storm. Before leaving orientation, each inmate had to decide to work or attend school. With my knowledgeable of word processing software, I selected to enroll in the newly implemented computer and business class that would begin in mid-January. Waiting for the class to start, I chose the position to prep food and clean in the special dining room area. Even though I was thankful for the assignment to work in the small dining room and enjoyed working there with the other inmates, I was looking forward to attending school. After high school, I had taken a few classes at Cuyahoga Community College and considered enrolling at Cleveland State. Regrettably, I never pursued further education after meeting Herman. By mid-January I was excited the class would begin within the next few days. Fellow inmates told me it was considered a big deal to be selected to take the new course. A few said for me to be accepted this quickly being a new inmate was especially unusual because only twenty students were accepted. After hearing this I thought to myself it was the required paperwork I completed to be considered for enrollment into the class that helped with my acceptance. I had answered the question of why I desired to enroll in the class by stating to enhance my current skills in the secretarial field with additional word processing training. On the other hand, the Holy Spirit confirmed to me this was another flicker of the glory of God in my life. How else could I explain my acceptance – I had arrived at the reformatory two weeks before the enrollment for the class ended and was selected out of hundreds of inmates that applied. It was no mystery, it was only by the grace of God answering me and my loved ones' prayers for grace and mercy during my incarceration.

The first day of class I anxiously walked into the classroom. The classroom looked remarkable. Each student had their own nice new desk and chair with a new computer terminal. The instructor was a nice young lady. After the basic introductions and a brief synopsis of the course, she began instructing the class. Within a few hours of her instructing it was obvious she was having trouble with the information set forth in the textbook and workbook. Her knowledge of how to apply the computer functions and the software applications was extremely limited. It was obvious of her inability to comprehend the various applications and worksheets. When she noticed I was proceeding with completing the assignments outlined in the textbook and workbook, she requested my assistance. I gladly said, yes. After several days of attending the class it became apparent to the other students that the instructor was seeking a substantial amount of assistance from me to instruct the class. A few days later, I was told Superintendent Arn wanted to meet with me. Knowing I had not committed any violations against the rules and regulations, I hoped she was meeting with me about a miraculous release. Once in her office, Superintendent Arn asked how the new B.O.S.S. computer program was going. Disappointed the meeting was not about an early release, I respectfully told her great, that I enjoyed the course. To my surprise, Superintendent Arn inform me a couple of the inmates had spoken to her about their concerns. The inmates were complaining the instructor was not knowledgeable about the course. They had told her the instructor was regularly requesting my assistance on how to teach the course and use the computer software applications. Superintendent Arn asked me if this was true. Stunned and nervous not knowing why she was asking me these questions, I replied the instructor at times was requesting my assistance. Superintendent Arn asked me several questions about how I obtained my knowledge. I answered from working in the secretarial field since 1975. She then let me know the State had invested a substantial amount of money into this program. Then to my unbelief Superintendent Arn asked did I have the experience, fortitude, and dependability to teach the course to my fellow inmates until another teacher could be hired. Trying to maintain my composure I said, yes. She explained the instructor would be terminated later today. Then she asked the amount of time needed for me to prepare to instruct the class. Although not sure I replied, about two days. Superintendent Arn briefly discussed the transition. Her last words pertained to how she was placing me in a unique position. She was trusting me to conduct myself in a respectable and honorable manner while adhering to the rules and regulations of the reformatory. With much gratitude I promised not to disappoint her, the students, or the reformatory. Superintendent Arn then instructed me to keep our discussion confidential until she talked to the class. Her plan was to speak to the instructor within the next few hours, followed by talking to the students. She then told me I could return to the classroom. Leaving her office walking back to the classroom. I could not believe what had occurred in the past ten minutes. I said to myself, Jesus Christ what did you just do? Am I dreaming or was I just asked to teach the B.O.S.S. program. What an amazing miracle had occurred in my life. Yes, once again a flicker of light from God of His omnipotence power. My heart was beating fast while a verse from the song *Since Jesus Came into My Heart* by Rufus H. McDaniel echoed in the soul. Quietly I repeatedly sang the one verse *what a wonderful change in my life has been wrought since Jesus came into my heart*. That day a sinner like me in the midst of despair the Lord bestowed upon me an unforeseen immeasurable blessing. Sixty days ago, on that freezing day in November when I was arrested, no one could have convinced me I would be asked to teach my fellow inmates.

Walking into the classroom I resumed working on my assignments. My feelings were mixed thinking my blessing was at the detriment of the instructor. I prayed for God to strengthen and bless her with a new job. After lunch I returned to the classroom to find the instructor had packed her personal belonging. Once all the students had returned, she stated this was her last day. Preparing to leave she wished us the best in the future and said we were to wait in the classroom for Superintendent Arn. Once the instructor left, some of the inmates made comments. While others wondered what would happen with the course. One of the inmates that had been incarcerated for more than twenty years said she had talked to Superintendent Arn about the instructor and Superintendent Arn had things under control. Shortly thereafter Superintendent Arn walked into the classroom. She informed the inmates it had been brought to her attention and confirmed the instructor lacked the experience to teach the class, because too often the instructor was seeking advice from inmate, DeBorah Washington. For these reasons the reformatory had terminated her employment. Superintendent Arn went on to say the State was working on hiring another instructor, but pending the hiring of an instructor, she did not want the inmates training to be disrupted. Shen went on to say to prevent any postponement in their training, she had asked me to instruct the class. Superintendent Arn then let everyone know what she expected from each of us. Any problems incurred or reported would result in the suspension of the class until a permanent instructor was hired. Each of the inmates agreed to the conditions for the continuation of the course. Several of the inmates stated the instructor did depend on me too much to teach the class. The inmates expressed their appreciation to Superintendent Arn for not letter the classes be interrupted. She let us know for today we would remain in the classroom until the normal dismal time. There would be no classes the next day, which was a Friday, to allow me time make preparation to instruct the class. The regular class schedule would resume on Monday. After Superintendent Arn left, the inmates congratulated me and expressed their appreciation the course was not suspended. I expressed to them my appreciation for their expressing confidence and support in my ability to instruct them. The remainder of the day was spent briefly outlining the goals for the program.

By the time I arrived back to the cottage, several of the inmates and guards, congratulated me on my new work assignment. Surprised how quickly the news had travelled, I said, thank you to everyone. Upon returning to my room, I was still in reverence of the almighty power of God. Even in prison God was utilizing my gifts to help others. Once in my room I began working on lesson plans. Thoughts of how teaching the class would help my emotional state by staying busy with preparing for and teaching the class. At that point the idiom *an idle mind is the devil workplace* came to mind. Thinking about that saying was probably because often when I had down time and was alone my mind would consume on my self-inflicted sins, the anguish I have caused many innocent people, and how I had been abused. This in turned caused my feelings of depression and remorsefulness to increase. Keeping busy helped eased those thoughts and feelings. With the teaching assignment I prayed my idle time would be reduced by being busy with preparing for and teaching the class. I would have less time for self-condemnation and despondency. Not only would it help me mentally, it was an opportunity to help and hopefully be a blessing to others. Remembering as a little girl helping and doing charitable deeds for others gave me joy. The older I became and the more iniquities I committed, helping, and giving to others was a way of atoning for my sins. I could not bring Herman back to life or take away the pain I had caused others, but what I could do was try to be a blessing to others. At this point in life, I praised God for the ability to instill into the twenty students' knowledge that someday might aid them in securing employment upon release, which in-turn might enable them not to become repeat offenders and be re-incarceration.

Hold on Just a Little Longer. As winter turned into spring, I continued trusting and depending on God for strength and guidance. Thankfully I had the support from family members and friends with visits, phone calls, and mail that was an essential part of my mental stability. It was also a blessing to be able to attend the worship services that were spiritually uplifting, together with teaching the class that was helpful in reducing my stress levels. By May 1986, I met the six-month requirement to apply for shock parole. While completing the application I prayed the shock parole board would agree to grant me a hearing. Many of my family members and friends were earnestly praying with me for my early release. The thought of being released early brought a new outlook and hope. Praying that I would not be separated from Syl, Ivy and Sylvia and other loved ones for the 4 to 25 years of my sentence. In the midst of praising God for the new hope of an early release, I received sad news that Bro, Adrene's husband, had died from lung cancer. I knew he would be missed by all his loved ones. Being away from the Taylor family during their time of bereavement was difficult.

Awaiting a response for the parole board each day through prayer and thanksgiving, I tried hard to think only positive instead of negative thoughts. I knew to stay strong I could not lean on my own understanding of why things occurred in my life but had to depend on God for understanding and direction. Yet Satan still tried to use the weak periods of my time to fill my mind with negative thoughts about the shock parole, my family, and future. This is when while reading the Bible the Holy Spirit guided me to Proverbs 3:5-6 (KJV), *Trust in the Lord with all thine heart; and lean not unto thine own understanding. In all thy ways acknowledge him, and he shall direct thy paths.* That day this became my primary scripture for my life. I must trust that God was in control of my destiny.

The first weekend in August was going to be my visit alone with Syl. On these visits I tried to dress especially nice. For that visit I clearly remember wearing the beautiful red top and white culottes that Linda Faye had sent in one of my boxes. Having received spectacular news, I walked as fast as possible without getting in trouble with the guards to the visiting hall. When I walked inside the room to my surprise, Syl was not alone. He had brought two youths from Assembly, Stacy, and Pam with him. Greeting each other with a hug and kiss, his demeanor appeared different. He seemed a little withdrawn. That day I was too excited to wonder why. When we sat down I began to eagerly tell him how this week we had received an answer to our prayers. Again, another bright flicker of light from God had been bestowed upon us. The parole board was going to meet with me in September to consider my request for shock parole. If the parole was granted I would be released by the end of the year. Even with that news Syl seemed withdrawn. I thought to myself something is wrong. I wondered if he was getting tired of waiting for my release and the burden the incarceration had placed on him. I prayed the news would be encouragement that I soon might be released. The rest of the visit we discussed how the girls and other family members were doing. I asked how Adrene and the Taylor family were doing since the passing of Bro. We talked about upcoming events at the church. This was the first visit for Stacy and Pam, and they updated me on everything going on in their teenage lives. We had a pleasant visit talking, eating, and taking picture. Before they left I talked to Syl about the parole hearing and if granted our anticipation for release. Leaving the visiting room, I remained disturbed about the behavior of Syl. Being overjoyed with thankfulness for God blessing me to receive the shock parole hearing, there was no way I was going to let Satan steal my praises to God. Whatever the problem I claimed my favorite scripture Proverbs 3:5-6 over the situation.

After receiving the notice of the parole hearing, some of my closest inmate friends suggested I and my family members and friends write letters in support of my potential release. I wrote a letter and asked family members, friends, and co-workers to write letters in support of my parole. Additionally, my inmate friends warned me to make sure not to have any confrontations while I awaited my parole hearing. They said although not too common at times some inmates became envious of other inmates pending hearings with the board. These inmates would attempt to cause trouble that would jeopardize my parole. Thanking my friends for all the advice, I became more mindful of my surroundings, while continuing to obey the rules and regulations of the reformatory. My friend Helen, although she did nothing to jeopardize my hearing with the board, withdrew from talking and spending time with me. My speculation was with more than 20 years of being incarcerated she had become friends with several inmates that had been released. For this reason, she might withdraw her friendship instead of preparing to say goodbye to another friend. To respect what I thought might be her decision to withdraw, I would speak and wait to see how she reacted before pursuing a further conversation. The next several weeks with renewed hope, I praised and glorified the Lord with humble acknowledgement for all the mercy He endlessly bestowed upon me and my loved ones. Throughout my incarceration I was strengthened by spiritually inundating my mind, heart, and soul with the word of God. I prayed, fasted, studied the word, sang praises to the Lord, attended worship services, and watched my inspirational television programs. My favorite program was *The Love Special Telecast* with Nancy Hermon. The other shows I watched were Tammy and Jim Baker, Kenneth Copeland, John Hagee, James Robison, and Charles Stanley. Not only did I watch my inspirational shows, I watch my favorite sitcom *The Golden Girls, Benson, The Love Boat, 227*, among others. With my loved ones knowing about the parole hearing, during the weekly visits we optimistically talked about my meeting with the parole board. Besides the members of Assembly, Pastor Judie asked every pastor he knew to pray for me. Linda Faye and Darrell also were praying and fasting with me. The inmates in the classroom were happy for me. Some said if my parole was granted, they were glad the course would be completed before I was released.

Finally, in September 1986, I met with the parole board. I remember nervously walking to the main building. Similar to the members of my jury, I have tried to remember the parole board members faces but cannot. The only visual I have is people sitting at a table. I do not know how many people were there, their gender, age, or race. What I recall is someone asking if my incarceration had reformed me. I replied yes, incarceration had taught me that everyone must be accountable when they break the law. When asked did I regret committing the crime. I emotionally expressed my true feeling that every day for the rest of my life I will regret and be sorry for shooting the gun that took the life of my husband and the pain and suffering I caused to our daughter, his two sons and other family members. That every day I must live with the guilt of causing the death of the father of our child. Someone asked about my teaching the inmates. I explained why Superintendent Arn asked me to instruct my fellow inmates and how I believed it could be helpful to them in the future. The final question I recall is what my plans were for my future if granted parole. I stated to return home to love, care for, and provide for Ivy, my other daughter, Sylvia, and my husband. Attend worship service at Assembly Baptist Church. Obtain employment and be a law-abiding citizen. Then someone said, thank you, and told me I could leave. The meeting with the parole board had went very quickly. Walking back to the cottage I was not sure if the parole board was convinced I met the requirements for an early release. Wondering if I said enough or too much, I thought back to what Ernest said about the tone of my voice during the trial, and it made me worry about the tone of my voice. Several inmates asked me how the meeting went, I told them I was not for sure. Most of them told me not to worry because they were going to grant my release. Others said not to get my hopes up. Needing to stay spiritually strong, I intensified my daily personal spiritual worship with praying, meditating, studying, and trusting in Proverbs 3:5-6. Diligently I continued to teach the class and adhered to the rules and regulations of the reformatory. During weekly visits we talked nonstop about plans upon my release. Everyone was praying and believing for victory while we anxiously waited for the decision from the parole board.

    A few weeks later, I was instructed to go to the main building to receive a letter. It was from the parole board. My heart was racing amazingly fast while I opened the envelope. Glancing over the heading to the body of the letter, I saw the words, *we are pleased…your request for shock parole has been granted*. Without reading the entire letter, I silently screamed inside while tears began running down my face. Glory and praises be to my Almighty God. Walking back to the cottage I wanted to shout and dance praises to the Lord for delivering me. The flickers, beams and bolts of lights were radiating from the heaven above while I repeatedly thanked God for blessing me with the early release. Overjoyed and gratefulness, I could not stop praising the Lord for all He had done for me. My heart full of joy I reminisced on the song *Call Him Up* by Keith Pringle.

One verse says *can't stop praising His name, I just can't stop praising His name, Jesus, Hallelujah, Jesus.* I would forever praise the Lord for all He had done for me.

When I finally calmed down I read the entire letter. The parole board had granted my early release with a one-year probationary period. My inmate friends and students were happy for me. Thankfully another blessing was the day I received the letter, I was scheduled to make a phone call. When Syl answered the phone, eagerly with joy in my soul I said, *I am coming home, they granted my shock parole.* I could hear the relief and happiness in his voice as he said, *thank the Lord.* We both gave praise to God. He called Ivy and Sylvia to the phone saying happily that your mommy is coming home. Their little voices sounded like sweet music to my ears while they said, *you are coming home mommy.* Elated, I said, *yes babies, Mommy is coming home.* That was the best phone call I ever had in my life. Several inmates and staff stated how happy they were for me. I said, thank you. A few of the inmates told me with my parole granted within a few weeks they would transfer me to one of the pre-release centers in my county where I would serve the rest of the 60 to 90 days of my sentence to prepare for reentry into society. That weekend the visit was spirit filled with praises to God, prayers of thanksgiving, tears of joy and discussing the glorious homecoming.

The next week, I was called to meet with the lady that handled the release of inmates. She informed me that because I was still teaching the class and the newly hired instructor would not be starting for several weeks, Superintendent Arn had requested I remain at the reformatory until the instructor began teaching in late November. Of course, I said, yes. Another blessing that I would not be sent to the pre-release center. The end of October was the completion of the first B.O.S.S. course. They were as appreciative of my teaching them as I was of having the opportunity to teach them. A new class began the beginning of November. I was still teaching the class until the newly hired instructor began in late November. When the instructor began working, the reformatory assigned me to assist her as needed until my release in late December. Anxiously waiting to be released it seemed like each day was getting longer and longer. Once the new instructor started, there was a minimal amount of work for me. The last few weeks most of my time was spent at the cottage instead of the classroom. During this time, I helped the other inmates with the upkeep of the communal areas of the cottage, attended bible study classes, and spent time in my room in prayer and meditation. Prior to my release Superintendent Arn sent me a note that said, *without you the program could not have succeeded.* That day and throughout my life, those words meant a lot to me. A few days before my release I gave many of my personal items to fellow inmates. They were happy and thankful.

Finally, it was the day for my release. Sitting waiting for Syl to pick me up, I thought even though imprisonment was an agonizing and intimidating time in my life God had brought me through. When the van from the Cuyahoga County jail had pulled up to the reformatory in mid-November 1985, what I thought would be impossible for me to endure, the mighty power of God made it possible. I had not seen this storm coming, nor the great spiritual intervention of God to calm the storm. He just did it. During those stormy moments in prison I bear witness how God supernaturally blessed my sinful life. Even during this difficult storm of incarceration, flickers of light of grace, mercy, glory, hope, strength, love, understanding from God sustained me. Since my release I know those flickers of light from God is what brought me out of darkness and bondage. Paraphrasing Psalm 107:13-15 (AMP), *Then [I] cried out to the Lord in {my} trouble, And He saved {me} from {my} distresses. He brought {me} out of darkness and the deep (deathly) darkness. And broke {my} bonds apart. Let {me} give thanks to the Lord for His lovingkindness, and for His wonderful acts to {me}!* Praise be to my Lord and Savior Jesus Christ my sentence went from 4 to 25 years to twelve months. With all my self-inflicted sins, faults, failures, and mistakes God still showed me favor. He expediently delivered me from one of my worst storms. Each time I reminisce about my time in prison with certainty I only survived by the miraculous intervention of my Lord and Savior Jesus Christ.

Chapter Nine – Home Sweet Home

That freezing day in December 1986, when I saw the car drive past the cottage to the parking lot, my heart leaped for joy. When they called me to come to the pickup area, I said my final goodbyes to the inmates in the communal area. Walking out the door, I praised God that never again would I pass through that door. Entering the release area, I signed my final release papers. The guard said good luck and happy holidays while opening the door where Syl, Pastor Judie and the girls were waiting for me. We hugged, kissed, laughed, and cried while trying to make our way to the car. Getting into the back of Pastor Judie's car I grabbed Ivy on one side and Sylvia on the other. As Syl drove off I hugged and kissed on my girls. Looking back at the reformatory I prayed all the women in the reformatory would seek God for forgiveness, strength, and encouragement. For those eligible for release, I prayed one day soon they would be reunited with their loved ones. Ivy and Sylvia had begun to talk nonstop about everything they could think of I had missed. Ivy was beaming with happiness that I was finally feeling better and able to come back home. We talked and laughed while Syl drove down Interstate 71 towards Cleveland. Looking out the window at the scenery I thought how often I rode up and down this road to visit Linda Faye and Darrell, each time never giving a thought about the car I was riding in, the nice drive or the beautiful scenery. I took it all for granted. In fact, I would often complain about drive, the weather, traffic, or something else. Now riding in the car seeing the beautiful winter day, I knew no longer could the simplest things of life be taken for granted. Incarceration had taught me another lesson of how to cherish and appreciate even the tiniest aspect of freedom in my life. Still cuddling with my girls, we continued to talk, laugh, and sing praises of thanks to God. Anxiously I looked forward to seeing the sign that read *Entering Cuyahoga County*.

When Syl pulled into the driveway, he blew the horn. The side entrance door to the house opened, and I was greeted by Adrene, Cha and other loved ones. While hugging and kissing we said to each other, praise the Lord. They were saying to me, we are so glad to see you. We missed you so much. Walking into our home I knew I would *never, ever again* take any aspect of my freedom for granted. As we entered our house, I gratefully overjoyed talking and walking with Ivy and Sylvia through each room listening to Ivy tell me about and showing me everything new. When Syl had brought the boxes of my personal belongings in the house, Ivy wanted to open each one of them. Over the months I had often made them little items at the arts and craft activities. Some of the items I had sent home, while a few I had saved to bring home with me. Ivy found the few items. She showed Sylvia and they played with each item for a few moments, then they started unpacking the other boxes. There were about three boxes of letters, cards, and pictures I had received. They each meant too much to me to discard. Adrene and Syl had prepared a nice dinner for me. How happy I was to finally be able to eat home cooked food. Several people stopped at the house or called to welcome me home. Seeing and feeling the love from my loved ones meant more than any of them could ever imagine. Hugging each person, I said it was their love and support that was a one of the primary reason I was able to endure those months away from everyone.

As the evening approached, Syl let me know he had made plans for us to stay at a hotel. Although I had looked forward to spending my first night at home with him and the girls, it made me feel exceptionally special and happy that he had thought to get us a hotel for tonight. Around 5:00 p.m. after we had eaten, and I had spent time together with the girls and other visitors, Syl and I prepared to go to the hotel. Ivy and Sylvia were clinging to my legs, saying, *Mommy do not leave again.* I kneeled down and embraced them, while assuring them I would be back in the morning. Ivy said, okay, *Mommy.* Syl had made reservations at the *Hilton* hotel in Independence, Ohio. It was a beautiful hotel with a lovely room. As soon as we laid in the bed and Syl placed his arms around me all the heartache and loneliness from not being able to lay next to him for months faded away. Finally, I was reunited with my husband. Our intimate reunion was filled with ecstasy. I was in a state of euphoria and utterly mesmerized as I snuggled in the arms of my husband. Syl then said, *things will get better with time.* Stunned and not knowing how to reply, I did not say anything, but to myself I said, *huh, why did he say that*? Immediately my sensitive and insecure emotions were stirred up. But I pushed those thoughts to the back of my mind, saying to myself, not today, I cannot ruin this special moment by overthinking what he said. Determined not to let my negative thoughts go into overdrive, I thought, yes, the comment was confusing to me, but I did not want to allow it to damper our reunion. Instead, I decided to hope and pray that my sensitive and insecure feelings were wrong, and what he said was not that serious; and that in fact Syl did enjoy our reunion of intimacy as much as I did.

The next day was Saturday. We went to breakfast then headed home. Ivy and Sylvia ran to us giving big kisses and hugs. I spent the remainder of the day bonding with my girls and preparing to attend church the next day. Linda Faye and Darrell arrived later that day. It was another joyous reunion. My sister and Darrell had been an enormous blessing to me, Syl and the girls throughout my incarceration. I would forever be appreciative for their love, support, and encouragement. Linda Faye had even began writing and supporting Genevieve, one of my dearest inmate friends. Even after my release, Linda Faye wrote and supported Genevieve. I was glad to see Hattie who brought over a cake. She told me to let her know if I needed anything. When Linda C. and Jan came to visit, I hugged and thanked them for everything they did for my family and me. The next day we went to Assembly. Once more, I was profoundly grateful to return to my house of worship. During the service Pastor Judie welcomed me home. Prior to the dismissal he motioned for me to come to the front of the church. He said how happy it was to have his daughter home. Pastor Judie then asked me to say a few words. I expressed my heartfelt gratitude for the many kind acts of love and support given to Syl, our daughters and me while I was away. Appreciatively I let the members know how the many letters and cards of encouragement helped me survive many lonely and sad days and the thoughtfulness of each member would always be cherished. To the parents that allowed their children to visit me, I said how much I looked forward to the visits and was thankful they allowed them to visit. Conveying how their love, kindness and support inspired me to stay strong during one of the most arduous times of my life. Pastor Judie then collected a love offering for me. Humbly I thanked each member for their generosity. After the worship service, many of the members were sincerely glad I was home. There were a few that I was told felt I still was a felon who had killed someone. This made me recall when Herman first died what my Lenore's mother said to me that day we saw each other in the store, *one of your classmates killed her husband.* Hearing now how some members felt reinforced in my mind that some people would always have negative thoughts towards me and believe I was a bad person. Although it was painful to accept the negative way some people thought about me, I knew there was nothing I could do or say to change their mind or prove my regret, sorrow, and guilt for causing the death of my husband or how many days I wished that it would have been me instead of Herman that died. I prayed one day those that felt negative about me would forgive. In the meantime, not wanting to dwell on the negative, I was determined to focus on Pastor Judie and most of the other members who unconditionally loved and supported me. On the drive home from the reformatory and during worship service that day, Pastor Judie told me to get back to working on the committees and positions I had previously held at Assembly. I planned to be obedient to Pastor Judie, because even with all my sins, he proudly continued to declare me, as well as Linda Faye his daughters and likewise he was our God-given father who I would always love and support. Therefore, there was no way I would let him down because of a few naysayers at Assembly.

On Monday, Syl took me to meet with my parole officer. She gave me guidelines and expectations the Parole Board expected me to adhere to and achieve during my probation period. She also provided me with a schedule of the days I was to meet with her. As Syl drove us home, for the first time since returning home, I thought about how being taken away abruptly from my daughters, especially for Ivy who was six when I was arrested, had to be tremendously confusing and emotionally disturbing for them. Although Ivy seemed a little timid, it appeared she and Sylvia had survived our traumatic separation and were mentally and physically healthy little girls. Later in life to my dismay I would learn there was a reason for Ivy being a little timid. Once we were back at the house, I held Ivy and Sylvia tightly in my arms singing our favorite song *You Are My Sunshine, My Only Sunshine*, while in my mind I promised from that day forward I would do everything possible for Syl and me to provide our daughters with a loving, stable, supportive home.

Deception or Weakness. I was very content to be able to get back into my routine in the free world after months of the rigid reformatory schedule. Syl and I had not yet discussed when I would return to work. I had talked to Eddie a few times, but we had not discussed my returning to WJC. A few weeks after being home, I was looking through some papers needed to prepare our 1986 tax forms. Mixed in the papers was the *American Express* card year end summary of purchases. Because it was the last year to write off as a tax deduction the interest from credits cards, I began to review the statement to find the interest amount we paid. Suddenly I noticed charges for stays at hotels and the purchase of expensive women purses and clothing. Uncertain why the charges were on the summary, I asked Syl. He asked why I was going through the papers. I told him to get the information needed to prepare our taxes. After much back and forth about the charges, then came an unexpected bombshell. Syl said he *did not know when I would be released, and he was getting lonely, which lead to an affair*. Devastation took over my heart, mind, and soul. No, Lord Jesus, no, not this soon. It had been less than a few weeks since my release from prison. Please do not let my world be shattered this soon. When I pointed out to Syl some of the charges was when he knew I was about to be released, he had no response. Even more hurting was the hotel we stayed at the night I returned home was directly next door to one of the hotels he had stayed at with another woman. I asked why he would take me that close to the same hotel. Again, did not give me a reason, but Syl did firmly say in a stern tone, *the affair was over, and he wanted us to get on with our lives*. I began to ask, *do I know her, what is her name*? I had to know because I did not want any woman smiling in my face who was the woman he had the affair with. Syl refused to tell me. No matter how much I begged him to tell me who she was, he would not tell me. Instantly emotions of being deceived, rejected and insecure surfaced. For several days discreetly, we quarreled about the affair, and more important to me who was the woman. It troubled me to the point I became obsessed with finding out who she was. Why did I have to find the credit card statement? Prior to finding the credit card statement, I would never have thought Syl had been unfaithful because he was always there for me. He visited two to three times a month, wrote letters mostly every day, answered my weekly phone calls, except for one time that happened to coincide with one of the hotel stay dates. Negative thoughts began to unrelenting consume me. Then I remembered in August when he did not come alone on his visit but had brought two of the youths from Assembly. My mind then went in overdrive. Was that going to be when he was planning to tell me he was getting tired of waiting for me? The negative thoughts increased my insecurities. Repeatedly thinking the woman was prettier and smarter than me and that Syl really did not love or want to be with me but her. That he only was with me because he felt sorry for me. I tried again to persuade Syl to tell me the name of the woman. He refused to tell me. I had to resort to my norm of living in my pretend world that life was great, while within my soul I was emotionally dying. Because there was no way I was going to let anyone know about the affair for that would be too embarrassing. Plus, my negative thoughts made me think even if I talked to someone that person might be the one with whom he had had the affair. This became another stormy part of my life that I would have to weather alone.

The affair and not knowing who he had the affair with affected my ability to be intimate with Syl. This resulted in me withdrawing into my private shell. After several days Syl harshly told me how he was sorry, and that either I forgive and forget what happen or our marriage would not survive. I asked him to please tell me the name of the woman. He refused. Knowing that another broken marriage was not what I wanted and definitely did not need, I suppressed my own personal feelings. Then I began to rationalize his actions thinking: how he supported me during my incarceration; it was not his fault but my own that I was incarcerated; I was the one not there to perform my wifely duties; he took care of and kept Ivy and Sylvia together; and he had taken care of our home. Considering all this, even though I was heartbroken, I knew it was not only about me but what was best for the entire family. With this in mind, I succumbed to his request to not let the affair have a negative effect on our marriage. Trying not to think about the affair, all my momentum was put into caring and providing for Ivy and Sylvia and reviving our marriage. Yet, privately within not knowing who Syl had the affair with continually aggravated me emotionally. It was also hard to understand the purpose of Syl keeping the statements with the information, and why did I have to find the statements. Once released I had prayed to have a loving peaceful home with my family. Unfortunately, this had to happen.

<u>Time to Get Back to Work.</u> Dealing with the affair, I discovered we were in financial trouble with excessive credit card debt. This surprised me, and it was difficult to understand, because when I was arrested most of the money from the life insurance from Momma was in the account. The during my incarceration significant amounts were received from the money withdrawn from my retirement plan and our

1985 tax refund check. Plus, the monthly social security benefits that Ivy received was more than enough to cover her school tuition expenses. In addition, Syl had received money from Linda Faye and Darrell, and his brother and sister in law, Tommie, and Vicki. All these funds were more than what I would have earned on my job if I had not been incarcerated. Therefore, during my incarnation, I thought he had ample funds to maintain the household. Yet again, I was wrong. Taking into consideration our financial situation, it was necessary for me to seek employment right away. Once more I registered with Kelly Girls. In mid-January 1987, I was offered and accepted a temporary job at Jones Day, a top five international law firm, as a floating legal secretary. In this position I would cover the work assignments for secretaries that were on vacation or taking personal time off. After a few months, I was assigned to the tobacco litigation cases where I worked for several staff attorneys. By April 1987, Jones Day permanently hired me. This was the beginning of my employment blessings. In mid-1988, I was assigned to work for two litigation associates. I always received outstanding evaluations and was considered an exemplary employee. A year later, I was assigned to a more prestigious secretarial assignment with a patent litigation partner, Richard (Dick) Sayler. I continued to work for one of the associates who was practicing in the bankruptcy department (the BK Attorney). Within four years, I was promoted from legal secretary to paralegal for the bankruptcy department. For a brief period of time, I worked as secretary for Dick and the bankruptcy department paralegal. Surprising after the earlier debacles with my spelling and grammar, I had become known as the proofreading go to person for the bankruptcy department. The attorneys considered my proofreading, together with writing, spelling, and attention to detail skills superb. Of course, after the previous embarrassing moments with my former employers and the military exam, this acknowledgement meant a lot to me. I had worked hard to become proficient in my writing skills, which I continuously strive to enhance.

Over the years at Jones Day I met and became close to several people. Initially I met Tresa and Gail. Later, I became friends with Debra and John. When I meet Tresa and Gail, they were lunch buddies. One day they invited me to join them. Thereafter we would usually have lunch together. Eventually we talked and attended events together outside the office. When Gail was getting married, Tresa and I helped with her bridal shower. For her wedding Teresa was one of the bridesmaids, while I assisted with the coordination. Tresa and I later supported Gail with her baby shower. I would invite Tresa and Gail, and they attended several programs and banquets we had at Assembly. During the Christmas holidays we exchanged gifts, and we celebrated each of our birthdays, and at times even the birthdays of our children. During times of sickness and bereavement we supported each other. For years we were spent a lot of time together, but eventually we began to spend less time together. Still over the years we would stay in touch for birthdays and during the loss of loved ones. Since around February 2015, I have not been in contact with Tresa or Gail.

Shortly after meeting Tresa an incident occurred that caught me completely off. We were sharing pictures of our families when I showed Tresa and Gail pictures of Syl, Ivy and Sylvia. Teresa looked perplexed as she said, *Syl looked familiar.* Then she said I remember meeting him at the wedding of my brother to Wretha, who happened to be a member of Assembly. She told me that the wedding was actually held at Assembly, *note this was before I invited Tresa to Assembly.* Tresa went on to tell me that one of Wretha's sister, Jackie D., also a member of Assembly, had told her she was married to Syl. With my mouth wide open, I said, *what*, then I asked Tresa if she was sure. She replied, yes. Trying to laugh off the conversation, I let Tresa know Jackie was lying. We then started looking at other pictures of their families. Of course, in the back of my mind I had plenty of questions for Syl. Did he have the affair with Jackie D., because it was too ironic that the wedding was in August of 1986 the same month Syl had visited with the two youths. In addition, I had seen a picture of Syl, Doris Faye and even Jackie D. in the driveway the day of Wretha's wedding. When I got home that evening, I told Syl what Tresa had told me. Once again Syl adamantly told me to forget who he had the affair with because he was never going to tell me. This did nothing but increase my suspicious and lack of trust. Knowing I needed to concentrate on our family staying together, I put all my disappointed feelings in the back of my mind where I hid all my heavy emotions from my stormy life. Regardless of my emotions, Ivy and Sylvia were innocent little girls that did not deserve to live without both parents. My girls living in a loving, happy, supportive family outweighed any pain I had to endure.

Months later, I met Debra (Deb), also known as Bubbles by her family, who has the most outgoing personality of all the people I know. There is not a person she will not befriend. This is how we met around late 1989. The firm had hired her to work as a computer analyst. There had always been few African-Americans at the firm, so when an African-American began to work for the firm, we tended to become acquainted with each other. Deb and I would often speak. One day one of us suggested going to lunch. After having lunch together that one day, we became good friends. Within months, our friendship grew into a sister relationship that remains the same today. She introduced me to her family who instantly I fell in love with and they graciously accepted me into the family as if I were one of their own. Her mother, Addie, became my God-given mother. Even to this day Momma Nunn as I fondly call her, loves me as her own. Deb's brothers Clarence, Michael and Gregory and sister, Mary, as well as Deb's son, Maurie always supported me and my family, especially Ivy and Sylvia. I also would be there for whatever or whenever the Nunn family needs me, something that I continue to do even to this day. Before getting too close with the Nunn family, I told Deb what had occurred in my life resulting in the death of Herman and my incarceration. I let her know I wanted the family to know from me before they could hear it from someone else. Deb with concern and love told me, *no one needed to know about my past, because it was not their business*. What she said that day and the way Deb accepted me into her life and family with all my faults, sins and shortcomings will forever be appreciated. Over the years, we shared a lot of wonderful times. We were together for births, weddings, graduations, trips, and holidays. Then during times of sadness, sickness, disappointments, and bereavement, we were there to support and encourage each other. Momma Nunn like my Momma would wake Deb and Greg up for work every day. To my delight, soon Momma Nunn included me in the list of people she called to wake me up each morning for work. Momma Nunn and I still talk often every day. Throughout the years, Deb and I might not talk for weeks, but know that we are always only a phone call or text away from each other. I thank God for blessing me to meet Deb and become a part of the life of the beautiful Nunn family.

John Barnes who worked in the cafeteria at Jones Day, also became a special person in my life. I do not remember exactly when or how we started talking but John became one of the dearest persons in my life. He is a handsome, thoughtful, funny, good natured person who brings much joy and laugher to the lives of my family and me. Early in our relationship John frankly shared a special part of his life with me. Without hesitation I told him regardless my love for him is unconditional, because repeatedly God had bestowed upon me grace and mercy for the life shattering sins I had committed. Thus, what stones could I throw at anyone? Absolutely none, there was no way I negatively could judge any one. Lovingly I began to call John my brother and he called me his sister. Eventually the same way John had shared confidences with me, I let him know about the death of Herman and my incarceration. Like it was with me, it did not matter to him. His love was unconditional even with my dark past and shortcomings.

We became and remain to this day an integral part of each other lives. Though we are not blood family, we are God-given family that love, care, and support each other wholeheartedly. Over the years we have been there for the difficulties of our journeys through life. Together we have prayed and worshiped God. Shared times of laughter and sorrow. We also encouraged and upheld each other. We have celebrated births, graduations, weddings, and many other good times. John and I have consoled each other during sickness and when loved ones have passed away. Each birthday Syl, Ivy, Sylvia and I know if we did not hear from anyone else, we will receive from John a card, sometimes with a thoughtful gift. Each year my family looks forward to John celebrating holidays with us. They have loved John from the moment they met him. When I met his family members, especially Marva and Sketta, they embraced me and my family like we had been family for years. John and I make sure we do not let too much time pass without checking on each other. I am extremely grateful that God blessed me to have John in my life.

In 1988, a lovely young lady with charming big beautiful eyes, smile and dimples named Lisa Hudson came roaring into the firm ready to take over the accounting department. One day Lisa walked up to me and began to talk. I admired her enthusiastic spirit. We hit if off from the moment she said, *hi, I am Lisa*. We made a date to have lunch. A few days later at lunch, I learned she was eleven years younger than me. We instantaneously became close. She felt comfortable talking to me about any issue she had, from work related matters to her personal life. I would listen to Lisa and try to give her sound advice. However, trying to keep Lisa on the right path was at times quite difficult. It took lots of prayer and patience to get through to Lisa, because she was very stubborn and hardheaded. She wanted things her way or no way. Then batting those big eyes and those dimples appearing with that heartwarming smiling, I would say to myself she really is a sweet, kind young lady, she only needed a little help to transition into a mature young woman. We began to spend more time together both at work and socially. As time went by we grew close. She even began to call me her god-mother. Like my other friendships that began at Jones Day, Lisa and I shared a lot together. We attended each other's family events and social outings. Many birthdays and holidays were celebrated together. I eventually told Lisa about my past with Herman and my incarceration. She became even more compassionate towards me, loving me unconditionally with my stormy life. One day Lisa came to my office needing to discuss an issue she had in the accounting department. I suggested how she should handle the matter. That day no matter how hard I tried to keep her *know-it-all* attitude under control, she did not listen. Sadly, this eventually resulted in her termination from the firm. Thankfully she was smart, young, confident, and ambitious. Lisa went on to acquire gainful employment. Even when she left the firm we stayed close and was happy when she asked me to be the god-mother of her first-born daughter, Ashley. Of course, I gladly said, yes. Later she married and had three other children. Over the years Lisa and I have been there for each other with love and support. Lisa knows whenever she needs encouragement or a tough love reality check, I am only a phone call away. Most recently, Lisa accepted her calling into the ministry. She received her master's degree in divinity. Currently she is the pastor of a church and one of the clergies for a county jail. I am proud of her accomplishment and to know that she will always be my lovable bright-eyed god-daughter who I love dearly.

Chapter Ten – Lots of Sunshine Then Abruptly a Storm

Undoubtedly in my life the most severe storms were the unforeseen deaths of Herman and Momma. Each time I think how they both abruptly died my heart aches to the same extent it did the day they passed away. Coming home to the immediate disappointments of the affair and our financial situation caused an emotional storm with severe scarring. Turning to God, I had to depend totally on Him to strengthen me. Physically I was functioning normally, while mentally I was in excruciating pain. When the shock parole was granted, without a doubt I knew God had truly blessed my family and me, and I had anxiously looked forward to reuniting with my family. Upon returning home I was completely blindsided when I found the credit card statements and financial situation. To go from the storm of incarceration, then to the sunshine of being granted an early release and coming home, only for another storm to almost immediate start had given me little time to enjoy the sunshine. This caused emotions of disappointment and sadness to intensify within me all over again. Undoubtedly, it seemed to me that Satan was mocking me with negative thoughts of now what are you going to do, and where is your God – did your God bring you out of jail only to face this new storm. Even with those negative thought and the heartache from the emotional agony, I knew that all God had brought me through, I was not going to let Satan have victory over my life. Regardless of the affair and finances, I was determined Ivy and Sylvia would live with both parents in a spiritually anointed home filled with love, joy, support, and encouragement. To keep our family together, I realized it would be impossible without the intervention of God. No question it would be a mentally challenging battle to contend with the emotional scarring from the affair and Syl refusing to let me know the identity of the woman, but to stay mentally strong, I spiritually saturated my mind, heart, and soul by constantly reiterating and applying Proverbs 3:5-6 to each aspect of my life. Instead of focusing on the things that happened, I concentrated on all the blessings God had done in my life. I knew each storm in my life that had endured was not only from me trying hard to make it through the storm, but from the much mercy and grace from God. Working hard and inundating myself with praying, studying, mediating, worshipping and praising Jesus Christ, while trusting and believing in God, I grew stronger each day. Although at times a certain thought would cause the emotional scars from the affair to resurface, thankfully there were flickers of grace and mercy from God to give me the fortitude to withstand the emotional discomfort. This enabled me to keep our family together. As I learned to live with my stormy life and related scars, I worked towards bringing more sun shiny days to our family.

In January 1988 the sun shined brightly when praise be to God I completed my one-year parole obligations without incident. With the fulfillment of the parole obligations my debt to society and the State of Ohio for causing the death of Herman had been satisfied. What would never be satisfied was the emotional scars within my soul for causing the death of Herman. For the rest of my life I would live with aftermath from self-inflicted storm of regret, guilt, shame, pain, and heartache. In addition to the aftermath, was the pain of living with knowing I caused the grief and pain of Ivy and her brothers living without their father, as well as his family living without their loved one. This pain and void I caused each of them is a perpetual life sentence of longing to go back in time to reverse that one second when I shot that gun. Impossible to turn back the hands of time, inwardly I had to thrust the mental agony into the private depths of my mind and heart hidden away for everyone. Outwardly I turned all my focus on the care of my family, serving at Assembly and working diligently on my job. Working hard to get our family life back to normal, Syl and I both earnestly strived to resolve the tension from being separated during my incarcerated, his infidelity and our financial problems. With much prayer, studying the word of God, and learning to be led by the Holy Spirit we grew stronger as a couple and as parents to our children. Slowly but surely with the passing of time our efforts to bring spiritual, emotional, financial, and social restoration to our family were gradually materializing.

Bright Days Fellowshipping and Serving at Assembly. Upon returning to Assembly, I gradually began to diligently work again as the choir director of the youth choir and church clerk. In addition, started to once again work with the children and youths with the performance of several Easter, Christmas and other special occasion plays and skits. The most memorable play was the renowned short play, *Tom Thumb Wedding*. The play is based on the marriage of midgets Charles Sherwood Stratton aka Tom Thumb to Lavinia Warren in an elaborate church in 1863. The play mocked a wedding ceremony with a cast of children ranging from ages four to twelve. The wedding party consisted of the groom, bride, bridesmaids, groomsmen, the minister, singers, and wedding guest. Dressed in traditional adult-styled formal wedding attire the children looked funny and adorable. Before the play began the bride arrived in a limo. Their performance of the comical script was hilarious. The audience laughed throughout the play. Following the performance there was a cake and punch reception. Following the reception, the wedding party was given a ride in the limo. I was very appreciative to my co-worker Alesica who assisted me with the flowers, cake, and dresses. My friend Roberta and her husband who helped with the donation of the limo. Besides directing the choirs and presenting plays and skits, Syl and I resumed organizing and escorting the children and youths to various outings such as: skating and bowling parties; and trips to amusement parks, sporting events, the circus, Christmas parades, tobogganing and overnight camping trips.

Assembly would sometimes be invited to fellowship with a few out-of-town churches. Pastor Judie would have me organize and coordinate those yearly trips to Chicago, Illinois and Flint, Michigan. The members of Assembly would also like to take a few leisure trips to Niagara Falls that I coordinated. When Pastor Judie and the members decided to attend the National Baptist Convention to celebrate the opening of the Baptist World Center in Nashville, Tennessee, Pastor Judie asked me to secure bus transportation, hotel arrangements and handle the registration for the more than forty attendees. During the trip Jessie and I chaperoned the girls, while Syl chaperoned the boys. For many of us this was our first time attending a major convention. It was inspiring to see thousands of people praising God. The classes and worship services attended by the adult members were uplifting and motivating. The children and youth enjoyed attending their classes and were amazed at the number of other children attending the convention. After their classes they rehearsed with the Children's Choir that had over one hundred children, who would sing at the closing evening worship service. We ran into a little snag when learning the Children's Choir attire was all white. Only a couple of our children had white outfits. Determined not to disappoint the children without white outfits, I went to *JCPenney* to buy the needed outfits. The evening the Children's Choir sang, the adult members were pleased to see our children singing in the huge choir. Returning to Cleveland everyone had been spiritually revived. This enthusiasm of the members uplifted the entire church, and the church grew in all aspects. The Holy Spirit was moving in the lives of members like never before. The membership increased, record numbers of members were tithing, and Assembly was growing spiritually and financially with its old and new members. It was a truly blessed time at Assembly.

Since the passing of Momma and my return home, no one had taken over as president of the Missionary Society. Pastor Judie asked me to carry on in place of Momma. There was no way I could say no. The Holy Spirit inspired me to do several things with the Missionary Society. The first was each month to take the youths to visit members of Assembly that were sick or unable to attend church. Around the holiday season we would visit members and non-members of Assembly at nursing homes and children's foster homes. During those visits the residents would appreciate us praying, reading scripture, singing, and talking to them. If allowed, we would give bags of fruit and other snacks. The elderly would say how much joy our visits brought to them. The foster children would also appreciate the visits and gifts we brought them. These were special times for me to give back to others less fortunate in appreciation for all God had done for me. When I asked Pastor Judie for permission to have the monthly Missionary meetings at the homes of members instead of at the church, he said that sounded like a clever idea. The first meeting was held at our home. We had devotional service with praying, scripture reading, and singing a few songs. Following the devotional service, anyone was welcome to give testimonies of the goodness of God in their lives. Then we studied and discussed the ways we could improve the mission of the church. After the closing prayer, refreshments would be served. The monthly missionary meetings were a blessing to Assembly, because it enabled members to fellowship with each other at each other's homes. More importantly we would minister to other family members, friends, and neighbors that were not members of Assembly. Witnessing to some of these people resulted in their uniting with Assembly by confessing Christ as their Lord and Savior and being baptized or uniting by Christian experience. For several years, the Missionary Society held meetings at various members homes.

    Besides Syl helping me with the children and youth, he was a member of the male chorus and served on the Trustee board. Prior to my incarceration, Syl had went on trial to become a deacon. Following months of training, he was ready to be ordained. As his wife, I contemporaneously became a deaconess. In May 1987 the Ordination and Installation service was held for Syl and Leroy Williams. The ordination was spiritually uplifting with us taking the vows to serve the members of the church in accordance with certain Biblical guidelines. Becoming a deacon and deaconess further helped to strengthen our marriage. Similar to us, Ivy and Sylvia actively served at Assembly, by being active in the youth ministries and programs, including the choir and usher board. Pastor Judie received a vision to incorporate into the Sunday morning worship a reading pertaining to black history not only in the month of February but every week. He asked Ivy to select and read a quote by Dr. Martin Luther King, Jr. each week. At the age of ten, each week Ivy select a quote from Dr. King, then would efficiently read an inspiring quote to the congregation each week. Besides our individual responsibilities at Assembly, we attended bible study, vacation bible school, evening services and various church related outings. Later in life Ivy and Sylvia teased how they spent Saturday afternoons at Assembly rehearsing and the evening preparing for Sunday school. Sundays we were at church at 9:30 a.m. for Sunday school, followed by morning worship at 11:30 a.m. Most of our Sunday afternoons were spent at evening services at Assembly or other churches that started around 3:30 p.m. Then on Wednesdays we often would attend Bible study. Church was truly an essential part of our lives. Worshiping and serving at Assembly, became the second home for our family. For me personally serving at Assembly eased a lot of the emotional scarring from my stormy life.

A New Little Ray of Sunshine. From the day Cha had moved in with us, our bond steadily flourished. Instead of a cousin-in-law, Cha was more like a little sister. We encouraged, supported, and protected each other. Together we shared a lot of great and tough times together. Through it all we were there for each other and could depend on each other to be genuinely honest and reliable. During my incarceration she was another flicker of light from God with her kindheartedness by being tremendously supportive in helping Syl with the girls. She was one of the people who was sincerely affectionate, supportive, and empathetic towards my baby girls. In July 1987, Cha filed for a divorce from Don-Don and asked that I appear with her at the hearing as her witness. Of course, I agreed. Shortly after her divorce Cha met Steven (Steve). They soon began dating. Several months later, Cha found out she was expecting. Things were going good for the parents-to-be. Suddenly to the dismay of Cha, Steve began to gradually stop coming around. For the remainder of her pregnancy I helped Cha as much as possible. On May 18, 1988, Cha went into labor. Driving her to the hospital pretending not to be scared, I tried to act calmly while she twisted and turned in labor pain. Upon arriving at the hospital, Cha asked me if I would stay with her. I said, most definitely. Usually I was the one in labor. This time being on the other side was different. As Cha laid in the bed in labor, suddenly the nurse and I jumped back when fluid unexpectedly squirted out. Cha with a confused looked said to us, *what is wrong, why are y'all jumping*. Laughing the nurse and I told her how the fluid came out. Cha seriously said, *see y'all jumping and that could have been the baby coming out*. Cha and I still to this day laugh about the nurse and me jumping. Several hours later Cha delivered her bundle of joy, Steven, Jr. (Little Steve). Even though I had given birth to my girls, it was still amazing to see the birth of Little Steve. Cha asked me to be his god mother, which I happily accepted. A few days later I brought her and Little Steve home. He became the ray of sunshine to everyone in the house. Ivy and Sylvia adored him. Prayers were answered when a few months later Big Steve called and came to see Cha and Little Steve. He quickly began to come over more often and eventually would stay overnight. I was very thankful Big Steve and Cha were working on their relationship and being great parents to Little Steve.

Sunny Days with Family and Friends. In September of 1988, Sylvia began kindergarten at Cedar Hill. She was excited to be attending school with Ivy and Nathan. Jessie, her mother, Syl and I were still coordinating transporting the kids to and from school. Each year the school would present several programs. The Grandparents Day program was attended each year by Pastor Judie and Mrs. Bessie. They were always excited to attend, as they were elated to see Ivy and Sylvia perform and to meet their teachers. The other big events were the yearly Christmas program and end of the year musical concert. The family members would enjoy attending. Linda Faye and Darrell were able to attend several programs. It was fun to watch how each year the girls changed. Sylvia had a memorable moment her first Christmas play when she made it to the stage. Within a few second of looking at the crowd, she bolted off the stage running directly to Syl and me. By the second grade she was ready to stay on stage. The programs presented were very enjoyable. A few of the songs and ideas from these programs I would teach the youth choir at Assembly. The affiliated and adjacent church of the school, Cedar Hill Baptist Church was part of the international nonprofit faith based *Approved Workman Are Not Ashamed Club* (AWANA). The AWANA club is for boys and girls from two to eighteen years of age. The goals of AWANA are for club leaders to teach children the gospel of Jesus Christ and train them how to be disciples for Christ throughout their lives. The girls, Nathan, and at the time family members and friends attended the weekly AWANA Club meetings on Tuesday evenings. The children were taught ways to have a personal relationship with Christ through interactive Bible based curriculum. Following the lessons, they participated in various games and team athletic activities. At the end of the year, the Cedar Hill AWANA club would attend the regional field day where they competed against AWANA clubs from throughout the state of Ohio in a variety of team athletic activities. This was always an awesome experience for Ivy, Sylvia, Nathan. They looked forward to traveling to different cities throughout the state of Ohio for the field days. It was good to see them learn to compete for medals in a competitive yet honorable manner. Syl and I were very thankful to be able to send Ivy and Sylvia to a Christian school with a good academic program that taught moral values in a Christian based atmosphere. I was also incredibly happy to be able to fulfill a dream of my Momma.

In summer of 1989, the sun and shield of the Lord shined brightly upon us. *For the Lord God is a sun and shield: The Lord will give grace and glory: no good thing will he withhold from them that walk uprightly,* Psalm 84:11 (KJV). Within the past thirteen months Syl and I were blessed to once more be financially sound. This enabled our once in a lifetime vacation to become a reality for us. It was extra special for me because it was a dream Momma had for her, Linda Faye, and me, which was coming true through us. Syl, the girls, Linda Faye, Darrell, and I were taking a four-week vacation to California, Nevada, and New Mexico. We were excited about the trip. This would be the first long distance flight for Linda Faye and me, and the first flight for Ivy and Sylvia. Both Syl and Darrell had flown on long distance flights while serving in the military. Syl had talked to Tommie and Vicki who lived in Pomona, California about us staying with them. They excitedly agreed to us staying with them. Tommie and Vicki are the ideal perfectly matched couple that truly exemplify the fruits of the spirit of true *love, joy, harmony, patience, compassion, integrity, thoughtfulness, and dignity.* When the six of us arrived, they greeted us with big hugs and kisses, saying their home was ours, as they freely opened their home to us. The first day we rested from the jet lag. The next day we went to meet Vicki's parents, Mr. and Mrs. Thomas, her sisters, brother, nieces, and nephews. Each of them extended the same generous hospitality as Vicki and Tommie.

Over the next few days we visited the Los Angeles tourist sights.

We went to Disneyland were the girls had a magnificent time. Then to the famous Venice beach where we saw many diverse sights. Tommie and Vicki went with us to Hollywood Boulevard where they showed us the Hollywood sign. We visited the Chinese Theater, Hollywood Walk of Fame, and the Hollywood Wax Museum. That Sunday we went to church with Tommie and Vicki. On Monday morning we loaded up the van we had rented and headed to Las Vegas. Tommie and Vicki told us what to look out for on the drive through the desert. As we rode through the desert, it made me reminisce of when I was a child watching *Wagon Train* and *Gunsmoke*. To see the exquisite beauty of the mountains was breathtaking. We saw signs saying *cut off engine* for a certain number of miles. Tommie had explained that those signs were to prevent cars from over-heating. When we stopped at a rest area, there were signs with watch out for snakes. Syl went out where the sign was to take a picture. I kept wonder, how did the pioneers make it through the deserts. When we drove into Las Vegas the hotels, lights and sights were unbelievable. We were fascinated by the lights and excitement of the city. We stayed at the *Flamingo*. This was Linda Faye and my first time at a casino and putting coins into slot machine. The main entertainment for Ivy and Sylvia were the pools and the carnival rides at *Circus-Circus* hotel. Everyone enjoyed our meals at the buffets. We stayed in Vegas for two days. On our return to Pomona we stopped at the Hoover dam. It was a beautiful sight. Everyone but me went up close to look at the view. With my fear of height, I could not muster up enough courage to go up close. The girls kept telling me to *come on*

Mommy it is not that bad. I said, *no, that is okay.*

We then returned to the beautiful home of Tommie and Vicki that Wednesday evening, we stayed there until that Friday morning when everyone heard Syl saying get up. Syl then started singing the song he sang each time we started a new trip, *on the road again, goin' places that I've never been* from the song *On the Road Again*, written by Willie Nelson. This time we were headed to San Diego. Following our routine prayer for safe travels, Tommie and Vicki said they would see us in a few days. Arriving in San Diego we were stunned to see the planes flying remarkably close to the tall building. It was like they were flying between the buildings. Later we learned the airport was in the middle of the city. I thought you really had to be an excellent pilot to fly into San Diego. When we checked into the five-star hotel, Ivy and Sylvia were wowed. Ivy said it looks like the *Contemporary*. Although Sylvia did not remember the *Contemporary*, she said I love this hotel. We had a two-bedroom suite separated by a living room with a view of the ocean. The girls cheerfully ran between each room. The first day we visited the San Diego zoo. The next day we went to Tijuana, Mexico. We had two lasting family memories from that trip. First was Ivy and Sylvia taking a cute picture wearing large sombreros while sitting on a donkey. The second was going through customs when we were returning to state side. Syl had instructed the girls to stay with us, be on their best behavior, and not to say anything. Syl was carrying a small handheld cooler as he approached the custom officer. The custom officer began to ask Syl the routine questions, which Syl answered. The custom officer was waving Syl through, when suddenly Ivy said, *Daddy what is in that cooler?* The custom officer stopped Syl saying, *what did she say?* Syl said nothing. Although there was nothing illegal in the cooler, Syl was happy the custom officer told him to keep going. When we were on the other side of the gate, everyone was relieved Ivy's questioning did not cause a ruckus for us. It became a family joke to tease and laugh about how inquisitive Ivy almost got Syl locked up in Mexico. We returned to San Diego where we stayed one more night. The next morning, we drove back to Pomona.

Our final trip was to San Francisco. Tommie and Vicki joined us on this weekend trip. It was another beautiful ride with incredible scenery. Surprisingly there were huge windmills scattered in large groups throughout the country side. The visit to San Francisco was nice for everyone, except for me coping with my fear of heights. I closed my eyes praying each time we rode over the Golden Gate Bridge and definitely the Bay Bridge which to me was the scariest. It was fun sightseeing the city by hopping on and off the trollies. The hills were very steep exactly as portrayed on television shows and in movies. Although we did not visit Alcatraz, we were able to see it from the pier. We spent time eating and shopping at the Fisherman's Wharf. For the return home, everyone had decided we would drive the scenic State Route 1 Pacific Coast Highway back to Pomona. We were looking forward to seeing the beautiful scenery and might even see the Hearst Mansion. Linda Faye insisted on driving. With the exception of Linda Faye, who was driving, Ivy and Sylvia because they were too young to understand what was taking place, and Darrell, the drive back to Pomona turned into the longest, quietest, tense, and nonstop praying ride for Syl, Tommie, Vicki, and me. We began the six-hour drive in the daylight it was great with breathtaking scenery. Unfortunately, we had a late start resulting in the sun setting much sooner than we anticipated. It was soon nighttime. The road changed from a two-lane highway to one lane. The ocean was on our right side. On-coming traffic on our left side. The darker it became; the slower Linda Faye drove. Drivers behind us attempted to go around. This was the beginning of a terrifying ride. As Linda Faye drove too slow maneuvering around the extremely winding road of the pitch-black highway with no street lights, the tailgating by drivers intensified. Besides Linda Faye and the girls, everyone in the car could sense that these drivers were familiar with the road. They aggressively were tailgating to force Linda Faye to speed up from the ten to fifteen miles she was driving. Most of the drivers would finally pass when it was safe to cross into the oncoming traffic lane. Others blinked their high beams or hooked their horns until they could safely pass. Tommie and Syl asked Linda Faye several times if she wanted them to drive. She adamantly said, *no*, insisting she was okay. When we finally reached the main highway to Pomona we gave thanks to God for safely bring us through the narrow winding one-lane road. Even to this day Tommie, Vicki, Syl and I talk about that night being one of the scariest times of our lives, as we recall how each of us were silently praying that we would safely arrive back to Pomona. After that night, none of us have had a desire to drive the scenic route from San Francisco.

Even with the Pacific Coast Highway experience, it was truly a spectacular vacation. Not only did I get to see beautiful sights and have a wonderful time with my family, it was the beginning of a loving and enjoyable relationship with Tommie and Vicki that remains the same to this day. The only sad part was this was the vacation that Momma had dreamed of for many years. Several times while enjoying the vacation, I knew Momma was looking down on us smiling and happy we were blessed to have a dream come true vacation to the West Coast. Preparing to return to Cleveland, we thanked Tommie and Vicki from the bottom of our hearts for their superb, heartwarming hospitality. Syl and I discussed with Tommie and Vicki the possibilities of us moving to Pomona. Syl promised to check into his job transferring him to the regional transit in Pomona. Vicki asked that we consider letting the girls visit next summer. Before boarding the plane, we hugged and kissed Tommie and Vicki good-bye saying how much we appreciated and loved them.

The following summer Ivy and Sylvia did visit Tommie and Vicki. The girls loved and missed their favorite Aunt and Uncle. I was nervous with that being only their second flight and they would be flying without Syl and me, but one they took off, things went well. It was prior to take off that our girls had another family memorable event. They both were given snacks and juice boxes. Ivy and Sylvia explained that Sylvia had decided she did not want to share her juice boxes with Ivy during the flight. To prevent Ivy from taking her juice box, Sylvia emptied all her boxes of juice into her plastic cup with a pop on lid and placed the cup into her bag. When the flight attendant came to make sure they were okay, and their seat belts were secure, she placed their bags in the overhead bend. A few moments later a red sticky liquid was flowing from the overhead bends onto passengers and some wires had gotten wet. This caused the plane to be delayed for about an hour. To this day we laugh about Sylvia delaying the plane to prevent Ivy from drinking her juice. Once the girls arrived in Pomona, Tommie, and especially Vicki showed the them one of their most exciting summers, including taking them on several outings, which most of the time Vicki's other niece, Brandi would go with them. This not only allowed time for the girls to bond with their other family members, it gave Syl and I time to bond. Ivy and Sylvia continued visiting Linda Faye and Darrell, but they seemed to not enjoy those visits like they did with Tommie and Vicki. Ivy and Sylvia complained Linda Faye and Darrell were too strict. Sylvia began to tell me how Linda Faye made her sit at the table for hours for not eating all her food. Linda Faye also began only allowing the girls to watch Christian programs and listen to spiritual music. Syl and I decided this was a little too strict for our seven and ten-year-old girls. After that year we no longer let the girls visit Linda Faye and Darrell without us.

Late 1988, the owner of the home we rented sold the house without letting us know. We had spoken with the landlord a few times about purchasing the house but had decided it required too much work. The new owner gave Syl and me the option to remain tenants. To our dismay, Adrene was given a notice to vacate the premises in 30 days. Syl and I decided it was time to move into a more diverse neighborhood, closer to where the girls attended school. Wanting to move as soon as possible, we decided not to buy but keep leasing. We were blessed to find a lovely home in the suburb of Cleveland Hts. The house was only a few moments from the girls' school. Adrene and her family moved to the suburb of Warrensville Hts. Cha, Big Steve, and Little Steve decided to move with Adrene, instead of us. The move on the one hand was poignant because I had grown close and would miss the Taylors, Cha, Big and Little Steve. On the other hand, we were happy to move into a beautiful three-bedroom home in a nice community. The new home brought many years of joy. Syl and I were constantly growing spiritually while actively serving at Assembly. We were working hard to support our family, which included enabling us to afford the Christian and eventually parochial education for the girls. Keeping Ivy and Sylvia busy with church activities and in non-public schools we believed would made a difference in shielding them from some of the negative aspects of adolescence.

Holidays were incredibly special times for our family. Christmas always was the favorite time of year for our family as we celebrated the birth of Christ, and Syl and I watched our daughters impatiently await a visit from Santa Claus. We participated in Christmas programs at Assembly. This was also the time of year the Missionary Society would visit the nursing homes and foster homes. On Christmas mornings the girls would wake up early, especially when they were between the ages of five and twelve years old. They would rush down the stairs to the Christmas tree. It was exciting to see their happy faces and hear the joy in their little voices. Their cheerful laugher and excited screams as they opened their gifts to see many of the toys they dreamed about throughout the year was like sweet music to my ears. One Christmas instead of buying their toys I decided to take them to the toy store and let them select what they wanted for Christmas. It took hours for them to decide what they wanted. It was wonderful to see them happily go throughout the store. On Thanksgiving and Christmas, Pastor Judie, Linda Faye, and Darrell would still spend at least one of the holidays with us. On a few holidays we would celebrate with Auntie and her family.

In early 1990, Syl and I began discussing a family vacation for the summer. We decided to plan another trip to Disney World for the girls, because before when we went Ivy being only five years old could enjoy the parks a little bit and remembered a little bit about the trip; but Sylvia did not get to enjoy much and had little memory because she was only two years old. With Ivy and Sylvia being older, they would have more fun at the parks together with memories of the vacation. Mark, of course, in his late teens, was not interested in going with us this time. In my wanting to help others frame of mind, I asked Syl if we could invite, Kelly to go with us, he said, okay. Adrene was glad we invited Kelly to go with us. A week before we were to leave on our trip, Ivy broke her arm while playing at the home of one of her friends. When we were at the emergency room, Ivy was more concerned about if she would still be able to go to Disney World than her arm. The doctor assured Ivy she would be able to go and would have lots of fun. He gave us a prescription for a plastic covering to go over the cast to allow her to get in the pools. This put a big smile on Ivy's face. A week later we rented a luxury size car and headed to Orlando for our two-week trip. Syl drove to Atlanta where we stayed the night before heading to Orlando. On the long ride, we sang, played games and made up nicknames for each other: Ivy was the *one arm bandit* because of her broken arm; Kelly the *laughing hyena* since she laughed all the time; Sylvia, *two fingers*, because she sucked her fingers; Syl was *la di da di*, because he was constantly singing, *la di da di, I like to party*, which was from a song by Doug E. Fresh; and I was *Mrs. Weaver* because I had recently had my hairstylist give me my first full sew-in hair weave which turned out entirely too much hair on my head, like one of the 80s big hairstyles. I had made plans to stay at one of the newer Disney World resorts, the Grand Floridian, an elegant Victorian styled resort with beautiful rooms and great amenities. We spent four days at that park enjoying the rides, character shows, parades, exhibits, and food. It was another memorable vacation with lots of family bonding filled with fun, good times, laughter, and many beautiful memories.

A Sudden Unexpected Grievous Dark Storm. In November 1990 Mark stopped by to visit us. Now twenty years old it was typical for him to visit at any given time. The girls were always thrilled to see their big brother. The moment he entered the house he would bring joy and laughter with his humorous nature. Mark always affectionately played with Ivy and Sylvia. While bonding and being around his father brought them happiness. He would give me big hugs while fondly finding something to tease me about. The Marshall household was enlightened with joy and laughter each time Mark was in our presence. From the age thirteen to eighteen, he frequently visited and spent the night. He was baptized at Assembly and served on the junior usher board. Besides our dream vacation to Disney World, Mark went on other trips with us. We attended his graduation from middle school. He later attended Shaker Heights High School where he played football. One of my most memorable memories with Mark happened when, as he often did, was staying at our house for the weekend. I woke up that Saturday morning to the delicious aroma of food coming from the kitchen. I wondered if Syl was preparing breakfast for us, but to my surprise when I went into the kitchen, Mark was standing at the stove cooking. I sat down talking to him while he cooked bacon and sausage. After he finished cooking the meat he crumbled it into small pieces. I asked Mark why he had crumbled up the meat? He said, you will see, and he began to place eggs in the frying pan. That day when I bit into the omelet with the crumbled meats, cheese, green peppers, and onions it was lip-smacking delicious. Mark had made the most scrumptious omelet I have ever tasted. I would ask Mark each time he spent the night to cook me an omelet and tell him he must be watching his mother cooking to cook that good. Each time I have eaten an omelet, none have compared to the ones Mark cooked.

When he came to visit one day in November, I opened the door to Mark in his typical humorous manner. Walking in he immediately started saying things to make us all laugh. Closing the door, I saw a SUV parked by the house. I asked him was he driving the SUV. Mark replied, yes. This seemed odd to me because Mark was not working. We had a nice fun-filled family visit. Before he left we gave each other big hugs. Early in December, Syl received a call that Mark had been arrested. Mark had previously been arrested in June 1990, and that case was still pending. The first arrest caused Syl and me to be concerned some of his associates were involved in illegal activities. After the first arrest, Syl talked to Mark constantly about what he was planning to do with his life and staying. Syl insisted that Mark stay away from the fast money street life. The second arrest bond was set for $20,000. Syl discussed with me the money needed to bail Mark out. On the one hand thinking about the lifestyle Mark was living, I thought it might be best to not bail him out as quickly this time. Reasoning that if he stayed in jail a little longer this time, it could prevent him for further trouble with the law because of not wanting to stay in jail. On the other hand, I completely understood Syl and Barbara wanting to bail Mark out of jail, because knowing under the same circumstances, I would bail out Ivy or Sylvia. In January 1991 Mark and one of his friends came to visit us. It was our usual enjoyable visit. Before he left we hugged and kissed each other as usual.

On January 31st at approximately 2:00 a.m., I was awakened by the ringing of the phone. I quickly grabbed the phone trying to avoid waking Syl since he had to get up for work in a few hours. I quietly said, hello. It was Keiasha. She asked if Syl was home. I said, yes. Then came the absolute unbelievable words. With concern in her voice Keiasha told me, *someone called her saying they heard Mark had been shot*. Sitting up in the bed, I said, *what*. Keiasha again said, *someone told her that Mark and his friend had been shoot*. In disbelief, I turned to wake up Syl to tell him what Keiasha was saying. Syl turned to me still looking drowsy and said, *what is wrong*. Still in shock, I started telling him what Keiasha was saying. Syl asked me several times, *what are you saying*, as if he was in a daze trying to understand if what I was saying is what he was really hearing. He then told me to hand him the phone. I told Keiasha that I would call her back. Syl took the phone and began paging Mark. He did not receive a call back. He repeatedly paged Mark several more time. After no response from Mark, Syl called Barbara several times. Finally, Barbara answered the phone, and she told Syl that Mark and a friend riding with him had stopped at a gas station and they had been shot and killed. It was the beginning of another very grievous dark stormy time for our family.

Our family was overwhelmed with sorrow and disbelief as we tried to accept that Mark was gone. For me, it was inconceivable to envision the pain and grief Syl and Barbara were suffering with the abrupt and incomprehensible murder of their son. That morning and several days thereafter, accepting the death of Mark was made even more painful by each local news station steady airing coverage about the shooting. The local news channels were reporting Mark was getting out of an SUV when a car drove up. The newscasters were saying there were four men inside the car that opened fire upon Mark who was standing outside the SUV and his friend who was sitting in the passenger seat. They reported that both Mark and his friend had died on the scene from the more than twenty bullets that had hit their bodies, and that a city-wide police search for the shooters was underway. Besides from us repeatedly hearing the news reports, it was heartbreaking to constantly see the airings of the crime scene with the body of our beloved Mark laying on the cold ground covered with a white sheet and the body of his friend still in the front seat of the shot-up SUV. The television reporters and newspapers were also reporting that moments before the shooting these two friends from the neighborhood that had attended Shaker Heights High School together, unexpectedly bumped into each other at a restaurant. They left the restaurant together in the SUV. Less than a few blocks away, Mark simply stopped to get gas. Immediately he and his friend were ferociously gunned down. Listening to these news accounts over and over we all were crying, why Lord? Why?

The families were overcome with grief by the senseless deaths of Mark and his friend. I prayed to God for guidance and strength on how to comfort and support Syl and Barbara. I was also seeking the words to explain to Ivy and Sylvia that their brother had gone to be with the Lord and console them. They also needed to be shielded from the media stories and negative comments from people. Outwardly I focused all my attention on comforting my distraught husband and confused daughters. Privately within my mind I was in a state of déjà vu. Silently I wrestled with reliving the death of Herman. I was grieving the death of Mark, while also realizing and experiencing the pain and sorrow Herman's family suffered from his sudden death. Satan attacked my mind to the point I began to believe Mark had died because of my shooting Herman. Innocent people were again suffering because of my sins. The loss of Mark and the negative thoughts that my sins caused his death became another gloomy dark storm. Simultaneously the emotional scars from the death of Herman resurfaced. It became a spiritual battle to overcome the taunting from Satan. With much prayer I finally reached a point where I released and turned over to God my feels of guilt and shame. I can now say at that moment there was a flicker of light from God of peace and strengthening of my mind that gave me strong enough to endure this storm. With faith and strength from the Holy Spirit, I began to rebuke the negative thoughts from Satan. The glory of the Holy Spirit instilled in my soul strength to accept the reality. Yes, Herman and Mark both died under violent circumstances, and the emotional scars from shooting Herman would forever be with me. But, the Holy Spirit revealed to me that my guilt from causing the death of Herman, now the grief from the death of Mark it would enable me to empathize and bear witness to others the after-effects of violent deaths from both perspectives, as an assailant and as a family member of a victim. This let me see that what Satan had tried to destroy me mentally with feeling guilty about Herman's death and at fault for Mark's death, with the help of the Holy Spirit those feelings were eased, and my soul lifted to another level of spirituality.

Pending the release of Mark's body from the coroner, we began the arduous funeral arrangement. Syl decided to have Martin Funeral Home handle the funeral arrangements, who was also handling the arrangements Mark's friend. Syl let Mr. Martin know he wanted to see Mark's body before it was prepared for burial. A few days later, the funeral director called Syl to let him know Mark's body had arrived at the funeral home. I went with Syl to view the body. Syl looked at his only dearly beloved son as he looked at and pointed to some of the gunshot wounds that were visible. Standing by my husband with his eyes filled with disbelief and anguish, I wanted to take all his pain away. However, that was impossible, because I knew from the death of Herman and Momma how the heartache he was feeling was only the beginning of a perpetual void. I prayed for God to strengthen him while I personally consoled him. Over the next several days, the funeral arrangements were completed. After the death of Momma, thankfully Syl and I had the foresight to buy more life insurance which included a rider that insured our children until the age of twenty-one. The rider was ample enough to cover the funeral expenses and headstone for Mark. The service for Mark's friend was held a day before his service. The funeral for Mark was held at Assembly with Pastor Judie officiating. The service was filled with sorrow, tears, and anguish. Syl endeavored to be strong for Barbara and all the rest of us that were weeping in a grief-stricken state of mind. Many family members, friends, and co-workers attended. The next morning, we prepared to bury Mark. I held Ivy and Sylvia tightly to me as the car followed the hearse to the cemetery. The pain I felt as the step-mother to Mark was nothing compared to agony and emptiness I could see Syl and Barbara were suffering. Thoughts of how unthinkable it is that parents must bury their children, my heart ached not only for Syl and Barbara, but for Mrs. Ethel. That day I sensed the death of a child far exceeded any tribulations I had contend with. Especially when the death occurred by the acts of another human being. I understood more clearly that regardless of the circumstances of why a person causes the death of another person, the family of the victim would want justice for their loved one. As the Holy Spirit had instilled in me several days ago, I now would experience how Herman's family experienced the sorrow and sought justice for what I did because now I felt the same way. I too wanted legal justice for those that caused the death of Mark and his friend.

Over the next several weeks, Syl and I returned to work. The police had arrested and charged one minor and three adult men for the death of Mark and his friend. We later were told the shooters were not even looking for Mark that night. They were looking for his friend who was at home. The trial began a few months later. Syl and Barbara were mentally unable to attend the trial. This reiterated the spiritual intervention of the Holy Spirit to prepare me for the mental dual-track of attending the trial in the exact building under similar circumstances that I had once been tried and found guilty. Only God and I knew how difficult those days were for me. God alone gave me the strength to be strong for Syl in his time of need. Several family members, friends and I attended the trials each day. Two of the shooters were brothers, one was a minor. The older brother reached a plea agreement with the prosecutor to plead guilty to murder. In exchange for his plea he would be sentenced to a specified amount of time, and his minor brother would not be tried as an adult but as a minor. In addition, the older brother would testify against the other two men. The two other men were tried, found guilty and sentenced to lengthy terms in jail. Those were very dark days especially for Syl and Barbara. The death of their cherished son changed their lives forever. Life was never the same for either of them. Thankfully even with a broken heart, Syl stayed faithful to the word of God, and continued to take care of our family and diligent work. I prayed for Syl and Barbara to have the comfort and peace that only God could give them.

Chapter Eleven – When Blessed Be a Blessing to Others

There have been many people who have been a blessing to me throughout my life. Many of these people are recognized throughout this book. Thankfully God has enabled me to reciprocate blessings to others. As a child even before I knew about blessing others, Momma would say, *you cannot share or help everybody*. This came from me routinely inviting people to meals without letting Momma know. At other times Momma would be looking for some my clothing, shoes, or toys only to find out that I had given or lent them to one of my friends. I realized many years later how hard Momma had to work to provide us with our minimal necessities. Although not always happy with me giving away things, Momma was proud of how I did try to help others. Mrs. Mudd, an elderly neighbor was one of the ladies that would let Momma know how much she appreciated me helping her with yard work and going to the store. Throughout my teens and prior to the death of Herman, helping others continued to come naturally for me. Often when others needed help, encouragement or advice with life issues pertaining to family affairs, relationship problems, financial issues, emotional concerns, or employment matters, I would volunteer to assist them. Following the death of Herman and the abortion, feeling guilty for being a terrible sinner, I became passionate about helping others. I threw myself wholeheartedly into serving others to help ease my guilty conscious caused by my many self-inflicted storms. Then after being incarcerated and blessed with miraculous grace during and after my incarceration, I knew without a doubt I had to be a blessing to others. Once released from prison, I committed to God to be a blessing regardless of how difficult it might be.

Over the years each person God placed in my life to be a blessing was a two-way street. Whether they knew it or not the little bit of sunshine I might have brought to their lives was nothing compared to the brightness they brought to my life. God has used me to bless different people in various manners. Some for a brief period of time and others for a lifetime. For this reason, embedded in my heart is another one of my favorite scripture, *In everything I showed you [by example] that by working hard in this way you must help the weak and remember the words of the Lord Jesus, that He Himself said, 'It is more blessed [and brings greater joy] to give than to receive*, Acts 20:35 Amplified Bible. I thank God for everyone that blessed my life and those who allowed me to bless their lives.

Unforeseen Awesome Blessings to and from Desmond Howard. In November 1990, while watching a football game between the University of Michigan and Ohio State, I noticed Desmond, Hattie's son, playing. When the camera focused on him he said, *hi, Mom*. I called Hattie to let her know Syl and I were watching the game. We extended her our congratulations to her and the family. Then not having talked to each other for months, we briefly caught up with what was happening in our lives. I later spoke with JD, Desmond's father. Unfortunately, JD and Hattie had divorced years ago. After that night periodically, I would talk to Hattie and JD. When the Michigan 1991 football season began, JD invited me to attend a game with him and Hattie. I gladly accepted. Even though I had been to a few Cleveland Browns football games and loved watching the Browns on television, I was not prepared for a Michigan college game. The football game played at Michigan Stadium, known as *The Big House*, in Ann Arbor was like nothing I had ever seen. The college students, alumni and fans made the *Go Blue* atmosphere mesmerizing. It was absolutely incredible to see over 100,000 fans in *the Big House* cheering in the huge stadium while the awesome band played. Following the game Desmond welcomed me with his adorable smile and a hug. Before heading back to Cleveland, we had dinner where we discussed how good Desmond had played. After the first game, I was regularly invited to the games. Desmond was playing superb. Sports newscasters began talking about Desmond potentially being considered for the Heisman Trophy and drafted into the NFL. Soon family members and friends were beginning to get excited about and discussed the possibility of Desmond winning the Heisman trophy and being drafted. Each week his football team, coaches, together with the student body, alum, media, and football scouts were taking notice of his excellent playing abilities. Before long the media were seriously reporting the possibility of Desmond winning the Heisman trophy and being drafted in the first round of the NFL. After each game his life was quickly changing as he dazzled the college football world with outstanding plays. Michigan was winning with Desmond being an integral part of the team. Each week he was being noticed more by the media and scouts with his remarkable footballs skills, phenomenal million-dollar smile, well-mannered personality, and professional mannerism. With more attention Desmond, JD, and Hattie included me in certain discussions concerning his potential future in the NFL. I answered questions to the best of my ability. Once it became apparent I could not address all the issues they were confronting, I suggested they speak with one of the attorneys at the law firm. I decided to talk to Dick, primarily because I knew he was an alum of the University of Michigan law school. I asked Dick if he could talk to the Howards concerning preparing Desmond for his potential NFL future. Dick agreed to talk to them. Once Dick talked to the Howards, Dick agreed to help the Howard family for me on a *pro bono* basis. With Desmond each week playing more spectacularly, momentum for him to win the Heisman increased. Then at the rival game between Ohio State and Michigan at *the Big House*, not only the 100,000 plus fans but the media world was given an unexpected surprise when Desmond had spectacularly punt return into the end zone for a touchdown. Once he entered the end zone, Desmond did a pose of the Heisman pose. The crowd went crazy. After the game, Desmond asked us did we see the pose. We excitedly said, yes. Within hours, the media nationwide was discussing the pose, and it was being featured in many newspapers and magazines. This astronomically propelled Desmond into the spotlight. Sportscasters were discussing more on the probability of Desmond winning the Heisman Trophy. To add even more anticipation, days before the Heisman trophy winner was to be announced, JD and Hattie were featured on a nationally televised news program. They talked about Desmond's childhood and their lives as his parents. While Desmond prepared to attend the announcement of the Heiman trophy winner, he invited me to attend the celebration to be held in New York City. I felt it an honor and was thankful for the invitation. Even though Syl was unable to attend, he was supportive of my working with the Howards and glad I was invited to attend the celebration.

Usually family members of the Heiman trophy candidates could attend the announcement of the winner held at the Athletic Club in New York. That year due to an incident during the prior year's ceremony, the family members were not allowed to attend the announcement of the winner. Dick, as the lawyer for Desmond, could attend. In Cleveland we prepared to watch the results on television. I had sweat shirts made for the immediate family with Desmond's name, the Heisman trophy pose and the respective relationship to Desmond. The night of the announcement, Hattie and her husband Floyd had invited people to their house to watch the broadcast. Anxiously Hattie, JD, Jonathan, Chad, Jermaine, Floyd, Syl, Ivy, Sylvia, and I, and some of Hattie's family members and family friends, awaited the announcement. A local television news reporter was also at the house to simulcast live the reaction of Hattie and JD that would be televised nationwide if Desmond was the winner. As O.J. Simpson walked to the podium to make the announcement, we anxiously awaited, we heard O.J. Simpson say, *the 1991 Heisman trophy winner is Desmond Howard*. Everyone in the house was shouting, *yeah* and hi-fiving each other. It was amazing. I was so happy for the Howard family. Following the announcement of the winner, the speech from Desmond, together with the simulcast of the reaction from Hattie and JD was filled with their genuine love and gratitude to each other. It was an incredibly special time for me to be a part of this huge one in a million achievement of Desmond. We flew to New York the next day. From the moment we arrived in New York, we received celebrity treatment. Although I had visited New York on several occasions, it was never for such a prestigious event. To add to the excitement of the event it was great to see the city merrily decorated in celebration of Christmas and the other holiday traditions. We stayed at the Downtown Athletic Club. The evening we arrived, and for the next several days the Howard family, Desmond's mentor, a few close friends, Dick, his son, and I attended the Heisman formal dinner celebrations and various other events. Beside the events it was great to see Desmond appear on several television shows. One of the favorite photos that I took was of Desmond seating on the set of the *Today* show during his interview with Bryant Gumbel. I expressed my sincere appreciation to Desmond, Hattie, and JD for letting me share in this extra special occasion. More importantly, I praised God for His blessing me to be a part of this phenomenal once in a lifetime event. On the plane ride home thoughts of how I never could have imagined on June 13, 1980 while sitting in the police car looking out the window at Hattie holding Ivy that I would be a part of this wonderful celebration with her.

Prior to and after the Heisman celebration Desmond received several other awards. With winning the Heisman and other prestigious awards Desmond had totally captivated the media world, and each day his popularity and fan base grew. He then received his first football card sports deal. This would require more legal work than the *pro bono* services Dick was rendering. Dick met with Desmond, Hattie, and JD to discuss the retention of the firm. The firm would represent Desmond in the negotiation of the pending sports card deal, assist him with the potential retention of his agents, financial advisors, and accountants, and advise him as needed on other legal matters. Desmond agreed to the retention of the firm.

Days after returning from the Heisman celebration, everyone begin to prepare to attend the Rose Bowl in Pasadena, California. Hattie, Floyd, JD, Chad, Jermaine, Syl, the girls and I would fly to Los Angeles for the game. Syl had spoken with Tommie and Vicki to see if our family, as well as if Hattie and Floyd could stay at their home. Tommie and Vicki said, of course. They later let us know Syl, the girls and I would stay at their home, while Hattie and Floyd would stay with Mr. and Mrs. Williams, the parents of Vicki. Desmond was taking care of the plans where JD, Jonathan, Chad, and Jermaine would stay. On Christmas Day, Hattie, JD, Chad, and Jermaine joined us for dinner. A few days later we flew to Los Angeles. I had asked Desmond if he could obtain extra tickets to the game for Tommie, Vicki, and her brother, which he graciously did. Before the game most of us, including our children, went to watch the beautiful Rose Bowl Parade. It was another fun-filled time for us. After the parade we went to the game. Ivy and Sylvia stayed with Vicki's sister and Brandi. Even though the Huskies beat Michigan, it was a very memorable event.

In late January 1992, Desmond introduced me to his friend Angie who was experiencing some family problems. He asked me to speak with Angie to see if I could give her some helpful suggestions for her situation. Over the next several weeks, it became apparent Angie and her young daughter Brittany where encountering housing problems. My helping nature kicked into gear. With the approval of Syl, we opened our home up for Angie and Brittany to stay with us. It was a joy having Brittany a bubbly adorable six-year-old in our home, who began to attend Assembly with us and sang in the youth choir. Although Angie was nine years older than Ivy, they became good friends. In about six months Angie and Brittany moved in back in with Angie's mother. Angie and Brittany stayed in contact with us for a few years. Nowadays Angie, Brittany, Ivy and Sylvia sometime communicate via social media.

After the Rose Bowl, Desmond focused his attention on finishing his classes in preparation for graduation, prepared for the NFL scouting combine, and contended to matters related to preparation to enter the NFL draft as one of the top picks. Dick and I worked diligently to assure that Desmond had an efficient, constructive, economically feasible and successful transition into his NFL profession. Desmond, Hattie, JD, Dick, and I conducted interviews at the firm with various sports agents. One of the sports agents invited Hattie and I to an event in Hollywood. We both accepted. Although a short two-day trip it was fantastic to stay in Hollywood and attend the sports event. After several interviews and follow-up meetings a decision was reached. We all agreed Desmond would have two agents: Leigh Steinberg for football contract matters, and David Falk for matters relating to marketing. Other critical issues were decided, including where his state of residency would be, it was agreed to be Florida; setting up trust accounts, obtaining Lloyd's of London insurance policy and other business matters. Interviews were held with potential investment advisors and accountants. It was agreed to retain Glenmede as investment bankers and Manohar L. Daga, CPA as the accountant.

Desmond had decided instead of attending the draft in New York, he would stay in Cleveland to be with family members and friends. He decided to have a draft party that Hattie and I planned. The two-day event was organized as a fundraiser with the proceeds to benefit Villa Angela St. Joseph (VASJ), formerly known as St. Joseph High School, where Desmond and Jermaine graduated from. Later Ivy and Sylvia would attend and graduate from VASJ. The event was held at a local downtown restaurant. On April 26, 1992, Desmond was the first round fourth draft pick by the Redskins. Immediately after the draft, Desmond went to Washington for his initial meeting with the Redskins coaches and management. When I was shown a picture of him in a newspapers article arriving at the Redskins football facility, I was happy to see him wearing the African styled Kufi cap I had given him. Later, it was troubling that he received hate mail regarding the cap. Those letters corroborated the fact racism and discrimination towards people of color are all encompassing. No matter of your accomplishments, economic status, or educational background prejudice sadly is still a part of our society. Knowing how to have the will-power to not allow the negative views of hateful people affect your journey in life is what I expressed not only to Desmond, but to my daughters and anyone confronted with bigotry.

A few weeks later Desmond proudly graduated. It was an accomplishment he achieved in four years instead of the typical five years of many athletics. Although I did not attend the ceremony, Desmond made a profound statement that received media attention. On his gown he wrote the words, *a scar for life*, in response to the not guilty verdict in the case against the police officers that had beaten Rodney King. After Desmond's graduated, I continued to be an essential part of his career and personal life. I worked with Dick on many legal issues. Assisted Hattie and JD on purchasing residential properties for Desmond in Reston, Virginia and Boca Raton, Florida. Later in the summer, Desmond was invited to attend a sports award ceremony in Las Vegas. He invited Syl and me to attend with Hattie, JD, Jonathan, Chad, and Jermaine. This was another incredible event that was attended by several celebrities. We were able to take pictures with a few of the celebrities. My most memorable are pictures with Danny Glover and Ella Joyce. When the NFL 1992 season began, I attended several games with the Howard family. Desmond gave me tickets to a few games. I took Syl to one and Deb Nunn to another. In 1993, Syl, the girls, and I while visiting Hersey Park, attended a few days of Desmond's summer training camp in Carlisle, Pennsylvania.

Assisting Desmond with his initial years of his career were a special time in my life. It gave me the opportunity to share in the superstar status of his NFL career. I worked with Desmond for several years with sincere devotion. Each time Desmond requested me to aid him in a matter, I strived to successful complete each matter to the best of my ability. In 1995, Desmond had certain requests that were questionable to me. At that time, I had to make a morally correct decision. This was especially true due to my previous shattering dark storms. Weighing the potential adverse consequences if I agreed to the request, it was necessary to make the correct decision. I had to say, no. Desmond understood and respected my decision. We remained cordial, then slowly our communication became less and less. Invitations to games and events stopped. Telephone numbers changed without receiving new numbers. Desmond stayed a client of the firm with Dick as his primary attorney and their relationship grew. Desmond later became close with David, Dick's son. Sadly in 2015, Dick died, and Cha went with me to the memorial service, which was the last time I saw Desmond. Throughout the years and even to this day, I still stay in touch with Hattie, Chad, and JD.

I will always cherish the close times with Desmond. It was a pleasure to have the opportunities to be a part of the beginning of his career. Sharing in the once in a lifetime extraordinary events were incredible. Working very diligently to get his career on the most positive path, I honestly must say at times I now feel like I was *kicked to the curb*. It emotionally stings to know Desmond and Dick, until his passing, and others I introduced Desmond to maintained close contact over the years. But, despite the regret of how our relationship fizzled, to know I did what was spiritually correct and have a clear conscious outweighs the disappointments. More importantly I thank

God in this instance I made the correct decision even at the cost of losing someone I cherished. The flicker of light was by the grace of God, I was growing stronger. *Yet shall the righteous (those upright and in right standing with God) hold to their ways, and he who has clean hands shall grow stronger and stronger*, Job 17:9 (AMPC).

Supporting Adrene Taylor in Her Time of Need. Around 1993, Adrene, her sons, Rodney, Donald and Cedric, and younger daughter, Kelly moved across the street from us. A few months later Mama Lula moved in with Adrene. It was nice to have Adrene again living close to us. In 1996 Kelly gave birth to her daughter, Dajsha. Adrene would babysit Dajsha while Kelly attended high school. In March 1997, while I was at work Syl called to let me know Adrene had passed out, was unconscious and the ambulance had rushed her to the emergency room. I told Syl that I would met him at the hospital Upon my arrival at the hospital, Syl said she had a massive stroke and was unconscious. Even though she was unresponsive the medical staff asked that we still communicate and caress her. Not wanting to leave her alone we altered staying with her overnight. Two days later the doctors stated she had a fifty percent chance to survive and it was uncertain how the stroke would affect her physically and mentally. The hospital case workers explained that immediate action was required to obtain medical coverage for Adrene. She further let us know once Adrene reached a certain level of stability, she would have to be discharged from the hospital and depending on her condition, she would either have to be admit to a long-term rehabilitation facility or return home and receive daily care from an in-home health care provider. After receiving this information from the hospital social worker, with me being aware Adrene was indigent with no income or health insurance and in dire need of medical care, I knew time was of the essence to get some type of medical aid from the government to cover the mounting medical cost Adrene was and would be incurring. Adrene had no insurance because before Bro died, he had always taken care of the financial needs of her and their family, while Adrene always had been a homemaker who never worked to earn her own social security benefits. Although Adrene could receive widow's benefits under Bro's social security benefits, she had not yet reached the age requirement. The only way she could receive the benefits at her current age, she would have to be disabled. Adrene had discussed with me how hard it was to make it financially, and she hoped she could make it a few more years when she would reach the age requirement to receive the widow's benefits. I would often help her financially when she struggled to live on only the money she received for living expenses from Mama Lula and her adult sons. With Adrene facing this crisis, it propelled me into urgent help mode. I thought back to the time Ivy and I walked into Assembly that chilly day in November 1980. Adrene was the first person to befriend us with kindness and became a loving vital part of my life. Immediately I began working with Doris Faye, her oldest daughter, to get benefits for Adrene. First, I went to the social security office to apply for disability benefits for her as the widow of Bro. After the application was submitted to Social Security, the representative explained due to the unpredictable rate for full recovery of a person who has a stroke, the application would not be considered for six months. The representative instructed me to call back in six months to report the progress of Adrene's recovery. He let me know at that time her application would be reviewed, and a final decision made. Next, I applied for Medicaid benefits through the Cuyahoga County Department of Employment and Family Services. She was approved for temporary Medicaid benefits pending further review of her case. The application was later approved for full benefits for a year with instruction to reapply each year, and I was named her authorized representative. Approval of the Medicaid was truly an answer to many prayers. Without either Medicare or Medicaid she would not be considered for admission into a rehabilitation facility.

After two weeks, the hospital informed us Adrene would be released in 72 hours. All her loved ones were praying for her recovery. Thankfully she had made enough progress to the point she could be discharged. However, even with the improvements Adrene was making the medical staff discharge instructions specified she needed intensive round the clock rehabilitation care and treatment. The social worker for the hospital let us know a bed at a rehabilitation facility had to be secured within three days. She let us know that she was sending faxes to each rehabilitation facility in the greater Cleveland area to request a bed for Adrene. Unfortunately, without private insurance, only lower tier facilities would consider accepting Adrene. Doris Faye and I visited several of the rehabilitation facilities that would accept Adrene in time for discharge deadline. Each of those facilities did not seem well kept and appeared to supply give services for a diverse group of residents from the elderly, substance abusers, mental handicapped, dementia, and rehabilitation patients. Each facility had little to no designated rehabilitation staff and equipment. The thought of her staying in any of those facilities was disheartening. We expressed our concerns and dismay to the social worker. She asked if we would consider a Catholic facility that she personally knew had an excellent rehabilitation program. The only downside was it was located on the other side of town. We said, of course, please let us know when we can take a tour. She faxed Adrene's information to the facility and arranged for us to visit. The next day Doris Faye and I visited the facility. It was much better than the other facilities. I called the social workers and asked her to please send the admission application to the St. Augustine Nursing Facility. She told me she would. The next day the social worker called to let me know the nursing home had accepted the application for admission. We praised God for answering prayers.

Adrene was transferred to St. Augustine with little expectation from the medical professionals of her ever talking or walking. Six months later her condition had not improved. I contacted social security regarding her pending application and was instructed to submit updated information on the medical condition. Within a few weeks I received a letter stating she was approved for social security disability. Miraculously within weeks of receiving the approval letter from social security, Adrene's health began to slowly improve. Initially she began to regain her memory, followed by muttering a few words. Although impeded, with each passing day we understood more of what she was trying to say. Gradually she gained limited use of her hands and legs. Adrene had always received a tremendous amount of support from family members, friends, and members of Assembly. The physical and spiritual support encouraged her to work harder to improve her memory, speech, and mobility. As her condition improved, the case workers for the rehabilitation center informed us Adrene could soon be discharged. Doris Faye and I began to make plans for her discharge. After discussions, we determined it would be best for Adrene to live with Doris Faye and her family. The social workers for St. Augustine began working to secure the equipment and supplies needed for Adrene to be discharged. I worked with her Medicaid social worker to obtain the necessary daily in-home personal health care services. It was agreed that Doris Faye would receive Adrene's social security benefits check to cover at least some of her living expenses.

Once the equipment, supplies and home heath aid providers were in place, Adrene was discharged from St. Augustine to Doris Faye's house. Things went well for a while, but after a few months the living arrangements for Adrene staying with Doris Faye became perplex. Although Adrene's memory, speech and mobility was still impeded, she was slowly improving, so I did not want her to have to return to the nursing home. Pondering the few options, I discussed with Syl the options of Adrene moving in with someone else or into her own place. The only practical choice was her own place. I found an apartment for Adrene to lease where Adrene could live with enough room for Kelly and Dajsha who had been living with Doris Faye after Adrene became sick. I was able to get everything in place for Adrene the only problem was financial constraints. I talked to Syl about the financial shortage, and he agreed we would subsidize Adrene income to help cover her living expenses. I completed the paperwork. The management had informed me the apartment would have to be in my name because of Adrene's credit score, and Adrene would be listed as the co-tenant. Within the next few days, Adrene moved into a two-bedroom apartment not too far from our home. Adrene was overjoyed with thanksgiving to be in her own apartment with her baby daughter and granddaughter. Before long she was able to attend church and go on short outings. Six months later Kelly and Dajsha moved into their own place. Adrene lived alone for a brief time before her daughter, Terri and her children, Terrell and Natasha moved in for a few months. After two years of subsidizing the living expenses for Adrene it was becoming too expensive for our budget. When it was time to sign the next year lease, I asked her son, Donald to move in with her to help with the rent. He said, yes. During that lease period we paid a smaller amount for her living expenses. Two years later with Adrene's living expenses increasing each year it became too much financially for us. Syl and I discussed the alternative of living with another family member. The only person that could accommodate her was Uncle Willard who lived alone in a three-bedroom home. Syl and I explained our circumstances with Uncle Willard, in particular how it was now a financial strain for us to subsidize her income. We asked him if Adrene could move in with him. She would pay him rent from her social security benefits. Initially Uncle Willard was hesitant to give up the independence of living alone. Finally, he agreed. Adrene was doing much better, but still required daily assistance from a care giver. Having strangers come into his house to care for Adrene became an issue for Uncle Willard. After several months, Uncle Willard and Adrene living together had become challenging for both of them. Several family members and I started to discuss alternative living arrangements. In January 2001, Cha called me saying she had located a senior citizens apartment where the rent was based on income. We immediately submitted the rental application to the Musician Towers leasing office. Within days Adrene was approved for subsidized rent at the apartment. Once Adrene moved into the apartment with the lower rent payment based on her income she quickly became financially self-supporting. Adrene was very thankful for all her many blessings. Her health had improved to the point she: had regained most of her memory; was able to get around with the aid of a walker or wheelchair; talked with only a slight impairment; and was able to live alone in her own adorable apartment. Her prayers, and those of many others, had been answered.

To this day, I assure that Adrene is financially sound and medically stable. Sadly in 2015, a few of her children had tried to viciously undermine the aid Syl and I have given to Adrene to make her life comfortable. Praise be to God, Adrene always speaks the truth to those that spread lies against us. More importantly we and others know from the beginning of her health and financial situation who was there to make sure she was cared for in the best way possible. Above all God alone knew how Adrene blessed my life when I first joined

Assembly and while I was incarcerated. Years later I was merely expressing my appreciation for her acts of kindness and assistance to me.

Helping Michael and Valerie in a Time of Crisis. In July 2006, my cousin, Jay called me from North Carolina to let me know Auntie had passed. Even though Auntie and I had not spoken in several years it grieved me to hear of her passing. I had no idea she had been sick. Letting Jay know how sorry I was to hear about Auntie, I asked how Michael, David and Valerie were doing. As far as she knew everyone was okay. David was handling the arrangments. I asked if she and other family members were coming to Cleveland. She was not sure yet if she would be attending, but was sure her mother, my favorite Aunt Sue and Aunt Lib would be coming. I asked if she knew David's number, she said yes, and gave to me. We promised to talk to each other in a few days.

Hanging up the phone my mind went to thoughts and memories of Auntie. I thought about her visit to me while I was incarcerated. Then when I came home she had me over for dinner and had cooked my favorite food and I met Karen's baby girl, Valerie. Over the years we gathered for several Thanksgiving or Christmas holidays and birthday celebrations, which a few times Linda Faye and Darrell had come to celebrate with us. Very unexpectedly Karen passed the next year at the age of 20. Auntie then was appointed the guardian of Valerie. After the death of Karen, Auntie and I talked a few times a year. By 1996, we very seldom spoke unless out-of-town family members were visiting Cleveland. By 1999, we rarely spoke. I was unsure if this was due to a situation between Linda Faye and me that had occurred in 1997.

The next day after talking to Jay, I called David to extend my sympathy. I asked him if I could bring food to the house. He said of course. Upon arriving at the house, David greeted me outside. We hugged each other. We talked about memories of Auntie. He told me how she was ill over the past few years requiring her to be admitted into the nursing home. We updated each other on what was going on in our lives. He informed me that he and Michael, who is severely mentally disabled, were living in the house, but Valerie, who is mildly mentally disabled, had developed behavioral problems and was living at a nursing home. That day I did not see Michael or go inside the house, but the visit with David went well. Over the next few days, I spoke with Jay several more times and called Aunts Sue and Lib. I let them know anyone coming to Cleveland could stay with me. A few days later Aunts Sue and Lib and cousins, Sherry and Vanessa drove to Cleveland from North Carolina for the funeral. Aunt Sue stayed with me, which was a joy for me. My second cousin, Francis flew in the day before the funeral. The day of the funeral, Aunt Sue and I picked up Cousin Francis from her hotel. It was good to meet Cousin Francis as Momma often talked about and visited her when visiting Aunt Sue.

The home going service for Auntie was held at her church. It was good to meet the pastor and other members that had been in the life of Auntie over the past few years. At the close of the service I met Mr. and Mrs. Castle, the god-parents of Valerie. Mrs. Castle informed me she frequently talked to and sometimes visited Valerie at the nursing home. We exchanged phone numbers. I let her know my intentions to check on Valerie. The church had arranged for a nice repast for the family. Following the repast Aunt Lib asked David if she could have a few pictures of Auntie. David agreed. We all went to the house, but Aunt Lib was the only one that went into the house. After dropping Cousin Francis at her hotel, Aunt Sue wanted to get some rest. Later that evening I asked Aunt Sue if she wanted to go to the hotel to spend time with Aunt Lib and her nieces, she said no, but for me to go. The rest of the evening I spent time with Aunt Lib and my cousins. They were staying at the Holiday Day Inn which had a nice adjacent night club. I had a blast with my family that evening. Aunt Lib was a lot of fun. The next morning Aunt Lib asked me to take them sightseeing before they left. She wanted to see the old neighborhoods where we lived when she would visit us, downtown Cleveland, and Edgewater Park where she could see Lake Erie. Aunt Lib enjoyed seeing the places she remembered visiting with my Momma and Auntie. Although it was a sad occasion with the death of Auntie, it was good being with my aunts and cousins. As we kissed, hugged, and said our goodbyes, we promised to stay in touch.

 A few days after the funeral, David's ex-wife, Michelle called to inform me he had been arrested. She told me Michael was alone in the house with no one to care for him. Knowing Michael was incapable of caring for himself, without a doubt I would have to make sure he at least had meals until David was released. The only problem was Auntie and David always had big dogs. From childhood I was very afraid of dogs. I called Michelle to see if she and her children David, Jr., Antoinette, and Christopher would assist me with Michael by taking food inside the house. Michelle said, of course. That day and several days thereafter I picked up David Jr. to take food inside the house to Michael. I introduced myself to several of the neighbors who knew Michael was mentally handicapped. I asked them to please keep a watch on Michael until David returned and gave them my phone number if they needed to contact me. Within a few days one of the neighbors called to let me know Michael was outside naked. I went to get David Jr. to help me get Michael back into the house. The neighbor called within a couple more days saying the dogs were running wild outside. Once more I picked up David Jr., to get the dogs back in the house. At that point I still had not gone into the house. A few days later I went to visit David at the jail to determine when he would be released and to discuss the issues I was facing with Michael and the dogs. David was unsure when he would be released. He suggested I contact the landlord to see if he could help me with the dogs and the house. Upon contacting the landlord, he worked with me to have the dogs removed by the city dog pound. Finally, I was able to enter the home with the landlord. My heart dropped when I went into the house, it was deplorable. Michael was laying on the couch in horrible physical condition. Naked, dirty and his legs swollen with cuts and bruises he was unable to get off the couch. He weakly said, *hi Debbie*. After all these years, Michael immediately recognized me. I was glad to see Michael, but in shock by his physical appearance. The horrible condition of the house made me sick. I could not understand why David Jr. did not tell me what was taking place with Michael. Immediately I called 911 to have Michael taken to the hospital. Like me the paramedics were surprised and concerned about his condition. Once examined at the emergency room, Michael was diagnosed with malnutrition, dehydration, and severe inflammation to his feet and legs. Initially the medical staff did not know what the particles were all over his legs. Further evaluation revealed the skin of his legs were embedded with dog hair. The doctor told me Michael had to be admitted for a substantial amount of medical care. The medical, physical, and mental condition of Michael was of such concern to the medical staff that social services was notified. The social service representative wanted to know why Michael was in such terrible physical condition. I explained to her in detail the circumstances of how I recently became involved in the life of my cousin. Discussing Michael with the representative without a second thought my help mode was activated when I told her my intention to take responsible for his future well-being. Within the next few days I was able to visit Valerie at the nursing home. Prior to the discharge of Michael, I arranged for him to be admitted to the same nursing home as Valerie. I visited Michael and Valerie several times a week. On occasion Michelle and her children would visit. Each time I visited Michael and Valerie consciously I knew if at all possible my cousins could not be confined in a nursing home. This started my journey of caring for Michael and Valerie.

My first goal was to obtain guardianship of Valerie and Michael. Second, I would then attempt to get Valerie and Michael back into their home. The final goal was to provide the best possible stable life for them. To reach these goals, initially I contacted social security to become their representative payee. Until they were discharged their combined benefits of $1,400 were payable to the nursing home. Then I contacted the landlord for help to make their house livable. The house required an extreme deep cleaning. New carpet and tile would have to be installed. Each room required painting. New or used appliances, furniture and household items would have to be purchased. Knowing this was a huge undertaking that would be costly, financially I would do all I could but would need financial help. I had kept Jay updated on what was happening with our cousins. After explaining the financial needs for Valerie and Michael, she provided me with phone numbers and e-mail addresses for some of our family members that might help. I called, texted, or emailed the family members seeking donations of items or financial assistance to help with revamping the house. Unfortunately, no one could assist. Not to be deterred from not receiving support, I sought assistance from social service agents for appliances, furniture, and other household products. Whatever I could not obtain through the social service agents, I purchased personally. The last necessity for Valerie and Michael to come home was a person who would reside with and take care of them. The caregiver would be provided free room and board, meals, and other necessities. The downside was I would not be able to pay any monetary compensation to the person because the expenses exceeded their social security benefits. This meant I would have to pay the difference, which was a considerable increase to my personal budget, therefore, leaving nothing at this time available for compensation. To locate a caregiver, I sent out *help* texts and emails to family members and friends requesting the referral of anyone needing a place to reside with free board and all essential while caring for Michael and Valerie. A member of Lee-Seville church, Florine, recommended her niece, Angela. Without a doubt Angela was truly a flicker of light from God for my cousins and me. Not only did we need her, she needed help as well. She agreed to care for Michael and Valerie if her four children could live at the home. I gladly agreed. Finally, Michael and Valerie were discharged and happily returned to their newly refurbished home.

For about five days things were going great. Suddenly things went awry. Valerie started to misbehave by refusing to respect and obey Angela and threatening to harm herself and others. One evening she ran out the house and Angela had to chase after her down the street. Angela would call me to talk with Valerie. Even after I talked to her she would be defiant and even lie that she was not doing anything wrong. Merely ten days after moving back into the house, Valerie had run out the house three times. Then the fourth time Valerie ran, when Angela tried to get her back into the house, Valerie was more rebellious than ever. She cussed at and tried to hit Angela while running down the street. When Angela called me, I said, let her go. I asked Angela to call the police to let them know she was mentally handicapped and needed medical attention. The police found Valerie and took her to the emergency room. After examining her the doctor admitted Valerie to the mental health unit. Days later she was discharged to the nursing home. Once Valerie was admitted to the nursing home her social security benefits would be paid directly to the nursing home. Without Valerie's financial part towards the expenses I could not keep the house. This meant I needed to make alternative housing arrangments for Michael and Angela. I spoke to the landlord explaining my dilemma, he understood saying they could move at my convenience.

Angela spoke with her Aunt Florine, regarding renting the extra area on their second floor. Florine agreed to let them rent the upper area of her home. Shortly after they moved, I happened to be discussing my situation with another church member. She suggested I contact the Cuyahoga Board of Mental Disabilities (CBMD) regarding my situation with Michael. Yet again a flicker of light from God of an overflowing goodness. *And the Lord said, "I will cause all my goodness to pass in front of you, and I will proclaim my name, the Lord, in your presence. I will have mercy on whom I will have mercy, and I will have compassion on whom I will have compassion*, Exodus 33:19 (NIV). Jesus Christ my Lord and Savior came to the rescue. Upon contacting the CBMD, I was informed that Michael and Valerie were clients. Their case workers immediately began working with me to update their files. Within weeks I was informed that Angela would be compensated for providing services to Michael after the required paperwork and training was completed. Angela successfully completed all the requirements to become a compensated permanent caregiver to Michael. To this day Angela remains the caregiver for Michael. Without Angela and the various agencies, Michael would be permanently confined to a nursing home where he would not receive the love and care he receives from Angela and her family. I am so very thankful for Angela, I call her our angel from God. She in turn calls us her angels.

It was a great peace of mind to know that Michael was in a safe and loving home. Now I needed to focus on the problems with Valerie. Over the next several years, she became more uncontrollable. I had to have her placed in several group homes because each time I believed she would behave in one home, she would misbehave and have to be placed in another one. Her stays in these group homes were always short lived due to Valerie was constantly making threats to commit suicide, intimidating roommates, and employees, threatening to harm her roommates or herself. She would even runaway where several times she began to talk to a strange man. After a few hours of talking to the man, she would falsely accuse them of sexual assault. A few times when she ran away, I had to seek help from the police to find Valerie. Some family members and friends thought I should simply make her a ward of the State. They did not understand the silent battle within that I could not turn her over to the State. It was because of always remembering how God had never given up on me. This made it impossible for me not to continue helping Valerie. CBMD persistently worked with me to locate a suitable group home for Valerie. With much prayer and patience, in 2014, the CBMD located another group home for Valerie. The group home was in a rural area outside of Youngstown, Ohio which is 75 miles from Cleveland. Praise God to this day Valerie successfully resides in the group home and has had very few minor incidents. Valerie and I talk on the phone four to five times a week. We visit with each other as often as possible. During our visits we go to her favorite restaurant and buy a baby doll to add to her collection of baby dolls. Often when we talk Valerie laughs while saying remember when I use to run-away all the time. I said, *yes, I am glad you stopped running away*. She then says, *there is no use of me running away now because there are only hillbillies and coyotes out here in the country*. Laughing I say, *you are right*. I am very thankful to have Valerie with an excellent group home where she receives support, encouragement, and a structured lifestyle. It is a blessing to have peace knowing Michael and Valerie are safe, healthy, and happy.

With regards to David, he was sentenced in December 2007, and served his time and was released in 2011. Upon his release, David did not try to see Michael or Valerie, but he did ask me for financial help which I provided. His daughter, Antoinette even asked me to co-sign for a student loan for funds she needed to return to college. Wanting to help her improve her life, I said, yes. A year later Antoinette stopped attending college, and the loan went into repayment status. With several failed attempts to contact Antoinette, I had to begin to repay the loan to protect my credit score. In November 2016, while visiting Aunt Lib and Jay in North Carolina, Aunt Lib asked about David, Michael, and Valerie. I let her know Michael and Valerie were doing great, but I had not talked to David in years. I told Aunt Lib that I would try calling David. His son, David Jr. answered the phone. I said, hello and asked how he was doing. He said, good. Then I asked him if his father was home, he said, yes. Then I heard him calling out, dad phone, followed by him telling David, Sr. it was Aunt Lib, Jay and Debbie calling. I could hear David, Sr. in the background saying, *who died*. I said to David Jr. to let his father know *Aunt Lib and Jay wanted to say hello*. David, Sr. refused to answer the phone. I told David, Jr., okay and we said our goodbyes. To this day I have not heard from David, Sr., or his children. This was a reminder of the statement *you cannot save everyone*.

Chapter Twelve – Unexpected Healing and Adversity

Over the years after my release from prison, there were frequent periods I privately battled with the emotional scars from my stormy life. Knowing I must keep going on for my girls I hid behind a facade of living a great life, hiding my personal emotions deep within. I had to depend on my spiritual faith to keep me focused that one day the light from the bright sunshine would outweigh the darkness of my stormy life. Even with my personal and emotional issues, I was very thankfully Syl and I were able to raise our daughters in a spiritually sound household filled with love, encouragement, and joy. Besides a sound upbringing, we were able to send our daughters to an excellent parochial education; live a good suburban lifestyle: and recently each year we were able to take vacations. Making my girls happy eased the agony from my personal and emotional battles.

Family Restoration and Deterioration. By 1994, Tim had come back into my life. His heath was diminishing. This required him to stay with Aunt Mary. Tim began to try to make amends with me for all the years he was not a part of my life. It was like he wanted to atone for the fatherly love, inspiration, and financial support I had been denied for many years. He spent quality time with me and my family. By spending more time together, we began to work on our father-daughter relationship. However, at times it remained very emotional for me to be with him because his absence from the lives of Momma and me, had made me resent and despise him. This made me one day appreciate him, then the next day his presence annoyed me. I prayed to God to subdue these negative feelings. The Holy Spirit constantly brought to my memory what Momma always would say to me, *Tim was not only my father but an adult*, and she had raised me to always be respectful to adults. She would also tell me regardless of how Tim behaved I had to respect him. Reflecting on how I had been forgiven and loved through all my transgressions, I had an instant reality check. Who was I now not to forgive? It was clear by Momma's willingness for me to have a relationship with Tim that she had forgiven how he had violated her body that resulted in my birth. At this point in my life it was up to me to do the same. The flicker of light from the Holy Spirit gave me this candid revelation – I had Momma to lovingly carry me through my first twenty-five years of life; and in my latter life Tim would give the fatherly love and affection I deeply longed for as a child. The closer Tim and I became, gradually my animosity against him began to lessen. Nonetheless similar to my other permanent scars, the scarring from the absence of Tim in my earlier life lingered. But I tried to tuck this scar privately away with the rest of the emotional scars. The challenge is that even to this day those scars resurface bringing anguish within my soul and mind, and I still become baffled as to why for all those years Tim was not there for Momma and me. Gratefully with the passing of time the flickers of light from God was peace of mind. *Finally, brothers and sisters, rejoice! Strive for full restoration, encourage one another, be of one mind, live in peace. And the God of love and peace will be with you*, 2 Corinthians 13:11 (NIV).

While my relationship with Tim was improving, by the end of

1994, Linda Faye's demeanor seemed to be changing. She was not call or visiting me as she normally did. When I asked her if something was wrong, Linda Faye upsettingly told me she felt I no longer had time for her, because I now had my father in my life while she did not even know who her father was. Listening to Linda Faye, I realized for the first time, just like me, she too had been emotionally affected by not having her father in her life. All these years of being with my sister, I never thought about how she also must have been silently suffering about her father. In all likelihood, Linda Faye was hurting more than me because her situation was even more direr than mine since, with the exception of his name and that he went to college with Momma, she had truly little information about her father. Then I found out how much Linda Faye wanted to find her father, when one of our family members told me, Linda Faye and Darrell had taken a trip to North Carolina to visit our aunts and their families, and also seek information about her father, but sadly she did not find any information about her father. My heart ached for my sister being unable to find her father. The heartache I experienced from the absence of Tim in my life during my childhood through my early twenties had emotionally crushed me. Because of this, I could earnestly imagine how much more devastating it was for Linda Faye to have the name of her father but be unable to find him. Every child deserves to know their biological father regardless if that father is in the life of the child. Simply finding the father of my sister could relieve her feeling rejected, insignificant and unloved.

Beside telling how she felt about me now having Tim in my life,

Linda Faye told me instead of spending time with her, I was too busy helping Desmond and other people in my life. To hear my beloved sister who had been with me my entire life felt this way was upsetting and disappointing. I deeply loved my sister with my whole heart and soul. Our entire life we had been a significant part of each other's life journeys. We had been the pride and joy of our Momma, we were her girls, and after Momma had passed away it was only the two of us. With Momma gone, Linda Faye and I, together with our husbands and the girls, had clung onto each as a loving family. But now Satan was trying to wedge us apart. I prayed to God to remove the negative thoughts Linda Faye was having and to restore our family back to His glory. I began to work hard to communicate and show Linda Faye how much I loved, appreciated, and needed her in my life because there was no way I was going to let Satan have the victory over my sister and me. With everything I could do, I tried to show my sister how much I loved and needed her in my life. Linda Faye always being strong-minded and uncompromising drew further away from me, isolating herself from me by saying she was business. Because Syl and I had visited several church services with Linda Faye and Darrell at World Harvest Church in Columbus, Ohio, when I heard they were having three days of revival services, I called Linda Faye to let her know Syl, the girls and me were going meet her and Darrell in Columbus to attend the revival services with them. Linda Faye said that sounded like a promising idea, and she would look forward to seeing us. Although we had a spiritual uplifting time during the services, and good bonding time together, it did not seem to fully improve the way Linda Faye was feeling about our relationship. A few weeks later instead of talking on a weekly basis, she suggested we talk once a month. We no longer had our yearly visits during Thanksgiving or Christmas. With the passing of time it appeared Linda Faye was drifting further apart from me. I endlessly prayed to God to help restore our relationship. To keep our communication lines open, I sporadically reached out to her. During those times we would have amicable conversations. In the meantime, I continued to pray believing and trusting in God that our relationship would be made whole again.

No Not My Baby. In May 1997, another intense deplorable dark storm abruptly commenced. In excited anticipation of the high school graduation for Ivy, we were preparing the invitation list. Suddenly Ivy had tears in her eyes. She was obviously upset about something. I asked her what was wrong. Ivy startled me by saying she did not want Darrell to attend her graduation. I did not understand why. I knew Linda Faye and I were still struggling with our relationship, but I did not believe it was affecting the girls. Within seconds, Ivy tearfully revealed to me the horrendous incidents she had endured as a child. My first-born baby girl solemnly began to tell me *how she clearly remembers being sexually molested between six and seven years old by Darrell.* My heart dropped listening to Ivy tell how it happened when I was in the special place when she and Sylvia would stay with Linda Faye and Darrell during the summer months and school breaks. Ivy went on to tell me she remembers Darrell *fondling and rubbing his penis against her vagina, and that he would sit in a* *chair on the side of the dresser watching her get undressed for bed.* She went on to say how he would *threaten to hurt me and keep me in the special place if she told anyone.* With tears in my eyes, I wanted to cry out, why Lord, why my baby girl, because there was no doubt I totally believed my daughter. What exactly happened to me was tragically happening to my daughter just like I did not realize the molestation I had suffered as a child until I was older, and the same was true for Ivy. Trying to comfort Ivy in my arms, I wondered how Darrell could have done this to my baby. Did he think his sexual abuse of my child would not be brought to the light? How could he not know that his evilness would one day come back to her remembrance? Still cuddling Ivy in my arms, she asked me *if I was mad at her?* Kissing my baby's forehead and holding her tighter, I exclaimed to her, *no, you are the light of my life, and I'm only sorry I was not able to protect her.* Ivy said, *so you understand why I do not want him at my graduation,* and I told her, *of course.* The Ivy asked me *what we were going to do about what he did to her.* I told my daughter, *I was going to talk to Syl about what we should do.* I told Syl and asked him what should we do? Should we call the police? Confront him personally? What I really wanted to do was to hurt Darrell for what he had done to my baby. Then coming to my senses, I knew I could never physically harm another human being no matter what the circumstances were, but this made the pain in my heart worsen as I felt helpless to avenge the harm caused to my child. Then I began to wonder how did I allow someone to harm my child? I asked God, hadn't my child suffered too much already. Praying and seeking guidance from God, Syl and I decided to first contact Linda Faye to find out what she knew. When I called Linda Faye informing her what Ivy had told me, right away Linda Faye vehemently refused to believe Ivy. Linda Faye said, *Ivy was evil and lying on Darrell.* She went on to say, *she did not understand why Ivy was being this deceitful, and if this had really happened, why Ivy did not tell anyone until now.* I told Linda Faye that I completely believed Ivy because the same exact thing had happened to me. I went on to tell Linda Faye about the two times I was molested as a child and when the memories came back to me. I even reminded Linda Faye that she was a social worker with a degree in social services and was knowledgeable about molestation, and that children who are abused may not recall an incident until later in life. For about ten minutes Linda Faye and I argued about our separate points of view. The call ended with Linda Faye calling *Ivy a liar and Darrell a good man that would never do anything like this.* Once off the phone, I went to Ivy and pulled her into my arms. I hugged and encouraged my child. I let her know she had done nothing wrong. What Darrell did was terrible, and he would have to answer to God for his sins. Assuring Ivy, she did the right thing in letting me know what Darrel did to her, I shared with her how the two boys had sexually abused me when I was around her age, and that we both had to depend on God to strengthen us. Holding Ivy in my arms the *why questions* quickly surfaced in my mind? Why did Darrell hurt my innocent baby? Darrell had been smiling in our faces all this time knowing he had done these disgusting acts to my baby. I struggled to be strong for Ivy while inwardly feeling the pain she suffered from

Darrell violating her little body. Darrell knew my child was too young to defend herself. The how could he be so very devious to use my child's love for me to scare her into his acts of sexual molestation. He did this knowing I was unable to protect her from him. What a sick man. I begin to prayer that Darrell would one day realize the eternal physical and mental damage he inflicted on Ivy, my innocent child, and that Linda Faye would come to know the truth that her husband had sexually abused her innocent niece. I hoped while they were attending services at World Harvest each Sunday, they would think how Darrell's sins affected my innocent baby. The flicker of light even through this appalling storm is God still blessed Ivy to become a beautiful woman even with the emotional scars caused by Darrell. His hateful acts did not have the victory in her life, God did. The fact that I was unable to protect my child from his vulgar acts will forever haunt me. This became an enormously incomprehensible heavy storm for me.

That day was the last time Ivy, Sylvia and I have spoken with Linda Faye. Years later I tried several times to reach out to Linda Faye, but she never responded. Ivy and Sylvia also reached out to her to no avail. Over the years, I learned Linda Fay had contacted other family members stating Ivy and I were spreading lies about Darrell. This was confirmed when I was cleaning Auntie's house for Michael and Valerie to move back in, I found letters to Auntie from Linda Faye telling Auntie that Ivy had lied on Darrell. She wrote that I really was not her sister because we had different fathers, and when she died, no one was to let me know. Linda Faye has spoken to or visited other family members, including Syl, Bessie, Jay, Aunt Lib, and cousin Gregory.

The day Ivy told me about being molested, I was full of shame and regret that I could not protect my oldest daughter. The fact of failing my child consumed my mind. Glory be to God that His anointing power delivered me from being consumed on why it happened, feeling ashamed, and contemplating vengeful thoughts, and the Holy Spirit gave me peace to realize accountability is a two-way street. Both the boys who molested me and Darrell who molested my daughter will be held accountable for their acts against us in the same manner as I am accountable for my acts against others. For Romans 14:12 (KJV) says, *so then every one of us shall give account of himself to God.* Furthermore, the Holy Spirit imparted to my heart that vengeance was not mine. *Do not repay anyone evil for evil. Be careful to do what is right in the eyes of everyone. If it is possible, as far as it depends on you, live at peace with everyone. Do not take revenge, my dear friends, but leave room for God's wrath, for it is written: "It is mine to avenge; I will repay," says the Lord. On the contrary: "If your enemy is hungry, feed him; if he is thirsty, give him something to drink. In doing this, you will heap burning coals on his head." Do not be overcome by evil, but overcome evil with good,* Romans 12:17-21 (NIV).

After letting me know what Darrell had done to her, Ivy shared how three daughters of Adrene had physically and mentally abused her while I was incarcerated. One callously told my innocent Ivy when she was only six years old several things that were not her place to tell, such as: that Syl was not her real father; that I killed her daddy; and I was in jail and never coming back home. This was downright mean and hurtful. I was furious because hurting my daughter took me to another level of revenge. I could tolerate people hurting me, but never my innocent child. The fact that Ivy knew about her father was not the issue, because it was never my intention for Ivy not to know about her father. I merely did not want Ivy to learn in that harsh manner when she was so young. The other daughter had placed a knife on her tongue several times threating to cut it out. This too, I have no doubt happened, I had personally seen the harshly discipline to her own children and other children in the family. If she disciplined her children in that manner, she would not hesitate to be that mean to my baby girl. Then the other daughter had sexual abused my baby by penetrating her with various objects. Whether this daughter actually knew what she was doing at that age, I will never know. Looking at the life of that daughter as an adult, I believe she abused my child. Enraged that these same people had been smiling in my face for years infuriated me. I spoke with Syl and others regarding what happened in that house to Ivy while I was incarcerated. To my dismay no one, of course, said they were aware of what was happening to my baby.

Forever this will break my heart. How could people be this cruel to my child; then pretend like nothing happened? Why didn't these people understand sooner, or later Ivy would remember their hideous acts? Did they believe I would be in jail forever? All of this added more to my emotional scars, because as a mother, I should have been there to protect my child. My sins had caused me not to be there for my baby. Yet understanding why my baby had to suffer for my sins continues to be an inconsolable storm for me. Looking back, I should have attempted to prosecute those that abused my child. Prayerfully this will let each of them and others like them know although they are young innocent children, one day they will remember and recall the cruel, despicable acts. Today looking at my daughter still struggling with the violence the assailants, who were supposed to family, afflicted on her during her childhood, I truly regret not obtaining mental health therapy for Ivy. Her spiritual belief together with mental health therapy could have given Ivy the ability to emotionally process the traumas she suffered and could have made a significant difference for her adulthood stability.

Chapter Thirteen -- Blessed Despite it All

A New Job Opportunity. In June 1995, the BK Lawyer that I had worked for resigned from Jones Day. He was beginning a new corporate bankruptcy practice at a smaller law firm. During the seven years of working for the BK Lawyer, we had an excellent working relationship. He always gave me superb yearly evaluations. Over the years we supported each other outside of the firms. Syl and I attended his wedding. He had attended the funeral services for Mark. When his wife faced a medical crisis shortly after they were married, I was able to encourage her because I had dealt with the same situation. On several occasions Ivy would babysit their children. When his wife started teaching paralegal classes at Lakeland College, she asked me to make presentations two to three times a year to the classes. One year the BK Attorney graciously extended to me the use of his vacation home in Miami. After leaving the firm, the BK Lawyer called me in August 1995 to ask if I would meet with the paralegal assigned to work with him at the new firm to discuss the duties and responsibilities of a bankruptcy paralegal. I gladly agreed to meet with her. A few days later she called me, and we decided to meet over lunch. During lunch I discussed with her in detail the duties of a corporate bankruptcy paralegal and provided her with copies of written information, outlines and guidelines. She was extremely appreciative. A few weeks later the BK Lawyer called to ask if I would consider joining him as the paralegal for his new practice. I told him, yes. His firm's Human Resource Manager (HRM) called me the next day to schedule a time to meet. A few days later I met the Managing Partner (MP) and the lady for HRM. It was a good meeting. They appeared to be impressed with my resume, knowledge of corporate bankruptcy, and that the BK Lawyer held me in high regards. Subsequent to the interview, I received a call from the HRM director extending me an offer of employment. I let my managing attorney at Jones Day know I had been offered a position as a paralegal for the BK Lawyer. The managing attorney asked me to take the weekend to think about resigning from an international law firm to work for such a smaller law firm. He was correct it was something to consider because my current employer was one of the top five international law firms with over 1,000 lawyers in twenty-four offices throughout the United States and abroad. The BK attorney's law firm had only two offices in Ohio with less than 100 attorneys. Over the weekend, I prayed to God to guide me in making the correct decision. I discussed the employment options with Syl, compared the salary and potential benefits. By Monday I had decided to accept the employment offer with the BK Lawyer's firm.

I started working for the new firm on October 1, 1995. On my first day at work, I completed the typical paperwork consisting of forms for payroll and emergency contacts. The law firm did not require me to complete a written employment application and no background check was required. Since no one questioned me about my past, I did not divulge any other information, including details about my incarceration. I believed I did not have an obligation to voluntarily reveal my past because upon being released for the reformatory I was told, unless asked by the employer I had an obligation to make know information about my incarceration. Accordingly, I began to work at the new firm in the same manner as with the previous firm.

The bankruptcy department initially consisted of the BK Lawyer, an associate and me. Over the years at one time the bankruptcy department was comprised of ten attorneys, two paralegals, a project assistant and five secretaries. From day one, I worked harder than ever to make the newly established bankruptcy department a stellar, well-respected, competitive part of the corporate bankruptcy world. As with the former law firm, adapting to the individual demands, dispositions and routines of multiple attorneys needed me to exemplify patience, understanding, and versatility. My work ethics and dedication earned me outstanding reviews each year. Within a few years I was promoted to Senior Paralegal. Together with my assignments to the bankruptcy department lawyers, I supervised at various times from one to five secretaries and project assistants. Besides the lawyers and employees of the firm, I an excellent rapport with clients, court personnel, and third-party vendors and professionals. Often times I, as well as the lawyers I worked for, would be told, or received notes from clients, court personnel and third parties of their appreciation for my professionalism and work ethics. In addition to my day to day work assignment, I organized several successful firm fundraisers on behalf of the United Way yearly campaign. The first few years at the firm, similar I had done for the other firm, I coordinated a soft ball team for the firm that played in the City of Cleveland softball league.

Economically accepting the position at the firm proved to be a tremendous financial blessing for me and my family. When I initially began working for the firm my billing rate was at $125 an hour, by 2015 it had increased to $240 an hour. My billing rate was the hourly amount clients were charged for the work I performed on their cases. Each paralegal for the firm were expected to bill a minimum of 1,500 hours a year. Except for three years, I would typically bill 1,800 to 2,100 hours per year. During the period of 2010 to 2015, I generated yearly revenue of $250,000 to $375,000, and earned more than six figures each year. I was able to be this successful because the lawyers I worked for and the clients I served recognized my dedication, diligence, and work ethics of going beyond the call of duty to produce superb work-products. My employment with the firm was a true blessing from God. I will always be grateful to have received the favor of God which allowed me to be an excellent employee that in turn enabled me to be respected co-workers and client, as well as highly compensation.

Bless with More Loving Friendships. While at the firm in 1996 I befriended Nicole Perry, who became like a daughter to me. Nicole is a beautiful, lovable funny young lady. Even though she is fifteen years younger than me, she has always been mature for her age. When people initially met Nicole, they thought from her demeanor she was mean. Quite the opposite. In fact, she reminds me of her favorite fictional character, *Winnie the Pooh*, because they both are friendly, considerate, reliable, creative, and have a love for food and socializing. Nicole quickly became one of the dearest, dependable, and caring persons in my life. Often, I was focused on the well-being of others that my own welfare was put on the back burner. Nicole was the person in my life I could always rely on to make sure I was okay. She would persistently tell me she did not want me to become burned out by helping others. If she thought I needed something, she would bring it without me asking. Her caring and loving spirit gave me strength through many days when I wanted to throw in the towel.

One of my most memorable moments with Nicole was one evening when I was working hard to meet a deadline. I typically parked my car in a lot several blocks from the office building. Not being able to take a break, I asked Nicole before the parking lot closed to move my car from the parking to the front of the building. Without a second thought, I handed her my keys. Nicole returned my keys about twenty minutes later. She told me the car was in front of the building. A few moments later one of the secretary came by my office. She wanted me to know Nicole asked her to move my car. The secretary said Nicole did not know how to drive, but because I was busy working she did not want to disappointment me by not moving the car. I thanked the secretary for letting me know. That incident let me appreciate two things about Nicole, how much she cared about me and she was a very smart young lady. With even a small request like moving my car, Nicole cared about me enough to figure out how she could help me in order not to let me down. Then she was smart enough to actually figure out a way to get the car moved. This is one of many fond memories of Nicole.

Not only has Nicole been close to me, she loves Syl, Ivy and Sylvia and others in my life. When Syl and I hosted a birthday party for Maurie, she met the Nunn family, and they adopted her into their family in the same manner they did for me. The day of the party, Nicole met Yul Perry. Several years later Nicole and Yul became husband and wife. Nicole like me is always willing to help others. I recall her being helpful in assisting several members of the Nunn family obtain employment with the firm. When Nicole's position with the firm was eliminated after a third-party company was hired, I was upset and spoke to the HRM director. Unfortunately, there was nothing anyone could do as the decision had already been made. Even after Nicole was no longer with the firm we remained especially close. Later in life there were a few matters I placed Nicole in the middle of that I earnestly regretted. If I could take those times back, like so many other events in my life, I would without hesitation. Without question, Nicole is another God-given person in my life that loves me unconditional. I am truly thankful to God that even today I have her in my life.

Charisse Vance was the other lady I became close with while working at the firm. Although she only worked for the firm about a year, we instantly became friends. Soon she, her daughter, Little Charisse, son, Michael, and grandchildren became another absolutely loving God-given family to me. Charisse made me laugh within moments after we first met and many days thereafter. Her witty personality has brightened up my days on many occasions, while her feisty attitude defended and shielded me during certain stormy times.

There is a saying *some people come into your life for a reason.* In my life when I need an honest opinion I go to Charisse. She always honestly tells me like it is no matter how difficult it is for me to accept. Whether I accept or refuse her opinions, I love her for being honestly blunt with me. Throughout the years we both know we can count on each other for support during the good or rough situations, be it for work, family, or personal matters, we have each other's back. We have an unspoken bond to do whatever we can to make a situation better. Charisse and I have many memorable memories. My most unforgettable memory of Charisse occurred at the firm. Anyone close to me knows that I love shoes. By the time I was in my late 40s I had more than 200 pairs of shoes. At the office, especially during the winter months, I would have at least fifteen pairs of shoes under my desk. One day in December when returning from lunch I had removed my boots and started to put on my shoes. Each shoe I picked up to put on I could not find a match. I kept going through the stacks of shoes. There were no matching shoes. Suddenly Charisse was at my office door. She asked, *what is wrong.* I looked at her I was about to say I could not find any matches for my shoes, but seeing the expression on her face, I knew she had taken one of each of my shoes. We laughed so hard that day to my stomach ached. Now, any time we think about that day we laugh. Charisse is another blessing in my life of unconditional love. With my stormy life, she still embraces and calls me her sister.

Momma's Dream for Her Granddaughters. From the day Ivy and Sylvia were born they became precious bundle of joys to our families. Momma's dream was for both of her granddaughters to have a happy childhood while receiving an excellent education. She wanted Ivy and Sylvia to grow up to be strong spiritually grounded women with excellent moral whose education had prepared them for successful careers in order to support a prosperous lifestyle. Sadly, Momma was called home to be with the Lord before she could see her dreams for Ivy and Sylvia come true. After the pasting of Momma, I tried to do everything possible to make sure Momma's dreams for our beloved Ivy and Sylvia become realities.

Throughout the mid-1990s Ivy and Sylvia steadily excelled in school. I was grateful that they seemed to be on the right track to fulfill Momma's dreams that each generation elevate higher in education and obtained better employment. Ivy graduated from VASJ in June 1997 with honors after making significant accomplishments during her high school years, including being on the honor roll several times; held leadership positions with student council; was on the cheerleader squad; and her senior year she was homecoming queen. Ivy also organized several events at VASJ. One of her most memorable events was for the Black History Month when she asked Desmond to be the guest speaker. Desmond agreed and delivered a highly motivating speech. Upon graduating from VASJ, Ivy received a scholarship to Xavier University, where she attended for two years. After her sophomore year, Ivy returned home and obtained employment. A few months later she moved into an apartment and enrolled at Lakeland College where she earned her associate degree. Syl and I were proud to attend her graduation. Immediately thereafter,

Ivy enrolled at Cleveland State University, where she obtained her bachelor's degree. Again, Syl and I were thrilled of our daughter. Prior to graduating from Cleveland State, Ivy applied for admission at the University of Akron Law School. She was accepted and received a scholarship. In 2009, Ivy earned her Juris Doctrine. This accomplishment put the icing on the cake for Syl and me as we happily beamed with joy for her accomplishment. Upon graduation the University of Akron Law School offered Ivy a position as a director in the admission's office. She was later promoted to associate dean. In 2011 Ivy became a licensed attorney when she passed the Ohio State Bar examination. Although Ivy continued to work full-time for the University, she and her girlfriend, Ashley formed a law firm, where she worked part-time. Looking at my oldest child, I smile outwardly and inwardly with joy and thankfulness for the blessings God bestowed upon her. I believe that not only my Momma, but Herman as well are always smiling down on Ivy enormously proud of her fortitude in pursing her education and her successful career. Throughout all the pain and sorrow my innocent child suffered during her childhood, she stayed positive, strong and focus on not letting that pain control her destiny. For this I respect and love my oldest child for her strength in the midst of the storms she had to bear as a child.

Sylvia graduated from VASJ in June 2001, where she had been a good student who took part in various after school activities. Before graduating, Sylvia applied to Ursuline College in Beachwood, Ohio. She was accepted and received scholarships. Sylvia majored in early education, and in May 2006, she graduated with a bachelor's degree.

Syl and I were extremely pleased with the achievement of Sylvia, especially when two months before graduating she was hired as a first-grade teacher for South Euclid-Lyndhurst School District. A year later, Sylvia enrolled at Notre Dame College where we happily watched her walk down the aisle to receive her master's degree. Sylvia later attended Virginia Polytechnic Institute and State University (Virginia Tech) via internet classes where she earned her second master's degree in May 2014. Syl and I gratefully went to Virginia Tech to attend her graduation ceremony. A few years later, Sylvia earned tenure status. Currently she teaches second grade students in a low to median income community in a suburb in the greater Cleveland area. In addition to me, many others will attest that Sylvia is an exceptionally compassionate, dedicated, and generous teacher. Her primary goal is to provide each student with not only a thorough education, but a secure, nurturing, comfortable learning environment. Sylvia is constantly seeking ways to address and aid with the educational, social, and family concerns she is confronted with on a daily basis by her diverse student body. Each school year she goes above and beyond to provide her students with a classroom decorated to enhance their desires to learn. The classroom is equipped with state of the art technology equipment. She maintains throughout the school year an ample amount of supplies and snacks for students who forget or are unable to afford their own. Although Sylvia personally funds a sufficient amount to equip her classroom, she requests financial donations from family members and friends. She also solicits donations via official online fundraisers for teachers and through educational grants. Each year she introduces Syl and me to the students as the classroom grandparents. For holidays and special occasions, we often give each child a gift. Besides being an awesome teacher in the classroom, Sylvia often prepares presentations and proposals for the school administrators. She has successfully organized after school events for the students, staff, and community. For her relentless efforts to instill into the students how to become successful and respectful citizens Sylvia has received recognition from school administrators, co-workers, local media, and the community. Like her big sister Ivy, Sylvia made my Momma's dreams come true for which I am so thankful.

People often ask what Syl and I did to encourage Ivy and Sylva to succeed in their education and careers. As for me, I constantly insisted they: fulfill the dreams of my Momma for their lives; not to become pregnant before graduating from high school; after high school to become gainfully employed or attend college; have productive lives as good citizens; and most importantly to never forget their spiritual upbringing by always depending on Jesus Christ for guidance in all aspects of their journeys through life. All the other accomplishments of Ivy and Sylvia are the tremendous overflow of answered prayers and blessings from God. Because exactly like I did my Momma when I was a teenager, during the teenage years of my girls we had the typical mother and daughter clashes. It became difficult for me to get them to listen and understand the goals they needed to focus on without being met with their know-it-all opposition. During those times I would often laugh to myself while reminiscing that I had the same identical clashes with Momma. There were a few more clashes with Ivy than Sylvia, just like Linda Faye had more clashes with Momma than me. Later in life Sylvia would say when Ivy was in trouble it taught her not to follow Ivy's footsteps. This resulted in less squabbles between Sylvia and me, like Momma and I had fewer disagreement. Being the youngest child, Sylvia learned how to stay on my good side, the way I had with Momma. Even with are few disputes, overall my daughters were terrific little girls and teenagers. They both learned at an early age the more you achieved in school and behaved at home and in public, the more you were rewarded. This incentive helped motivate them to succeed. One of the most sought-after reward was to drive their own car. Like most teenagers, driving was on their minds as soon as they turned fifteen. Ivy and Sylvia both learned to drive six months before their sixteenth birthdays. Right after they completed their driving training classes, each of them took their driving test, which they passed and received their driver's license. As promised for their excellent grades and behavior, we were blessed to purchase cars for each of them shortly after they received their driver's license.

Relationships Enhanced and Developed. Once Herman and I lost our first home, it was no longer my desire to be a homeowner. Then in early 1997 because I was tired of walking up the stairs in the home we leased, Syl and I began discussing buying a home. Initially Syl inquired about purchasing through his veteran benefits. However, since he and his ex-wife had bought their house with the benefits, none were available to use for another home. Even though the veteran benefits were unavailable, we were financially able to afford the conventional mortgage down payment. In mid-1997, we began looking for a house. By September 1997, we had financed and moved into our ranch styled home.

Before moving, I knew that Tim's health was progressively deteriorating causing him to be primarily confined to a wheelchair. He had recently fallen down the stairs several times at Aunt Mary's home resulting in him being hospitalized a few times at the Veterans Hospital. It was apparent to Tim, Aunt Mary, Gregory, and me that he required additional care. I talked to Syl about letting Tim live with us due to his health, and he agreed that with me. When I talked to Tim about moving in with Syl and me, without hesitation he happily said, yes. Before Tim could move in, I arranged for him to receive daily personal care services from the same health care provider I used for Adrene. I was blessed that Syl was extremely helpful in assisting with the care of Tim. Tim living with us further enhanced our father daughter relationship. The more time we spent together, my love for him grew. Yet like each of my other storms of life, although I had forgiven Tim the emotional scars were still embedded in my memories. As a result, when certain words were spoken, or acts done it would trigger sudden thoughts of how Tim neglected Momma and me. This would cause the reemergence of the emotional scars that would cause emotional dismay, until eventually the emotional scars would subside until the next time.

A few times prior to 1998, Tim, Syl, Sylvia and I, travelled to Bowie, Maryland to visit Kim and her family. Each time we visited

Kim, Tim was happy. He smiled non-stop full of joy for his two daughters to be bonding with each other. July of 1998 was the first time Kim, her daughter, Kimola, and son, Karrington visited our home. This was the beginning of a devoted sister relationship filled with love and support. Within a few years we were there for each other through good and not so good days. The closer Kim and I grew, I could see the contentment in the eyes of Tim. Each time he looked at us together or even heard us talking on the phone always made him content. Our first big celebration together was attending Kim's graduation from community college. Syl drove Tim, Sylvia, and me to Bowie for the graduation. This was the first time I met Kim's fiancé, Darcy (Mo), her mother, Mrs. Elaine and her fiancé, Billy. Later Kim would attend the graduations of Sylvia for VASJ and Ivy from law school. It became a tradition for me to celebrate Kim's birthday on April 1st, each year. My most memorable birthday celebration for Kim's birthday was flying to Maryland on a Friday to attend her party that Saturday night. Then the next morning we flew to Miami where we spent time relaxing on the beach for a few days.

    The next big occasion was her destination wedding to Las Vegas. Beside Sylvia and me the wedding was attended by Kimola, Karrington, Kim's two aunts and younger brother, and Mo's two sisters. Kim let me know that instead of her mother attending she was going to help finance the wedding and allow her sisters to attend while she stayed with their mother. Sylvia and I where part of the wedding party for the beautiful Vegas styled wedding. It was a spectacular time. Kim had selected a charming hotel where we stayed. There was limo transportation the day of the wedding. The ceremony venue was beautiful, and the reception dinner was held at a nice restaurant with excellent service and food. There were two hilarious recollections from the wedding. The first was when the entire wedding party was running through the Venetian Hotel to arrive in time for the romantic gondola ride that I had scheduled for Kim and Mo. The second was Mo, who has a small physique, trying to carry Kim, his lovely bride who weights several more pounds than him, over the threshold of the door to their hotel room. We were all in the hallway cracking up laughing at the newlyweds. Kim had a very buffy wedding dress with lots and lots of layers. This made it difficult for Mo to pick her up because he could not find her waist or legs under all that dress and undergarments. Every time I think about Mo struggling to lift and carry my sister in the room still bring tears of laughter to my eyes.

A year later on July 19, 2007, Kim gave birth to my niece, Miracle. Her name is a testament that she is a blessing from God because Kim had to endure and overcome significant health issues for Miracle to be born. Because Miracle was under-weight when she was born, she had to be receive special medical care. Even when Miracle was discharged, she needed special treatment and care. Shortly after Miracle was discharged from the hospital, I went to help Kim for a week. Two weeks later, Ivy went to help Kim with Miracle. These were special bonding times for all of us. A few months later in September 2007, Kimola gave birth to my great-niece, Jordynn. Throughout the years, Kim and I were always there for each other. We confronted life's journeys together, the joyous times of weddings, births, birthdays, graduations, vacations, and promotions. We held each other together during sickness, death, legal concerns, employment matters, and marital problems. A few years ago, when facing too many storms in our lives, we adopted the motto *you still riding?* This is based on the movie *Thelma and Louise*. As long as we are riding in the car and not at the end of the cliff, we were okay. Over the years, all knowing God blessed me with Momma and Linda Faye in my earlier years. Then God knew that Momma would leave this life and Linda Faye and I become estranged, therefore, God blessed me with Tim and Kim to be a major part of my latter years. What an awesome God I serve.

Another special person came into my life during Sylvia's junior year at VASJ she met Brianna Banks who was a freshman. Brianna not only became a close friend to Sylvia but an integral part of the Marshall family. I immediately fell in love with her bubbly happy go lucky demeanor. I fondly called her my BriBri, embracing her as a God-given daughter. BriBri would stay at our house for several days, only leaving when her mom insisted she come home. For years if you saw Sylvia, not too far behind was BriBri. Frequently they would spend time together after school and during the weekends. She began to attended church with us and sang in the youth choir and took part in other youth activities. Two times prior to BriBri reaching adulthood, she and Sylvia caused me to get on their cases. The first was before Sylvia graduated from VASJ, and the two of them went out. It was after their curfew, and BriBri's mother, Dineen, called to see if she was still at our house. I said, no. When Dineen explained that BriBri was supposed to already be at home, I told her not to worry I would find them. I began to page Sylvia. Shortly thereafter, they pulled into the drive way. Immediately after coming out the front door, I swiftly went to the driver's side of the car and started scolding them for breaking curfew and fussed at BriBri for not informing Dineen of her whereabouts. I told Sylvia to go into the house. Getting in the car, I took BriBri home. This was the first time I personally met Dineen. Months later when the aftermath of the incident began to diminish, Sylvia and BriBri started teasing me about how terrified they were that night. They claimed even before the car totally pulled into the driveway, within a split second, I was out the house and flew literally in the air down the porch stairs to the car. They laughed about this for years. The second memory occurred after Sylvia had graduated from high school. She was taking her first road trip to Connecticut to visit a friend. BriBri of course wanted to go. This being Sylvia first road trip without Syl and me, I checked on her every hour. Dineen was also checking on them. When Sylvia called to let me know they had arrived safely, she was concerned BriBri had told Dineen that I went with them. Sylvia had heard BriBri saying to her mother, right now she is sleep and she is still sleeping. When I talked to BriBri she admitted not telling her mom I was not going. I reprimanded her for being dishonest to her mother. Not wanting Dineen to be worried for the next two days, I decided not to tell Dineen. Thankfully they had an enjoyable time and returned home safely. I am not for sure if BriBri ever told her mother that I did not go on the trip.

BriBri and Sylvia had several things in common. One was their love for Beyoncé. During the *Beyoncé Experience* concert tour in 2007 my cousin, Drew Williford was part of the production team. He called to say hello and let me know he was in Cleveland working the Beyoncé concert. When I told Sylvia, she said, *please Mommy you got to get me tickets*. I called Drew to ask about tickets. Without hesitation he said, *of course, he would have two tickets waiting for her at will call*. I thanked my cousin for being so kind to me and my daughter. It was no doubt, BriBri was going with Sylvia. When they arrived at the venue, Sylvia called me excitedly saying that Drew not only had two tickets for excellent seats, he gave them backstage access passes to meet and take pictures with Beyoncé. This was a dream come true for them, they were ecstatic about that night and talked about it for several months thereafter. In 2012, Sylvia, BriBri, and I went to Atlantic City, New Jersey for their second and my first Beyoncé concert presented by Revel Casino and Hotel. It was an awesome concert and exciting time in Atlantic City. I had not visited Atlantic City since 1983 with Syl. Since that time there had been a lot of improvements to the Boardwalk and the surrounding areas which was very impressive. There were serval new casinos and many new retail stores and other attractions. The concert was spectacular. I had not been a fan of Beyoncé but became one after the concert. The day after the concert we were walking through the main lobby heading outside. Sylvia and I had not noticed that BriBri was not behind us, until she ran up too us saying she spotted Beyoncé's mom, Mrs. Tina Knowles. BriBri was whispering to us that Mrs. Knowles and her friends spoke to her. BriBri continued to whisper that they think she is the actress, Gabourey Sidibe and wanted to take pictures. Laughing, we played along with BriBri as we walked back to their table and we all took pictures together. Mrs. Knowles was very friendly, as I told her how much I enjoyed her daughter's concert.

 Whenever we travelled, BriBri would often travel with us. Later in life when I became a member of Lee-Seville Baptist Church, I chaperoned BriBri and the other youth members of Lee-Seville to the Full Gospel Conventions in Baltimore, Maryland and Atlanta, Georgia. When I wanted to visit Kim in 2008, I asked Ivy and Sylvia to help me drive. Of course, our BriBri went with us. Of all our trips with BriBri, my most memorable one was the cruise with the Williams family that Rosemary Williams Grantling organized. It was the first time BriBri traveled by plane and cruise liner. We had an exciting time on the beach in Miami before and after the cruise. The cruise and the port of calls were a blast for everyone. Over the years, BriBri celebrated birthdays, graduations, holidays, weddings, and births with us. She also supported us during times of sickness and bereavement. Although Sylvia and BriBri do not communicate as much nowadays, they know each other are only a phone call away. Every Mother's Day and birthday, BriBri is one of the people I can count on to sends me a thoughtful message. I will always have a special place for BriBri in my heart.

Chapter Fourteen – Pinnacles and Nadirs of Life

Needing to Feel Special. Years after my release from prison, there had been some significant dark storms, profoundly the regrettable death of Mark and becoming aware of the hideous abuse of Ivy. Even with those storms, and the others throughout my stormy life, there were times of many bright sunshiny days. I continued to have loving family members, friends, and a church family. Was blessed to attend a spirit-filled church where I served the Lord. My health was good. I was successfully employed. Syl and I were financially able to provide our family with both necessities and other materialistic wants. Even with all my blessings, my emotional scars would abruptly cause my heart to become heavily burden. At times the silent battles within my mind, heart and soul became overwhelming. Outwardly it appeared, I was on top of the world, as I constantly smiled and pretended that I was happy and acted like my life was grand. But, deep inside, I was despondent from the grief my life had caused innocent people, especially my loved ones. Shameful for my past transgressions, I coped with the guilt of breaking so many of the Ten Commandments. My lack of self-confidence to ever be considered a good person because of my sins and shortcomings made me feel alienated from people without stormy lives. During these times I missed my Momma more than usual because I just needed her to comfort me with a hug and hear her say everything was going to be okay. I even began feeling like a disappointment and embarrassment to Syl because he was becoming very disparaging and callous towards me and nitpicked about the most trivial things I did.

People always thought Syl and I were the ideal couple because our marriage to the outside world appeared perfect. No one knew that since the mid-1990s, at home Syl's demeanor of being a complainer and criticizer had gradually intensified. He had started to nitpick a lot about many things I did, including, how I cooked, cleaned, talked, walked, drove, styled my hair, and the clothes I wore. With each passing day his criticism and negative comments were affecting my self-esteem to the point of being overbearing for me. Then what became even more difficult for me to deal with was Syl began to unnecessarily criticize Ivy and Sylvia. To witness my babies being criticized was more hurtful than his critique of me. His behavior was very disappointing because I would have to listen to Syl talk politely and kindly to other people on the phone or in person, yet at home, it was so different. Everyone on the outside of our home enjoyed his comradery, friendly and joking personality, while behind closed doors at home Syl would shout when speaking in a harsh, coldhearted tone. It was like he had a *Dr. Jekyll* and *Mr. Hyde* personality.

Similarly, to the criticism, the love and compassion we enthusiastically shared prior to my incarceration had never truly rekindle. The permanent scars from his affair burdened me with severe insecurity issues. This caused me to ache more than ever before for excessive acts of affection. I needed to be assured Syl genuinely loved me more than he did the other woman. I craved to hear more words of encouragement and desired to receive acts of kindness. I even began to more freely express to Syl the type of compassion I needed. But that did not work, in fact it became very lopsided because Syl began telling me less than before that he loved me; my attempts to hug him were met with him pushing me away; talking had dwindled to only when necessary; and one-on-one time together was getting less frequent. All the while Syl was stifling his love and affection from me, silently in my mind I was yearning so much for the affection displayed by other couples. I would look at couples out shopping or dining together holding hands and cuddling. Some couples would be walking side-by-side talking, smiling, and laughing, then spontaneously they would peck their mate on the cheek or lips. I longed for this type of outwardly affection. It got to the point when seeing couples showing this type of affection, I turned from being happy, to becoming envious of the woman. This would cause me to begin my wondering questions. Was it wrong for me to want to receive a complimented in the same manner I was criticized? Was wanting to feel love as much as I was being rejected asking too much? Did my desire for affection upset Syl because he really did not want to be with me? After fifteen years of being together was the flame dwindling? Why couldn't Syl sense my needs, see my desires, and sense the loneliness and pain I was feeling? Didn't he see how much I needed his approval and encouragement, or had he grown tired of me because he preferring to be with the other woman?

Syl also knew I still had serious issues with him never telling me who he had the affair with. Why couldn't he put me out of my misery by just telling me the name of the woman? Was it because it was someone I knew? Was it Jackie? He knew his affair unrelentingly consumed my mind. It got to the point I began to believe he really did not enjoy being with me or even making love to me. Then my constant thinking of his purchase of the designer purse and clothing for the woman made me become obsessed with purchasing designer purses and clothing. Before I found those receipts, I had never known about $500 purses. Foolishly, I thought by getting my own Louie Vuitton purse, mink coat, expensive jewelry and clothing would ease the pain. It did not. No matter how hard I tried to heal the scar from the affair it would reopen. Like most of my scars a spoken word or act would bring it back to my memory. The unknown woman steadily increased my insecurity and decreased my self-esteem. It was like an invisible presence eating away at my thoughts. Was she prettier than me? Did she perform better in bed? Have a better job and more money? Did not have as many sins? Even though Syl had threatened if I continued to ask about the women it would affect our marriage, every now and then I would ask the name of the woman. He would again get very irritated of why after all this time I was still dwelling on this. His response made me even more introverted. Why couldn't I shake off the affair? Why not knowing who the woman was consumed my mind and caused me to be suspicious of any woman around us? Was my being too sensitive and apprehensive causing me to worry about things I was unable to control or change? Yes, I had forgiven Syl, but it was the emotional scars that made it impossible to forget because the slightest word or incident could trigger a memory. Plus, I believed if I knew who Syl had the affair with it would ease some of my heartache.

Temporary Fixes Are Not the Answers to the Problems. All these issues and lack of self-confidence resulted in my trying to enhance my outer appearance by apply extra make-up, dressing more fashionable, and wearing trendy hairstyles. Many family members, friends and even strangers told me how nice I looked. The one person I needed to hear a complement from was Syl, but he never gave many any. Instead I received negative remarks from him. One day in 1993, while at the grocery store this man said, hello, you are gorgeous. When I turned with a look of surprise on my face, there was this handsome man smiling saying, yes, I am talking to you. Somehow those few words instantly smoothed a little of the loneliness and insecurity bottled inside of me. Never could I have imagined those few words would turn my entire world upside down. For twelve years I had not even thought of, yet along spoke or looked at another man. Yet suddenly I was swept away to the fairytale of being Cinderella with someone finally noticing me. The ugly duckling was being told she was a beautiful swan. Standing there in a trance he asked to walk with me. Still mesmerized by his looks, voice and what he had said to me, I began to walk with him. We had general conversation until I finished shopping and headed to the checkout counter. Helping me with my groceries, he asked for my phone number. Absorbed in the moment of being noticed, I gave him my number without hesitation. Leaving the store, I thought talking to another man was totally unlike me, but it had been exciting. Wondering of all the people in the store why did he pick me to approach. Why did I give him my real name and work phone number? What if he really called me? Once I walked into our house and heard my girls say, *hi Mommy*, meeting the man vanished from my mind. A few days later I answer my work phone. The voice said, hello gorgeous how are you. The sound of his voice sent chills through my body. We talked for about an hour. He told me he was divorced, had two grown children, worked as a sales representative, and had lived in the Cleveland area since a young child. I let him know I was married with two daughters, and that in all the years of being married, I had never given my number to a stranger, which made talking to him usual for me. What I said did not deter him because he was an assertive conversationalist, which was good for me because once he started a conversation it motivated me to talk nonstop. I loved to talk but found it difficult to start a conversation. This is might be why Syl and I did not have long conversations, because we both were sort of introverts – we did not often start conversations but could be talkative once a conversation was started. After the first few days of talking to him, I begin to look forward to our daily conversations. About a week later, he asked if I would go to lunch. Without hesitation, I agreed. When I walked outside, he was waiting outside the car. He opened the car door as I approached the car. This was a complete surprise. I could not remember the last time a man had opened a car door for me. He took me to a nice restaurant overlooking the lake. Lunch was terrific, and he was the ideal gentleman. In that little period of time his kind words, compliments, mannerism made me feel on top of the world. It was how I dreamed and desired Syl would treat me. Upon returning to the office, he insisted on opening my car door and helping me out the car.

I told him I really appreciated the lunch and his company. The next day a bouquet of flowers were delivered to me at the office. This put the icing on the cake. Flowers had never been delivered to me at my office from either of my husbands. Assembly, employers, and friends had sent flowers several times when I was in the hospital. A few other times people sent flowers in appreciation for helping them with matters. After that day we talked more on the phone and went out for lunch and dinner dates. I began to visit him at his house. All this time together was drawing us closer together. We were going from hugging to holding hands. From a quick kiss on the cheek to passionate kisses. It had gotten to the point, I was dreaming of him making love to me while sleeping in the bed with my husband. The more I prayed to resist talking and seeing him, it seemed Syl would say or do something negative towards me that I could not wait to talk to my friend the next day. By this time, I was not only listening to my gospel music but my favorite R&B artist Mary J. Blige. *What's the 411* was always playing in my car, singing *Changes I've Been Going Through*, *Real Love* and *Sweet Thing*.

One evening while at my friend's house amid a long-heated kiss and lots of fondling resulted in my first night of infidelity. Once it ended, immediately my feelings fluctuated. One moment I felt guilt and shame. The next second happy and satisfied. When I arrived home, looking at Syl in the bed I felt another feeling, a sense of revenge and vindication. He did not even know about the affair, but it still gave me a sense of now you see how I feel attitude. Within a few weeks the affair became an emotional roller coaster for me. When

I was with him I was filled with the romantic desires for compassion, affection, and happiness. Each time we were together the inward loneliness and lack of self-confidence in my life vanished for those few hours, making me feel desired and adored. Then returning home I was overcome with feeling hypocritical, shameful and had a guilty conscience. Worse than anything was knowing I was being an adulterer while going to Assembly serving God. Several weeks after beginning the affair, I begin to have second thoughts. My guilty conscience of cheating was beyond what I anticipated. Hiding the affair became more difficult. The thoughts of the ramification of what would happen to my family if I was caught was frightening. Most importantly I felt spiritually guilty of committing adultery with the possibility of destroying and ruining my family after the many blessings God had bestowed upon my stormy life. Feeling torn between what made me happy and knowing what was best for my family, without a doubt I would choose my family. Despite how good the affair made me feel, it was only a temporary fantasy world. For a few hours it took me far away from my real life, then it was back to reality. The bottom-line was I had to accept the truth of being wrong. My own personal desires had allowed me to succumb to temptation. I knew without question having an affair could never negatively affect Ivy and Sylvia. Regardless of what I personally had to experience inwardly and with my marriage, the well-being of Ivy and Sylvia had to come first. The thought of them living without both parents was not worth a temporary trip to fantasyland. A stable ideal family household is what I had prayed and dreamed for my girls and that is what they would receive regardless of how miserable I was in my marriage. By the grace of God, I came to my senses. Acknowledging my negative feelings of lusting to be with another man and seeking revenge and the vindication of the affair by Syl, had lead me down a path of transgression. The affair had to end, and I had to seek forgiveness from God. The flicker of light was forgiveness from Jesus Christ by repentance for my wrongdoings. *Repent therefore of this thy wickedness, and pray God, if perhaps the thought of thine heart may be forgiven thee*, Acts 8:22 (KJV).

<u>Realizing the Characteristics My Heart is Craving.</u> After ending the affair, thankfully to my knowledge Syl had no idea. Even though Syl remained in the same emotionless, negative, critical demeanor, I constantly prayed for strength to not dwell on my personal discontents with our marital life. Instead I was determined to look beyond the negative and concentrate on the positive aspects of the marriage. I threw all my efforts back into working on making our home a loving, happy, stable dwelling place for us, especially for Ivy and Sylvia. Concentrating on the girls while working harder at Assembly and the firm enabled me to have less time to dwell on the inwardly emotional battle for affection. I began to wonder how one man could give certain aspects like physical and emotional happiness in a relationship, while another man gave financial security and spiritual support. This made me wonder if something was wrong with the way I chose my husbands. Throughout the years I would hear how girls who did not have their father during childhood struggled with romantic relationships. Did this cause me not to know the agape love, devotion, security, and support my husband should exemplify? Was this why I had no idea of the true characteristics for a husband. Why did it take me until reaching forty years old to realize the characteristics I wanted for my husband? At this point of my life I knew the characteristics I needed from my husband were: to be a *provider* for spiritual, emotional and financial needs; a *romantic lover* who is mentally and physically attentive to me that is willing to not only express his love privately, but publicly by spontaneously holding my hand, giving me kisses on the cheek, hugging, cuddling, and opening the doors for me; a *visionary* leader for our family with current and future goals and purposes for us; a *communicator* to enable us to talk and listen to each other; be my number one *supporter* by cheering, uplifting and encouraging me through ups and downs; the primary *compromiser* who works through conflicts and differences for the betterment of our family; a *socializer* that enjoys get-togethers with family and friends; and an *interactor* during family and social gatherings. Looking over my characteristics list I knew our marriage needed to improvement. I began to talk, plead, and cry out to Syl for at least a few of the desires and for him to tell me the desires he needed from me. It was too bad my efforts fell on deaf ears. With a determination to keep our family intact, I decided to apply a quote one of the elder members of Assembly, Mrs. Bank would often say, *you can catch more flies with honey than with vinegar*. Instead of nagging Syl about what I needed from him emotionally, I would place that on my back burner and focus on being more patient while surrounding him with a positive loving atmosphere. I knew Syl was capable of being a better husband to me, because it was clear by how he expressed his admiration to the woman during his affair.

With the passing of time the grace and mercy of God my longing for a lovey-dovey marriage had to become secondary. The happiness of our daughters was far more important. With steadfast prayer and seeking spiritual intervention, my desires to seek affection from other men was kept bottled up. Over the next several years, besides concentrating on being a faithful wife and mother, serving at Assembly and working at the firm, there were changes and new opportunities in our lives.

Times of Pinnacles Even in the Midst of Nadirs. During one of Assembly business meetings, Pastor Judie suddenly informed the members he was marrying a member of Assembly. It stunned me since there was no indication he was dating. Initially it was emotionally upsetting because I had always wanted him to marry my Momma. Now with him getting married, I felt I would be losing him to his fiancé and her family. Once he made the announcement, the meeting became very heated, when I and several other members expressed our discontent with the upcoming wedding. Following the meeting, Pastor Judie and his fiancé, Sis. Marie personally talked to me and eased my concerns. Following our discussions, I supported their marriage wholeheartedly. Sis. Marie even asked Sylvia to be her flower girl. Although Sylvia was not your typical two to five-year-old flower girl, she was a lovely addition to the wedding party. Sis. Marie was a God sent blessing for Pastor Judie. She faithfully took great care of Pastor Judie until he passed away on November 16, 2009.

Talking to Hattie one day she let me know she had started driving part-time for the Wills Funeral Home. She asked if I would be interested in driving. I said, yes, while thinking this is the funeral home that handled the services for Herman. Once I talked to the owner, he let me know they would call me when they needed extra drivers for family cars or the hearse. I would typically work three to four times a month. Eventually Syl and Big Steve began to also drive. Working for Wills lead us to becoming acquainted with American Limousine Service, the largest limo company in the greater Cleveland area that rented limos and hearse to Wills and many other local funeral homes. Syl, Big Steve and I soon began driving for American. Soon Wills and American would ask me to refer additional drivers. Several family members and friends would drive for one or both companies. In September 1995, the Rock-n-Roll Hall of Fame opened in Cleveland and a big event was planned for the city of Cleveland. Many limos would be required for the event. American requested my services in providing drivers for the event. I retained and coordinated over thirty drivers. The drivers chauffeured many celebrities like James Brown, Little Richard, Al Green, Aretha Franklin, and many others. It was an exciting time for us.

For the next few years I remained committed to making sure I was doing all I could to make Syl satisfied and happy. Loving and supporting him together with taking care of our family matters was my focal point. I believed Syl eventually would reciprocate the affection I deeply desired. To my dismay it did not ever happen. From time to time I would ache within for the love, affirmation, and attentiveness I felt when having the affair. Slowly but surely the longing for the temporary excitement, fulfillment and satisfaction began to reoccur. By early 1995, I foolishly succumbed to another man that showed me affection and attention. Again, it was short lived. The temporary happiness did nothing to lessen the roots of my problems. No matter how hard I tried to convince myself what I was doing was okay, my conscious admonished me. The flicker of light from the Holy Spirit would questions where was my hope, patience and understanding? How could I be unfaithful to Syl? Why was I putting the happiness of my girls in jeopardy? Would this man really be any different than Syl in a couple of years? Once more I was torn between wanting our daughters to live in a content home with both parents and needing my personal feelings met. My girls had to come first. My personal needs had to be denied. For the second time, I sought forgiveness from Jesus Christ for my indiscretion and prayed for strength to defeat the negative emotions that caused my feelings of insecurity, discontentment, and neediness.

As time went on, I lived in my pretend world of happiness with an outwardly appearance of living a great life, when in fact inwardly I was silently now battling the dark secret of infidelity that added to my stormy life. In desperate need of spiritual deliverance, I cried out Psalm 51:1, *have mercy upon me, O God, according to thy lovingkindness: according unto the multitude of thy tender mercies blot out my transgressions.* The flicker of light was the mercy of God despite my many transgressions. This made me fixated more than ever to get Syl to realize the problems I was having in our marriage.

Each day I prayed and hoped he would finally show some sign of meeting a few of the things from my characteristics list. The other flicker of light was by the grace of God Ivy and Sylvia had no idea of our marital problems. To them they were teenagers still growing up in a loving supportive home with both parents.

By mid-1995 Cha, Big Steve and Little Steve had been staying in an apartment. Due to some unforeseen problems, Cha asked if they could temporarily stay with us. Of course, we said, yes. While staying with us Cha and Big Steve decided to get married. On January 14, 1996, coincidently the same date Syl and I were married, they exchanged their vows at Assembly with Pastor Judie officiating. They followed in Syl and my footsteps by simply going to Assembly one evening with me, Syl, and a few other family members there to witness the ceremony. After that day the four of us would celebrate our wedding anniversaries together.

We were still working with Wills and American when the City of Cleveland would be hosting the 1997 NBA All Star Game. American again asked me to help with drivers. I retained and coordinated over fifteen drivers for this event. It was exciting for the drivers to chauffeur many NBA stars and their family members. We continued to work for Wills and American for several more years.

By April 1997, we had sadly learned of the horrible abuse Ivy had suffered through. Praise be to God Ivy kept her faith as she tried to cope with the emotional scars caused by the abuse. In August of 1997, Ivy had graduated and started her freshman year at Xavier, while Sylva was beginning the ninth grade at VASJ. My daughters were becoming beautiful intelligent young ladies. It was amazing to see my girls growing up. Syl and I purchased our home and Tim moved in with us. Cha and her family had moved into an apartment. In our new house, it was my prayer for us to live happily ever after. For months our lives seemed to get better. Several months after moving because of a family crisis Doris Faye asked if she and her son, Marc could temporarily live with us. Syl and I agreed to let them move with us. It seemed like the house brought joy to Syl. He immediately began to work on minor to major updates to the house. Big Steve would often help him with the repairs. The first few years, holiday celebrations were held at our house. It was always an enjoyable time to be with family members and friends. Each day Syl and Tim had fun talking and watching television. I could see the obvious contentment of our family. It was a no-brainer for the benefit of my family I had to suppress my personal emotional concerns deep within my soul. A content home had to take precedence. Even though our family life was good, the lack of attentiveness from Syl towards me remained the same. To my dismay there was no indication he wanted to satisfy the affections I desired on my characteristics list. Tired of complaining, I steadily put on my outwardly with the I am great attitude and added to it a *fake it til you make it* approach to my marriage. But, inwardly I was screaming for real affection and attention from my husband.

My mental pain was further agitated because not only was Syl not trying to fulfill my needs for affection, he still would not tell me the name of his mistress which relentlessly haunted me. Yes, I was absolutely wrong for having affairs, but sadly the affairs only gave me the much-desired attention and affection I longed for, but it was only temporarily fixes. Absurdly what satisfied me more from having my affairs, was the sense of payback for the affair Syl had. It also eased the pain caused by Syl not destroying those receipts that allowed me to find them resulting in this mental storm and emotional scarring. Albeit, Syl did not even know about my affairs, it still made me feel vindicated. Deep down inside I knew I could not continue to allow my vindictive feelings to override my common sense, but no matter how hard I prayed, the emotional scars would resurface to negatively consume my mind.

Mild Rainstorm Slowly Brewing into an Unexpected Thunder Strom. Dealing with the emotional scarring from my earlier storms, between 1997 and 1999, other storms were on the horizon. This storm unbelievably was brewing at my spiritually revered Assembly. Our dearly beloved Pastor Judie was nearing eighty years old. Over the years he preached and taught spirit-filled optimistic inspirational sermons and classes that were Bible based. Instead the sermons and teachings became more discouraging, uninspiring, and scornful. Not only were the sermons and teaching changing the administration of Assembly and the officers had to be his way or no way. This caused a rift among the members. Gradually the membership begins to dwindle. Eventually the strife became too much for me. The atmosphere to me had become borderline like the idiom *drinking the Kool-Aid,* which refers to the November 1978 Jonestown deaths of hundreds of members of the *Peoples Temple* religious organization that were under the leadership of Jim Jones that died from drinking Kool-Aid mixed with cyanide and other drugs. Powerlessly seeing the stagnation of the spiritual growth of Assembly was another mental, heartbreaking storm of my life. Since November 1980, the essence of my spirituality was strengthened by worshipping and serving God at Assembly. Pastor Judie was my cherished loving God-given father who was an integral part of my life. Then my husband was a devoted deacon of Assembly. Also, many members of Assembly were like family to me and we loved and supported each other. For months I took consideration my love and devotion to Assembly, Pastor Judie, my husband, and the members, while contemplating my need for uncompromising biblical teaching and spiritual growth. It felt like I was between a rock and a hard place. Did I have a moral obligation to stay at Assembly only to be a people pleaser? Or was I obligated to remain a member out of feeling a sense of personal obligation instead of seeking spiritual inner peace. Was it wrong for me to want to attend a church were my spirit would be spiritually feed?

In August 1999 Willie Mae (Tiny) Williams, the beloved mother of Trina and LaTisha and the cherished daughter of Mother Ida Mae, and Assembly much-loved spirit-filled director of the music department, suddenly passed away. It was a traumatic loss not only to her family members, but to the entire membership of Assembly and her many friends. Tiny was one of the most profound gospel singers I have ever heard. With wholehearted dedication she directed the choirs and presided over the music department. Her witty personality and big smile warmed the soul of everyone she met. Tiny impacted my life shortly after I became a member of Assembly. A few months after I had joined, Tiny simply said to me one night at choir rehearsal, *you have not been to any of the church fellowships with other churches.* Those words had a positive effect on me. The fact she called me out made me feel welcomed and needed and was one of the primary reasons I became a faithful member of Assembly. Those words from Tiny unknowingly were a flicker of light of God that encouraged me to become an active member at Assembly. Unexpectedly, the first week of July 1999, Tiny asked me to help with planning her upcoming birthday party. I gladly agreed to help. Sorrowfully instead of the birthday party, the weekend of her birthday was her home going service. Weeks later I thought of how Trina and my life mirrored each other with our mothers. Both of our mothers had diabetes and now following a brief illness our mothers suddenly passed away when we both were in our twenties. Following the passing of our mothers, neither of our lives were ever the same. Then to further confirm how our lives mirrored each other several years after the passing of our mothers, incredibly both our fathers permanently came back into our lives. When our fathers came into our lives they gave us the love and support we both had deeply long for when we were growing up.

The death of Tiny resulted in another void at Assembly. I was already struggling with the gloominess at Assembly, the passing of Tiny was personally for me the end of my rope at my beloved church. Slowly I began to visit other churches or stayed at home. During this time added to my mental distress was longing for the good times at Assembly when the membership was one big happy family. My marriage and church life were plummeting out of control. The high-spirited services with my Assembly family were gone, and Syl the love of my life refused to give the much-desired love and affection I wanted. He showed no signs of ever meeting a few of the needs from my characteristics list. This steadily caused my mental scars to intensify. Previously I would immerse myself into serving and worshipping at Assembly to help me to contend with my marital and infidelity problems. Now that was gone.

Played with Fire Too Long and Got Burned. Until I Pathetically in 1998, I become involved in another affair. Even more shameful, I had several affairs. It was like I became addictive to finding true love and contentment that I perceived many other couples were experiencing. Comparable to any other addiction, each affair was only a temporary fix. Unfortunately, the sayings go, *if you play with fire you will get burnt* and *what happens in the dark will come to light,* became front and center in my life, when Syl became aware of one of my affairs. One evening Syl caught me with a man in my car. It was one of the most embarrassing moments of my life, because not only was Syl in his car, Sylvia was with him. Being caught by Syl was terrible enough, but more atrocious was for Sylvia to see me in the car with another man and the arguing between Syl, the man and me. The disgusted look on Sylvia face is still embedded in my memory. This incident shocked me back into reality. Syl, though terribly upset, he did forgive me. I believe perhaps because the man was only in the car he could only speculate the extent of our relationship. Syl assumed I had an affair, yet he and I both knew there was absolute proof of his affair with the unknown woman. When Syl caught me with the other man, it scared me into reconciling my marriage. I had always expected if I was caught with another man it would adversely affect my life, especially my daughters. When Syl saw me in the car with the other man, I learned there is an enormous difference between expecting and actuality. Seeing the expression on my daughter's face and confronting the aftermath at our home, I faced the actual damages of my infidelity. I had allowed self-gratification to come before the welfare of Ivy and Sylvia. It was not worth the pain it could cause my daughters. Deep down inside I had to again admit after risking losing and disappointing my family, the affairs did not remove any of my inward battles. As before, the feelings from the affairs were only temporary relief because afterward I always felt even worse with deceit, shame, and guilt. Once again, I prayed for forgiveness of my infidelity and healing of my related emotional scars, as well as strength to stay faithful to Syl and for his demeanor towards me to improve. I needed us to stay together for my daughters that was of the utmost importance to me.

Ending the affairs and committing to my family, I asked myself had the affairs been worth the risk of losing my daughters? Definitely, no, and I would never recommend an affair. Revenge sex or trying to find a substitute for the lack of affection from Syl only caused more painful emotional scarring and did not heal the hurts and pains of my marriage. Instead I needed to soul search on how to be content with my life without self-inflicting pain upon others and myself. Like my other self-inflicted heavy storms, I also had to take responsibility for my actions. In addition, I had to get it in my head that the actions of others should not affect how I responded and accept the fact that I could not change Syl or anyone else into the desires of my characteristics list. I had to admitted that my adultery behavior, which mirrored reverting to my teenage ways of promiscuity, added to my self-inflicted storms of misery in my life.

Eventually I realized even through this self-inflicted sinful behavior, the flicker of light from God was mercy, forgiveness, and deliverance. *Withhold not thou thy tender mercies from me, O Lord: let thy lovingkindness and thy truth continually preserve me. For innumerable evils have compassed me about: mine iniquities have taken hold upon me, so that I am not able to look up; they are more than the hairs of mine head: therefore, my heart faileth me. Be pleased, O Lord, to deliver me: O Lord, make haste to help me*, Psalm 40:11-13 (KJV). Not only did my Lord and Savior Jesus Christ have compassion on me, Syl showed compassion for my indiscretions and our marriage survived those extramarital affairs. Looking back on those days of my life the thoughts of the loving compassion of God brings my soul to tears of gratitude. Another time in my life that God never left me. Even when I turned away from what I knew was right, God patiently waited for me to recognize and relinquish my sinful ways.

Chapter Fifteen – Went Too Far Stayed Too Long

Over the many years of all the sermons I heard Pastor Judie preach, the one most unforgettable is *Went Too Far Stayed Too Long*. Like most of his sermons this one incorporated a song. For this sermon Pastor Judie referenced the blues song of the same title by James Peterson. The main point of the sermon for me was when you go astray from what you know is right and do not return to what you know is right for days, then weeks, which turn into months, and even years, the longer you stay the harder it is to get back to what you know is right. Subsequently the title from Pastor Judie's sermon and the song by Mr. Peterson song became a reality in my life.

At the beginning of 2000, Ivy was still attending Xavier and Sylvia was completely her junior year at high school. After being caught by Syl with the other man, I kept my promise not to have another affair and it remained important to me for my daughters to continue to have both parents in our home. Periodically I would mention to Syl how his negative personality affected me mentally and physically. I even admitted that although it was me that decided to have the affairs, it had a lot to do with his unwillingness to express his love towards me in the same manner he criticized me. I even restated to him that it perturbed and continued to hurt me that he would not let me know who he had his affair with. Even with these discussions Syl did not show any intention on working to meeting me half way in reconciling our differences. His refusal to address our marital problems resulted in my ongoing withdrawal into a depressed world of discontent, insecurity, and hopelessness. Then the flicker of light from the Lord gave me hope through a sermon I heard at a convention titled *My Latter Will Be Greater Than My Past*. That sermon spoke into my life restoring and strengthening my spirit. For the first time in many months I believed that marital bliss would come into my life if I waited, trusted, believed, and served Jesus Christ. Even if it did not come right away, I had to believe the promises of God that it would materialize. Until that time, I would try to be content with my marriage.

Going Too Far and Stayed Several Hours Too Long. In July of 2000, Kim called to let me know she planned to visit us August 2000. Since this was several years before she married Mo, Kim had made it clear to me she wanted to go dancing at a nightclub. Since I rarely went to nightclubs, I asked a few friends who suggested several places. One place was the *Coupe One Club*. We were glad to see Kim when she arrived in Cleveland the first Thursday in August. That Friday evening, we went to the *Coupe*. Because I had never been to this club, I asked the police officer and door attendant that were at the door if this was a cool place. They stated, yes. Kim and I then went inside, and it was a decent club, even though there were few people inside, most of which were women. Kim asked, why isn't there a crowd, where are the people? I relied, it was probably because it was still early in the evening. The police officer who was a nice looking, tall, chestnut brown skinned, and well-built man came near our table several times. Kim asked, *why is this rent-a-cop following us?* I answered, *I do not know*. A few moments later the police officer stopped at our table and begin to talk to us for a few moments. I remember he asked us if we liked the place and let us know the crowd would pick up later in the night. Kim and I stayed a little longer while she had a few drinks. I drank juice since I never drink and drive. Kim said, the club was boring, and she wanted to go somewhere else. The only other place familiar to me was the *Mirage Nightclub*, which was in the warehouse district of downtown. I asked if she wanted to go there, and Kim said, yes. Walking out the door, the police officer said, *you all leaving already*? I said, *yes*. He then asked for my phone number. Hesitating, I thought about the night Syl and Sylvia caught me in the car with my male friend, and how I had not given my number to a man since that time. Thinking I had no intention of being unfaithful and should not be giving my number to another man, yet, I still gave the police officer my phone number. After leaving the *Coupe*, I took Kim to the *Mirage Nightclub*. We had a wonderful time together that night. The next day while shopping at Randall Park Mall, the police officer called, and we began talking. His name was Jerome Barrow, and he was a sergeant with Cleveland Police Vice Department who worked part-time at the Coupe. He was five years older than me and had been divorced for over ten years. I told him a little about myself, such as age, where I was employed and although it was a little rough at times between me and my husband, we were still married. Our conversation lasted about ten minutes before he told me he was not really a phone person, but that he would call me again soon. Over the next few days we talked briefly on the phone. We discussed our jobs and it appeared we were both workaholics, and about what we enjoyed doing when not working. Little was discussed about our family life or my marital problems. That following Thursday, he asked if I wanted to go out for a drink. I agreed. We met at *Joe's House of Blues Club*. It was a nice evening. We talked, listened to the band and disc jockey, and danced a few times.

A few weeks later, Nicole planned to take me out for my birthday. Over the years, Earl and I had sporadically remained in contact with each other. He would contact me regarding matters related to his bars or rental properties. Sometimes I would visit his bars with friends. On a couple of occasions, he had given me birthday parties. That evening Nicole and I went to his bar for drinks where a few other friends met us. Jerome called me while we were at the bar to invite us to the Coupe. Nicole and I decided to go. From the time we walked through the door it was the beginning of a wonderful evening. Even though Jerome was working, he made me feel incredibly special the entire time. He assured that the staff gave Nicole and me whatever drinks we wanted. The club photographer took several pictures of us. Everyone that we met was very cordial. Once the club closed, the only people in the club were the other police officers that were working with Jerome, a few of the employees, Jerome, Nicole, and me. One of the police officers began to play music from the disc jockey booth. Jerome took my hand leading me to the dance floor where we slow danced under the sparkling disco ball. Even though I was turning 43, I felt like a fairytale princess with her prince dancing the night away. It was nearing 3:30 a.m. Nicole who had patiently waited for me was getting tired and was ready to leave. Jerome told her, I got her, she is going with me. I had been drinking, was feeling good and he got no argument from me. Nicole in her normal very protective manner asked me several times if I was sure that is what I wanted to do. I confirmed with Nicole that I was okay, and it was alright for her to leave. This was the beginning of another self-inflicted adultery relationship. The problem was this one became different than any other affair because never had I stayed out all night. Then, not only did I sleep with Jerome and stayed with him until the next morning, when it was time for Jerome to take me home I had the gall to have him drop me off where I lived with my husband and daughters. As we pulled up to my house, Jerome asked *is this Nicole house*. I replied, *no, it is my home.* He looked shocked and in disbelief that I had him bring me to the house I shared with my husband. Truthfully, I was looking foolish too, because I could not believe that I had allowed the entire evening and morning to happen, let alone his driving me home. As I got out the car, Jerome told me he would talk to me later, and I said, okay. When I entered the house upset was not the word to describe how Syl was feeling about me staying out all night, it was more like, total perturb and pissed off. Seeing his demeanor, that day I lied telling him I stayed with Nicole because we had been too drunk to drive. Even to this day I am unable to explain my nonchalant actions that day. Now looking back, it is without a doubt what I did the night and morning was irresponsible and disrespectful. Why I repeatedly behaved in this manner I am unable to figure out or explain. I think it might have been because I was no longer committed to my marriage. Unless it was because by reaching my early 40s I was experiencing the *mid-life crisis*. Or had I simply lost my mind. Whatever the reason, I was going too far and had stayed several hours too long.

Gone Too Far and Stayed Weeks Too Long. Regardless of the reason for my behavior and lying to Syl, after that day it still did not stop me from talking to Jerome. Instead, we regularly talked and saw each other once or twice a week. As we grew closer, I did something else that I had never done during my other affairs, I told Jerome all about my first marriage to Herman, including what happened to me after his death. I also let Jerome know what led to my being unfaithful to Syl, in particular, his infidelity and how his negative and critical disposition caused me to have low self-esteem and be insecurity. Jerome seemed earnestly seemed moved by and concerned about what had happened in my past as well as my current emotional well-being. As time went on Jerome's character seemed to be that of a quiet, considerate, respectful, and responsible man. Although he seemed a little introverted because he did not talk just to be, but when he did talk he was a truly knowledgeable intellectual communicator. In fact, he was one of a few men I had seriously talked to that had earned a college degree. Jerome let me know he had four children, three daughters and a son. His daughter, Jazmyn was in high school and his son, Otis who was about nine years old where with his ex-wife Corrine. His oldest daughter, Markita was twenty, and her mother was Pat, his former girlfriend. Sheriese was his youngest daughter who was only four years old, and her mother was his former girlfriend, Sheron. Jerome's mother, Mary (Hootie) Moore lived with him, but had not been home the night I stayed all night because she was in the hospital.

Weeks turned into several months with me becoming closer to Jerome and lying more to Syl about my whereabouts. Previously my infidelities were primarily to uplift my confidence and self-worth and lasted only a few weeks. This time my emotions were all over the place. I was living in an imaginary fantasy world. To have these types of feelings for Jerome was not good for my family, because I had made a commitment to be there for my daughters. Thus, I was fully aware my feelings for Jerome could not disrupt that commitment. Yet, I continued to live a double life – there was my real life with Syl and my daughters and then my make-believe life with Jerome. Knowing I could not deal with the feelings that were developing too rapidly for Jerome, I had to face reality. As before, I could not think of my feelings, I had to do what was best for my daughters. At that point, I tried to break up with Jerome. For several weeks, I stopped calling him and answering his calls. One day he called from a number I did not recognize. Once I answered, and heard his voice saying, what is going on, I felt all warm and fuzzy inside, I replied, my usual, working. He said, you have not called or returned my calls. I told him that I had just been busy. Jerome then said, *if I did not want to see him anymore just let him know*. Knowing I had missed him and feeling on an emotional high from hearing from him, I told him that I still wanted to see him. Following that conversation, we began to see each other even more regularly than before. Our relationship steadily grew. By Christmas of 2000, I spent a part of Christmas Eve with

Jerome. Before I left he gave me a lovely card and a beautiful gold and diamond necklace. Christmas Day and New Year Eve were spent at home with my family.

In March 2001, Jerome let me know his brother, Otis (Moochie) was getting married in the spring. He asked me to ride with him to Canada to purchase liquor for the bachelor's party. I agreed. During the drive we talked, laughed, and listened to a variety of music including, rock, soul, jazz, pop, and blues. I was amazed Jerome knew all the words to a lot of the songs. That spring, Jerome asked if I could travel to Toledo, Ohio with him to attend the three days statewide police and fire competition games. He would be coaching one of the police basketball teams. Of course, I wanted to attend. Since sometimes I would travel out of town for work-related matters, I decided to lie to Syl by saying I would be out-of-town working for a client. The trip was filled with fun and watching exciting competitive basketball games. Being with Jerome while we socialized with team members and his co-workers was enjoyable. Then our alone time was filled with much needed affection and compassion. To top things off Jerome took care of all the finances. This was relief for me to be taken care of financially. In both of my marriages most of the time my income exceeded my husbands and I handled the finances. To not have to take the lead financially was great. During those few days he fulfilled some of my characteristics including, being romantic, socializing, interacting, supportive, and handled the finances. Each day I talked to Syl and the girls, while I pretended to be working. Three days later even though returning home was back to earth for me, I remained aglow from the days spent with Jerome. Several weeks later, Jerome asked me to attend Moochie's wedding with him. I said, yes. Prior to the wedding, I helped Jerome prepare for the bachelor's party to be held at his house. The day of the wedding I met Jerome at the church. Following the ceremony, the reception was held in the church dining hall. Jerome formally introduced me to several people. I finally was introduced to his mother, Mrs. Hootie, who would be at the house when I sometimes visited, but we had not formally been introduced. I also met his son, Otis, Aunt Artilla (who he called Aunt Mill), and several other family members and friends. Otis was a charming nine years old boy. We became friends from the second we met. Many of Jerome family members told him I was a beautiful young lady. Jerome agreed with every person. Of course, this did my soul good because compliments were rarely received in my life. It was a momentous day with Jerome and his family. The only exception that concerned me was one of the members of Assembly attended the wedding and she knew Syl and I were still together. As we amiably greeted each other, there was no hint that she would let anyone know I was at the wedding with Jerome.

Our next special day was on the 4th of July. Jerome asked me to go to dinner with him at his sister's house. I was introduced to his sister, Jane (Mooney), his daughter, Markita and some of his other family members. Mooney said that I must really be special to her brother because I was the first lady Jerome had brought to her house. This made me feel wonderful. What was confusing to me is how everyone there was surprised that I had not met Jerome's daughter,

Jazmyn. They told me that she was Jerome favorite child and the love and joy of his world. That day was all I had wished for in a holiday. It was a pleasant time spent with family, cooking, talking, and having fun. Afterwards, Jerome and I returned to his house. With him tightly holding me in his arms as we made love, Jerome asked me to be his girlfriend. I was a little surprised because Jerome knew although I was not happy being with my husband, I was still married with a family. Yet he stilled wanted me to be his girlfriend. Without hesitation I said, *yes*. A few weeks later, Jerome asked me to help Mooney and him with the 21st birthday party for Markita. I worked with Mooney to plan the party. The party was full of yummy food, drinks and lot of fun talking, laughing, and dancing. Jerome introduced me to several other family members. Without a doubt, like the sermon by Pastor Judie, I had gone too far and stayed weeks too long.

Gone Way Too Far and Stay Months Too Long. At this point I was living a life full of deceit. Living as the wife of Syl and the girlfriend of Jerome. I did still love Syl. He was the father of our daughters and we had shared over twenty years together with many beautiful memorable times. During some of the saddest times in our lives we were there to support and encourage each other. Understandably, things became difficult after I found out about the affair that I forgave, but the emotional scarring could not let me forget. My obsession of not knowing the name of the woman even to this day is a thorn in my side. In some respects, I remained in revenge mode because he refused to tell me her name. Our relationship further deteriorated when his demeanor became obnoxiously disparaging and negative. Even when I showered him with loving affection, compliments and encouragement while begging for his positive confirmation of me physically, mentally, and emotionally he refused to meet me even halfway. If only he would have shown a little interest and effort towards a few of my desires, I believe we would have been able to celebrate our 50th anniversary.

Unlike in the past where my indiscretions were temporary, my relationship with Jerome was detrimentally affecting my marriage. My feelings for Jerome intensified each day. He uplifted my self-esteem and made me feel confident about myself. Many of the desires from my characteristics list he was displaying by being attentive to my emotional needs and very affectionate. He would put a smile on my face by saying or doing something nice that made me have a better day. Jerome had the attribute of leadership and was a hard worker and financially stable. The few times spent at social gathering he was friendly and sociable. We were going out to restaurants and clubs where we had fun, danced, and listened to DJs or live bands. The few places we travelled were enjoyable. For special occasions he showered me with beautiful thoughtful gifts. More importantly we had a lot of one-on-one time. These were things that over the years I had begged Syl to do me, to no avail. This caused me to go way too far and stay months too long.

<u>Gone Too Far and Stayed Years Too Long</u>. Although living a dual chaotic life, my primary focus was still my daughters and taking care of our household. During May and June of 2001, Syl and I prepared for Sylvia prom's and graduation from high school. Just like we did for Ivy's prom and graduation, we did the same for Sylvia to make her dreams come true. After her prom we made preparation for her graduation. Kim made plans to attend the graduation which made me happy. Prior to graduation, we gave Sylvia a graduation party. She then began to prepare for college.

Granting I was living an adulterous life, but my faith and trust in God never waived and not attending Assembly was causing a spiritual void in my life. Besides myself, several other members were no longer attending Assembly. Among them were Mother Ida Mae and her family members. Her daughter, Big Sylvia had joined Lee-Seville Baptist Church and Trina was frequently visiting there. In December 2001, Big Sylvia and Trina invited me to a Christmas program at Lee Seville that I attended. Beside myself, Mother Ida Mae and several other former members from Assembly attended the program. Following the program, I attended Lee Seville for several more weeks. By February 2002, Mother Ida Mae and I united with Lee-Seville. Shortly thereafter I was serving at Lee-Seville as the director of the youth choir and assisting with the preparation of programs. Before accepting the positions to serve at Lee-Seville, I met with Pastor Newton to let him know about my tragic past. Pastor Newton, just like Pastor Judie, told me my past life was not an issue for him and assured me if any members had an issue they would have to deal with him. His support and understanding were appreciated. Even as I contemplated and dealt with my double love life, being able to again worship and serve at Lee Seville was much needed for my spiritual stability. The flicker of light was the Lord knew all about my past and current sins and yet the favor of the salvation of God was still with me. *You, God, know my folly; my guilt is not hidden from you. Lord, the Lord Almighty, may those who hope in you not be disgraced because of me; God of Israel, may those who seek you not be put to shame because of me....But I pray to you, Lord, in the time of your favor; in your great love, O God, answer me with your sure salvation*, Psalm 69:5-6 & 13 (NIV).

Even though things were going good with serving at Lee Seville and the heavy case load at the firm, my personal life was in shambles. It was getting more difficult for me to manage my real life at home and make-believe life with Jerome. With the girls at the beginning of their own adult lives, there would be no need for me to continue living in an unhappy marriage. This made me begin to wonder if I would be with Syl or Jerome. Even with everything Syl and I had done wrong to each other over the years, I honestly did love Syl and believed he loved me in his own way. My problem was for years I had expressed to Syl how unhappy I was, but he refused to change his attitude of being uncompassionate, condescending, and unsupportive. I had concluded that he did not show affection either due to masculinity issues; he could not because he just did not know how; or he just did not want to because he believed it was unnecessary. Syl also knew protecting the identity of the woman he had the affair with always made me feel inferior. Yet he refused to help me overcome that issue. This made me believe he did not care about how it made me feel. With all the negative and hurtful emotional wounds that we had afflicted upon each other from our adverse behaviors, I did not know if those wounds could be healed.

Trying to balance my unconventional and immoral love triangle and all the other aspects of my life, I became exhausted morally and physically. Juggling my time between our home and Jerome's house, I found myself torn into two pieces. I constantly pondered do I stay with Syl knowing the girls were grown and about to start their own lives; or alternatively take on the idiom of *me, myself, and I*, and fulfill my desires to be with Jerome? After wrestling mentally for weeks, once more I put my desires behind and begin to spend less time with Jerome and more time at home. I told Jerome there were family issues I needed to address. Unlike my previous affairs, Jerome never stopped pursuing me. Each time he called, and I heard his voice, I would see him again. Before long I found my evenings and weekends at Jerome house once again increasing.

In August 2002, Syl gave me a surprise birthday party. It was the first time I had a surprise birthday party. Shocked and happy he had thought enough of me to give the party. It was a beautiful celebration at the house with family members and friends. I thanked Syl and everyone that attended for making my birthday such a special day. The only downside of the party is that it brought back memories of when I was giving Syl a surprise birthday party years ago. As I was trying to get him to leave with me for what he thought was merely a dinner with me, his behavior was so discouraging, by the time we arrived at the venue, I was in tears. When Syl walked in the door and saw many family members, co-workers, friends, and members from

Assembly, he had a big wide grin on his face. The guest blessed him with nice gifts and a good amount of money. On the way home, he told me how nice it was for me to give him the party and he was sorry for his behavior before the party. This was another time when I forgave but could not forget his behavior.

My next unexpected surprise from Syl was a few weeks later when one morning in September, he called asking me to bring him a sandwich on his bus route. This was something he regular asked for when we first met in 1981, and I would happily take breakfast or lunch to him on his bus route. It had been years since he had asked me to bring him food, so that day I was caught off guard, but I of course said, yes. After I handed him the sandwich while getting off the bus, Syl told me, *you look nice*. My heart dropped, thinking to myself now you say what I have been begging and longing to hear for all these years. Still stunned, I said, *thanks*. Then my why questions took over my mind. Why didn't he give those types of compliments before today? Why did he say this today when he knew our marriage was in trouble? Why couldn't this even small act of affection be expressed even a few months ago? Just a little compliment like that would have healed a lot of emotional pain. He finally complimented me, but it was too late, because weeks before I had decided to move into an apartment. I now had gone too far and stayed years too long.

Gone Too Far and Stayed Way Too Long. Initially I planned for Tim and me to move together. After speaking with his case worker, she informed me Tim was only approved to receive four hours a day of health care aide services. With the hours I worked, this number of hours were insufficient. She let me know with the continual deterioration of his health it had reached the point of a safety issue for Tim to stay alone. She brought up the fact Tim had fallen several times at our house when no one was home. Even though he was able to push the help button, the falls out his wheelchair had become more frequent and caused him to be hospitalized several times. Following my discussion with the case worker, I called Kim, Gregory, Aunt Mary, Uncle Andrew, and a few other family members to let them know I was separating from Syl. I explained that due to the hours I worked it would be unsafe for Tim to stay with me. I let them know we needed to decide a plan for his care. Because no one was able to take full-time care of Tim in their home, it was decided that an assisted living home would be the best option for him. Once I spoke with several representatives of assisted living homes I knew those facilities were too expenses. Again, I spoke with everyone. Agreeing it was obvious Tim could not afford assisted living, everyone concurred the alternative was to locate the best nursing home. Once I secured Tim acceptance into a nice and well-maintained nursing home, I begin to look for an apartment. In mid-September, with the help of Nicole, I moved Tim into the nursing home. By this time Syl knew my intentions. We were barely speaking and had not slept together in months. Sylvia and Ivy were now aware we were having marital problems, though I was unsure they knew the extent of the problems. It was a point of no return. I had now *gone too far and stayed way too long*.

Chapter Sixteen –Jerome Barrow

After I had looked at a few apartments, I called Jerome to let him know I intended on moving by the middle of October. He replied, okay and that we would discuss it later. That evening as I talked to him about which apartments I preferred, to my astonishment he said, his mother had moved into her own apartment. He then suggested I move in with him because we were together most of the time and it would allow me to save money. After discussing my moving for a more few days, we agreed it would be more financially best for me if we lived together. This was because he knew when I initially made plans to move into an apartment my budget was planned with Tim living with me and his income being used to help supplement the expenses of the apartment. When it became necessary for him to live at the nursing home, it made a significant difference in my anticipated living expenses. My financial concern also was primarily due to already knowing Syl would be unable to keep up the house unless I paid a percentage some of the expenses. If I moved into an apartment, my living cost together with the expenses to assist Syl would result in an extremely tight budget and might would cause me to live from paycheck to paycheck. Moving in with Jerome alleviated my financial concerns, especially since he said I did not have to pay expenses until I was more financially stable. Although my financial concerns had been lessened, it created another dilemma. Not only would I be dealing with leaving Syl and the potential ramification thereof, but what would my daughters and other loved ones think about me leaving Syl and moving in another man. I knew my decision to move in with Jerome was in the best interest for me in many ways. However, the thought of contending with what would be said and the negative impact of my actions on my daughters triggered a lot of stress and anxiety. This made me begin to second guess my decision. Wondering if again I was making the wrong decision, I prayed to God for guidance and strength. While praying thoughts of the sermon *went too far and stayed too long* came to my mind. The Holy Spirit revealed the sermon applied to both me and Syl, that emotionally we both *went too far and stayed too long*. It was clear Syl was not fulfilling my desires and vice versa I was not giving him what he needed and had unfaithful to him. Our personal issues were preventing us from having a happy marriage. The saying *two wrongs don't make it right* applied to our marriage. Was I more to blame? Most definitely, yes. Was there any way our relationship could be healed? I did not know. But not wanting to keep on going down the same road with Syl when Jerome had come in my life like a knight in shining armor to carry me away like I was a princess, I was leaving Syl.

On October 7, 2002, while Syl was at work, I moved out of the house. After what happened when I planned to divorce Herman, I vowed never to leave a man when he was at home. I thought Sylvia would be at school, but unfortunately, she did not have school that day. When the moving van arrived, Sylvia said little to me. She called Syl and Ivy. Syl called saying he could not believe I was doing this to our family. The call ended with him saying if I left don't try to come back. Ivy was extremely upset. She stated how could I break up the family and take another father from her life. I tried to explain my position to Ivy and Sylvia. Neither were hearing a word I was saying. After the reaction of Ivy and Sylvia I was too afraid, embarrassed, ashamed, and reluctant to tell them I was moving with another man. Instead, I told them I was moving in with Charisse. A few weeks later they discovered I lived with Jerome. In this grievous self-inflicted storm, the flicker of light from God was of His glorious forgiveness and compassion. *When I kept silent about my sin, my body wasted away through my groaning all the day long. For day and night Your hand [of displeasure] was heavy upon me; My energy (vitality, strength) was drained away as with the burning heat of summer. Selah. I acknowledged my sin to You, and I did not hide my wickedness; I said, "I will confess [all] my transgressions to the Lord"; And You forgave the guilt of my sin. Selah....Many are the sorrows of the wicked, but he who trusts in and relies on the Lord shall be surrounded with compassion and lovingkindness*, Psalm 32:3-5 & 10 (AMP). Despite my igniting this self-inflicted adulterous dark storm that resulted in the end of my second marriage, my daughters being hurt, dismayed, and disappointed in me, and causing me emotional scars of disgrace and guilt, my Lord and Savior Jesus Christ with compassion forgave me once again.

Unintentional Pain. Initially Syl was furious with me for leaving, especially in the manner I left. Thankfully he slowly became civil towards me. Regrettably though, the day I left him I lost a part of my girls that I would never regain. The separation hurt my girls more than I expected. Ever since my marital problems had started, I thought if I was to leave Syl, it would be better to do it after Ivy and Sylvia were out of high school and starting their own adult lives. Like many other decisions in my life, I was wrong. My daughters were devastated. Sylvia my quiet baby, not only was emotionally affected it caused her to suffer in college that year. Ivy felt not only had I taken her first father from her, now I had taken away the only father she had known all her life. They both believed I had deceived them and lived a deceitful, and a fake life. Most importantly, that hated that I had hurt their father. All those years, I thought waiting to leave Syl would be better emotionally for my daughters when they were grown women instead of little children was so very wrong. My logic had been once they had an opportunity to be in their own relationships they would understand the ups and downs of relationships. Somehow, I thought over the years they would have detected my unhappiness and sense the emotional effect my marriage with little compassion and lots of inattentiveness was having on me. Of course, again I was wrong. In hindsight it was not in the best interest of Ivy and Sylvia for me to stay married primarily for their sake because I believed leaving when they were grown would be better. It would have been better for me to leave when they were under the age of twelve, because they would have been happy-go-lucky children without such strong viewpoints about our marital problems. This might have allowed my daughters to better handle the separation in a childlike blasé open-minded attitude, and I could have more easily appeased our daughters. Instead waiting until Ivy and Sylvia were adults they now totally had their individual thoughts, opinions, and point of views about me leaving our family that made the separation much harder for them to accept. This was especially true because there were no visual signs of any martial problems perceived by them. If they were aware, it was not until they were in their late teens, and they did not realize the severity of the problems in our marriage. This resulted in my daughters believing for all those years I deceived them by living a phony life. They believed I had broken up our home because I was only thinking of my happiness. They thought they had beaten the statistics of a broken home with divorce parents. Ivy and Sylvia said how proud they had been that their parents were still married when they graduated from high school, because statistically most students graduated with divorce parents. I had even ruined their dreams of not being a part of that statistic. My decision to leave Syl initiated unintentional pain upon my two daughters, the joys of my life. Hurting my daughters was another heavy self-inflicted load to bear. Not only had I hurt my daughters, I had emotionally damaged and let them down. What have I done to my daughters? My selfish actions yet again were wreaking destruction upon them. Why didn't I continue to put them first instead of myself? Why did I obliterate my darling innocent daughters? Would they ever forgive me? How would this affect their future relationships? Would I be able to regain their trust? Hurting my daughters is something I will forever regret. To this day, I still try to heal the hurt I caused my girls by leaving their father.

With much prayer and asking my daughters to forgive me for hurting and letting them down, eventually my relationship with Ivy and Sylvia improved. With each passing day our talks were more friendly and thoughtful, and we were able to see each other with less tension. Even though Ivy and Sylvia did not like my leaving Syl, they slowly began to respect my decision. This allowed us to begin to heal our relationship. The reconciling of our relationship was the flicker of light from God's steadfast blessings upon my life that I deeply appreciated. With time Syl and I became more amicable than ever before. In the beginning, we reached an agreement for me to pay forty percent of the maintenance of the house. This was necessary because Sylvia was still in college and staying at the house, and eventually Ivy again lived at the house, and I never wanted my girls to be concerned with where they would live. Moreover, the guilt I felt deep down inside for being unfaithful and not staying with Syl through the good and bad made me have a sense of financial obligation to him. Although not to the same extent as when I first left to this day I still help pay the expenses for the house.

By going *too far and staying too long* there were consequences I had not planned to face. Unfortunately, I had not totally trusted in the Lord with my marital problems. In many instances I had stepped out on my own feelings and emotions. I knew after leaving Syl from that point forward instead of leaning on my own understanding, I needed to reaffirm my focus on Proverbs 3:5-6, making it the central not peripheral aspect of my life.

Third Time's a Charm. After moving in with Jerome, I was determined not to have another failed relationship. To sustain and insure the healthy growth of our relationship I was fully committed to devote my love, energy, and dedication to Jerome. Then to prevent our relationship from becoming boring I was determined to be flexible to change. I would be open to different ideas and strive to meet the needs of Jerome. Most importantly, to always precisely communicate my thoughts, desires, and ideas to Jerome, rather than assume he would know what I was thinking or needed from him. Jerome and I had discussed my characteristics list and the attributes he was looking for in me. We promised to work to fulfill each other's needs. Getting settled in, Jerome did not complain as I gradually turned the bachelor pad into a cozy home. Wanting more than ever for this relationship to last, I was intent on keeping Jerome happy by being very attentive to him. One thing different I plan to do was to prepare home cooked dinners on weekdays, and on the weekends breakfast, lunch, and dinner, if he wanted it. I even decided he never would have to make his own plate. I made his plate and brought it to him on a nicely prepared tray.

The following weekend after moving in was my first test of how I would react in situations. That Saturday it was Sweeties Day, a day comparable to Valentine Day celebrated primarily in northeast Ohio and few other areas in the United States. From the previous gifts Jerome gave me and the fact I just moved in, I knew without a doubt he would give me a card, candy, or flowers. To my surprise he did not get me anything. He did not even say, Happy Sweetie Day. I was disappointed. To assure our communication remained healthy, I had promised to promptly and directly address my concerns. It was my hope that by addressing the problem would prevent me from my old habits of assuming or trying to figure out if something was wrong, wondering why something happened, or becoming upset and pouting. Determined not to revert back to my old habits, I asked Jerome why he did not at least say Happy Sweeties Day to me. Jerome replied, he typically *does not celebrate all those made up days*. I expressed how important it was to me. He then said he *would work on it the next time*. It was refreshing to promptly address a concern, and have it amiably resolved. Even though this was not a major issue, the fact that it was resolved with communication instead of assumptions meant a lot to me. For the first time I believed in the expression, *communication is an important part of a relationship* was true. Too many years in my marriages and other aspects of my life I would not say exactly what was on my mind. In the past I would as the saying goes *beat around the bush* about what was bothering me, instead of being straightforward with my concerns. Then I would assume my concerns were clearly understood and would be addressed, when in fact the person really was unaware of my underlying problems or concerns. This would lead to a lot of unnecessary misunderstanding, because I would become frustrated when my concerns were not addressed. Determined to communicate much better with Jerome, this was the beginning of changing how I thought and communicated. Assuming had to be eliminated from my thoughts, because *when you assume you make an ass of you and me*. In addition, no longer would I assume people knew what was on my mind. I had to start speaking precisely what I wanted and *stop beating around the bush*.

Attending Lee-Seville, I was again spiritually growing and

working diligently with the youth and assisting the church clerk. I also was busy at the firm with several cases requiring that I often had to work of extended hours. My relationship with Ivy and Sylvia was gradually healing, Syl and I were on friendly terms, while my relationship with Jerome steadily grew stronger and closer. Thankfully once again I was happy and content with my life. I was also grateful that starting my life with Jerome, I did not have to worry about the status of my appeal lingering in the background like I had when I started my life with Syl.

The second weekend when I returned home from church on Sunday, I entered the house to hear voices coming from the basement. I said, hello, and heard a few responses in startling tones say, hi. I went upstairs to change clothes, and when I returned downstairs to the kitchen to begin cooking, several men came upstairs from the basement. Besides Jerome, it was Moochie, and their friends Rico and Larry that I had met at the wedding. As Jerome begin to reintroduce me, they each said they met me at Moochie's wedding. Jerome then let me know they were over watching the Browns' football game and whatever I was cooking could I cook enough for everyone. I answered, of course. The next week, when I returned home from church, the guys were there, and again I cooked dinner for them. When Rico, Moochie and Larry were preparing their plates, each of them told me how shocked they were last week when I opened the door to the house with a key. They were even more surprised when I went upstairs and came back downstairs and started cooking. Each of them went on to teasingly tell me they could not believe

Jerome had allowed a woman to move in with him. Those words made me feel extra special just like the day at Mooney's house when she told me that Jerome had never brought a woman to her house. It further assured me of the feelings Jerome had for me of genuinely wanting me to be a part of his life.

People coming over to watch the Sunday football games and having dinner became a weekly routine at our house. Eventually other people, including Mooney, Jerome nephew Michael, Trina, Cha, Nicole, Ruth, and Charisse, sometimes would come over on Sundays. Mooney would often help with the cooking. The Sunday gatherings were enjoyable for me because it was one of my characteristics list desires of socializing with loved ones. Each Sunday the house would have an atmosphere likened to the movie and TV series *Soul Food*. Although for years Jerome has been a four-seat season ticket holder with the Browns, he would usually watch the game at home and either give or sell the tickets. If the weather was not too cold, we sometimes would go to games with family members or friends. We even attended one game with Hattie when Desmond's team played the Browns. Although Jerome attended games when the weather was cold, I never would attend those games.

November of 2002, Jerome was turning fifty years old. I decided to give him a surprise birthday party at the Coupe. I asked Mooney to help me and she gladly agreed. She obtained the names and addresses of family members and friends for the invitations. Mooney also agreed to prepare most of the food, which I was glad because she was an excellent cook. She planned to prepare barbeque ribs and chicken, baked beans, greens, and potato salad. I told Mooney how much I appreciated her help with all the arrangements for the party.

Jerome had previously introduced me to his first patrol partner, Kennedy, who was also still worked for the police department, so I asked Kennedy to help me obtain the names and addresses of their co-workers. Kennedy said he would be glad to. I was excited about surprising Jerome. I was imagining the surprised reaction when he walked through the door to see his family members and friends there to celebrate his birthday. I was looking forward to meeting his other family members, friends, and co-workers. The plan was for Rico and Moochie to bring him to the Coupe. They had called him earlier in the week to let him know they were taking him out for drinks on Saturday. A few hours before the party Rico called to tell me Jerome was refusing to go with them. A few moments later Jerome called me stating he had received a phone call from Sheron, his youngest daughter's mother. He said she knew about the surprise birthday party and was threatening to come make a scene with him and me at the Coupe. Jerome went on to tell me he did not want any problems for me as Sheron could be very confrontational. Even though assuring him I could handle myself, Jerome insisted he did not want to take any chances of her embarrassing us. Unable to convince Jerome to change his mind, I had to cancel the party. I called the manager of the Coupe to let him know the party was unfortunately cancelled, and if any people showed up, to let them know I was sorry but I had to cancel the party. When I called Mooney, she was upset that Jerome allowed Sheron to ruin his party. She then helped me call as many people as we could to let them know about the cancellation. Nicole had been with me all day getting things together and tried to calm me down and get me to understand that Jerome was only doing this to protect me. I tried to get that through my head but was still disappointed. Nicole and I then went to Mooney's house to get some of the food, so it would not go to waste. Mooney also tried to console me by explaining that Jerome was thinking about me not getting mixed up in a messy situation with Sheron and her family. Nicole assured Mooney no one was going to bother me. I was really upset that Jerome had allowed Sheron to make him cancel the party and livid by the audacity of Sheron to threaten him and me. Thinking about and trying to rationalize the events of the night, I was listening to what Mooney and Nicole were saying an attempt to make me feel better. They kept asking me if I was alright and saying how wrong it was for Sheron to do what she did, and Jerome should not listen to her. I put on my fake persona saying, I am alright. We placed as much of the food as possible in Mooney's refrigerator and split the rest of it between Nicole, one of Mooney's family members, and me. While I drove home my mind kept on replaying how I had planned a wonderful surprise birthday party, but the surprise was on me. I was the one caught off guard with the biggest surprise. Less than six weeks of living together this incident ignited anxiety and questions. What was the true status of Jerome's relationship with Sheron? Were they still involved romantically? Had I been fooled again into believing I was the only woman in a man's life? Immediately I felt a flood of emotional defensiveness. Then there were flashbacks of how Herman and Syl both betrayed me with other women. Was Jerome already cheating? Had Jerome ever been faithful? Had I brought pain and suffering to Ivy and Sylvia only to be in the exact same situation as I was with Syl?

When I arrived at the house, Jerome was already home sitting in the kitchen. As I began to bring in the food from Mooney and other items for the party, Jerome came outside to help me bring the items in the house. He began apologizing for having to cancel the party and telling me how he appreciated everything I tried to do for him for his birthday. He then explained how he wanted to avoid any problems that could have escalated out of control at the party. He told me how it would have been difficult for him to have a fun time while constantly checking to assure the guests and I were okay. He did not want me or any other guests to have to deal with any adverse confrontations. I told him I could not believe that if Sheron was his ex-girlfriend she could cause this type of havoc in our lives. Jerome assured me that he was not romantically, or any other way involved with Sheron except for the care of their child. I believed him because my past experiences with Syl had made me an expert in snooping for telltale signs of cheating. So far there were no indications that Jerome was being unfaithful. Though still disappointed we had to cancel the party I knew from my life with Herman it was best not to knowingly place myself and others into confrontational situations. This was one of the times in my life that I did not realize the flicker of light of the grace of God that did not allow me to walk blindly into an adverse situation that night. Days later I was thankful the evening ended peacefully. More importantly I was grateful for the direct open communication that allowed Jerome and me to positively handle this situation.

For Thanksgiving, Jerome and I went to see Mrs. Hootie. We ate and had a nice visit. It was always entertaining to be in the presence of Mrs. Hootie. She would keep me laughing sharing stories about her life, although her talking about family members and their various situations caused me to raise my eyebrows. Some her family members often described Mrs. Hootie as a stern woman who said exactly what was on her mind regardless if it might offend or hurt your feelings. For this reason, some people could not handle her personality. When I was around Mrs. Hootie, she did speak what was on her mind, even at times talking harshly about Jerome and Mooney. I would say, Mrs. Hootie *they are not that bad*, and she would always say, *you will see*. As I witnessed her blunt abrasiveness towards family members, I was happy she always was kind to me. The more I got to know Mrs. Hootie I loved and admired her for being herself. To me Mrs. Hootie just had a *no holds barred* personality.

That Christmas I helped Jerome wrap gifts for Sheriese, Otis and his grandchildren from his step-son Charles (CJ), the older brother of Jazmyn and Otis. At this point I had not met Sheriese or Jazmyn, only Markita and Otis. Early Christmas morning Jerome left to take the gifts to his children and grandchildren. Later that day I spent time with Ivy and Sylvia at their house which I now called *my old home*. We exchanged gifts and had a good visit. For New Year Eve's 2003, Jerome was working at the Coupe where I was to join him before midnight. We brought in the New Year under the stars while he and others shot off a few rounds in the parking lot. I thanked God for bringing in another year, and I prayed this would be the first day of a year filled with reviving, increasing and blessings for my daughters, loved ones, Jerome, and me.

Different Mate, But Still Problems. At the beginning of each committed relationship, I had faith that this time everything would go right. Thus, I believed I had learned from my other marriages what to do and not to do for Jerome and my relationship to withstand adversities. So, surely the expression the *third time is a charm* had to be a good omen for me. Plus, as I previously mentioned, from the moment I moved in with Jerome I knew communication was going to be vital part of our having a successful relationship. I hoped our communication with each other would balance out, because as previously noted, Jerome was not a big talker. Usually Jerome would only talk extensively if discussing a topic that interested or pertained to matters concerning him. On the other hand, for me once I began talking, I could go on for hours often repeating what I said several times, to the point I would be *talking just to hear myself talking*. When I moved in with Jerome, I thought if we at least talked when needed we would be okay, but unfortunately, after the first few months of living together, I realized Jerome talked even less than I thought.

By February 2003, Jerome's personality began to change. I thought this is *déjà vu*. No way was this happening to me, again. My love life history could not be repeating itself. Everything was supposed to go right. Then suddenly it was, *oh no, not again,* my fairytale life could not be shattering with his true demeanor of being insensitive, controlling, secretive and condescending surfacing? These thoughts were arising in my mind because Jerome did not believe in giving an account of his whereabouts. He would walk out the house without saying where he was going or even goodbye. Yet he always wanted to know my whereabouts. If I was unable to answer the phone when he called, he would call nonstop. When I answered he would not accept my reason for not being able to answer, but instead he accused me of being with another man. Then he began belittling me. Not only did he do this when we were alone he did it when guests were visiting. Often the way he talked to me was in an impolite demeaning tone. This was especially true when he wanted me to fix his plate, get him a beer or simply see what he wanted. Even though it was me that willingly started and enjoyed bringing his meals to him on a tray and getting beers and other things for him, at times he would be very insensitive and unappreciative. It became so bad that my loved ones started calling me *Edith*, the wife to *Archie Bunker* from the television sitcom, *All in the Family*. Even though it was said in fun by loved ones, mentally it made me feel degraded. Initially I thought his secretive and condescending demeanor was due to him not living with a woman for such a long time. I began to believe it was because Jerome was not used to sharing his space. His controlling demeanor I presumed was on account of how our relationship had started with me cheating on Syl to be with him, and he thought I would be unfaithful to him. I explicitly had let Jerome know why I had been unfaithful to Syl was because of his lack of showing compassion, inability to express his love for me, and the harsh manner he treated me. I had assured Jerome if he did not treat me in the same manner, there would be no need for me to be unfaithful. When I discussed my concerns with Jerome about his recent negative behavior, as I thought it would be, he told me it had been a longtime since he had lived with anyone, and I needed to give him an opportunity to get acclimated to living with me. Listening to him explain the reasons for his recent negative demeanor, I decided at this junction in my life, I did not want another failed relationship. It would be too hurtful and embarrassing to fail again this soon. Moreover, I knew I also had issues of my own of being insecure, low self-esteem and a habit of blowing things out of proportion that I needed to work on. After talking, we agreed to work harder on making our relationship better by working on communicating and being more patient with each other.

Then an incident several weeks later left me in shock. The phone rang, I answered it saying hello, it was Markita calling to talk to Jerome. A few seconds into the conversation, I heard Jerome talking very cruelly, yelling, and using profanity. I could not believe the way he was talking to Markita. I could faintly hear her in the background crying and hollering. He hung up the phone and mumbled profane words. Within seconds Markita called me on my cell phone. Upset and crying she told me she was pregnant and had told Jerome. She went on to tell me how he became enraged and degraded her by cussing and calling her profane names. I tried to console and assure her I knew how she felt. I shared how at times he spoke to me in a comparable manner. I encouraged her to be strong for her baby. Then

I let her know that Jerome eventually would come around to support her and the baby. Although Jerome and I never mentioned the conversations we had with Markita, that day the way he spoke to his daughter revealed another dark side of his character. When Markita had her baby girl, Cameron, Jerome was there for her birth to support her and Markita. From that day forward, he was the ideal loving and supportive grandfather to Cameron.

Joyous Times Together. The next several months, Jerome and I worked to improve our relationship. When our work schedules allowed, we spent quality time together. In August 2003, we made plans to attend his family reunion being held in a suburb of Detroit, Michigan. Otis, Jazmyn, and Mrs. Hootie were going with us. Because all of us could not fit in Jerome's car, Mrs. Hootie rode with me in my car. This was the first time I met Jazmyn who I had been looking forward to meeting. The anticipation was due to family members and friends being shocked that I had lived with Jerome for a year and had not met Jazmyn. Everyone repeatedly told me she was his favorite child and the love of his life. They let me know o be totally accepted by Jerome she had to like me. This was mind-blowing that my future might be in the hands of his young daughter. Once we arrived at the hotel, everyone wanted something to eat. Jerome suggested Jazmyn and I go pick up some food. We of course said yes, and while we waited for the food, Jazmyn and I had an opportunity to talk. I let her know how concerned about meeting her I had been due to everything the family members and friends had told me. Jazmyn was very polite and kindly replied, she understood. She then let me know that Otis had asked her if she liked me. She told him, yes, and Otis then told her he was glad because he liked me too. From that day forward Jazmyn and I had a pleasant relationship. The family reunion was nice. There was another coincidence when I saw one of Jerome's cousins, Montana Davis who was a former member of Assembly. When I talked to her I let her know that Syl and I were no longer together, and I was dating Jerome. Mrs. Montana was happy for me

Several months later after the reunion, Mrs. Hootie began to have health issues. Jerome let me know due to her health she would be moving back into the house, I said okay. It was good to have Mrs. Hootie there for companionship. She still had no problem saying what was on her mind, regardless of whether it hurt or insulted you. Being around Mrs. Hootie you had to have tough skin to deal with her. The primary people she continued to criticize were still Jerome and Mooney. One day I learned firsthand about her saying exactly what was on her mind when abruptly she asked me, *why was I with her son with his mean self.* I would tell her, *because I loved him.* She would reply, *you will see he is a mean cruel man.* Her saying this to me was like déjà vu of when Christina warned me about Herman. Like I ignored, Christina, I ignored the warnings of Mrs. Hootie. As time passed, I had to agree with Mrs. Hootie, at certain times Jerome was downright mean and then other times he was the perfect gentleman. Thinking about the saying *you have made your bed, now lie in it,* I knew if I wanted my dreams of celebrating many years with Jerome, I had to work on staying together through the good and bad. I knew without working through our problems there would be no fairytale happily ever after ending for us.

    After Mrs. Hootie moved in the Sunday gatherings for football games and other events faded out. Mrs. Hootie would regularly receive visits and phone calls from family members and friends. Prior to Mrs. Hootie moving in with us, Mooney and I had become good friends. We would visit each other and frequently talked on the phone. She had met several of my loved ones. We would go out to eat, shopping and visited each other churches. I always looked forward to her superb cooking because I really enjoyed her barbeque ribs, greens, potato salad and desserts that were always awesome. Suddenly one day Mooney began shunning and acting cold towards me. It was disappointing as I had always enjoyed being with Mooney and the family gatherings at her home. I asked Jerome why Mooney was acting ticked off with me. He said, he had no idea. Mooney did not talk to me for weeks, then unexpectedly she called like nothing had happened. This type of behavior occurred several more times. One day she would like me and the next day she would detest me. It came to the point I became use to our seesaw relationship. When Mrs. Hootie moved with us, Mooney became even more hostile towards me. She completely ostracized me and told people how much she loathed me. I could never figure out why she was temperamental with me. At one point I thought it was due to Mrs. Hootie living with us and we had a good relationship resulting in us bonding, while Mrs. Hootie continued to speak unkindly about Mooney. Being aware of the animosity Mooney had towards me, I would make sure I was not home or left when she came over in order to keep the peace.

In November 2004, Jerome and I became officially engaged when he placed a one and one-half carat princess cut engagement ring on my wedding finger. The ring was beyond my dreams, it was magnificently exquisite. I was excited, happy, and thankful as I hugged Jerome telling him *I would never again doubt his love for me.* He said, *yeah, we will see.* Then I thought how several months prior Nicole had went with me to buy my dream wedding dress in anticipation of marrying Jerome. Suddenly I said, *oops,* I am engaged to Jerome but not divorced from Syl. My crazy logic was now that I was engaged, Syl would have no problem with us getting the divorce. Later that month we had our first Thanksgiving dinner with our blended family gathering. All of our children were there except for Sheriese. For our children to meet made me extremely happy. The next month we celebrated our first Christmas as a blended family. It was filled with love, laughter, and more family bonding. Mrs. Hootie had a beautiful Christmas with her grandchildren and her great-granddaughter, Cameron. With Mrs. Hootie living with us Jerome demeanor was more thoughtful. This helped us to further enhance our relationship and look forward to uniting in holy matrimony. Even though I realized that our relationship was far from my fairytale dreams, I was committed to working through any problems instead of running away from them. Without a doubt I knew Jerome exemplified several of the characteristic traits that I wanted because he was an excellent provider that worked hard and was financially conservative, could be romantic when he wanted to, had a vision for our future, when necessary was compromiser to work through our problems, and was willing to socialize. His being financially conservative was appreciated. In my previous marriages at times there would be financial problems. Herman had not been a good provider, while Syl was a good provider, he would sometimes live above our means. On the other hand, Jerome was a good provider to his children, and during the beginning of our relationship he also helped me financially to support my daughters. His financial help was immensely appreciated, and in some ways, it helped me not to dwell too much on his pessimistic behavior but on his optimistic traits. When I assessed our entire relationship from his and my point of views, there was no doubt we loved each other. Our problem was we were both emotionally scarred with excessive baggage from past relationships. My being unfaithful to Syl certainly would be forever a major concern to Jerome, while his negative dominating mindset was of concern to me. Meditating on how we could be more on one accord, I committed to praying for both of us. Clinging to Philippians 4:6 (KJV) *Be anxious for nothing, but in everything by prayer and supplication, with thanksgiving, let your requests be made known to God.* I asked God to instill in me confidence, patience and understanding, and for Jerome to be more thoughtful, amicable, and respectful. Although Jerome and I did not pray together, and seldom attended attend church, he would often kneel to pray before going to bed. This was a flicker of light from God revealing to me that Jerome believed in God and the power of prayer. At times when I saw him kneeling to pray, thoughts would run through my mind to ask him for us to pray together. Regrettable I never asked him because I was too afraid he might reject the idea. Nowadays I wonder how heeding to those thoughts from the Holy Spirit would have affected our lives.

<u>A Storm is on the Horizon.</u> Mrs. Hootie unexpectedly became ill during her dialysis treatment in January 2005. She was taken to the emergency room and admitted to the hospital. For several days Mrs. Hootie appeared to be doing better. Suddenly her health began to decline. The doctors asked for a conference with the family to discuss her medical condition. The meeting was attended by Mooney, Phyllis, one of Jerome's sisters, Moochie, Jerome and me. The doctors let the family know that Mrs. Hootie was extremely sick. Her vital signs were very weak, and she was barely breathing on her own. The ventilator was breathing for Mrs. Hootie. The medical staff believed there was little chance of her recovering. The family was requested to decide how long they wanted Mrs. Hootie to remain on the ventilator. After the doctors left the conference room they stayed in the room to discuss what was best for their mother, while I returned to Mrs. Hootie's room to pray. When everyone returned to her room, to my surprise Mooney begin to talk to me. Immediately I forgot about the rift between us, and thankful we were able to be civil to each other in this time of uncertainty. As always, talking to her again was appreciated because her presence in my life had been missed. Later that evening with the family by her side Mrs. Hootie entered her eternal rest. Because Jerome knew I had worked part-time for a funeral home, he asked if I would call the funeral director I worked with about making the arrangements. I said, of course. The next day Jerome, Mooney, Phyllis, and I went to make the funeral arrangments.

When leaving the funeral home, Mooney abruptly began an argument with me saying, that *Mrs. Hottie was her mother, not my mother*. I was completely stunned by her actions considering we had just reconciled less than twenty-four hours ago. I told Mooney that I knew Mrs. Hootie was her mother, and that I was only there because Jerome asked me to help him. She continued to talk negatively to me. Seeing that she was determined to argue with me regardless of what I said, I walked away. When I got in the car with Jerome I asked him what her problem was with me. In his usual manner he responded he did not know and wanted nothing to do with whatever Mooney and I were going through. Later that day Mooney called me to further argue with me and let me know what she thought about me. She said I thought I was *Miss Goody Two Shoe*s and thought I knew everything. The more she talked about me, I strongly defended myself my telling her that I cared for her mother while she lived with us only because Jerome asked me to and there was no one else at the house to do it. I reiterated to her that I was only at the funeral home because Jerome asked me to be there. I told her if she had a problem with whatever I did for her mother, she needed to take it up with Jerome. The more we talked the conversation escalated into a shouting match. Mooney then began to threaten to jump on me when she saw me. This resulted in me hanging up the phone. I was livid. If that was her opinion of me, why did not she let her mother live at her house. Honestly, I knew Mrs. Hootie would have never lived with Mooney. It was simply the fact of Mooney making these false accusations against me. I called Phyllis to let her know what happened between Mooney and me. Phyllis told me Mooney had called her fussing about me. Phyllis let me know not to worry about Mooney. Phyllis told me how she appreciated all I had and was now doing for her mother. I was glad and grateful for the support from Phyllis. I let Jerome know what Mooney had called saying to me, and how she threaten me. Jerome sternly let me know he was not in the mood to deal with Mooney and me. He even began to blame me for the situation. It was to the point he became inconsiderate and unsupportive of my perspective. Knowing Jerome was grieving the death of his mother together with contending with the funeral arrangements I refused to take his negative comments and attitude to heart. Under the circumstances I fully understood why he did not want to contend with an uncalled-for problem between Mooney and me. Still her intimidation concerned me. In my mind I was unsure if Jerome fully understood how worried I was about the threats from Mooney. Remembering hearing from Mooney and others the aggressiveness of her and her children, I felt vulnerable. The thought of a confrontation with them frightened me. Considering the comments and attitude of Jerome, I began to wonder if he would support or protect me from his family. Uncertain of what to expect, I let my family members and friends who planned to attend the funeral know how Mooney had intimidated me with her threats. In the meantime, Jerome requested I see if the funeral service could be held at Lee-Seville and for me to prepare the programs. Even though Mrs. Hootie was not a member of Lee Seville, Pastor Newton gave the approval for the funeral to be held at the church. The morning of the funeral, I ask Jerome did I need to be worried about Mooney. He stated, I got everything under control. I asked what that meant. When he said, huh, I knew it was best to not push for any further explanation.

That Saturday when we arrived at the church for the funeral service there were many people there to support the family. During the wake period, I greeted and met family members, friends, and co-workers of the family. Although I did not have an opportunity to personally meet them, I did see Sheriese, Sheron and some of their family members. When the home going service began even under the circumstance it was an uplifting service. Jerome spoke fondly sincerely about his mother. He ended his remarks with loving words of encouragement for family members and friends. Although Pastor Newton never personally met Mrs. Hootie, he delivered an inspiring eulogy. Praise be to God everything went very smoothly with no incidents. At the repast, many people said they did not know Jerome and I were engaged as they admired my engagement ring. I thought they knew either by the ring or the obituary in which I listed myself as Jerome's fiancé. They asked if we had set a date. I replied, no, but they would receive an invitation. In the back of my mind I was thinking, I cannot get married yet because I am still married. That evening Jerome told me he had also received congratulations on our engagement.

The day after the funeral, I woke up to another unexpected confrontation. I said to Jerome, *good morning*. Jerome replied, *yeah*. Then to my astonishment he bitterly said, *some of my people who attended the funeral were being disrespectful to him and he did not appreciate their behavior*. I could not believe he was saying this to me. I told him *there was no way what he was saying was true that none of my people had disrespected him or his family.* Feeling offended and upset by his accusations, I asked Jerome, why he was accusing my family members and friends of this type of behavior. I adamantly reminded him that barely a few days ago, Mooney not only was being spiteful towards me, she scandalized my name and threaten to beat me up. I let him know how he would not even stand up for me. Jerome told me, *he had it all under control.* He asked me, *did I think with all the police officers there that Mooney or her daughters would have been able to get something like that off.* I replied, *he had said nothing to me to show he even cared how his sister was treating me, let alone telling me he had did anything to prevent an incident.* I complained to him there was no indication he would protect me. How could he now after the fact tell me he had it under control? By this point filled with disbelief of what he was saying, I had begun to cry as I said, *it was ridiculous for him to think my family members and friends would disrespect him at the funeral of his mother when they were there to support both of us.* Thinking to myself even when my family members and friends recognized how he disrespected me, they still were always polite and respectful to him. That was because all my loved ones knew that regardless how they felt about Jerome since I was with him they would respect him for my sake. Yet on the other hand Mooney had not only disrespected me, she threatened to harm me while he did nothing. He refused say or do anything to defend, comfort or protect me, instead he blamed me for her rude behavior. He had pissed off, because his hurting and demeaning me was one thing, but there was no way he was going to insult and falsely accuse my loved ones. This was totally on a different level that I would not tolerated. We ended the argument with him insisting he knew what he observed. While I maintained my people never behaved in such a childish manner.

A couple of days after his tantrum Nicole came to visit me. Lately when I had guest, Jerome would typically have a *bump on a log* disposition. That day I noticed it was worse than ever. There was also residue tension from our argument a few days prior. This made me jittery because I did not want Nicole to detect the tension between Jerome and me. I was also worried that Jerome might say something to Nicole. To prevent any awkward unpredictable situations, I put on my fake happy go lucky attitude while Nicole and I sat at the kitchen table talking, Jerome walked in and out of the kitchen several times and I could hear him mumbling something to himself. Unsure of what he might do, I pretended to be getting tired. I was glad Nicole noticed me getting sleepy and said she was going to leave so I could get some rest. Immediately after Nicole left, Jerome started talking to me in a threatening demeanor saying, *Nicole was the main person that disrespected him at the funeral*. He went on to tell me to *never again let her in his house*. I tried to reason with him that he was wrong, explaining Nicole was our number one cheerleader and thought we were the perfectly cute couple. I let him know that Nicole does not even like attending funerals, but wanted to be there to support us, and she had told me after the funeral how good we looked together. This is the reason I could not understand why he was saying Nicole was disrespecting him? The more we talked the discussion was turning into an intense argument. I was aware Jerome had been drinking throughout the day. In his present state of mind, I was not willing to argue with him. To stop the argument from further escalating, I said *okay, she will not ever come back to his house*. At that point I realized this was not *our* house but *his* house.

Together with his drinking and mourning the loss of Mrs. Hootie each day Jerome became meaner. On February 24th, he left the house early in the evening without saying a word. No goodbye or I will be back. It was nearing 11:30 p.m. when I called his cell phone. When he answered I could hear a woman in the background laughing saying, *you in trouble now, you better go home*. I asked, *where are you?* He said, *visiting Sheriese*. Instantly furious I said, *this time of night*. Then I hung up the phone. There was no way he could justify at this time of night visiting a daughter who was five years old. Fuming at the thought of all his mess I was enduring. It was hard enough putting up with his ruthlessness, mean demeanor and obnoxious intimidation he inflicted on me. Now he had left the house without saying a word and at midnight had the audacity to be at his ex-girlfriend's house, the woman that had ruined and made him cancel his surprise birthday party. No way could I take another second of this treatment from Jerome. I was through with him and he could have *his* house because I was getting out of there. In a state of dismay with tears in my eyes, trembling, I called Charisse. Talking hysterically, I asked her if *could stay with her for a while*. Sounding halfway sleep she said without hesitation, *yes*. I asked her to please come help me move out. She said, *okay, I am on my way*. I then called Nicole, Trina, Maurie, and Gregory. Still in a state of panic when they each answered their phone, I asked each of them to please come help me move. They each sounded sleepy and asked, *now*. I fervently replied, *yes, I needed to get out of this house tonight*. Waiting for everyone to arrive, I placed all my clothing and other personal items in garbage bags. Jerome called several times. Initially I refused to answer. Finally, I answered saying, *what do you want*. He again told me he was only visiting his daughter. I told him to stay where he was because I was moving out and would be gone within the next hour then he could have *his* house. I then hung up the phone. When he called back, I refused to answer. Gregory arrived first. He was in shocked because he had visited with me earlier that day and there were no signs of any problems. I thought to myself that was because earlier I had put on my usual pretend life is good attitude since I never wanted to let my family members and friends know the turmoil that I inwardly suffered behind closed doors. Gregory asked what happened. I briefly explained to him what had occurred before and after Mrs. Hootie's funeral. He said, okay what you want me to do. Trina, Nicole and Maurie arrived within five minutes of each other.

As they were helping load my items into their cars, Trina came inside to tell me Jerome had pulled up. Within a few minutes Jerome came into the house. I heard Trina and Gregory say, hello to Jerome. He asked Gregory, *what is going on man*. Gregory replied, he did not know. I entered the kitchen asking Jerome to let me get my stuff and leave. In his usual, I am the man demeanor, he confronted me.

Grabbing my arm, he tried to lead me out the kitchen into the living room saying, *let us just talk*. I was saying, *no, just let me go*, when Nicole who had been upstairs with me, came downstairs. Nicole started telling Jerome to let me go. They started arguing. Jerome told her to get out his house. He started shouting at me, why did I let her back into his house. While they argued, he was backing Nicole towards the front door while still holding my arm on his other side. I was begging for him to stop and to just let me leave. When we reached the doorway, with his free hand he shoved Nicole out the door. I could hear Nicole shouting at the door to let me leave. She then said she was going to call the police. Jerome ignored Nicole, shut the door, and started talking to me as he tried to reason with me, but it was too late. I no longer wanted to hear his excuses.

Once Nicole had called the police with us living in the suburb of Shaker Heights the police came in full force. Initially, when the police knocked on the door saying open the door, Jerome would not answer the door. I pleaded with Jerome to please open the door for the police. When he finally did open the door, the police asked him to come outside. He identified himself as a police officer and talked to them from the doorway. The police repeatedly asked him to come outside. Eventually when Jerome did walk outside, police officers apprehended him by tackling him to the ground, searching him, followed by placing him in handcuff. They had searched him for a weapon because Nicole had informed the police dispatcher that he was armed with a gun. I later found out the police had also handcuffed Trina and Maurie, and Gregory who had gone to sit in his car when

Jerome came home was instructed by the police to stay in his car. The police officers then entered the house. They asked if I was okay and whether anyone else was in the house. I replied, yes, I was okay and no one else was in the house. The lead officer asked me what had occurred. I informed him how I was moving out when Jerome came home and became confrontational with me and especially Nicole. The lead officer asked if his gun was in the home because it was not on his person? I replied, I did not know. He then asked if I knew where he kept the gun? I replied, yes. He asked if I would see if the gun was in the house. I looked but it was not where it usually was kept. I heard Charisse downstairs telling the other officers to let her in the house. I ran down the stairs and told them that was my sister and to please let her in the house. The officer opened the door for Charisse. The lead officer really wanted to find the gun to the point he asked me if the house could be searched. I replied, no, there is no reason for the house to be searched. The lead officer continued to persist on me allowing the house to be searched and encouraging me to press charges against Jerome. Once again, I stated, no, while explaining to him and the other officers that the recent death of his mother could account for part of his behavior. Charisse hearing the discussion suddenly vehemently told the lead officer, *she said no, so it is time for y'all to get the hell out of the house right now.* With that statement from Charisse, the lead officer looked at Charisse then me with a look of appall, then he said to the other officers standing around, *we are no longer wanted here,* so *let us go.* He turned to the officer standing next to him taking my report and instructed him to stay to complete the incident report.

Trina and Maurie were finally released from the handcuffs and Gregory allowed to get out of his car. They came back into the house, where the officer told them he would take their statements after he completed mine. Nicole remained outside giving her statement to an officer. Trina told me that Jerome had been placed in the back of the police car and officers had driven off with him. Shortly thereafter Kennedy called the house phone saying that Jerome had called him from the police station and he was on his way to the station. Kennedy asked me what was going on. After telling him what happened, he asked me not to press charges because Jerome would be in trouble with his job if I did. I told him I had no intention on causing Jerome any problems with his job. A few moments later Jerome called saying he was sorry and asking if I would not leave until we had a chance to talk. He also let me know that pressing charges would cause serious problems with his job. Jerome asked me to consider how it would affect him and his children's financial future. I knew from prior discussions with Jerome, police officers could be subject to disciplinary actions for inappropriate behavior. Hence pressing charges might result in him being suspended or losing his job. This could cause a financial hardship for him and the children. Of course, I never wanted him to lose his job or suffer financially. For this reason, I told Jerome I would not file charges. When the police officer requested Nicole to file charges., I asked Nicole for my sake not to press charges. She agreed not to proceed with the complaint. Kennedy called again to ask me if it was okay to bring Jerome back to the house and encourage me to give Jerome another chance.

Following speaking with Kennedy and Jerome, emotions of remorsefulness overwhelmed me. This resulted in being torn between leaving and staying. Consciously how could I leave Jerome when he had been arrested without agreeing to his request to talk to me? Deciding to give Jerome a chance to talk, I chose not to move out that night. Although everyone was in shock and disbelief that I planned to stay, they said okay, if that is really what I wanted. I said, thank you for everything. Giving each one a hug saying I loved them and appreciated their always being there to support me. Charisse laughing with her hardy laugh said *yeah, yeah, yeah, we love you too, that is why at midnight we got out of our warm beds as cold as it is outside to come help your crazy butt.* Everyone else laughing agreed with Charisse.

    A short while later Kennedy brought Jerome home. Kennedy talked to both of us for a few moments. Before leaving he asked me if I was okay. I told him, yes. Uncertain of what Jerome would say or how he would react, I waited for him to start talking. Although I could tell he was upset his voice and behavior was not hostile. He told me how stunned and perplexed he was that I had allowed this to happen to us. I had no emotional or physical strength to dispute with Jerome that it was in fact his out-of-line behavior that triggered the tumultuous situation, I decided to sit quietly and listen to him. When he finally stopped talking, I merely interjected how sorry I was he had been arrested. As he began to talk again, he restated how this could affect his future and job. I assured him I would do whatever to prevent him from being charged. After he finished talking, I let him know being over Sheron house that time of night was unacceptable. Although he agreed, he maintained he was only visiting Sheriese. Once we finished talking about what had occurred that night, we discussed ways to prevent a repeat of this type of situation. Before going to bed we agreed to make personal adjustments for the betterment of our relationship. Praying that night, I asked God for Jerome and my relationship to be healed and blessed, that Jerome would not get in trouble with his job, and my relationship with Nicole not be affected by the situation.

When I woke up in the next morning, I understood even through Jerome and I would work towards healing our relationship, the storm from last night would leave both of us with permanent emotional scars. Although I prayed it would not happen, the most painful scar for me was my relationship with Nicole became strained. Regrettably, it resulted in us being estranged. This was heartbreaking because I loved Nicole. Even though she had become my God-given daughter, it was more like she was my guardian angel. I always could depend on Nicole. In a moment's notice she would be there for me through my good and troubled times. I prayed to God that one day Nicole and I would reconcile our relationship. The other scar was wondering if deciding to stay with Jerome was another mistake. Was he truly capable of loving me? Reflecting on my past, I thought how Herman loved me, but never stopped the mental and physical abuse and cheating. I believed Syl loved me. Yet he let me find out he had an affair and refused to honor my request for the name of his mistress. Now being with Jerome, he was not physical abusive like Herman, but he could be mentally abusive. It seemed my life was heading down the same path with Jerome at times being mentally abusive. Could I trust Jerome to be a man of his word and stop being mean and intimidating? Feeling at my wits end, I turned these emotional scars over to God. I knew only His intervention could begin to heal these scars.

After the incident with the police, Jerome's demeanor improved but he was drinking more than usual which I attributed to his mourning the death of his mother. Slowly but surely Jerome again started communicating harshly with criticism of what or how I did things. Even when he asked me a question it became a problem. When I answered his question, he would ask me the same question several times. Then he would treat me like a child by saying, *are you sure*? A question from him was like being interrogated. It reached the point that when he repeatedly asked the same question that I had already answered I would simply stare at him. Another problem was being blamed when things went wrong or there was a problem. Even when the problem was caused by the actions of him or other people it was still my fault. Like when Mooney threaten me, it became obvious that Jerome would not defend or support me regardless if I was right. Instead of protecting and standing up for me, he sided with the other person. If he was not complaining about something I did or did not do to his satisfaction, he had little to say to me. Like my life with Syl, I begin to wonder if he was this mean to others or only me. With all the unconstructive criticism and inconsiderate behavior towards me, I frequently asked him how he would feel it the companions of his sisters and daughters treated them the way he treated me. He would tell me *it would be their problem*. What became the most humiliating was when he started to routinely come home past midnight or later typically after he had been drinking. At that time of night, he would come upstairs to our bedroom waking me up and insisting I get up to cook him something to eat. If it was not something to eat it was given him some *shorts*, his word for sex. At time he would want something to eat and shorts. Most of the time I would adhere to his request to keep the peace. Then occasionally I would be too sleepy and tired. When I told him I was too tired, Jerome would badger me non-stop with negative comments and calling me derogatory names. Several times, he would pull the bed comforter and sheets off me, grab my arms, and shake me. If I tried to resist, Jerome would forceful pulled me out of bed. This behavior would go on until I had no choice but to do whatever he wanted. His tightly grabbing and forcefully pulling on me would sometimes cause bruises on my arms and legs. After times Jerome would put me through all that agony to get up, and once I cooked the food and brought it to him he would further insult me by having the audacity to be sleep and would not wake up. I could not understand the purpose of waking me up and demanding I do things for him knowing he was sleepy. This behavior was upsetting and mortifying. In my usual fashion I hid from the world this part of my life with Jerome. On occasions when asked by people about the bruises on my arms or legs, my answer would be I do not know how that happened. Ivy on several occasions asked if Jerome had caused the bruises. Of course, I would say, no. The look in her eyes let me know she did not really believe me. Fortunately, there was only one incident when Jerome actually slapped me in the face. This caused me to have a total melt down because that one hit was like reliving all the abusive years with Herman. Although no way near on the level of abuse from Herman, that one slap was still frightening. After hitting me, Jerome immediately promised never to hit me again. Thankfully it was a promise he never broke.

Realizing There is One Persona When Dating and Different One When Living Together. It came to the point of facing the fact once I started living with the men I dated and fell in love with, that man vanished. Their personalities would be one way while dating, then drastically different when we moved together. Three times I had fallen in love with men I believed were my knights in shining armor. Upon committing to live my life with each of them, they changed from my knight in shining armor, and their true personalities appeared. Repeatedly I was falling in love with the same man with a different face and name, but with underlying characteristics that were similar that they had deceivingly kept from me until I moved in with them. Tired of running from my challenging relationship, I decided not to give up this time. Instead I prayed for guidance from God to change either Jerome or me.

Typical of me, I prayed, but did not wait for an answer. Instead I began to contemplate it was only my fault the relationships deteriorated. Looking at myself instead of Jerome, I decided *by any means necessary* I would do what it took to make Jerome happy. With this renewed commitment I would focus more on the positive instead of negative aspects of our relationship. I was determined to keep us together even if that meant I would have to put on my fake it until I make it attitude. The sayings I had heard over the years of *I would rather have half of a man, than none* and *something must be wrong with a woman who cannot keep her man* began to resonate in my mind. These expressions became a part of my mindset. Beside me working hard to keep our relationship together, Jerome too was honestly working towards keeping his promise to change his behavior towards me. He strived to be more compassionate and sensitive to my needs. I concentrated on trusting that he loved me even when he refused to the words. I tried to be less suspicious of him being unfaithful. To enhance my self-confidence, I begin to personally address my feelings of insecurities and worthlessness. Even though our efforts did not result in my total dream come true relationship it did improve to the point I knew we loved each other and wanted to spend the rest of our lives together.

In November 2005, Jerome was promoted to Lieutenant. Everyone was happy and proud of him. The promotional ceremony would be held at City Hall. Several family members and friends planned to attend the ceremony. When I arrived home from work to prepare to attend the ceremony, there was this cute little girl seated quietly on the couch with Otis watching television. I said, *hello*. She said, *hi*. Otis said, *you have not met Sheriese yet*. I said, *no*. Finally, Sheriese and I formally were introduced. The ceremony was nice. Jerome introduced me to his co-workers as his fiancé. Following the ceremony, we went out to dinner. During that time, I had an opportunity to spend a little more time with Sheriese. She was a funny, lovable little girl. This was also the first time Sheriese and Cameron met. Sheriese who was eight years old was staring at Cameron, who was two years, if to say who is this little girl sitting on my Daddy's lap. Jerome sensing Sheriese observing him called her over where he was seating where he lovingly played and talked to them both. It was a special night of bonding for us. In celebration of his promotion and birthday, I planned a party at his friend's local bar. It was a pleasant time with family members, friends, and co-workers as we ate yummy food, had plenty to drink, danced, and had lots of fun.

    Devoted to still being in our relationship was not as trouble-free as I hoped. Struggling to keep our relationship amicable was more difficult than I ever imagine. This was especially true taking into consideration communicating was one of our primary problems. Trying more than before to initiate general conversation did not work. Jerome persisted to have little to say unless there was some sort of disagreement between us. Then he would complain for hours about what he believed were my shortcomings. Not only were we having communication problems, there was little one-on-one time together. Jerome worked evening on his regular job. When he was off, he would work part-time jobs. I worked days that included extended hours. This further impeded our ability to work on our relationship. With our work schedules I was usual alone in the house each evening and him during the day. With hours of idle time I would mope over my preventable and unpreventable mistakes. I was consumed with figuring out the underlying problems of my former marriages and my current life with Jerome. One thing I recognized was how I confronted some of the identical problems with each of them. The anxiety of my past and current relationships resulted in my frame of mind being extremely low. Trying not to become too depressed, I inundated myself with notes I had taken from inspirational conferences and books. I began to write in a journal my concerns and questions. What happens after the dating phase is over? Why do relationships begin loving and caring to only change? Why do my relationships change once we commit to live with each other? What was I doing wrong? Was there something wrong with me? Searching the scriptures for words of encouragement many verses encouraged me. A flicker of light from God was one of my favorite scriptures. *See that none render evil for evil unto any man, but ever follow that which is good, both among yourselves and with all men. Rejoice evermore. Pray without ceasing. In every thing give thanks: for this is the will of God in Christ Jesus concerning you*, I Thessalonians 5:15-18 (KJV). Determined to be good to Jerome regardless of his negative demeanor, I inundated myself in praying, studying, mediating, and serving at Lee-Seville. To my dismay Jerome's disposition stayed the same.

Unable to Let Go. Discouraged and mentally tired, I decided to seek spiritual guidance from a pastor. The sessions were initially helpful as I told the Pastor everything that occurred in my two marriages and what was currently happening in my relationship with Jerome. The Pastor instructed me on positive ways to work on forgiving myself for past mistakes, improving my self-esteem and figuring out if I was in a positive or negative relationship with Jerome. At the end of my fourth session, the Pastor asked me if I wanted to get something to eat. At dinner I was getting more than a counselor vibe from him, it seemed like his mannerism was flirtatious. By the end of the night my inclination was correct. He expressed his personal feelings and concern for my well-being. My common-sense instinct told me to nip this in the bud, while my illogical thoughts shouted enjoy the ride. After three more meetings, I had finished the counseling sessions. Though the sessions ended, the Pastor continued to regularly take me out to eat and on long car rides. We eventually began to talk daily on the phone. Once more in my life, I had met a man that was showering me with the positive attributes that Jerome no longer was expressing. He was a nice attentive gentleman who complimented and made me feel good about myself. Aware of my promise to remain faithful to Jerome, I found myself in another predicament.

In June 2006 when Ivy and Sylvia earned their bachelor's degrees, Syl and I gave them a graduation party. Many family members, friends, classmates, co-workers, and members from Assembly and Lee-Seville attended the celebration. Jerome was kind enough to bring Tim from the nursing home to the party. Kim and her family even drove in for the party not only to celebrate with us, Mo also brought his disc jockey equipment to DJ the event. Tim was happy to have his daughters, son-in-law, and grandchildren together. It was a fabulous day to see the many people that had touched the girls lives over the years. We enjoyed delicious food and entertainment.

At the end of the party, assuming Jerome would take Tim back to the nursing home, I asked him if he was ready to take Tim back. He was hesitant, saying *ugh, nobody else can take him*. This of course upset me, and I said, *fine, I will find someone*. I thought who I could get to take Tim back. Kim could not take him because her SUV was loaded down with luggage and the DJ equipment. My coupe Lexus was too small for the wheelchair. This caused me to have to find someone to take him back to the nursing home. I asked one of my friends to take him back for me. This was embarrassing and hurt me to know the man I was engaged to marry let me down in front of family members and friends. This was one of several incidents that caused the contention in our relationship in 2006. Even with the let down from Jerome, I refused to allow it to put a damper on our great celebration.

Following the way Jerome embarrassed and disappointed me by not taking Tim back to the nursing home, I was looking forward to having lunch with the Pastor. Over the next several weeks being progressively more disgusted with my relationship with Jerome, and more captivated by the outwardly acts of compassion, encouragement, and attentiveness from the Pastor, I went to bed with him. Being intimate with the Pastor took off like no other relationship. He took control of getting my life on the right track. He was insistent that I leave Jerome as soon as possible and began to make plans for me to leave him. It was astounding to me how quickly he wanted me to get away from Jerome. Typically, several times a week he would take me to lunch. One day when we went to lunch, he drove into the parking lot of the *Pier W* restaurant. It is one of the few five-star restaurants in greater Cleveland areas where we ate at quite often. Presuming we were going to lunch there, instead he turned into the parking lot of the Carlyle Condos. When he did this, I had a look of surprise on my face. He merely smiled while humming a song which was a habit of his. The Pastor parked the car and when we got out, he took my hand walking towards the apartment building. Really confused, I asked him where we were going. He smiled while still humming. We entered this fabulous lobby. He said hello to the lady at the reception area. She smiled saying, hello again, while waving us towards an office. Reading the sign *Real Estate/Leasing Office* on the office door, I became more perplexed. Entering the office, a lady greeted him saying, you returned sooner than I thought. He introduced me to the lady who said she was our real estate agent. The agent asked me if I was ready to see my condo. I know the agent was curious why I was looking at her so crazy. It was because, I could not believe what I was hearing. Following the agent out of the office, she told me how I was going to love living at the Carlyle. She said the residents were all nice and how the property was well kept. The agent then let me know there were superb amenities such both indoor and outdoor pools, mini convenient store, hair salon, party room, fitness facility, games room, racquetball court, putting range, secluded beach with picnic facilities, volleyball court, and a wooded picnic area with barbeques grills and picnic tables. We got off the elevator on the thirteenth floor. When she opened the door of the condo, I was taken aback. Immediately I saw a breathtaking view of Lake Erie and the downtown skyline. It was a beautiful one-bedroom condo, with a gorgeous kitchen and a spacious L-shaped living room and dining area. The balcony was the length of the condo with access from the bedroom or living room. The agent asked me when I planned to move in. Still in disbelief about what had happened in the past fifteen minutes, I looked at the Pastor smiling at me and said, whenever it is available. As we headed back to the rental office, I thought about how I had told the Pastor my dream of living in an apartment overlooking the lake with a view of the city's skyline. What had this man done? What was I supposed to do? Entering the rental office, the agent explained to me the condo would be in both of our names with me as the resident. She then said the Pastor had already signed his part of the paperwork and it was ready for me to sign. Wanting to holler what the heck is going on, I sat there with a dumbfounded look on my face. What made him just pick-out a condo for me and agree to lease it without saying a word to me. I was happy that he knew I had no plans of living with him, but I was confused why his name was on the lease? Telling the agent, I would like to review the lease before signing it but needed to get back to the office, I asked her if I could take the lease with me to review and return it to her tomorrow. The agent said, of course. Walking back to the car, the Pastor said, *well are you happy, do you like the condo*? I replied, *of course, it is beautiful*. Then I told him, *I do not believe I can afford that type of condominium*. Without hesitation he answered that he planned to pay any amount I was unable to afford. He added his would buy whatever furniture and other items I needed. This was unbelievable for me to have someone want to take care of me in this manner. I had often heard women speak of how men provided for them, but I had never experienced such treatment. Arriving back at the office it was like I was dreaming. Did this really happen? I told my secretary what happened. Though stunned, she was happy for me. My secretary was one of the very few people I shared many of the true good and troubled times of my life. Having her was a flicker of light from God to help me for she was my cushion of support and inspiration, and a true confidant that I could remove all the layers of my fake life and reveal my true emotions. Throughout the rest of the day and night, I shifted between the Pastor helping me to get the condo was one of the best things that had happened to me in my relationships with a man. Yet on the other hand, even with all our problems did I really want to leave Jerome? I decided to compare the positive to the negatives. First, I had only lived on my own with Ivy for a little over a year after Herman died. Most of my life I had lived with someone. I had gone from Momma to Herman to Syl to Jerome. Second, I knew my relationship with Jerome had barely improved after the altercation with Nicole. Then the flicker of light was that night when Jerome came home he was more obnoxious than ever before. Listening to him rant and rave and taking his horrible behavior confirmed it was time for me to get away from his mental abuse. The next afternoon I took the signed lease paperwork to the agent. A few days later, the Pastor took me shopping for furniture.

It was mid-September 2006, everything was going as planned for me to move into the condo in October. Jerome would be out of town with co-workers and friends for a Browns football game. It was the perfect time for me to move. I was thankful and excited about starting my new life. Once Jerome left for the airport on Friday morning, the Hardin Moving Company came to move my things into the apartment. The Pastor came to the condo while the movers were there. To our surprise the Pastor knew one of the movers. Once the movers left, I organized a few items before leaving to return to the house because it was not my plan to stay at the condominium that night. When Jerome called that night, I told him I was moving. He could not believe I was doing this while he was out-of-town. He asked me to think about what I was doing because he did care for me. He called several times over the weekend expressing how much he cared about me and asking me to wait until he returned for us to talk. Saturday and Sunday, I moved more smaller items from the house to the condo. On Saturday evening Sylvia, Trina and her daughter, Jessica came to the condo to help me set up and decorate. They loved the condominium and were happy for me. I had not yet let everyone know all the details behind my leasing the condominium. Of course, this was because I was too ashamed and frustrated by another failed relationship and not proud of leaving one man to be with another man. The truth was I had been an absolute failure when it came to my love life. The flicker of light was the hope in God that I could still find the loving mate I had longed for many years.

On Monday, I had taken a day off work to finalize cleaning a few things at the house and moving the final few items to the condo. The Pastor was insisting that this be the last day in Jerome's home. Jerome called stating he would return to Cleveland by 4:00 p.m. Telling me how he understood my wanting to move out, he only wanted to talk before I left. I agreed to wait. Trina called to see if I had left the house. I told her no. She said, *you are leaving right*. Even though I told her, *yes*, honestly, I was torn between leaving and staying. My heart was full of apprehension and hesitation about moving. Despite everything I loved Jerome. Besides he had asked me to wait until he came home in order for him to talk to me. Frankly I was eager to hear what he had to say. The thought of leaving without at least hearing what he had to say was making me feel heartless and selfish, especially since I had been intimate with another man. On the other hand, my mind was running rampant with the anticipation and gratification of moving on with my life because a new beginning was the best thing for me. Yet thoughts of fear and concern was running through my mind. Should I take the chance that the negative demeanor of Jerome would eventually improve? Or if I gave up my chance of a new lifestyle and dream condo would I only be let down by Jerome? In such a brief period of time the Pastor had done all these marvelous things for me. Everything he had done I appreciated. Despite all this, why was I even thinking about staying with Jerome? With all these questions swirling around in my mind and my heart split in half, I was in a state of discombobulation. I finally decided to stay to hear what Jerome had to say. With his plane landing at 4:00 p.m., I expected him to arrive by no later than 5:00 p.m. since the ride from the airport to the house takes twenty minutes. Aware of the importance of his coming home to talk to me, Jerome inconsiderately decided not to come directly home. Instead he had stopped at a bar. In the meantime, the Pastor was calling me non-stop asking what was taking me so long to get to the condo. I tried to explain to him why I was not there was because Jerome wanted to talk to me before I left. Instantaneously I could hear the change in his voice when he told me to call him once I was at the condo.

When Jerome arrived at the house, he asked me why I was moving. Because we were in the kitchen, he had not yet realized I had already moved my things out. I begin to tell Jerome I moved out because I showed him how much I loved him by my actions, but he refused to treat me in the way I deserved. I let him know that no matter how much I explained to him what I needed from him physically and mentally he refused to satisfy me. I went on to tell him how he would promise me he would do better. Yet he always went back to his old habits of being mentally cruel to me, refusing to support and encourage me, and rarely communicating with me unless we were having a disagreement. I went on to say beside the affection we shared in the bed, I felt no to little compassion from him. Jerome replied he did not have to tell me he loved me because he showed it was a joke, but the way he treated me is not the way you show you love me. Once I finished telling him why I left, he said, you know I care about you and we could work things out. He went on to tell me he expressed how much he loved me by moving me in with him. He had never let another lady live with him. He asked me how could I feel he did not care with the engagement ring he gave me in contemplation of marrying me? If he did not care about me he would not be planning to marry me. He insisted his planning to marry me while I was still married to Syl was proof of his feelings for me. I asked him why we could talk this much when there was an issue, but all the other times, he would not converse with me. Walking into the dining room, Jerome realized that my things were gone. He asked me, *did you do all this within these few days?* I answered, *I had made my decision several weeks ago.* He then asked me, *why did not I tell him I was going to move before he went out of town.* I told him, *because of what happened when I filed for the divorce from Herman, I promised never to leave a man when he was home.* He said, *I hope you Nicole and none of your other folks were in my house.* I told him, that *I had hired professional movers and none of my people were in his house.* We then turned back to discussing for hours our issues. I reemphasized my problems with him, recalling the way he spoke so harshly to me especially when other people were around which was hurtful and was disrespectful. I remained him the way he criticizes me made me self-conscious. I also let him know his waking me up late at night by grabbing, pulling, and shaking me not only hurt physically it made me inwardly regress to when Herman beat me. I ask Jerome, why he did not understand treating me in that manner would have an adverse effect on me? Jerome adamantly reminded me how he had previously apologized for pulling and grabbing me. He repeatedly said how he shows love by his actions and telling me he never believed in just saying love you all the time. He let me know that ever since we had lived together he went to work and came home, only stopping for a drink every now and then, and other than that, he was at home. He emphasized he never hesitated to help me with whatever I needed, including giving me access to his credit cards without any questions.

Jerome said we both needed to work towards how we treated each other. He wanted me to stop being so insecure while he would work to improve how he treated me. For the first time Jerome let me know how Nicole calling the police on him had a negative impact on him. He told me when I took her side over him it made him question my love and devotion to him. He then brought up how he never understood why I had to snoop through his personal belonging especially his cell phone when he never looked through my things because that made him think I did not trust him. After talking for about two hours, Jerome said he was going upstairs and asked me to come with him. When we got to the bedroom, hugging me he said, *I do care about you.* He asked me *would I stay the night, and if I wanted to leave in the morning, he would not argue or try to stop me.* My heart had already decided I did not want to leave and with those words, my mind decided I was not leaving that night. My cell phone rang several times. Jerome said, *is that your other man trying to reach you.* I lied replying, *no* and cut my phone off. Closing my eyes, I prayed to God that I had made the right decision. Unrest still spun around in my mind. Had my prayers for a knight in shining armor been answered for me only to reject him? The Pastor had told me God wanted him to be my cover. Was this further evidence he was the answer to my prayers? With the Pastor recently being a widow would people judge us negatively? Would they say it was too early for him to be dating? What type of woman would I be considered? Do I leave the man I absolutely love for a man I thought was nice but wasn't sure I loved? Thinking once again I could be running away from one relationship with problems to another one with unknown adversities made me doubt myself. What was wrong with me? Was the statement of the prosecutor during my trial of *why didn't I run* have a lasting effect on me? Was this why I gave up on my marriage to Syl and now Jerome when there were problems? With Jerome laying sleep holding me close to him, I battled between running and staying as I steadily prayed for guidance. Thankfully there was a flicker of light when the Holy Sprint brought to my memory the mercy and patience of God throughout my life. This led me to mediating on *now the God of patience and consolation grant you to be likeminded one toward another according to Christ Jesus* Romans 15:5 (KJV). Waking up in the morning my mind was at peace. Still holding me Jerome asked me what I had decided. I said to stay with him. I could sense his happiness and relief. Letting him know my only concern and problem was the lease for the condo, Jerome let me know we would work things out. He then prepared to leave to attend a court trial on one of his cases. During the evening I had already planned to take the day off. When Jerome left, I called Sylvia and Ivy to let them know I would be staying with Jerome. They did not seem surprised. Sylvia simply said she would be staying in the condo. I then called the Pastor. He asked me what happened. I let him know I stayed at the house with Jerome. Saying okay he asked if we could meet for breakfast. I agreed. At breakfast, although disappointed he understood and respected my decision not to leave Jerome. His main concern was if I made the best decision for my future. He promised to honor his commitment to pay his part of the rent and other expenses for the condo, which he did until the end of the lease. After that day we remained amicable speaking from time to time about the lease. The following Sunday, Jerome attended church with me as a way of showing me he was serious about improving our relationship.

Apart from one night I stayed at the condo for an early morning maintenance service call, I never stayed at the condo. Sylvia and BriBri periodically would spend time at the condo. The month before the end of the lease, I used the party room for a birthday party for Big Sylvia. Other than that, the condo was unoccupied. A waste of thousands of dollars. One of my not so very smart financial decisions. At the end of the lease, I moved the furniture back into Jerome's home.

Life Gets Better. With the passing of each month our love life was a daily work in progress. Some days required more work than others. Nonetheless it was evident that we would be together. In November 2006, Syl called to say it was best that we officially divorce. I was relieved that he had finally asked for the divorce. My hesitation in asking Syl for a divorce was because of several reasons. First, deep down inside regardless of his affair, I knew it was wrong of me to be unfaithful and I felt guilty for having the affairs. Second, leaving Syl in the manner I had and moving right in with Jerome was not right. Lastly and most important, I was the one that broke up our home to the detriment of our daughters. Syl had accepted that our marriage was over shortly after I left, and even more so when he saw the engagement ring. Thankfully despite not being together and now ready to get a divorce, we understood we always would be friends because together we would forever be bonded by our daughters. We prepared the dissolution papers and separation agreement and were officially divorced a few weeks later.

<u>Still Attempting to Make a Loving Home.</u> In mid-April 2007, I started discussing with Jerome, Ivy, Sylvia, Trina, Charisse, and Cha celebrating my 50th birthday. I decided on a Hawaiian luau theme and selected the Velvet Dog nightclub in downtown Cleveland that was a popular three-story club to be the venue. What made it the perfect location was the rooftop lounge had a Hawaiian theme. Jerome agreed to pay for most of the party. Invitations were sent to both mine and Jerome's family member, friends, co-workers, and members of Lee-Seville that had been a part of my life from childhood to present. A week prior to the party I received a call from a lady calling from an accident site outside of Toledo, Ohio. The lady told me she was calling on behalf of Cha who had been in a terrible accident. The car she was riding in had been hit by a truck causing the car she was in to turn over several times and landed upside down. Cha and her friend, Erica were being transferred to the hospital. I thanked the lady for calling. Instantly in a state of panic I tried to figure out what to do because I knew I had to be in the office that day for a major case filing. Knowing Syl was now retired, I decided to call him to inform him about the accident. I let Syl know I could not be away from the office because of a mandatory case filing and asked him if he could go to Toledo to check on Cha. He told me not to worry he would go. Trying to work, I nervously awaited an update on her condition. Finally, I received a call from a nurse at the hospital informing me that even though Cha had suffered significant trauma to her neck and back there were no broken bones, and she was in stable condition. The nurse further told me once the results from a few more test were received and if there were no underlining problems, Cha would be released. The nurse also let me know that Cha's friend, Erica was also in stable condition. When Syl and his brother, Ray arrived at the hospital Syl called to let me know Cha and Erica would be released shortly. He said it was a miracle they were not seriously injured because the car was totaled. I lifted my voice in praise to God for blessing them not to have any life-threatening injuries. Later that day they arrived back in Cleveland. I went to check on Cha when I finally was able to leave the office. Listening to Cha tell me the details of the accident, I knew the Lord had spared her and Erica from critical injuries.

With my birthday party days away, I was overly excited about celebrating it with loved ones. I had ordered luau tops and skirts with accessories for Ivy, Sylvia, April, Cha, and me. Ivy and Sylvia were taking care of the decorations. Trina had ordered a special theme birthday cake. My former hairstylist, Davilynn handled obtaining the traditional kalua pig. Charisse arranged for Little Charisse and her husband to take professional pictures. The agreement with the nightclub was I would have exclusive access to the club from 5:00 p.m. until 9:00 p.m. After 9:00 p.m. the club would be opened to the public and I would have a smaller reserved section. The earlier timeframe was good because it would allow the guests that wanted to get home before it was too late to still have time to enjoy themselves. The only bummer was Cha might be unable to attend due to recuperating. The day of the party Cha called me to say even in pain she would not miss the party. It made my day even more special to know that she still planned to attend. The day of the party I told Jerome we needed to leave around 4:00 p.m. He said, okay. To my dismay Jerome was not ready to leave on time. By 3:00 p.m., I became annoyed when it became evident Jerome was not planning to be ready to leave at 4:00. When I asked him if he was going to get dress, he answered, he would be there later. This of course irritated me. Why couldn't he go with me now? There were people I had not seen in years coming that I wanted to introduce my fiancé to. Instead of debating with him, I got dressed and left.

When I arrived at the nightclub, I was elated to see how beautiful the girls had decorated. Looking around to see many loved ones lifted the weight caused by Jerome before leaving the house. Hugging and talking to everyone made me reflect upon how they each played a prominent role in my life. Filled with admiration for them coming to celebrate with me, I thanked everyone and hoped they would have an exciting time. Our luau outfits were a hit. Several people also wore luau attire. When I made it over to the food table everything looked delicious. The pig added a great touch to the theme. Trina had gotten a fabulous cake with a shoe theme in honor of my love for shoes. It was a festive time with fun, dancing, food, and drinks. The only downer was being asked several times when Jerome would arrive. I keep saying he would be there soon. Little Charisse and her husband took many pictures of this special day in my life, but sadly my dude would not be in any of those pictures. Around 9:00 p.m. we changed from the luau outfits to party dresses. Finally, about 10:00 p.m.

Jerome arrived. By that time, I was totally pissed off. How could he do this to me? Many of the people that I had not seen for years that I wanted him to meet and some of his family members had already left. I felt truly embarrassed that my fiancé did not show up on time for my birthday party. When I asked Jerome, what took him so long to get there, I could not believe what he had the nerve to tell me. The reason was he had to mop the kitchen floor because it was filthy. If I had not been outraged about him arriving this late, I would have sarcastically busted out laughing. I said, *a dirty kitchen floor*. In the five years we had lived together he had not lifted a finger to do any cleaning. Why in the world today of all the days he would decide to mop was incomprehensible. I could not believe him. Determined not to let him spoil my celebration, I pushed his actions to the back of my mind. Sensing the tension between us, Jerome asked *was I and my guests having a fun time*. I replied, *yes*. He said, *that is good because it cost him enough money*. The rest of the night I danced and had fun refusing to focus on how Jerome had let me down.

Upon arriving home, Jerome reiterated I should not be upset with him because he had financed most of the party for my folks. It had been too good of a day to let it end with an argument. Instead I decided to tell him thank you for giving me the money to have a beautiful party. With that said he stopped ranting. The next morning, I read the many beautiful touching cards. I received lovely presents and an unexpected generous amount of money. Once more I thank God for everyone that helped to make my 50th birthday celebration spectacular and for everyone who came to celebrate with me. Later that week I sent everyone cards thanking them for attending the party.

In the summer of 2007 Otis moved in with us after his mother remarried. Otis was now 14 years old. The same as when we first met at Moochie wedding, Otis was a happy go lucky, lovable teenager with a cheerful funny personality. We always had a good relationship. Over the years we would be together at graduations, his sporting events and family reunions. I was glad he was living with us because he brought the joy and laughter a child brings to a home. Some of those quiet lonely hours at the house now were filled with caring for a teenager. Jerome enrolled him at Shaker High School where he would be in the ninth grade. Otis loved playing sports, especially basketball. He tried out for and made the basketball team. Often Jerome spoke of his hopes for Otis to play professionally. With Jerome no longer coaching the police basketball team, he eventually formed a youth basketball team for Otis and his friends. The team was part of a league that played tournament games throughout the city and out-of-town. These games were great family outings that allowed us to have bonding time.

A few months later all our children came over for Thanksgiving Day. Most of us were in the kitchen talking when unexpectedly, Cameron asked me, *when Papa and you getting married*? Several of us said, *what did you say*? Without hesitation she said, *Papa and DeBorah when are y'all getting married, because DeBorah said I was going to be the flower girl*? We were all startled by the five years old little Cameron asking when we were getting married. I turned to Jerome to answer her questions. Jerome said, *soon*. Everyone laughed. That night I said to Jerome we needed to set a date. Jerome said, *it was up to me*. A few days later I asked Jerome what about on May 31, 2008, since it was Memorial Day weekend. Jerome said, okay.

Even at 50 years old, I hoped my childhood fairy tale wedding would become a reality. I envisioned me in the beautiful dress I had bought years ago walking down the aisle towards Jerome looking handsome in a tuxedo, with our elegantly dressed wedding party at the altar waiting in gleeful anticipation of the exchanging of the vows. The church would be gracefully adorned filled with well-wishers. Our reception would be filled with succulent food, drinks, music, and lots of fun. The beginning of the year I began planning our wedding. The first task was to prepare and mail the save the date cards. My next task was to select the bridesmaid, maid of honor and flower girl dresses. After a few debates from the thirteen ladies in the wedding the dress was finally selected. Then the focus shifted to the venues. Jerome made it clear the wedding would not be held at Lee-Seville. He told me he planned to ask the chaplain of the police department to marry us. He got no argument from me. I visited the church were the chaplain was co-pastor. It was a nice church but too small. After looking at several churches, we decided to rent the East Side Christian Church for the ceremony. For the reception we selected Catered Elegance. My attention then turn to selecting the floral arrangments and decorations for the church and reception hall. The final major decision was the musicians. Ivy, Sylvia, BriBri, Trina and Cha were inspirational in helping me with various aspects of the planning. Kim was a tremendous help even though she was in Bowie. With her being my maid of honor, she was determined to host the wedding shower. Kim let Ivy, Sylvia, and me, know what her plans for the shower and what she would need. She arrived in Cleveland the first Friday in May for the shower. That Saturday she gave me a spectacular wedding shower. I will forever be thankful to my sister for the time, effort, and money she spent to make my shower a wonderful. For a little while Jerome had me worried about who would be the groomsmen. Three weeks prior to the wedding, those concerns were put to ease when all the men had ordered their tuxedos. Everything was going as planned. In anticipation like a child on Christmas Eve, I eagerly awaited my wedding day.

Tears in Between Happiness. Since 2002 when Tim was admitted into the nursing home, I typically visited him several times throughout the weekdays and either Saturday or Sunday. Kim and sometimes her family would come to Cleveland at least three times a year to visit Tim and me. In addition, Tim received regular visits from Uncles Andrew and Phillip, Gregory, Barbara, Chip, his nephew and other nieces and nephews, and a few of his friends. Periodically Jerome, Syl, Ivy, Sylvia, Nicole, members of Lee-Seville, and other family members and his longtime friends would visit. Before his ability to move around in his wheelchair was further restricted, I would bring Tim to the house for visits and holiday gatherings, and we would go to church and other family outings. When his brothers were in town they would take him to the family church for worship services. In 2006, Tim asked to unite with Lee-Seville. I let Pastor

Newton know the intentions of Tim. He promised to visit Tim to accept his request to unite with the church. Once Tim joined Lee-Seville he would receive visits from members of the Lee-Seville.

It was the day before Mother's Day and thirteen days before the wedding, when I visited Tim. In my typical manner I gave him a hug and kiss on the forehead. He appeared a little tired. I asked him if he was okay. Nodding his head, he said, yes. Holding his hands, I asked him about his week. He was not his usual self but responded to my questions by nodding his head while smiling. I talked about him getting fitted for his tuxedo for the wedding and how excited and happy I was that he and Gregory would give me away. Before leaving I gave him another hug and kiss. I returned home to prepare to attend the birthday party of the DJ for our wedding. Jerome and I were getting dressed when the phone rang. Answering it I said, hello. The lady asked to speak to DeBorah. I said, speaking. She then identified herself as a nurse from the nursing home. Then she said, *your father has died*. Screaming I dropped the phone while falling to my knees shouting, *no*. I could hear Jerome shouting in a worried voice, *what is wrong*, as he rushed over to me. Jerome was bending down trying to hold me as he took the phone from my hand and finished the conversation with the nurse. Sitting on the floor I was saying this could not be. I was with him only an hour ago. Thoughts of how my relationship with Tim had begun very hurtful, but then by the grace of God over the years Tim had become a loving father to me. The flicker of light from God had enabled the emotional scars of pain and emptiness caused by the absence of Tim in the earlier part of my life to become more bearable. Through the power of God, the presence of Tim in my life enabled my heart to become filled with forgiving love for him. At the end I became his beloved daughter and he my loving father. I knew Momma was smiling down from heaven grateful that we had become truly father and daughter, but now I was being told he was gone forever.

Jerome held me tight as I tried to face the reality of the past few minutes. Once I calmed down Jerome told me the lady had told him they were going to clean Tim up then we could come out in about an hour to see him. Tearfully I said, okay. Then I began the dreadful calls to Ivy, Sylvia, Kim, Aunt Mary, Gregory, and other family members and friends. Like me everyone was in shock. Kim of course was deeply distraught. It was barely a week ago that she was here to host the bridal shower and visited with Tim. Still in a state of disbelief, Jerome drove me to the nursing home. When I walked in the same room I had been in less than a few hours ago, Tim was now laying in the bed as if he was peacefully sleeping. They had shaved and cleaned him up. Touching his hands, I thought how Momma and Tim both had left me very suddenly. I called my friend Roberta from the House of Wills to arrange to have Tim taken to the county morgue because with him dying in a nursing home an autopsy was mandated. We stayed at the nursing home until Tim was taken to the coroner's office. Jerome and I returned home. That was one of the nights Jerome was truly my knight in shining armor.

The next morning, I left a message for the HR director about the passing of my father and called several other people. Then as Jerome and I had done for the past several years, we went to the cemetery to visit the grave sights of our mothers. Jerome cleaned the headstones and we placed flowers at the head on their stones. The next couple of days were spent preparing for the home going service for Tim. Kim asked that I try to have the service that Saturday. She planned to arrive in Cleveland the morning of the service. I told her of course. While I prepared to make the funeral arrangement, the thought of Nicole came to mind. I really missed her, and I knew she loved Tim. Frequently Nicole had went with me to visit him at Aunt Mary's house or when he was in the hospital. She also had visited Tim when he lived with Syl and me. Nicole and Tim would often tease each other about how much they loved hot dogs. I knew even though she disliked attending funerals, she would be right here to take my hand and help me through this challenging time. As God always did during my stormy life, I received a flicker of light that although Nicole was not there to help me, God sent Charisse to step in and help me. Charisse was beside me through everything from making the funeral arrangments to ordering the floral arrangements. When telling her I was going to buy Tim a suit, Charisse replied, *girl you better not*, with all the suits I have from Dean over here you better get one of these. Sadly, her husband, Dean had passed away in 2004 and she still had his clothes. That week where ever I needed to go, Charisse drove me. The way she drove took my mind away from the grief until I got out of the car. This was because Charisse drives extremely fast and would tailgate too close to cars. I would be a front-seat passenger driver the entire ride. Besides constantly praying, I put a foot imprint in the passenger mat from pretending I was applying the brakes. Charisse thought this was very funny and would laugh at me pushing my foot into the mat, saying, *you really think that is going to stop the car*. I will always be grateful for the love and support Charisse gave me during my time of bereavement. That entire week she was truly a blessing from God.

Tim's home going service was held at Lee-Seville. Uncles Andrew and Philip, Aunt Mary, Gregory, Barbara, Chip and several other nieces and nephews from Cleveland and out-of-town, other family members, friends and co-workers attended the service. Pastor Newton delivered a moving eulogy. Tim was laid to rest at the Veteran Cemetery. Jerome continued to my knight in shining armor during this time of grief by supporting and being by my side the entire time which I will always appreciate. Following the burial of Tim, with still a heavy heart, I had to return my focus to the wedding that was less than two weeks away.

Fairytale Wedding. If there is such a thing as mentally multitasking that was my current state of mind. Emotionally on the one side I was grieving the sudden death of Tim, while on the other side I was enthusiastically finishing the last touches to my fairytale wedding. The wedding rehearsal and dinner was held the Friday before the wedding merely a week after burying Tim. Over the years I had coordinated several weddings and believed that to have the wedding rehearsal and dinner the night before the wedding often resulted in a lot of unnecessary stress. Even though the out-of-town and a few of the in-town participants were unable to attend the rehearsal the rehearsal went well. Jan was coordinating with the help of Charisse and they did an excellent job even without the entire wedding party. The rehearsal dinner was held at the same club we had Jerome birthday and promotion celebration. Davilynn prepared the food and the dinner was a perfect end of the evening as the wedding party was able to become acquainted with each other and enjoyed delicious food and entertainment. The night before the wedding some of the groomsmen had a bachelor's party for Jerome at the same club. Instead of going out that night, some of the bridesmaids, out-of-town guest, and I stayed at the Embassy Hotel where we finalized a few details. Like most wedding days, it was very hectic that morning. Several of the bridesmaids and I had early appointments with the hairstylist and makeup artist. Once we finished at the salon, we returned to the hotel to get dressed. Trying to coordinate the prompt arrival at the church of the flower girl, maid of honor, and thirteen bridesmaids was more than a notion. When we finally drove out the hotel parking lot, we were already fifteen minutes late. Finally, we made it to the church, approximately thirty minutes late. When the limo bus drove into the church parking lot, Jerome met me at the door saying with a concerned look on his face, *what happened.* I tried to explain the delays while rushing into the church. As we got off the bus with the sun still shining there was a short sprinkle of rain. Later someone told me that was my and Jerome's deceased parents smiling down on us.

Within moments my fairytale wedding began. Our special guests were escorted to their seats as the pianist, violinist and drummer played music from the movie *Dream Girls*. Next was a beautiful memorial tribute with a slide presentation of pictures of our parents and other loved ones that were no longer with us. Simultaneously with the screening of the slide show a family member walked down the aisle to the music being played. Once at the alter candles were lit in honor of our loved ones. The musicians begin to play the bridal party song. My beautiful wedding party a combined total of twenty-eight groomsmen, bridesmaids, ringer bearer and flower girl began their procession down the aisle. Then the ushers opened the doors to the sanctuary where Gregory and I stood waiting to walk down the aisle. I was smiling from ear to ear as the minister asked everyone to stand. I looked up at Jerome. Our eyes met. and his eyes radiant in awe as he looked at me and there was the most incredible smile on his face. Seeing his face filled my heart with love and joy as Gregory and I began to walk down the aisle. Later I was happy the photographer had captured a picture of Jerome at that moment. Even to this day I can plainly see the loving look on his face. The minister commendably officiated the wedding. Jan and Arthur also had asked the minister to incorporate a special presentation to us which was very moving and encouraging. Once we exchanged our rings, Jerome and I presented a love gift to each other's children as a symbol acknowledging the blending of our family. Then the minister pronounced us husband and wife and introduced us as Mr. and Mrs. Jerome Barrow. On May 31, 2008, I officially became *Mrs. DeBorah Barrow*.

   Even though our wedding was spectacular with twenty-eight

people in the wedding, we did have a few bumps. There were two no shows for our wedding party. Moochie, the best man was a complete no show. Kim, the maid of honor never made it to the wedding, but later arrived at the reception. The reception was totally what I wished for with more than 250 people attending with delicious food and the cake was lovely. Jerome had made sure there was plenty of both alcoholic and non-alcoholic drinks. We danced the night away. It was an absolutely marvelous time with family members, friends, and co-workers. Following the reception, Jerome and I went to the Marriott Hotel where Rico, one of the groomsmen, and his wife had reserved the honeymoon suite as their wedding gift to us. Words cannot express how spectacular our honeymoon night was as we consummated the beginning of our life together as husband and wife.

The next morning while dressing I could not find my toiletry bag. It not only had my personal toiletry items, but my other jewelry. There was my Movado watch, a gift from Jerome. A heart shaped ring from Ivy and Sylvia. Two other diamond rings and a diamond necklace. Initially I thought it was in the car. It was not in the car. Then I called family members and friends that might have picked it up for me. Everyone said, no. I called the church, hotel, limo company, and the reception venue. The bag was not at any of those locations. Unfortunately, the bag was never returned or found. This was very disappointing. The jewelry had sentimental value especially the ring from Ivy and Sylvia and watch from Jerome. Coming to grips that a family member, guest, or someone assisting in this special day took possession of the bag was difficult. With the passing of time, I accepted that whoever took the bag needed the items more than me.

By the end of August 2008, Sheriese who was now ten years old, began to stay with us during the weekdays because Jerome had to take her to and from school. Her mother had been fighting breast cancer for several years, and sadly, it was now limiting her ability to care for Sheriese. Prior to Sheriese staying with us, I had only seen her at the promotion ceremony and the college graduation of Jazmyn. When she began staying with us, our bond grew into a remarkably close relationship. She was a very polite well-mannered little girl. Sheriese was ecstatic to be with her big brother, Otis. They would really enjoy being together as they talked, laughed, teased each other and horseplayed each day. She would be done with her homework when I arrived home, and we would spend the evenings shopping, cooking, and watching television. With her at the house it brought more joy and happiness to our home. Soon after Sheriese began staying with us, Sheron and I began to talk on the phone. We later met in person and this was the beginning of a polite relationship. Later I met Sheriese's grandparents, older sister, niece, nephew, aunts, and cousins. I had met her uncle years earlier as he and Jerome were good friends.

By November 2008, the happily ever after was diminishing. Jerome's demeanor was reversing back to his old temperament. His intimidating, criticizing, humiliating, and lack of loving emotions were intensifying. At times his mentality could be profoundly heartless. It seemed I was a servant instead of a wife. No matter how hard I worked to make a cheerful home and assist in caring for Otis and Sheriese, Jerome would constantly complain that things were not good enough. Jerome regularly started degrading and talking negatively about *my fake family*, which he defined as any person not related to me by blood. *Fake Family* included my god-parents and their family members, god children, and relatives of Syl. He would say my *fake family* did not care about me. They were only using me. I was stupid not to realize those people were phony. Then he started to make hatefully rude remarks about Syl. He ranted, he was a real man, not a chump like your other men. These remarks about Syl enraged and I vehemently told Jerome how mean and evil it was for him to ridicule the father of my children, and that I never would degrade the mothers of his children. It became like he used my weaknesses to dominate over me knowing I had lack of self-confidence issues. Silently the hopes of my fairytale marriage began to fade away. This resulted in my withdrawal into a state of depression, self-doubt, and guilt. Then came the flood of emotional questioning. Why couldn't I have a happy marriage? What was wrong with me? What was I doing wrong? Why can't I get my marriages right?

Long Awaited Reunions. In the spring of 2009, out of the blue Mooney called saying she had made me a cake and was going to bring it to the house. Stunned by the call, I simply said, great. After hanging up the house phone, I thought, now what was that all about? It had been four years since Mooney and I had spoken. We had sent her an invitation to our wedding. Although she did not attend her son Jamel was in the wedding and her other son and daughters attended. When she arrived, she acted like nothing had ever happened between us. A little leery, I was still open to restore our relationships. Gladly I welcomed her back into my life. That day she visited for hours. We discussed events over the past four years. She had brought the CDs of Anthony Hamilton. I had not heard about this artist or any of his songs. As I begin to listen to the CDs, I became infatuated with several of the songs. I particularly loved *Can't Let Go, Please Stay*, and *the Point of it All*. Jerome gave me the impression he was okay with Mooney and me again being on good terms. For yet another time it appeared all was well with Mooney and me.

Shortly thereafter I was talking to a lady that knew both Nicole and me who informed me Nicole was getting married. I asked that she tell Nicole to call me. I was hoping Nicole would call since we had not talked after the incident between her and Jerome. She called a few days later. From the moment I heard her voice it was like we never were separated for those four years. Our god-mother, god-daughter relationship was rekindled within a second. Over the next several days we spent time together catching up on everything that had occurred in our lives. On a few occasions, I had spoken with Jerome about Nicole. Each time I mentioned her name, including after Mooney and I reconciled, Jerome would get upset. He remained adamant that Nicole was to blame for the incident that night. He accused her of trying to deliberately sabotage his life, saying to me he would never understand how I still wanted a relationship with Nicole after the problems she caused for him. I tried to explain to him in the same manner I accepted Mooney after her actions towards me, he should accept Nicole. He replied he would never forget what she did to him and his family. Repeatedly Jerome said he would never understand how I could be around her after what she did to him. Seeing how intense his animosity was towards Nicole, I stopped asking him to accept me being in her life. When Nicole and I had lunch, I explained to her how Jerome still held her responsible for the incident. Then hugging her, I assured her that regardless of what he thought never again would his views affect her and my relationship. Nicole agreed with me. We vowed to never let anybody, or anything ever separate us again. Nicole and I would meet at her home, the homes of other family members and public places.

As Nicole begin to prepare for her wedding, I assisted her with the wedding plans. When Jerome had to travel out-of-town for a work-related workshop, I asked Nicole to come to my house. Nicole asked if I was sure it was okay. I assured her Jerome was out-of-town and it would not be a problem. Sheriese came home while Nicole was visiting. I introduced them. A few weeks later, Jerome confronted me about Nicole being in the house. Irate he told me to never again let her in his house or around his children. Then over and over he angerly stated this was his house, and he could not believe I still want to be around Nicole after she intentionally tried to destroy his life. I pleaded with Jerome to understand regardless of how his family members mistreated me, I always forgave what they did to me, and consistently extended the olive branch, while my pleas to him for the same treatment were falling on deaf ears. No matter what I said there was no reasoning with him. Nothing was going to change how he felt about Nicole. His persistency that I agree with his point of view was relentless. He became aggressively overbearing to the point I agreed with him. I told him Nicole would never come to *his* house or be around his children. To myself I knew Nicole and I would never be estranged again in life. The only change would be Nicole would not come to *his* house.

Keeping the argument to myself, I focused on assisting Nicole on planning her upcoming wedding. She asked me to be the coordinator and I happily accepted. The support she had given to me throughout the years had always meant a great deal to me. Now I was able to express how much I appreciated her love and support. Both of our family members and friends were thankful Nicole and I were reunited. Nicole's biological mother, JoAnne, let me know how much Nicole had missed me. She even gave me insight why Nicole was so afraid for me that night. JoAnne shared how the incident with Jerome had reminded Nicole of another friend who was a victim of domestic violence that had ended in tragedy, and that was the reason Nicole was extremely concerned for my welfare that night. Over the next several weeks we prepared for Nicole's special day. On September 4, 2010, Nicole married the love of her life Yul. I was beaming with joy as I thought how in the late 1990s Yul and Nicole had met at my and Syl's house when we hosted a birthday party for Maurie. A few years after they met, Nicole and Yul began their love connection that lead to their beautiful wedding day. I was grateful to have played a part in their meeting each other. To this day Nicole is an integral part of my life and means more to me than she will ever know. Our bond and unconditional love for each other is truly a flicker of light of the grace from Jesus Christ.

Chapter Seventeen -- Ivy and Aaron

In October 2009, Ivy began dating Aaron. Aaron and Ivy met at St. Louis middle school where she was a grade ahead of Aaron. They later attended VASJ together. They knew each other only as schoolmates during those years. Ivy told me one day Aaron made a comment to one of her Instagram posts, which she responded to. Thereafter they communicated via Instagram and Facebook several times. Later they set a day for a date. The rest is history. From the moment Ivy introduced Aaron to me, he impressed me with his gentlemanly mannerisms. I learned that although they never talked, Aaron had a crush on Ivy in middle school. They dated for several months. One day Ivy came to me with a perplexing look on her face. She said Mommy I have to tell you something. Looking concerned, I said, *what is wrong*. Nervously Ivy told me she was pregnant. Grabbing and hugging my baby, I asked, *why are you looking sad?* As Ivy nudged her shoulders, I told her how happy I was for Aaron and her and knew that they would be terrific parents. Already feeling proud to be a grandmother-to-be, I let my oldest baby girl know how overjoyed I was at the thought of becoming a grandmother. With encouraging words, I told Ivy there was no need for her to hold her head down or be nervous, because she was a grown thirty years old woman who will be a great mother capable of loving, caring for and supporting her child. I further said to my daughter that she knew Aaron like her had no children, and I believed he would be excited to have his first child. I let her know that I was glad he was a responsible young man and they were both able to give the love and support to raise a child in a nurturing atmosphere. When Aaron and Ivy told other family members the good news, everyone was overjoyed. Thereafter, Aaron and Ivy began to prepare to bring their unborn child into the world. When the ultrasound revealed it was a boy we were all extremely happy. I was bubbling with joy that my grandson was on the way.

Sylvia and I planned an extravagant baby shower with all the bells and whistles. It would be held at the Landerhaven, one of areas premier banquet facilities. When we began to prepare the invitation list, Ivy talked to me about her relatives on Herman's side of the family. As I mentioned previously, following the passing of Herman, I had hoped his family would stay in touch with Ivy regardless of their opinion of me. However, Vet was the only one that initially stayed in contact with Ivy. Later in life, Ivy communicated more with both Vet and Dion. Her relationship with her brothers had on occasion resulted in her being in contact with some of Herman's other family members. The older Ivy became the more I had encouraged her to reach out to the Washingtons or to respond to some of their requests to see her. Ivy eventually began to communicate with a few members of the Washington family. This made me happy and thankful. Over the years I had prayed to God to soften and open the hearts of the Washington to allow Ivy to be a part of their family, instead of making her suffer because of me. So, when Ivy asked me if I would be alright inviting some of her father's family members, I told her of course they could be invited. Invitations were then sent to several members of her biological father's family.

Over 80 people attended the shower. I appreciated that from Herman's side of the family her aunts Annie and Eunice and a few cousins attended. This was the first time I had seen any of Herman's family members since the trial. Apprehension and remorsefulness plagued my thoughts, but when we greeted each other, I thanked God they were cordial towards me. I expressed my sincere gratitude for their support of Ivy.

Sylvia and I had worked with the staff of Landerhaven to create a unique baby theme décor for the room. It was a lovely baby shower with lots of comradery with family members, friends and co-workers of both Aaron and Ivy. This was a time for the families and friends of Ivy and Aaron to meet and mingle together. Personally, for me it was good to see many loved ones, including those that had known us from childhood, others that had known us for years, and those that recently met us. There were fun games with great prizes. A delicious luncheon with a barbequed theme was prepared by the caterers. They also prepared five fabulous cakes that spelled *Aiden*. Aaron and Ivy took tons of pictures with their loved ones. The guest blessed Aaron, Ivy and soon to be born, Aiden with many beautiful and thoughtful gifts. It was a very memorable blessed day for Ivy and Aaron, as well as their families.

Early on the morning of July 24, 2010, Ivy called to let me know she was in labor. Aaron took Ivy to the hospital. Syl and Sylvia followed shortly behind them. Aaron mom's, Eddie and I also headed to the hospital. Ivy's friend, Ashley met us there as well. With so many of us at the hospital, we had to take turns between being in the delivery room and in the waiting area. The closer Ivy came to having Aiden, Aaron called his father, Ivan who lived out-of-town. He stayed on the phone with us throughout the delivery. Finally, that afternoon our Aiden Winslow Banks was born. Looking at him I praised God for my handsome healthy grandson. He really resembled the Waters, Banks and Washingtons with a little bit of the Kithcharts. He had big eyes like Aaron and Eddie. Dimples identical to both Aaron, Herman, and Vet. A head full of slick black hair the same as Ivy had when she was born. His lips were full like Ivy and Herman. We were all in awe of the new addition to our family. The birth of Aiden was one of the most joyous days of my life. He sparked a new desire in my life. When Ivy and Aiden were discharged, they returned to Syl's house. Shortly after being home, Ivy suffered an unexpected seizure. The ambulance was called. She was rushed to the hospital where she was diagnosed with a severe case of eclampsia. It required her to be hospitalized for several days. During this time Eddie and I together with other family members and friends helped Aaron with caring for Aiden.

Once Ivy was released we continued to help Aaron with caring for Ivy and Aiden. Our prayers were answered several weeks later when Ivy was blessed to completely recover. Ivy and Aaron was soon able to care for Aiden without assistance. Once Ivy began planning to return to work it became a concern of who would babysit Aiden. Due to Ivy having been molested, she was extremely protective of Aiden. The flicker of light from Jesus Christ for my daughter and

Aaron was when Eddie and Mrs. Ethel Waters, Aaron grandmother, who were both retired, agreed to babysit Aiden. What an answer to our prayers. Everyone was truly thankful that strangers would not babysit Aiden.

Several months later Ivy and Aaron decided it was time to move into their own residency. I had always been supportive of my daughters comparable to how my Momma had been to me. Momma had instilled in me that the support of a mother to her child does not cease when the child graduates from high school. This made me believe that parenthood was also until death do you part. In addition, exactly like Momma told me, I would tell Ivy and Sylvia to strive to do your best. If my girls were trying, like my Momma I vowed to always help them out to the best of my ability to enable them to reach their goals. For this reason, I extended the offer to obtain the mortgage for their home with the agreement I would pay the mortgage for one year. Afterwards they would be responsible for all the expenses of the house. I believed the agreement would give them a jump start in life by allowing them to pay off some bills and college tuition obligations and would also allow them to work towards their nest egg. In September 2011, Ivy, Aaron, and Aiden moved into their charming home. Of course, I made it clear to everyone that the house was really Aiden's home. As Aiden grew older, he would remind everyone this was his home.

In the fall of 2011, Aaron, Ivy, Sylvia, and a few other friends went to dinner at the Pier W restaurant. Following dinner, Aaron surprised Ivy by proposing to her with a gorgeous engagement ring.

Ivy of course accepted. Syl later told us that Aaron had requested his permission to marry Ivy weeks before he asked. I praised God for blessing my oldest child with Aaron and was grateful he was a man of integrity that was born-again, caring, hardworking, and well-mannered. Immediately Ivy began planning her fairytale wedding. They set their wedding date for September 22, 2012. Ivy decided on an African-American theme. We initially went shopping for her wedding dress. The dreams of her story book wedding began to come true with the purchase of her gorgeous wedding dress. Aaron and Ivy decided to get married at First Baptist Church of Greater Cleveland. Although they were not members, the church allows non-members to get married at the church. The church offered a great wedding package which included members of the church's staff helping in the planning of the wedding ceremony. More importantly, couples had to attend mandatory premarital counseling for several weeks with a minister of the church to prepare them for marriage. Once the church was selected, Ivy and Aaron begin to decide where the reception would be held. Through Aaron's job, he knew about a cater that often catered lunches at his job. The cater also was the owner of an event center. Once they talked with the owner, it was decided to have the reception at his venue, the Terry Macklin Entertainment & Event Centre. They then begin to work on the other aspects of the wedding. Ivy and her bridal party selected their dresses and accessories. She worked on designing her exquisite floral arrangments. We worked with a cake specialize on the unique African-theme cake. The décor and backdrops for the church and reception venue were decided. Syl and I were blessed to financially help Ivy and Aaron make their wedding dreams come true. Sylvia and I planned a beautiful bridal shower. Sylvia later hosted a fun-filled bachelorette's party for Ivy. The wedding rehearsal was held the night before the wedding. Jan, with help from Stephanie Nunn, the wife of my god-brother Michael, and the wedding coordinator for the church, did an excellent job preparing the wedding party and other participants for the wedding ceremony. The rehearsal dinner was held at the host hotel, where everyone had a fabulous time eating and socializing with family members and friends.

On September 22, 2012, the wedding ceremony was held in the picturesque prestigious church before over 150 guests. Walking into the church I was flabbergasted. Ivy had created an incredible fairytale wedding atmosphere. I say this not because it was the wedding of my oldest baby daughter but because it was truly one of the most elegant and lovely ambiances I had ever seen. When the ceremony began I was even more overjoyed and thankful. The ceremony began with several songs being sung. Then with inspiring musical selections being played the parents and grandparents were escorted to their seats. Jerome escorted me down the aisle. Following the seating was a heartwarming memorial tribute for the loved ones of Aaron and Ivy that has passed away but were there in spirit. The tribute incorporated a slideshow presentation of pictures of the loved ones, while family members walked down the aisle with a floral arrangement they placed on a seat that stood for each loved one. I was grateful to have Jay travel to Cleveland to represent Momma. Vet walked on behalf of

Herman. Zelina presented for Mark. Carrington represented Tim, and members of Aaron's family presented on behalf of his deceased loved ones. When Aaron, the best man, groomsmen, and minister walked into the sanctuary, I smiled with much gratitude that my oldest baby girl had been blessed with a man of such good character. The wedding party procession began with the bridesmaids in stunning dresses accented with stylish shoes, jewelry and hair styles carrying bouquets of exquisite flowers walked down the aisle where the groomsmen looking debonair in their tuxedos met them at the altar. Our handsome little Aiden entered as the ringbearer. The distance down the aisle to the altar was quite long, so Aiden decided halfway down the aisle to stop and wait for his Auntie Sylvia, the maid of honor, to meet him halfway down the aisle. Once close to the alter, he ran to his Daddy. Then Miracle, Jordyn and Arilynn were the cutest little flower girls as they walked down the aisle holding hands. When Ivy looking like a gorgeous princess entered and began walking down the aisle arm in arm with Syl tears of joy filled my eyes. The minister rendered the traditional vows. What was inspiring was the minister incorporating the marital advice Aaron and Ivy received and agreed to during their counseling sessions. This resulted in the most unique vows I had ever heard. Once the minister announced Mr. and Mrs. Aaron Banks, we all begin to clap as the recessional march of the wedding party commenced. Ivy and Arron had planned for the photographers to capture pictures of the wedding party outdoors in the church meticulously manicured grounds, gardens and the balcony that overlooked the grounds. Unfortunately, it began to pour down raining once the ceremony had begun which prevented the outdoor pictures.

Their reception was just as beautiful as the wedding. The African theme with the backdrop, wedding cake, centerpieces and other décor at the reception looked spectacular. The wedding party were introduced as they entered the venue. After the introduction of the wedding party, Mr. and Mrs. Banks were seated in the center of the dance floor where an African dance troupe performed the traditional wedding dances. At the end of the performance, Aaron and Ivy jumped the broom. I often tell Ivy and others the dance troupe reminded me of one of the scenes in the movie, *Coming to America*. The reception was filled with the traditional toasts, food, drinks, and lots of fun. The entertainment included a photo booth with various props that guests could use to take pictures. After they took the picture, they were given a copy of their picture. Aaron and Ivy later received a photo book with a copy of all the pictures. The DJ kept the guests dancing throughout the night. Everyone mingled, talked, laughed, and had an unbelievable spectacular time. I had the chance to speak to Herman's family members, Annie, Robert and Nettie and a few other members of the Washington family. I had not seen Robert since the trial and Nettie since the evening Robert graduation. Again, it was both a remorseful as well as happy and grateful time to see Herman's family. Vet and his family, as well as Ivy's nieces from her brother, Dion attended. It was truly a joyous occasion with the Banks, Waters, Kithcart, Washington, Marshall, and Barrow families, together with Aaron and Ivy friends and co-workers. The next morning Aaron and Ivy left for their seven-day honeymoon cruise.

Several weeks after returning from their honeymoon, a pregnancy test revealed my second grandbaby was on the way. Later the sonogram let us know it was another boy. Both families were again overjoyed. Sorrowfully, Aaron's grandmother, Mrs. Waters passed away in February 2014. We banded together as a family to support Aaron and the Waters family during their time of bereavement. On July 13, 2014, the family was blessed with the birth of Ethan Marshall Banks. He came in just as handsome as Aiden but with his own individual looks. His eyes were bigger than Aiden's eyes. He had the same dimples with a captivating smile. My second grandson immediately became an additional joy of my heart. The Banks family was growing into a loving family. Ivy and Aaron both were spiritually maturing. They were flourishing in parenthood and financially they were accelerating on their jobs. I was happy for the Banks family. In late 2014, Ivy called me sounding distraught. She told me although she had been on birth control, again she was pregnant. I encouraged my daughter that everything would work out, while reminding her how blessed she was to be happily married. I further let her know that she and Aaron were gainfully employed and had family support and reiterated to her with their many blessings there was no reason for her to be worried. Most importantly I let her know the grace of God was with her, Aaron, their two sons, and unborn child. Once all the anxiety subsided, we happily awaited the birth of what I knew was a girl. Prior to the sonogram, Aaron politely told me it was only a thirty-three percent chance the baby would be a girl. This became a wait to see between Ivy and me because we really wanted the baby to be a girl, while Aaron and Eddie wanted another boy. A few weeks later the sonogram revealed Aaron and Eddie won, it was another boy. Ivy had the most difficulty with this pregnancy, but praise God on December 26, 2014, two months before his due date, Ivan Winslow Banks came roaring into the world to bless our lives. Ivan looked like his two brothers, handsome with beautiful eyes and those amazing dimples. God had truly blessed Ivy with a loving husband and three gorgeous boys. My heart was overjoyed with appreciation.

Chapter Eighteen – Blended Families

A blended family can be an enormous challenge for all parties. This was a challenge that I had to confront in each of my marriages because the men I married already had children with multiple women. When Herman and I were married, I became the step mother to Vet and Dion. My relationship with Vet and Dion has always been good. They may have been some issues with me after the death of Herman, but if there were, I was not aware. As mention in other chapters of this book, Vet's mother, Christina, and I always had a cordial relationship prior to and after the death of Herman. Christina and I had not spoken in years, until Thanksgiving Day of 2017, when she, her daughter, Vet, and his family, one of their family friends, and Dion, who I had not seen since the death of Herman, came to dinner at the Banks' home. It was a very blessed day to finally see Ivy with her both of her brothers. That day I was also extremely grateful when Christina expressed how happy she was I was writing this book and offered her support. Since that day, Christina and I have periodically been in touch with each other.

With Syl, as noted previously, my relationship with Mark was close, and he was a significant part of our everyday life. I will forever appreciate how graciously Barbara allowed me to be a part of his life. Her kind disposition towards me enabled us to have a very friendly relationship. Initially my relationship with Zelina and her mother, Christine began very well. Syl had even arranged for me to pick up Zelina from home to spend time with us. After we stopped by

Adrene's house, several family members asked *why I had her with me*. Taken aback by the question, I asked why. I soon found out it was due to Syl and some of his family members questioning her paternity. This was further mentioned while I was pregnant with Sylvia. On several occasions Syl said to me *how glad he would be when she was born to see if she looked like Mark or Zelina*. This of course caused a problem for me in my relationship with Zelina and Christina. Regrettably I took on the negative attitude that if Syl and his family do not believe she is his daughter, I do not either. Now in hindsight this was another self-inflicted storm that I should have prevented. How could I treat an innocent child wrong? Why I did not realize at that time it was only by the grace of Jesus Christ that Ivy had Syl in her life as a father figure. More importantly, I already personally knew from how Tim treated me the emotional scarring from not having your father in life. Thank God a few years later the truth was revealed through a paternity test that proved Syl was her father. Remorsefully the emotional scarring had already been inflicted. This remains one of those moments in my life that I wished the hands of time could be turned back. The flicker of light from Jesus Christ was mercy and grace given through seeking forgiveness as I sought forgiveness personally from Zelina and Christine. Thankfully thereafter Christina, Zelina and I had an amiable relationship. More importantly, Syl stepped up to become a devoted caring father to his daughter. In turn this enabled all of us to share many special moments together as a family. However, like me, I knew Zelina would forever have emotional scars from the actions of me, Syl and other family members. This made me feel even more horrible for being a part of causing her this perpetual heartache.

My life with Jerome and his four children was the most challenging. It was like a roller coaster ride, then up and then down, spinning around and then back around again. My relationships with their mothers were civil. Corrine and I had a decent relationship. The few times I saw Pat, we were cordial. Although it was a difficult start for Sheron and me, eventually things worked out for us to become pleasant with each other.

Each time I became a step-mother, I entered the marriage with hopes of loving and supporting the child while working with the father to provide a positive and caring family atmosphere when the child was with us. Albeit with Vet and Dion I really was a young step-mom, more like a much older sister, but I still wanted to make the time they spent with their father enjoyable. Unfortunately, under the circumstances, we had only a few years to bond.

With Mark we had lots of great times as a blended family, until his premature death. Unfortunately, with Zelina, taking into consideration how early in our relationship I behaved adversely towards her because of the negativity that had been instill in me, there was tension between us. Although I tried to rectify the problem and sought forgiveness, Zelina was still left with emotional scars which will always be a reminder of what she suffered through. When it seems like those emotional scars have resurface in Zelina's life, I have to not only respected how she handles her pain and heartache but remember that regrettably I was a part of causing this dilemma in her life.

Stated in the preceding and succeeding pages of this book, is my life with Jerome's children that has been filled at times with much love, happiness, and pride. Then at other times to my dismay they have been downright disrespectful, hurtful, defiant, and ungrateful. When I left Syl, I found out it would have been easier on my daughters if they would have been younger children instead of adults because as a child I believe they would have coped better. After being married to Jerome, it is my belief this also is true for a blended family. Blending a family with little children rather than teenagers or adults is much easier. It is my opinion this is what caused some of the problems with my blended family life with Jerome. Trying to have a harmonious bond with Jerome and his children was at times taxing. This was especially true taking into consideration in 2002 their ages ranged from six to twenty-two. Even though I did not personally meet all his children until 2006, Markita is Jerome oldest child and the first of the four children that I met. She and I had a great beginning to our relationship. It stayed that way for a few years. Then like Mooney, her attitude towards me would spontaneously change. When her disposition turned sour, I simply road the roller coaster until it leveled out again. My relationship with Jazmyn had been one of friendly toleration. With us both deeply in love with her father, we do what is needed to keep it peacefully moving. Jazmyn and my daughters are similar in this regard, that if their fathers are happy, it makes life better for me. Otis has always been kind-hearted towards me. Even when he is in the middle during those roller coaster rides between his sisters and me, he still greets me with a loving hug. Sheriese irrespective of the roller coaster ride of our relationship, will always hold a special place in my heart, because I cannot imagine the emotional scarring she confronts from seeing at such an early age her mother being gravely sick.

Two of the most problematic issues with Jerome and my blended families surprisingly was not instigated by neither one of us, but by Markita. During the planning of our wedding, Markita and Ivy started to frequently talk. After the wedding, they begin to spend more time together. One summer day in 2008, Ivy was on her way to visit Markita, but stopped to see me first. When Ivy said she was leaving to go to Markita's house, Otis asked Ivy if he could go with her. Ivy said, yes. About an hour later Ivy called me and I could hear in her voice that she was terribly upset as she began to tell me that Markita had abruptly started treating Otis really bad and saying mean to things to him. Ivy went on to tell me Markita had even said something very horrible which totally devastated Otis (due to the sensitive nature of what Markita said to Otis, it will not be divulged, but referred to as (mean words)). Ivy was in shock and disbelief, as she wondered why Markita saying such mean words to Otis. Ivy was also genuinely concerned about the way Markita was still taunting Otis even though he was being quiet. I told Ivy to calm down and bring Otis home. I assured Ivy, that although I had no idea why Markita was acting this hateful towards Otis and had said such mean words, I would talk to Jerome about what happen. When I called Jerome to informed him what Markita had did and said to Otis, in a surprised tone he said, he did not know why Markita would say such mean words. I let Jerome know Mooney may have told Markita, because shortly after I had met Moony, she had told me the same mean words that Markita had told Otis. I told Jerome I had kept what Moony said to myself because I thought such mean words were idle gossip which I refused to repeat. Jerome sounding frustrated said, he would talk to Markita but that regardless there was little to be done about what Markita had told Otis because at this point it would not change anything. I replied that I totally agreed and understood.

Whatever occurred after Jerome and I discussed what Markita had told Ivy and Otis is unknown to me. This of course, affected the relationship between Ivy and Markita. Then at certain times even though nothing was actually said to me, Jerome seemed to be questioning if Markita and Mooney actually said the mean words about to Otis to Ivy and me. Naturally even the slightest thought that Jerome doubted that Ivy and I had been told those mean words was upsetting to me because there was no reason for us to lie about something so serious. It seemed like *déjà vu* to me of when Syl and some of his family members told me certain things that started my doubt about Zelina, which turned out to be untrue gossip, but still caused unnecessary heartache. The emotional scars from that situation with Zelina had encouraged me to not spread deceitful gossip to the detriment of others. For without a doubt *once words are spoken, they can never be taken back even after an apology.* Years later around October 2014, Jazmyn and I were discussing the issues of our blended family. The incident with Markita and Otis was brought up. Jazmyn shared how she never understood why Markita would say those mean words about Otis realizing the hurt it could have caused the family. I whole-heartedly agreed with her. Why people speak ill-will of others for no reason other than to gossip will forever baffle me. I hope that gossipers that read this book will think twice about the emotional damage they can cause to innocent people before spreading their vicious lies.

The other issue happened during a family gathering at our house in November 2009. All five of our daughters, Otis, Jazmyn fiancé, Raishaun, and Aaron were visiting. At some point during the gathering I saw Markita pull Ivy to the side to talk. I hoped Markita was making amends from the incident with Otis. Later Ivy told me about the conversation. Markita informed Ivy she knew Aaron because he had dated someone she knew. Ivy let me know that Markita spoke negatively about Aaron, warning her he was no good. Ivy told me she politely listened to Markita. Ivy said being my daughter she knew to be respectful in our house and knowing Markita's personality there was no need in starting a ruckus with someone who had only months ago started such a terrible incident with Otis. After Markita finished her spill about Aaron, Ivy told me she had simply said, okay. I advised Ivy that she had to follow her own heart concerning Aaron. More importantly she had to take into consideration the known character of the person who was bearing the news. To this day, I am extremely thankful Ivy did not listen to the deceitful lies Markita spoke about Aaron. To this day, Ivy and Aaron are very happily married.

Joyous Days to Tears of Sorrow. In late 2009, Kim and I started to plan for our dream family vacation to Disney World. We planned to meet in Orlando in December 2010. Kim and Mo were arranging for our lodging at their Wyndham timeshare vacation club. Once Aiden was born in July 2010, I was very excitedly looked forward to the trip to Disney World, because after Syl and I had taken the girls to Disney World twice in the 90s, I had promised not to come back until I had a grandbaby. Often when talking to Kim on the phone, Sheriese would hear me talking about the trip and said, *I want to go*. In my typical motherly nature, I believed every child should experience Disney World. Since I was a young child, I loved to help others, especially children. Later that evening, I spoke with Jerome about Sheriese going with us. He said, *we will see*. He needed to first talk to Sheron to see if she was okay with it. If so, he would need her to help financially. Once he spoke with Sheron, she was happy Sheriese was invited to go with us. Sheriese told her niece, Neasia (NeNe) about the trip. Of course, NeNe wanted to go with us. Naturally, I extended the invitation for NeNe to attend. Sheron and her family members pulled together to pay for the airline fares, the park tickets for admission to the parks, and spending money for Sheriese and NeNe. Additionally, Jerome gave money towards the cost for Sheriese. The trip together with Sheriese staying with us fortified my relationship with Sheron, which I appreciated.

In December 2010 the family vacation became a reality. Kim, Mo, Kimola, Karrington, Miracle and Jordyn traveled from Bowie, Maryland to Orlando, Florida in a huge RV loaded with everything, including the kitchen sink. Ivy, Aaron, Aiden, Sylvia, Sheriese, NeNe, and I flew from Cleveland to Orlando. Otis and Jerome were invited to attend, but Otis had basketball obligations and Jerome was unable to go due to working. The vacation was a dream come true. Our lodging accommodations were awesome. Kim who loves to cook made us a few bountifully scrumptious breakfasts and dinners. We spent four enjoyable fun-filled days at Disney World and the affiliated parks. On the fifth day Kim and her family started their road trip back to Maryland, while we stayed a few more days. For those days, we stayed at the Nickelodeon Hotel where we enjoyed the theme rooms and activities. During the days everyone, except Aiden and I, went to Universal Studios. It was truly a once in a lifetime memorable vacation. I was grateful and thankful to God to be able to share this special time with my loved ones. To have quality time with my daughters away from my busy work schedule was a blessing. Then to be with my adorable five-month old grandson on his first visit to Orlando filled my heart with joy. It was uplifting to spend time with my sister and her family. Getting to know my soon to be ideal son-in-law let me know what an awesome addition he was to our family. Being able to spend time with my young step-daughter and her niece strengthen my bond with them.

Unfortunately, in retrospection for this family trip and many other family trips and events in my life I should have consulted with my two daughters before always inviting others to go with us. This was due to becoming aware several years later in 2015, that my daughters at times did not always want to share their Mommy with others, but to have me to themselves. They let me know that after a while they had gotten use to sharing me with others, but still wished to go places with only me and them.

My 2011 New Year started happy and appreciative. We had returned from the family Christmas vacation to our daily routines. Disappointingly, by mid-January Sheron had a relapse in her health. Eventually she was hospitalized. Everyone tried to keep Sheriese in as much of a normal routine as possible. This was especially true with her upcoming birthday on January 27th when she would turn fourteen. The weekend before Sheriese's birthday, I made plans to take her out to celebrate. On the 26th of January, Sheron's condition had further declined. The next day Jazmyn and Markita spent the day with Sheriese celebrating her birthday. Sorrowfully the next day Sheron passed. My heart ached for Sheron's family, especially for Sheriese. The thought of a child losing her mother being so young was inconceivable. When I saw her, I could only give her a big hug while saying how much she was loved by her mother and many others. I caringly shared with Sheriese that just like when my mother passed away her spirit is always with me, and her mother's loving spirit would live forever in her heart and soul, together with her beautiful memories forever etched into her mind. The parents of Sheron, Mr. and Mrs. McClain, were very gracious to me during the funeral. They even invited me to be there for Sheriese with Jerome by allowing me to ride in the family car to the service and sit with the family during the service. Over the next several months I would see how Mr. and Mrs. McClain are nice and caring people that love unconditionally.

Each time I visited them were always kind to me regardless of the circumstances. Even when Sheriese and I went through the roller coaster phases of our relationship or when Jerome and I had problems or Jerome, they stayed the same pleasant. Their steadfast kindness will always be appreciated.

After the passing of Sheron, I prayed for guidance in my relationship with Sheriese. We were extremely close, but I knew I had to be careful how I proceeded. Although not as young as Sheriese when Momma passed, I knew no one could ever replace my Momma. I was blessed with several beautiful loving God-given mothers that I love and appreciate. Nonetheless my heart, mind and soul were never the same since Momma passed. There are days I still cry out for Momma. I just need to hear her voice of reassurance or feel her touch. This caused me to pray for guidance to not overbear Sheriese, but nurture and support her as she allowed. With Ivy and Sylvia, I knew there were many things I would love to have a do-over when they were growing up, but that was not possible. Discussing how to be a good role model and step-mother to Sheriese with Sylvia, I remember her telling me, *I had made mistakes with Ivy and her, that could help me avoid those mistakes with Sheriese*. I let what Sylvia to abide in my heart and mind with a determination to adhere to the advice of Sylvia.

Trying Times with Teenage Step-Children. Going from living in a home with only Jerome and me to two minor teenagers was a major adjustment to my daily routine. Coupled with the fact that I was no longer a spring chicken but middle age, in my early fifties, it was challenging to adapt to the lifestyle of their youthful twenty-first century mindsets. It was necessary for me to focus on working with Jerome to have a loving and supporting home for his teenaged children. Eagerly I strived to blend us together. Regrettably, the efforts of Jerome towards a happily blended family never mirrored my ideas. Instead of working together to make us a happy blended family, he intensified the friction. The lackadaisical immature manner he handled situations between me and the children was disturbing. By Jerome working evenings, much of the time of Otis and Sheriese was spent with me. A typical evening with them entailed assuring they completed their homework assignments, were fed, prepared for the next school day, and went to bed at a reasonable time. Most of the times things would go smoothly. While at other moments it was an uphill battle. At times their behavior and attitudes became very obnoxious. Even though Jerome knew certain behaviors of Otis and Sheriese were inappropriate, he refused to work with me to improve the situations. When they did not want to adhere to what I asked, they simply called Jerome complaining. Once they talked to Jerome, he would give them instructions in contradiction of my initial ones. To my further embarrassment, Jerome would not even extend to me the decency of letting me know of his conversation approving whatever I had disapproved for them. His doing this caused tension. Otis and Sheriese knew they did not have to follow my instructions. They figured out calling Jerome would override anything I said. This resulted in their loss of respect for me. It came to a point that at certain times Otis and Sheriese would say, *you are not my momma*. I would reply, *no, I am not, but right now, I am the adult in this house*. This caused them to have an even more rebellious attitude towards me. They began to ignore whatever I said, while they laughed and said snide remarks. It was as if we were not even living in the same house. When I attempted to discuss the issues with Jerome, in his aloof attitude he would respond any problems I had with Otis or Sheriese was my fault. He would then accuse me of doing things the wrong way. If not that, he told me I really did not want to do anything for them. Once Jerome was stuck on what he believed, it was extremely difficult to get him to see he was incorrect, or another point of view. Then to boot, any conflicts in the house between Otis or Sheriese and me would often involve Jazmyn and Markita. Jazmyn and Markita would rudely interfere without any regards of what caused the situation. Emphatically this resulted in them treating me as the enemy. This added another layer of frustration that intensified the situations. It was more than a notion to live with the blatantly rude behavior of minor children. Couple that with Jerome not supporting and ostracizing me, together with the input from the other siblings it made me feel humiliated and exploited. All these actions caused me to go into my shell of insecurity, defeat, and withdrawal. It came to the point it was best for me to stay in my own lane. I would not say anything except hello and good-bye. Unless asked a question, I would be quiet. If not asked to do something, I did nothing. Deep down inside it was emotionally hurtful and upsetting to earnestly strive to make a happy, healthy, and loving home only to be treated in the manner Jerome allowed his children to behave towards me. I often thought what Otis's mother or Sheriese's grandparents would think if they knew the type of disrespectful behavior Jerome allowed. I knew talking to either of them was not feasible, because it only would cause more hostile reactions from everyone. Then aware of the proverb, *blood is thicker than water*, things could get worse which could result not only in my being further left out by the three of them, but by other family members as well.

Over the years, there were only three major adverse incidents with Otis. The first was leaving the house at the age of fifteen without saying anything to me. The other two involved inappropriate visits at the house with young females. The good thing with Otis was our disputes were resolved within a few days. He would apologize, then I would say okay, that I understood, and we would hug. Things would then go back to our normal routine. Most of the time Sheriese and I had a good relationship. Then without warning her attitude and the way she spoke to me would become extremely disrespectful. There were several incidents when her behavior was very inappropriate. Although not a quickly resolved like with Otis, I was always pleased that in time we would resolve and settle our disputes.

Chapter Nineteen -- Accepting the Reality of My Third Marriage

Throughout the period of 2008 through 2011, Jerome and I tried to make our marriage work. There were many days of unity and several days of disaccord. The disaccord was like a tenacious merry-go-round of repetitive issues with each turn becoming more intensive. Repeatedly he would let me know he had a problem with most of the things I did. Yes, this sounds familiar. Being berated by Jerome was liken to Syl. The difference was Jerome was five times more intensifying. This is when it felt like I had remarried a much harsher version of Syl. He complained the house was not maintained sufficiently. My caring for Otis and Sheriese was inadequate or insincere. Except for Ivy and Sylvia, he disapproved of my relationships with family members and *fake friends*. He belief that most pastors were hypocrites which caused him to think there was no need for me to attend and serve at the church. He had one standard for me and a different one for himself. Jerome insisted I inform him of each aspect of my life while he would not let me know what was occurring in his life. There were times he would intensely drill me about various matters. Yet when I questioned him about certain things, he would not give me an answer, instead he always said, *why you want to know*. As had been common for years, we rarely held lengthy conversations unless there was a disagreement. During those times Jerome would debate with me for hours. The next morning, he would continue discussing the matter. Months later Jerome would rekindle the same issues into a new dispute.

The blended family issue was likewise a significant obstacle. Jerome had his way and I had mine. As previously stated, it was my desire to thrive to unite our families. Jerome's efforts were more dissention. One of the major problems was he did not require his children to respect me in the same manner my daughters respected him. Ivy and Sylvia had been taught throughout their upbringing they must respect adults. Regardless of how they personally felt about Jerome, my daughters knew they were to be polite to him. Quite often, Jerome's children would treat me with respect, but when being disrespectful, they were very offensive. They would come into the house without speaking. Our bedroom was invaded without any regards to my privacy. Their attitudes were always like this is *my daddy house* not yours. At certain outings it was as if I was a stranger while they communicated amongst themselves. These situations caused me to often feel alienated in what I thought was *our* home and family. Not only did I have to deal with Jerome disregarding me, I had to cope with the opposition from his children. His inability to even talk to his children about their behavior towards me caused a lot of despair. It was like instead of *too many cooks in the kitchen* there were *too many children running a household*.

Trying desperately to make this marriage succeed, I would express my concerns and feelings to Jerome. Our inability to communicate without arguing, eventually made the feelings of being inept, undesirable, and unloved resurface. His resolution to our problems *was some shorts*. Trying to solve our problems with makeup sex changed nothing. When we finished, we got out of the bed with the exact problems we had before. This lifestyle was again steadily reopening my feelings of insecurity, defeat, and unworthiness. Next came the withdrawal into periods of despondency.

June of 2011, Otis was graduating from high school and had been accepted into a college in San Diego. Otis let me know because his mom was unable to take him, Jerome and I would be going with him to San Diego to help him get settled in before the beginning of school. The news of being a part of helping him move across country was rejuvenating. That evening I talked to Jerome about the trip. Over the next several days Jerome, Otis, Sheriese and I discussed the trip. With the time for Otis to leave approaching, I asked Jerome when we would make the arrangements for the trip. He informed me that he would be taking Otis to college in the next few days. Taken aback, I mumbled, the *next few days, what do you mean*? Looking and sounding dumbfounded, I stated, *I thought we were taking him*. He said because he needed help with everything, he had Jazmyn make all the arrangments for him and her to take Otis. In disbelief and unable to speak, I simply stared at Jerome while thinking, not again. Not only had he omitted me from the decision making, he totally excluded me from the trip. Never had I excluded him, nor Otis and Sheriese when proper, for going places with me, especially out-of-town. How betrayed I felt. Once more Jerome had built my hopes up only to let me down. How could he be this inconsiderate and mean? He knew for more than four years I had been good enough to work with him in raising Otis by, among other things: cooking; cleaning up behind him; doing his laundry; driving him to school and other events; allowing him to drive my car; and gave him money when he asked. I had helped Jerome in the overall daily care of Otis since he had moved in with us. Why couldn't Jerome have the decency to let me know the moment he had changed the plans? What a bummer, I felt completely shut-out by being uninvited from going with Jerome to help Otis get setup to attend college.

While they ecstatically prepared and packed, I helped Otis when he asked me to, never displaying the dejection and hurt I was experiencing to him. Otis was an innocent child that I would never begrudge because of the actions of his father. The day before they were scheduled to leave, Sheriese had begun to pack. I asked her was she going. She said, yes, she now was going. Yet again I was speechless. How could Jerome so easily brush me off? Gloomily I asked Jerome, *did you ever think about including me*. Irritated he replied, *he really was not thinking about that*. He told me his *focus was on getting Otis to college and he needed someone that could help get everything organized*. His remark frustrated me even more because he knew I had excellent organizational and logistical skills. Determined not to start an argument, I said, okay. On Saturday they prepared to leave on the one-week trip. Although Jerome did not believe I was good enough to go on the trip, he asked me to take him and Sheriese to the airport. On the ride he was unusually happy. He was smiling, singing, and even talking to me as he drove. He said to me, *you still my girl*. Even though my demeanor was withdrawn and dismayed, I murmured, *yes*. Then unexpectedly and out of character for Jerome, he reached over to put his hand under my dress and began sensual rubbing me. Speechless I sat there suddenly thinking I know this man is not trying to show this type of outward compassion while for years I had been begging him for some type of affection. Why was he doing this now? It made me think of the one day when Syl stated how nice I looked after all those years I had yearned for him to compliment me. This let me know Jerome, just like Syl were capable of being spontaneously compassionate, but simply had ignored or refused my requests. Jerome was only touching me in this manner today because he knew it was wrong the way he handled the situation of Otis moving to California. He had not treated me like I was his wife and knew I was upset and hurt. This gesture was not a sincere display of affection but done to pacify me. How dare him after I had begged and been rejected for his attention to think on this day he could make me feel better by doing this, he was wrong. When we arrived at the airport, Jazmyn, Otis, Corene, Rashawn and a few other family members were happily waiting at the curb for them. When I got out the passenger's side of the car to go to the driver's side, Jerome showed more compassion than ever before by pulling me towards him and hugging me and grapping my butt while saying he would talk to me later and not to give his *shorts* away. Nodding my head in a yes motion with tears beginning to form in my eyes, I thought if you really cared you would not be leaving me behind like a discarded rag. Not wanting everyone to see my disappointment, I got in the driver's seat and hurriedly drove off. He called a few minutes later asking if his wallet was in the car. It was. I turned around to take it to him. When he came to the car, I handed him the wallet. He said, thanks, and was about to say something else, but I looked straight ahead and speedily drove off because by that time I was crying, and my emotions were all over the place. I cried all the way home thinking of how happy everybody was, while I felt like a fool.

Once they arrived in San Diego, Jerome called to let me know they arrived. He then would call each evening. Our conversations were short because I really had little to say. Emotionally the pain of being disappointed and abandon had not subsided. This caused me to be standoffish when I talked to Jerome. Whatever questions Jerome asked, I barely answered. I would say, yes, no, or may be. During our conversation on Wednesday evening Jerome told me they had not finished everything and would be extending their stay until Saturday or Sunday. Feeling very depressed and wanting to hear something positive to uplift my spirit, I asked Jerome, do you really love me. He said, ugh. I told him if he did, I needed to hear him say it. Moaning in annoyance he answered like always, *if I did not love you, I would not have married you*. Beseeching him to say what I needed to hear, the actual three words, I said, *but why you just will not say you love me*. He began to get agitated saying, *look, I do not have time for this now and we will talk later*. Pissed-off now I said, *if you cannot tell me you love me, we are finished*. Angrily Jerome told me, *he did not have time for this mess*. Through with the conversation, I said, *okay*, then pressed the end button on the cell phone.

At that second, it was the end for me. I was no longer going to pretend my marriage to Jerome was alright. Instantaneously, all the mental agonizing pain from him that I had bottled-up within became unbearable. Falling to the floor, I screamed, *no*, while tears filled my eyes, I hollered out for my Momma and pleaded with God to help me. On my knees the pain consumed my heart while my mind whirled with thoughts of how I could not go through this again. Not again. Why couldn't I be loved in the same manner as other happily married women? What is wrong with me? Is this my punishment for all my self-inflicted sins? Was it because of the death of Herman and the abortion? Is this the cost I must pay for my sinful life? Did my transgressions prevent me from finding a man that loved me? Why was I still alive to only be hurt by people? I had done all I could to give Otis a home full of love and support, but now Jerome did not believe I deserved to go with them to California. Laying on the floor in the fetal position, I hollered out to Jesus Christ for mercy and help. That evening I was unable to eat or sleep, only persistently crying and praying to God for strength. That night the flicker of light from Jesus Christ was strength. The Holy Spirit imparted in my defeated spirit *The Lord is my light and my salvation; whom shall I fear? the Lord is the strength of my life; of whom shall I be afraid?* Psalm 27:1 (KJV). Even while praying, Satan was injecting negative thoughts in my mind that I had been used again, and nobody care about me. My mind was in warfare. Satan began saying it was time for me to permanently leave this life because I was not loved or appreciated. For the first time in many years, thoughts of suicide resurfaced, at the same time the Holy Spirit was saying to me be strong and trust in the Lord. With strength from God, I was able to realize there was much more to my life than Jerome. Primarily, there were my daughters. Even though they were now grown, I first-handed knew how hard it is to live without Momma. How could I even think they would not feel the same? At that moment I knew moving out of the house would be best for me and my loved ones. Picking myself off the floor, I wiped the tears from my eyes. I decided to phone Cha who had recently moved into an apartment to ask if I could move in with her until I could find an apartment. As soon as I asked Cha, immediately she said, of course. Cha stated how sorry she was for what happened between Jerome and me, but that I would be okay. I let her know how much her support and love were appreciated. The rest of the evening was an emotional struggle, but with the grace of God, I survived.

On Thursday morning, I sent a message to my secretary and the lawyers I worked with letting them know I would not be in the office today. Next, I called the mover, Mr. Hardin. I asked him if he could assist me in packing and moving my items to a storage unit. He was available to move me the next day. After talking with Mr. Hardin, I searched the website for storage facility. Once arrangement had been secured for the storage facility, I began packing. I talked to Ivy and Sylvia informing them of my decision to move. They both said, okay. They told me to let them know if I needed anything. I appreciated that Cha consistently checked on me. She even offered to help me pack. Although appreciating her offer to help, I could not let her come help me, because I knew from his insisting not to have other people in his house, I had to pack by myself. I planned to only take the furniture and household items that I had purchased. When the movers arrived the next morning, they helped me with finishing the packing. They then moved my belongings into the storage unit. Afterwards, I worked on packing the rest of my personal items that I would be taking to Cha's apartment. Jerome had called back, but there was no inkling he planned to tell me he loved me. In turn, I refused to inform him I was moving.

On Friday night I was packing the few remaining items to take to Cha apartment when abruptly depression and darkness overtook me. No longer did I want to be in this world, I wanted to be with my Momma, I wanted to be gone from this world. I even began rationalizing the idiom *worth more dead than alive*. My death would end my destructive journey in this world and enable my daughters to receive substantial amounts from my insurance policies and other investments. Completely in a depressed state and consumed with being too tired to live another second at 10:00 p.m. that night I got into my car. I drove to the 24-hour Walmart on Northfield Road and bought a bottle with the largest quantity of *Tylenol PM* tablets. Driving back to the house, with tears in my eyes, praying to God to end my life, I took several of the *Tylenol PM* tablets. Once back at the house, I took at least twenty-five more *Tylenol PM tablets*. I wrote short notes to my daughters and Jerome. Feeling the effects of the pills, I laid down on the couch in the living room to die. Sometime around 5:00 p.m. the next day I was awoken by my cell phone ringing. In a daze I answered the phone. It was Mommy Nunn. I must have sounded in a daze and not like myself as I remember her asking me several times if I was okay. Of course, I lied, saying, I was okay, just sleeping. After speaking to Mommy Nunn, I sat up on the couch feeling upset that I could not even succeed in killing myself. Years before I remember hearing how a young lady died from taking only fifteen pills, what I believed to be *Tylenol*. Why was I still alive after taking more than thirty-five? I called Cha to let her know I would be at the apartment soon. Getting up from the couch, I noticed a few things around me and in the living room out of place. When I went upstairs to my surprise the bedroom was awry. The bedding was flung throughout the room, the chair turned over, and other items scattered throughout the room. Still feeling discombobulated, I assumed Jerome returned home and threw everything around in the room. Though I wondered why he had not woke me up or touched the letters that I had laid beside me. Later I learned Jerome had not arrived home until the next day. This is when I realized it was me who had tossed everything around the house, it was similar to when I had taken the pills when married to Herman. Once more the pills had put me in such an unconscious state that I was unable to remember my actions. The flicker of light from Jesus Christ was two-fold mercy. It was not my appointed time to die nor was I physically hurt while in an incognizant state. While unconsciously moving about the house it was a blessing I remained in the house. I think about what if I had walked outside the house. Even worst what if I had attempted to drive. Facing the fact that once more I had survived another suicidal attempt, I pulled myself together. With the warfare persisting in my mind, emotionally despondent yet being obedient to the Holy Spirit, I loaded my car with the final few items. Locking the door to the house was painful, as I knew my dream that this would be my happily forever home would not come true. Thinking one more failed marriage with tears running down my face, I drove to Cha's apartment.

Chapter Twenty -- Living on My Own

When Jerome returned home, he called non-stop. For several hours I refused to answer the calls. Finally, I answered. He told me what I did was wrong, and he wanted to know who had been in his house to move me. I told him only the moving company, and that I had not allowed anyone else in his house. Jerome then asked what I was going to do about my credit card debt. I answered, pay my debt. Then he wanted to know if I made any extra keys to the house and his car? My reply was, no. His next question was if I had filed for a divorce? I responded, no. After answering his all of questions, I tried to explain he could have prevented this if he had only told me he loved me. He became more defiant, saying that made no sense. Jerome belligerently challenged my decision to leave, yet not listening to the reasons why I left. This lasted for more than ten minutes. Finally, I hung up on him. He then repeatedly called me stating I was wrong. Jerome told me we could have talked about things. Then he began telling me I must have another man. I repetitively told him of course he would say it was about another man or my fault, instead of acknowledging I left because of his behavior towards me and the way he allowed others to treat me. The more we talked it was obvious there was no reconciling because Jerome believed I was wrong and he had not done anything wrong. This let me know he had no idea of the disrespectful way he treated me as his wife. He had no clue of how mean and obnoxious he treated me. That night we ended the call with me hanging up the phone and refusing to answer any more of his calls.

With the passing of each day, I became more depressed. It became extremely bad to the point I was not even able to pray. Constantly crying out to God begging Him to please let me die. All the while outwardly acting like life was great with a fake smile on my face. Each day I talked to my girls and Mommy Nunn pretending like I was doing good. Working hard at the office helped pass a lot of empty miserable hours, especially because of being able to talk to my secretary and reveal to her my true emotional battle. It was also good that Cha encouraged me to attend church with her at Mt. Pleasant Baptist Church. The sermons by Pastor Harris and worship services were truly uplifting. Most importantly they always reinforced what my heart already knew, and my mind needed to declare, that God loves me. *For God so loved the world, that He gave His only begotten Son, that whosoever believeth in Him should not perish, but have everlasting life*, John 3:16 (KJV). In addition, I had to remember that Jesus Christ died for my sins. *Who gave Himself for our sins, that He might deliver us from this present evil world, according to the will of God and our Father,* Galatians 1:4 (KJV). My heart knew that from the moment my Momma conceived me the grace and mercy of God through Jesus Christ had brought me through a lot of tribulations. What I had to overcome was allowing my mind to be consumed with what I presently was able to see and feel that was causing me distress. Instead, I needed to envision and sense how I would have a triumphant future. I prayed to God to give me strength to help me strop vacillating from one moment being consumed with thoughts of my past and present stormy life, then the next moment being steadfast in believing

I would have a glorious future for me. The warfare inwardly kept me fluctuating from happily optimistic to depressingly pessimistic. It got to the point that I began to drink alcohol and even started smoking cigarettes to help mask my inward pain. For several weeks I went to clubs, usually with Cha where I met a few men. Some would ask for my phone number and I gave my number to a few guys. With a couple of the guys I would talk to them on the phone and went on a few dates. However, at that point in my life I had no desire for any type of relationship. Mentally beginning another relationship was the furthest thing from my mind. I was happy with just talking to someone since that at least helped pass the long hours of the day. Eventually no matter how hard I tried to substitute drinking, smoking, and pretending life was great at the end of the day nothing removed the inner pain. The fake smile slowly turned into tears of shame, fear, and dismay. Cha would see and help me through some of those awful tear-filled days and nights when my soul cringed in agony. She was a flicker of light from God during some very dark days and nights by encouraging me to trust in God, be strong and forget about Jerome.

I diligently attempted not to think about Jerome or answer his phone calls. Since I had not changed my address my mail was still being received at Jerome's address. To avoid any contact with Jerome, I went as far as to have Cha call him to get my mail. When he asked where I was, I told her to tell him I was in the hospital for a few days. Each day was a struggle not to try to commit suicide and not communicate with Jerome. One of the toughest times during my stay with Cha was the week she had to attend an out-of-town work-related conference. Being alone those six days was mentally challenging. Like before when I had tried to leave Jerome, thoughts of living alone haunted me. I constant thought again how I went from Momma to Herman, to Syl, then to Jerome, now over 50 years old could I survive living on my own? Those six days being mentally tired and scared of how my future would unfold, I persistently fought inwardly to not take a bottle of pills. My nights were always filled with weeping and moaning. The aching in my heart was immeasurable. Unable to pray, I would scream and cry out, *Lord, please help me*, because these were the only words I could get to come out of my mouth. The flicker of light from Jesus Christ during this despondent time in my life was the daily intercessory prayers for me by Gregory. Without a doubt I know it was his prayers that played a significant role in me being able to survive that week alone without trying to commit suicide. That week not only did I not try to kill myself, but by surviving those days, it rekindled my spirit and hope. Accepting the fact, it was solely the grace and mercy of God upholding me, I started to work on ways to get a grip on and accept the reality of my life. More importantly, I knew I had to begin to concentrate on being alive not trying to end my life. Through faith in God, I worked on believing that there must be a purpose for me to be alive. Then I knew through the darkest storms of my life, God had always given me flickers of light of grace and mercy that always saw me through to brighter days. Yet, despite all my renewed faith and hope, I still had moments when I would be full of joy and optimistic about my future, then suddenly I would be coping with depression, suicidal thoughts and worrying about my uncertain future. This caused me to mentally again begin to question why I was ever born and what was my purpose for living? Struggling to stay focus on positive thoughts more than negative ones, I worked towards being able to wipe the tears when they fell and praying when I could. The times when I could not pray, I still cried out to God for strength to make it through the next hour. *In my distress I called upon the Lord, and cried to my God: and he did hear my voice out of his temple, and my cry did enter into his ears*, 2 Samuel 22:7 (KJV).

Each day I strived to get adjusted to being on my own after living eleven years with Jerome. By late July, I began to look for an apartment. I decided because I did not have a chance to previously enjoy my apartment at the Carlyle that is where I would move. A few weeks later my desire became true with the lease of a gorgeous lake view chic apartment. Mr. Hardin moved my furniture from the storage unit to the apartment. Sylvia and Nicole assisted me with the decorations. In August, my 1992 Lexus 420 coupe that I was hoping to become an antique car needed too much repair. Still wanting one day to have an antique Lexus coupe, I purchased a 2000 Lexus 300 coupe that was in excellent condition. With some of my material desires coming true that aspect of my life began to look good again. Inwardly life was not as easy to get back on track as I hoped. Living alone was harder than I thought. Going to an empty apartment began to affect me mentally. I would often think of Momma living alone after I moved wondering how she handled living alone for all those years. Then with my apartment being on the other side of town it was thirty-five to fifty minutes away from my family members and friends which resulted in few visits. Each day I talked on the phone with Ivy, Sylvia, Mother Nunn, and occasionally a few other friends, pretending I was happy and doing great. These calls would help me temporarily, but the loneliness always quickly returned. Gratefully when I went to work, mentally I would be okay, basically because I would be busy working and was also able to vent to my secretary. The problem was staying emotionally positive once alone at the apartment instead of being restless and inwardly emotionally dying. I came to accept much of my anguish was because I had not gotten over Jerome, together with the fact I was on the verge of my third failed marriage and feeling miserable about my life because I did not want to be alone. My feelings were still going from one extent to another in a moment's notice: one second my heart: ached from missing Jerome; then it switched to hurting at the thoughts of how callous and disrespectful Jerome treated me; followed by me feeling stupid for falling in love with an unemotional man; then finally I felt hollow like nothing matter anymore, I felt completely void. Unable to sleep, I would try reading scriptures and spiritually uplifting books, watching TV, or playing video games. Doing one of those things would help make me sleepy, but then I would lay down to go to sleep only to toss and turn for hours. My mind would not stop pondering and reliving my life and its purpose. Exhausted with sleepless nights, I began to take over the counter sleeping pills and drink more alcohol. It eventually became a daily habit to take pills and drink. I even increased the quantity pills when it took too long to go to sleep. On the weekends when I did not have plans with family members or friends, I would take larger quantities of pills and pray to God please do not wake me up only to eventually woke up at some point the next day.

Jerome knew I had moved into the apartment when he received the verification from the U.S. Post Office about my change of address. He would periodically call late at night after 11:00 p.m. In his normal routine, if I did not answer the phone he would repeatedly call. This would further affect my inability to sleep. Some days he would call me at the office. Initially when I answered, he started the conversation asking me why I left the way I did. I would explain for the umpteenth time that it was because of the way he treated me, and not saying he loved me when I asked him. He would ask me if I was with another man. My answer would be no, I was not sleeping with anyone. Jerome would say he would understand if I was with someone else. He only wanted me to tell him the truth about why I left him and that there was another man. Again, and again I told him I was being truthful, about why I left him and there was no other man. Talking to Jerome was like it always had been throughout our relationship with him constantly refusing to acknowledge and accept his negative behavior in our relationship. Now more than ever with him not admitting to contributing to any of our marital problems, I knew firmly expressing my feelings was essential. By me talking over the phone or texting him I was able to speak more freely and clearly express my thoughts because I did not experience the intimidation I felt when talking in his presence. Without having to hold back, I would let Jerome know how his words and actions made me feel unloved, insecure, humiliated, and worthless. That his manipulation had negative effects on my relationships with my loved ones. The way he relentlessly interrogated me when asking questions made me feel like an idiot. How it was wrong of him to question my whereabout while he would come and go without any accountability. When he did not stand up and protect me as his wife from his family members and friends disrespecting me was disheartening. When I finish telling him these things, Jerome hit me a response that made me wonder about myself when he said, I was constantly going to church and praying but did not practice, trust, and believe what the Bible said. He told me instead I was insecure, needed more fortitude, lacked self-confidence, snooped too much, and tried to save the world. Jerome said my being unnecessarily insecure caused me to worry and question things for no good reason and not to trust him when he was one of the few people that genuinely cared about me, while my *fake family* could care less about me and really talked about me behind my back. He went on to say my not having fortitude made me run at the first sign of trouble without him having any opportunity to have any input, even though I had made a vow through good and tough times. Then he told me by lacking self-confidence, made me not believe in myself and I thought he and his family were always talking about or attacking me, and I took everything too personal. How it ticked him off when I snooped in his personal belonging because it made him not trust me and wonder if I was the one really hiding something. Jerome let me know that my trying to save the world made me look stupid and people were only using then forgetting about me. Jerome would then repeatedly tell me he would not have married me if he did not care about me. Discussing all our problems over the phone or text seemed to work towards improving our ability to communicate. The more we openly discussed our feelings it gave us insight about how we truly felt about each other. We agreed knowing each other pet peeves and working towards eliminating them was the first step if we wanted to heal our marriage.

On August 26th, Jerome called to say happy birthday. He asked what I was doing. I replied, there was nothing planned for my birthday. He asked if I wanted to go to dinner. Although we had talked on the phone and texted regularly over the past weeks, we had not seen each other since late June. I knew I missed and wanted to see Jerome, so I told him, yes, I would love to go to dinner. When he arrived, I was glad to see him. To my surprise he had Sheriese with him. It was really good to see her smiling face because I had truly also missed her. We both were bubbling with excitement, giving each other a big hug while saying how much we missed each other. I could see Jerome looking at us with the tiny smirk on his face that he had when he was happy or pleased. Jerome said with that same smile, are you all finished hugging, then he asked me where I wanted to go eat. I suggested a little restaurant around the corner. It was a very enjoyable evening as we talked and laughed a lot. Sheriese kept me amused with her usual funny comments and teasing of Jerome. She brought me up to date on things she had been doing, including how excited she was about being on a competitive cheerleading and preparing to attend high school. The restaurant had a bar with entertainment and that night the entertainment was karaoke. Sheriese and I decided to sing one of our favorite songs *Benny and the Jets* by Elton John. As we were trying to sing, Jerome joined in to help us. It was hilarious. Any stranger looking at us that night would have thought we were the ideal happy family. It even seemed that way to me. On our way back to the apartment Sheriese asked if she could spend the night. I said, yes. She turned to Jerome asking, is it okay? He said, yes. When he dropped us off at the apartment, he told me he had to work a part-time job that evening. Getting out the car, I said, okay and that I enjoyed the evening and would talk to him later, and he said, okay.

When Sheriese and I stepped into the lobby of the apartment, she said, *wow, this looks like a hotel*. After entering the apartment, she was even more excited, saying this looks like a picture in a magazine. The remainder of the evening we talked and watched a few of our favorite TV series until she fell asleep. Jerome called around 4:00 a.m. telling me he had finished working his part-time job. He said he was going to come back over to the apartment if it was okay with me. Without hesitation I said, yes, while thinking how good it was to be with Sheriese and him instead of alone in the apartment, and the nice evening we had together celebrating my birthday. When Jerome arrived, Sheriese was sleeping in my bed. Jerome and I sat in the living room talking and must have woken Sheriese as she came into the living room. We talked for a little while, then Sheriese said she was going to sleep on the couch. That night was the first time Jerome and I were intimate since the night he left for San Diego. In the morning I cooked breakfast for us. Before they left Sheriese asked if she could come back to spend the night next weekend because it would be a long week for Labor Day. I said, yes, of course you can.

During the next several days, Jerome and I had amiable phone conversations without any arguing and he made no sarcastic remarks towards me. I did not complain about his negative demeanor towards me. The following Saturday Jerome brought Sheriese to the apartment before he went to work. Sheriese and I talked and watched a little TV. Later we went to the pool. Once again, Sheriese said the apartment was like a hotel because of the pool, spa, game room, min-store, beauty salon, and exercise room. Once we finished playing around in the pool, we got dressed and went out for lunch and shopping. Jerome called when he finished working to see if it was okay to come over. I said, yes. From that night forward, we were more pleasantly civil with each other. We would talk several times a week. At time he would sporadically visit me. There were times we would not talk or see each other for several days. This was fine with me because at this point I was still unsure if our marriage could be saved. If it did not work out for us, I had to be prepared to move on with my life. What I was thankful to God for was after the birthday dinner, my bouts with suicide decreased and I was sleeping better with less sleeping pills.

No Third Time Charm. Ivy's employment with Akron Law School included often travelling for work-related matters. In October 2011, she had to travel to Philadelphia and New York. We discussed Aiden and me going with her on the trip, and we both agreed it would be great for us to go. A few days later I bought my airline ticket, Aiden did not need a ticket because he was under two and would sit on our laps. I scheduled a few days off from work and anxiously awaited the time away with Ivy and Aiden. From the moment we boarded the plane, we had an amazing time. When Ivy attended her conferences, Aiden and I enjoyed our time together. The second evening in Philadelphia we were happy when Aaron's father, Ivan and one of his colleagues were able to join us for a nice dinner. The next conferences were being held in New York City. Ivy let me know we would travel by train to New York. Thinking about all the movies about New York train and subway system I could not see my grandson riding on a train. Instead I arranged and paid for roundtrip limo transportation to New York. Even to this day Ivy and Sylvia often tease me how my first-born grandson was too good to ride the train. In New York, once Ivy finished her conferences we had a spectacular time. We took a carriage horse ride through Central Park, and shopped at Schwartz Toy store, Macy's Department Store, and a few other stores. It was like a breath of fresh air being away from Cleveland. Typically, whenever I was on vacation my real world always seemed to disappear. The same was true during this trip as I enjoyed the time away from Cleveland with Ivy and Aiden.

    Although Jerome and I had been seeing each other off and on, we had not seen each other for several weeks prior to the trip. When we were in New York, Jerome called. I let him know I was out-of-town with Ivy and Aiden and we would return in a few days. We had a brief friendly discussion. When we arrived back in Cleveland, I had previously made plans to have dinner with a gentleman I had been introduced to by a friend several weeks ago. The gentleman and I talked several times on the phone and before leaving on the trip, we had made plans for dinner. Prior to arriving back in Cleveland, Jerome called. He asked what I was doing. I said, still out of town because there was no way I was going to allow him to interrogate me about my dinner date. That evening Jerome called several times. I refused to answer his calls. After my date, I returned to my apartment without calling Jerome. Early the next morning Ivy called. She told me Jerome had called asking was I with her. She told him, no I was at home or work. Ivy asked me what was going on because she was not aware Jerome and I had been talking again. I told her not to worry, I would call him. I called Jerome asking him why he called Ivy. He said because he knew I was lying about still being out-of-town. This started his interrogation of where was I. Who was I with? Did I have sex with this person? I told him about my dinner date. This was not good enough for him. He insisted I went to bed with the man. This argument went on for days. He was determined to make me admit I had sex with my date. I denied his false accusation. After not budging after his non-stop intimidation, Jerome said that it would be best if we filed for a divorce, and a little stunned, but I agreed.

We decided to work towards reaching consensual terms to the separation agreement and file for a divorce without legal counsel. It became a problem for me when Jerome did not want to reimburse me for more than $50,000 I had invested in his house and his vehicle over the past eleven years. During our time of cohabiting and marriage, I had paid half of the cost for improvements and major repairs to the house from the installations of siding, windows, carpeting, interior and exterior painting, window fixtures and appliances. On top of that, for several years I paid one-half of the monthly car payment for his BMW. Jerome was vehemently adamant about not reimbursing me for the investments. This was even after I explained to him it was not fair that he and his children benefit from all my investments. We disputed the reimbursement issue for several weeks. I became too tired of arguing day after day with him. Jerome had worn me down to the point I no longer had the will-power or desire to fight anymore with him. At that point I would relinquish my investments and anything else he wanted to complete the separation agreement. Thankfully, I received a flicker of light from Jesus Christ to be still and let the Lord fight my battle. *And...Fear ye not, stand still, and see the salvation of the Lord, which he will shew to you to day:...The Lord shall fight for you, and ye shall hold your peace*, Exodus 14:13-14 (KJV). Peace of mind was far better than the material lost. In addition, my sanity was worth more than losing the $50,000 investment. With the guidance from the Holy Spirit, I called Jerome informing him it was not necessary for the separation agreement to include any reimbursement to me for my investment. A few days later the complaint for dissolution of marriage together with the separation agreement was filed with the court. After filing the complaint, Jerome again begin to repeatedly call the office during the day and my cell phone late at night. Whenever I did not answer the phone, he would call non-stop until I would turn the phone off or answer. His calls were primarily to let me know I could tell him the truth about the other man because he would respect me more if I would admit it. I constantly denied his accusations. Then his discussion would change to letting me know he still wanted us to be friends. I would tell him we should both move on with our lives, reminding him that he asked for the divorce and there was no need for us to be friends or to have any type of relationship. I told him we had no children that bonded us together and it was plainly clear we never trusted each other. Moreover, staying away from each other was in our best interest.

Waiting for the divorce hearing I strived to go forward with my life. I kept on working and trying to become accustomed to living alone. Thanksgiving Day our families had a blessed time celebrating at the Banks' home. After Thanksgiving Day everyone began to prepare for Christmas. Following a few more dates with my friend, I stopped talking to him. I had reached a point of not being in a mental state to begin dating, and it would be unfair to involve him or anyone else in my emotionally unstable world. Nights had once more became the worst part of my day. Unable to sleep I was more frustrated than ever. My routine each evening reverted back to taking many sleeping pills and drinking vodka or wine. My weekends were even worst. Adding to my mental anguish it was winter in Cleveland with the days cloudy, dreary, and snowy. The dreary weather and because it was getting darker earlier due to the end of daylight saving time, not only did those two things increase me feel low-spirited, I felt more lonesome and the evenings seemed to linger with morning nowhere in sight. Due to the frigid weather there were even less visitors because everyone stayed in the house. I would sit alone for hours in the apartment lonely and depressed, not feeling sorry for myself, but simply emotionally drained.

The dissolution hearing was held on December 11, 2011. The Judge asked if we wanted the dissolution. With tears in my eyes, I passionately responded, *he wants it*, and Jerome said, *it was for the best*. The Judge looked at us for a second before nonchalantly saying, complaint is granted. Leaving out the courtroom Jerome asked if I wanted him to drive me back to the office. Fervently I said, no and asked him to please just leave me alone. I started running away from him. Jerome followed me repeatedly saying, this was best for both of us, but that he still wanted us to be friends because he cared about me. Irritated I told him to please leave me alone. He kept saying over and over we could be friends, how he always would care about me, and would be there if I needed anything. I shouted as forcefully as possible to him, will you shut up and leave me alone. We finally reached the exit doors. Once more he asked if I wanted a ride to the office. It was extremely cold that day, but I refused to ride with him as I began to run down the stairs of the courthouse to the crosswalk. Once out of his sight, I stopped running and began to cry while walking briskly back to the office. My heart ached, and tears streamed down my face, I felt loss and empty as I tried to grasp how another husband I still loved was no longer my husband. Why did this happen again? Was it because I had asked too much of Jerome by wanting him to reciprocate the love I gave to him and desired in return. Then I thought it was not Jerome, but me who was unlovable. I even wondered if I knew how to love myself yet alone Jerome or anyone else.

Too Tired to Live. After that day, silently suicide became an essential part of my life. I begin to reiterate and convince myself the true unconditional loves of my life, Ivy and Sylvia were grown. They had established their lives. More importantly, the financial benefits from my death would justify my decision, because as I had previously declared and believed, I was *worth more dead than alive*. Each evening and weekend became a monumental emotional battle to live. My prayers were God please let me not wake up. Then I would take numerous pills, drink lots of vodka and go to sleep. Although very groggy, I always would wake up. Once I was able to get out of bed, I would dress. Then I would put on my life is great disguise to cope with the real world. Unlike my separation from Syl, Jerome persistently called like nothing had changed in our relationship. He would say, regardless you still are my girl. Despite not being able to stop loving Jerome, I begged him to leave me alone, but he would not listen. In fact, Jerome called even more. He would question if I was alone, and why he could not have some *shorts*. I repeatedly responded how hurtful it was for him to still want to be friends and ask me for *shorts* when he wanted the divorce. How could he claim he cared about me when he so easily asked for a divorce without any evidence of me being with another man. I reminded him when I was there with him all those years he showed little love and compassion. Why was he now acting like he cared so much? These conversations went on for weeks. Jerome knew exactly how to get to me and wear me down.

He was an expert in getting under my skin until I was exhausted. Eventually the constant calls were successful. Together with knowing deep down inside I loved and missed him, I succumbed to his request to see me. Even though Jerome and I resumed talking and being intimate, taking my life never stopped consuming my mind. In the presence of Jerome and everyone, except for my secretary, my life was a façade. I portrayed a happy go lucky life, smiling and talking as usual. I worked and helped whoever needed my assistant, all the while emotionally dying inside. Each morning as I woke up, I would ask God why He kept me alive. Why did I keep waking up? I had hurt and disappointed many people. My failed life had negatively impacted many innocent people. I no longer wanted to face another day of failure and disappointment to others. Again, this was no pity party. I was only tired of creating darkness for others and myself and was exhausted from living. Going through the motions of life was too much to bear. It had gotten to the point when hearing someone had died I would get upset with God that I was not the one that died. I believed those who died had no desire to die while I was daily begging to die. Without ceasing I prayed, Lord please let me enter my eternal rest.

Chapter Twenty-One – Trying Again

Initially Jerome would come to the apartment a couple of nights a week. By March 2012, I began to stay at his house several times a week. Once again, our relationship had improved. As usual he worked on being more compassionate and I focused on having more self-esteem and being less insecure. To my knowledge Sheriese was the only one of our children that was aware Jerome and I were again in a relationship. As a result, in the spring when Jerome told me Jazmyn was getting married, I was uncertain if I would attend. When Jerome asked me to attend, I said, yes. Jerome let me know I would be attending the rehearsal for the wedding and of course would be seated next to him at the wedding and reception. Subsequently to moving out of the house, except for Sheriese, I had not seen any of Jerome's family members or friends. This made me apprehensive of how I would be received. When we arrived at the wedding rehearsal, Jazmyn and the other family members were cordial with several of them hugging me. The next day Jazmyn had a beautiful wedding and reception at the City Hall rotunda. During the reception it was good to see other family members and friends. A few said they had missed me when I was out of town for the birthday celebration for Aunt Mill and the family picnic. Aware Jerome always was an extremely private person, I knew few people were knew we had been separated and now divorced. Even with handling the father-of-the-bride responsibilities and mingling with all the guest, Jerome managed to be exceptionally attentive to me, it was like we still were married. The entire weekend was remarkable. A few months after the wedding, Jazmyn asked me about a venue for her baby shower. I suggested the party room in my apartment building. After Jazmyn came to see the party room, she agreed it was the perfect place. In August she had a lovely baby shower.

In July 2012, it was time to determine if I would renew my apartment lease. Jerome and I discussed my moving back into the house. We decided living together would be more beneficial to the rekindling of our relationship. At the end of August, I moved back into the house. Yet once more we were living a more harmonious life. Both of us endeavored to communicate and express our love for each other more candidly. Sheriese was happy I was back, even though she wished I still had the apartment to visit because she loved the amenities. Things were good. It appeared we were finally on one accord. During this timeframe, Ivy and I had been planning her wedding. When Ivy found out Jerome and I were once more together, she was gracious enough to invite him, Sheriese, Jazmyn and her husband to attend the wedding. The night before the wedding, Jazmyn went into labor and her and Rashawn's first-was born son, so of course, only Jerome, Sheriese and one of her friends attended the wedding and reception.

Life with Teenager Once Again Was a Rollercoaster Ride. Jerome still worked evenings. As a result, Sheriese and I once again spent a lot of time together in the evenings. It was like I had never moved out with us doing a lot of things we did before I moved. We went back to our old routine of watching our favorite television shows, and she would complain when I talked too much during the shows. Sheriese and I also resumed are heart to heart talks discussing her dealing with peer issues and her future career goals, including preparing to attend college, dating and sexual relationships concerns. Besides being busy with high school studies, Sheriese was a cheerleader for the high school and on the competitive cheering squad. When she cheered for the school, many family members would attend. For the competitive cheering events that were held locally, in state and out-of-state, Sheriese and I would attend, and on several occasions Jerome, Jazmyn and Sylvia attended. In addition to cheering, Sheriese was interested in modeling. I encouraged her to pursue her dreams and she did by modeling in several fashion shows and enrolling in modeling classes. When there were parent-teacher meetings, I attend. Then would let Jerome know what the meetings were about and if the school needed any information.

Even before I had moved, Sheriese and I would have great days filled with some strenuous times. Over the years, I had become acclimated with my rollercoaster ride with Sheriese. One day she would be loving, sweet and respectful then the next day moody, mean, and disrespectful. Those difficult days at times caused a great deal of tension on our relationship. Trying to talk to Jerome was pointless because as in the pass he always insisted I was to blame for our problems. Consequently, he still did nothing to rectify the situations. During those difficult periods I would ask if she wanted to talk. If she did not, I would leave her alone. I presumed some of these changes in her behavior could potentially be caused from her grieving and missing her mother. This I totally understood. Even though it had been thirty years since Momma passed away there was a never-ending void in my heart and life that could never be filled. Every so often I would be in la-la land daydreaming about my Momma. Experiencing my emotions from missing my Momma allowed me to relate to the possible reasons for Sheriese's mood swings.

One of the most difficult incidents with Sheriese occurred several months after I had moved back in. On school days I would drive her to school then go to work. With the house only having one full bathroom each morning she would wake up first to shower. Following her showering, I would get up to shower. Either before or after I would begin showering, she would come in the bathroom to apply her makeup and style her hair. We typically had no problems in the morning, but one morning, she was already in the bathroom when I went to open the bathroom door to get in the shower. Abruptly Sheriese yelled, ugh, and said something else that was unclear, while forcefully slamming the door in my face. I could not believe this little girl had the audacity to slam the door in my face. Knowing that my own daughters would never be allowed to treat me or any other adult in this manner, there was no way this child was going to behave like this towards me. Upset and furious I stormed into the bedroom yelling for Jerome to wake up as I went on to say he better get Sheriese, and that I was not driving her to school. As Jerome got out of the bed still a bit groggy and confused, he tried to figure out what had happened. Still upset I repeated what I previously said and how Sheriese had slammed the door in my face. Jerome did not say anything to either of us as he put on his clothes and left to take Sheriese to school. I was upset, hurt, and more important, disappointed that Sheriese would behave in that manner.

Following that day Sheriese and I did not speak for days. When I would say, good morning or hello, she would barely mumble a respond. Undoubtedly, it was difficult not to communicate with Sheriese because I did love and care about her and did not like us not talking and missed our camaraderie. Instead of Jerome attempting to resolve the tension between us, he did nothing. Yes, I was the adult who could have said more. The problem was in this situation I was unable to handle it like I would've if it had been Ivy and Sylvia. The fact was clear I was only the step mother of a child whose mother had passed. There was no doubt I recognized and accepted that I would always be considered an outsider. For this reason, I knew there were certain instances and matters that I must handle with kid gloves. On the other hand, Jerome had the authority to put our home back on track. It was my belief that it was his duty to let his children know that irrespective of what they thought about me, I was the woman in his life and our house, even though we were no longer married. Like so many times before, Jerome let me down by not addressing the problem. With each passing day, then weeks, to my disbelief increasingly when Jerome and Sheriese were together they started to behave like I did not exist. Daily matters that I would normally do for Sheriese, he or her sisters now would do. Once more it became exceedingly mentally challenging to live under those conditions. My feelings for her welfare had not changed. It solely was her seesaw attitude from kindness to cruelty that needed to be addressed. A few weeks after the incident, Jerome called me on the phone to finally discuss what was going on between Sheriese me. He stated he was getting tired of it. When Sheriese got into the car, Jerome said, he would call me back. A few moments later I heard shouting coming from my cell phone. I put the phone to my ear and heard Sheriese shouting, *I am your daughter, she is nothing to you*. Jerome was trying to calm her down. I hung the phone up feeling the piercing sting and mental effect of her words. I called Jerome back to let him know I had heard what Sheriese said. When I returned home that evening before Jerome left for work, I did try to get Sheriese and me to settle our issue. Regrettably, it turned into a screaming match between Sheriese and me. In the end nothing was resolved. Upset I sought advice from a few friends. Several told me to leave her alone, because they believed as kind and nurturing as I had been to her that she was ungrateful. After several days of much prayer, there was a flicker of light from Jesus Christ of compassion. The Holy Spirit reminded me of 1 Peter 3:8-9 (KJV) [f]*inally, be ye all of one mind, having compassion one of another, love as brethren, be pitiful, be courteous: Not rendering evil for evil, or railing for railing: but contrariwise blessing; knowing that ye are thereunto called, that ye should inherit a blessing.* Yielding to the Holy Spirit I went to Sheriese with compassion in my heart asking to talk. She agreed. I told her my sole purpose in her life was to improve not upset it. Then I explained to her my intensions were never to harm or offend her, but if I had, I was sorry. I ended the talk by giving her a hug. With prayer, we were able to rectify our relationship and move forward.

A few months later it was Sheriese's sixteenth birthday, and she was anxious to learn how to drive. I started teaching her the basic driving skills. Eventually, I allowed her to drive my car short distances. Once she obtained her learners permit, Jerome enrolled her in a driving class. Regularly, Sheriese drove me around while she completed her driving classes. Upon completing the driving class, I took her for the road test. Sheriese was overjoyed that she passed and promptly called her grandparents. They were proud of Sheriese. Like Mrs. McClain always did, she thanked me for everything I did for Sheriese. In the spring of 2013, Jerome purchased Sheriese a brand-new Subaru car. She was overjoyed, and in true blissfulness. We all were happy for Sheriese. With the purchase of her car came a new set of problems. Like Jerome, at times Sheriese would leave the house without saying a word. Once I figured out she was not in the house, I would call her to ask where she was going. Irritated she would reply, *I told my dad.* I talked to Jerome about this problem. In his usual unconcerned attitude Jerome thought nothing was wrong with this behavior. He believed if Sheriese spoke to at least to one of us it should be okay. My issue with Jerome was Sheriese was a minor teenager who left out the house with me the adult in the house unaware by either of them what was going on. This behavior was not only wrong and rude, it was dangerous, because if something would happen to her, I would be the first questioned as to when and where she left the house going to. What harm would it be for one of them to keep me apprised of her leaving the house? After several incidents with

Sheriese leaving out the house without saying anything to me, I reiterated to Jerome if his children never saw him loving, supporting, and respecting me, he could not expect them to. Yet, Jerome did nothing to resolve our problems. And, of course, this is exactly what began to happen with Sheriese's attitude towards me. It would waiver from respectful to disrespectful in a split second. During those time I prayed persistently to remember to be compassionate and have patience with Sheriese.

In August 2013, when Sheriese began the eleventh grade one of her instructors extended an invitation for her to take part in the high school foreign exchange student program. Initially the students from London would visit Shaker Heights, and in June 2014, Sheriese and several other students would travel to London, England for two weeks. Although the trip was quite expensive, I believed it would be a once in a lifetime experience for Sheriese. After speaking with Jerome, he agreed it would be a good opportunity. Over the next months, Jerome and I together with family members helped Sheriese plan for the trip abroad. Sheriese had an excellent learning experience and loads of fun in London. During this time, it was amazing for me to receive text messages and a few phone calls from Sheriese Upon her return from London, we began to discuss preparing for her senior year.

<u>Not My Time.</u> By January 2014, notwithstanding the emotional rollercoaster ride with Sheriese, Jerome and I had tried to keep our relationship on track. Then gradually old habits began to reemerge. Jerome started to assert his earlier confrontational attitudes and behaviors with his negative criticism, suspicion, domination, emotionless demeanor towards me. It was even more intensive than previously. Watching him be easy going with others while being very harsh with me was unsettling. This let me know he knew how to be loving, supportive and considerate, yet he kept on withholding those feelings from me by repetitively choosing to revert to his adverse personality. It became crystal clear to me once more that Jerome had no intention of holding me in the loving high esteem he did others. Accepting this fact was disheartening. Together with facing the reality that after many months of our relationship improving to suddenly deteriorating made my anxiety levels be at an unprecedented high. Communication between us was at an all-time low. Another déjà vu moment filled with embarrassment and ashamed that I had believe this time our relationship would work out. I could not dare tell anyone, except my secretary, what was happening in the house because they would say, I should have never gone back to Jerome, as well as think I messed up again and was stupid because I had not learned he was not going to change. What was I going to do now? Depressed and feeling at the end of my road down, during the evenings and weekends I regressed to my old habits of drinking and taking large doses of pills. Then during the day, I went to work always glad to see my secretary; talked to my daughters, Momma Nunn and a few other loved ones acting as if everything was great. In the evening it was back to the bleak lonesome long nights and weekends of being depressed. Listening relentless to *Take Me to the King*, sung by Tamela Mann and taking enough sleeping pills, together with any of my prescribed medicine and even pills that were prescribed to

Jerome, I would pray that I would die in my sleep. The next morning, I would wake up and say, why Lord, why?

In the spring of 2014, I had taken pills throughout the night. In the morning, as usual I was woozy and upset about waking up. I took a hand full of more pills, put on my walking clothes and told Jerome I was going out to walk which was a usual routine for me. All the time knowing it was never my intention to go walking, I went directly into our de-attached garage. I opened and closed the garage door, got into my car, and started it. Reclining my car seat back, I then waited for carbon monoxide with the combination of pills to finally end my life. I was beginning to feel relaxed, dizzy, and barely able to keep my eyes open, I closed them. The next thing I realized was Jerome opening the door to the car. He said, *get your ass out the car*. Dazed I did not response but only wondered how he knew I was in the garage. The garage was far enough away from the house that he should not have heard the car running. Why had he found me? He grabbed my arm while pulling me out the car and dragging me into the house. Once in the house, he helped me to the bedroom where I laid down. Neither one of us had said anything since he told me to get out of the car. Laying in the bed I thought non-stop why did Jerome come to the garage. Then I knew it was only God that sent Jerome to the garage. Crying I buried my head into the pillow and said to God, I got it, I was not going to die until it was my time, and until that time I had to endure. Later that night accepting God was not ready for me to die, I picked up my Bible and searching for scriptures to help me, I looked at Jonah crying out to die in Chapter 4. *Therefore now, O Lord, just* take my life from me, for it is better for me to die than to live." Then the Lord said, "Do you have a good reason to be angry?" Jonah 4:3-4 (AMP). This became the words I began to focus on to give me strength and encouragement, because I had more good reasons not to be wanting to die than to die. Too put the icing on the cake, I read, *To every thing there is a season, and a time to every purpose under the heaven: A time to be born, and a time to die…*, Ecclesiastes 3:1-2 (KJV). I thought about how no matter how hard I tried to kill myself death would not happened until God said so. Knowing I might as well relinquish everything to God, I said to my Lord and Savior, I put my life is in your hands. By yielding to the Holy Spirit, I increased my praying, studying, and mediating on the word of God. The song *I Almost Let Go*, by Kurt Carr resounded in my heart. Working towards focusing every inch of my energy on learning to live with the personal letdowns in my stormy life that had left many permanent emotional scars, the desire to die subsided. However, thoughts of dying did not stop overnight, in fact it remained an inward battle. Especially right after Jerome found me in the garage, each day it was a fight to sustain my mental stability and not to try to kill myself. However, I was adamant not to act on my thoughts to kill myself, so I inundate myself daily with praying, meditating, and studying the word of God. I would also hum throughout the day the verse, *as God gives me grace I'll run this race until I see my Savior face to face*, from the song *Goin' Up Yonder* by Walter Hawkins.

Months later when thoughts of killing myself still were coming to my mind, there was a flicker of light from Jesus Christ of endurance and the Holy Spirit declaring to me, *No temptation [regardless of its source] has overtaken or enticed you that is not common to human experience [nor is any temptation unusual or beyond human resistance]; but God is faithful [to His word—He is compassionate and trustworthy], and He will not let you be tempted beyond your ability [to resist], but along with the temptation He [has in the past and is now and] will [always] provide the way out as well, so that you will be able to endure it [without yielding, and will overcome temptation with joy]*, 1 Corinthians 10:13 (AMP). Thankfully even to this day that flicker of light is always with me reminding me of the grace and mercy of God that kept me alive, and now strengthens me to make it through each day. Even today at times it is second by second to make it through a day. But glory be to God like the title of song by Bishop Paul Morton, *I'm Still Standing*, nowadays when thoughts of suicide attack my mind, I call upon God to spiritually renew my mind. All the time holding dear to my heart, *order my steps in thy word: and let not any iniquity have dominion over me. Deliver me from the oppression of man: so will I keep thy precepts. Make thy face to shine upon thy servant; and teach me thy statutes,* Psalm 119:133-135 (KJV) and humming the verse, *order my steps in Your Word, Dear Lord, lead me, guide me every day, send Your anointing, Father, I pray order my steps in Your Word*, from the song, *Order My Steps*, written by Glenn Burleigh.

Weeks later after trying to kill myself in the garage, Gregory, and Barbara, were visiting from Alabama. Gregory had called to see if I was available to see them before he returned to Alabama. I said, of course. Over the years as Tim and my relationship grew, Gregory and my relationship had also grown exceptionally close. This was in spite of when Gregory who had always been in contact with Linda Faye and she discovered Gregory was talking and visiting me she gave Gregory an ultimatum of being a part of her or my life. I was grateful Gregory never succumbed to Linda Faye's demand and remained a part of my life. This together with his unconditional love and support forged a close knitted bond between us. Throughout the years I shared my sunny and stormy days with Gregory. In turn he was steadfast in praying for me and my family members. Many times, it was his intercessory prayers for me that kept me when I was too weak to pray for myself.

When they arrived at the house that day, we hugged and greeted each other as usual. Sitting down in the living room, we started talking, initially it was my normal fake demeanor. Then, unexpectedly, my mask fell off revealing years of unspoken pain. Without any forewarning suddenly, I began sharing with Gregory and Barbara what only one other person, my secretary, knew. With my head looking down at the floor, tears forming in my eyes I emotionally began disclosing to them one of my darkest secrets. Words began to flow from my mouth revealing to them for years I not only had lived in an emotionally torment life but had tried to kill myself many times. Glancing up from the floor I looked at my cousins and saw the startled and astonish expressions on their faces. Turning back to looking down at the floor, I told them in detail about what took place the last time I tried to kill myself. Looking up at them I testified how the intervention from Jesus Christ and the Holy Spirit let me know it was not time for me to die and was now enabling me to resist acting on thoughts to commit suicide. I went on to tell my cousins, how each day with much prayer, meditation and studying the word of God, I was becoming stronger in my desire to live. Both of my cousins were staring at me with looks of shock and concern. I knew for Gregory this was very disheartening because many years ago, his brother, Reginald had committed suicide. They both began talking to me. One moving statement from Barbara was how suicide was a selfish act that leaves loved ones devastated. As they were encouraging and praying for me, Jerome walked in the room. Gregory and Barbara said, hello. Jerome barely spoke, then he walked into the other room. We resumed talking, during which time Jerome had walked in and out the room several times. Jerome walked again into the room, but this time he stood there staring at us. I could tell something was wrong with him. Attempting to defuse whatever he was feeling, I began to change the subject to a general discussion for all of us. That did not work. Abruptly Jerome very viciously said to Gregory and Barbara, they were *disrespecting him in his house*. Becoming confrontational with Gregory and Barbara, Jerome began to accuse them of excluding him from their discussion with me. Cold-bloodedly he then told my cousins they had to leave his house. Completely bewildered I tried to explain what we were discussing. That made Jerome even more agitated and his conduct became more offensive and belligerent towards my cousins and me. Gregory tried to explain to Jerome they were not trying to exclude him from the conversation or disrespect his home. Jerome was extremely irate and was not hearing anything we said. He furiously insisted they leave his house. Trying to resolve the situation, I again tried to get Jerome to calm down, explaining to him what we were discussing had nothing to do with him. Gregory told me it was okay that they were leaving. As they prepared to leave the house, even with Jerome hovering over them, Barbara unrelenting encouraged me. As we hugged at the door, I said, I loved them very much and would talk to them later. Once they were gone, Jerome fussed at me for hours about how my cousins and I were wrong and disrespectful to him. Besides his accusation, he said Gregory and Barbara were forbidden from being in his house. Yet again more of my loved ones that could not visit me. After Jerome left for work, I called Gregory to apologize for the behavior of Jerome. Gregory encouraged me to stay strong in the Lord, keep depending on God, and remember I had many people that loved me. He told me in the future when Barbara and he visited Cleveland we would meet at his mother's home.

More Drama Blended Family Commotion. In September 2014, Sheriese started her senior high school year. During the next few months we began to excitingly prepare for her final year of high school. We discussed plans for her graduation, prom, graduation pictures, and visits to colleges. She had a busy schedule with class assignments, preparing for college entrance tests and cheering on the school squad and competition team. During the earlier part of 2014 when we were out-of-town with the competition cheering team, Sheriese and I had visited several colleges. In the fall of 2014, we visited several more in and out of state colleges. Thanksgiving Day was very uneventful, although I cooked a small dinner, no one came to the house to eat. A few days later there was a major disturbing incident with Sheriese. She had asked if her boyfriend could visit. I said, yes. The curfew for him to leave was midnight. A few minutes after midnight I went downstairs to tell him it was time to leave. Going towards the room simultaneously I said, *it is time to go home*. and looked into the room and was appalled to see Sheriese and her boyfriend on the floor having sex. I hollered, *no y'all ain't doing this in this house*. In a very disappointing voice I said, *how could y'all*. All the time thinking I never would have thought Sheriese would have sex with me in this house. This was particularly true since we had discussed several times how important it was for her to behave when her boyfriend was visiting, especially, when Jerome was not at home. She and her boyfriend were fully aware of how extremely strict Jerome was when it came to her having company, because when Jerome was home, he would sit downstairs in the kitchen or living room for the entire time her boyfriend visited. But me, I was silly enough to have confidence in Sheriese and trusted that she would never have sex in the house. This was especially true since Sheriese knew I was upstairs and could come downstairs at any time. More disturbing is they knew her boyfriend had to leave by midnight. What was she thinking? It was after midnight. Did they just not care that I had told him that he had to leave soon? Reflecting on my high school years, I had not been a saint. However, never did I contemplate having sex when Momma or Linda Faye was home. Even if I would have had the nerves to try, I would never be in the act that close to curfew. Sheriese and the boy immediately told me they were really sorry. That it would never happened again. Sheriese pleaded with me not to tell Jerome. Even though extremely upset, I decided to firmly and thoroughly lecture her and the boyfriend about their behavior and question them about why they thought it was okay for them to have sex in the house. I also admonished them about how their actions were very offensive and disrespectful. Sheriese and the boy pledged not to ever again have sex in the house. Believing they would kept their promise, I agreed not to tell Jerome or the boy's parents about them having sex. They sighed a sound of relief as each of them thanked me for not informing Jerome or his parents.

Over the next several days, Sheriese's demeanor towards me was appreciative because she was profoundly grateful I had not told Jerome about them having sex. I was glad to see her happy and being more respectful than usual. I only wished she would have thought of respecting her father, me, and more importantly, herself by not having sex in the house. The next Friday Sheriese asked if her boyfriend could come over. Admittedly I was a little astounded she asked so soon. Nevertheless, I agreed to let him visit because I was overtly confident and trusted Sheriese to not repeat the same behavior. I said to myself there was no why they would be foolish enough to have sex again in the house with me home. This was especially true taking into consideration, her boyfriend and her knew how upset I was last week, the promises her boyfriend and she had made, and that I would not hesitate to inform Jerome and his parents if they broke their promise.

Besides agreeing to let him visit, there were certain guideline, including she would wear long pants not shorts, the lights would remain on, and there would definitely be no sex. When he arrived, I reiterated the guidelines with emphasis on no sex. He agreed. Over the course of the evening, I would go downstairs to check on them. They were watching TV, talking and on their cell phones. When it was nearing midnight, I went back downstairs to let him know it was time to leave. I almost dropped to the floor, but instead I shouted, *no, it could not be.* Unbelievable it was incomprehensible to see them again engaged in having sex. I lost it. Hollering again at them, *no you did not.* Sheriese jumped up, pulling up her pants and came running to me frantically trying to apologize and talk to me. I did not want to hear a word either one of them had to say. I went directly to the house phone calling Jerome. In despair I told him what had just happened and occurred a week ago. He asked to speak to Sheriese. While he talked to Sheriese, I called the parents of the boy letting them know what had happened tonight and the previous week. After speaking with his parents, they understood me being upset and disappointed. When I gave him the phone to speak to his parents, I could hear them scolding him. Once he handed me the phone, he apologized. I finished talking to his mother who apologized for his behavior before we ended the call. When Sheriese finished talking to Jerome, she handed me the phone. He told me we would talk when he came home. When he arrived home, Sheriese was sleep. He woke me up to discuss what happened. To my disappointment, it was in his normal interrogation attitude. I could see from his questioning, he was blaming me for what took place. The next morning, I did not hear him say nothing to Sheriese about the what happened the last night, nor was there any parental discipline by Jerome for her actions. That day and every day thereafter life went on for Sheriese as if she had done nothing wrong. She never missed a beat, because that evening she left out the house, got in her car and went out with her friends. Once more Jerome blatantly declined to stand up for what was right. Instead he blamed me for Sheriese having sex in the house by persistently scolding and reprimanding me. He did his usual steady chastising me like I was the child. With there being no repercussions for Sheriese's actions but she heard and seen the way Jerome blamed me for what she did, there was no doubt in my mind that she felt there was no reason to adhere to anything I said. This resulted in another rift and division in the house with Sheriese and I not communicating with each other for several weeks. Unbeknown to me this incident would precipitate a trickle-down affect resulting in another huge storm in my life that would bring my world to another destructive time in my life.

Decision to Keep My Sanity. Although Christmas was uneventful at the Barrow house, it was truly special at the home of Ivy and Aaron. Family members from both sides of the families came to celebrate the birth of Christ. It was a lovely day with great food and a good bonding time with our families. Even being seven months pregnant, Ivy cooked a scrumptious dinner and made it a beautiful day. I could tell my oldest baby girl was exhausted. My little grandson was not due for another six to eight weeks. However, Ivy had been six centimeters dilated for the past two weeks with no sign of the newest addition to our family coming anytime soon. We had eaten dinner and played fun games, followed by our yearly funny re-gift exchange. Taking a little break Ivy and I were sitting on the steps watching Aiden and Ethan play with their toys while everyone else was talking. Ivy started blowing hard. Several times I asked her if she was okay. She kept saying, yes. Aaron and others seeing her in a little distress asked Ivy if she was okay. Ivy told all of us she was okay. A few seconds later Ivy tried to hold in a scream. I said, Aaron it is time to go. Ivy continuously said she was okay. Aaron said, *babe it is time to go to the hospital.* Ivy, Aaron, Sylvia, and Dr. Ivan headed to the hospital. Eddie, Aunt Rachel, and I stayed at the house with Aiden and Ethan. Later Jan and Arthur came over to bring gifts for the boys. Once Aiden and Ethan were settled in bed, Eddie said she would stay the night. I then went home to await the birth of the new addition to our families. About twelve hours later, on December 26th, our bundle of joy arrived. The next day I went to visit Ivy and my third grandbaby, Ivan Kristopher Banks. Even though he was eight weeks early, he weighed seven pounds. He was healthy and stunningly handsome. I was overjoyed for the Banks family. It was hard to believe that my first-born baby girl was now a wife and mother of three handsome sons. Special days like this was when I wished Momma and Herman would have lived to see and enjoy.

New Year's Eve, Jerome had to work. I planned to stay at home. Around 8:00 p.m., I called Jerome to ask if on his break he could bring me some food from Whitmore Bar-B-Que restaurant. I wanted all my favorites a polish boy, shoulder (pull pork), and rib sandwiches, and a chicken wings dinner. Jerome asked if I was really going to eat all that food. I said, yes, it was comfort food for me to help me prepare to bring in the New Year alone. When I went downstairs to get the food from Jerome, Sheriese and her friends were preparing to leave out to celebrate. Although Sheriese and I rarely had talked after the incident with her and her boyfriend, that night I said hello to everyone, and told them they looked nice and to be safe. Sheriese and her friends replied, thanks. Minutes before midnight I begin to hear gunshots and fireworks. Jerome, Kim, Mother Nunn, Ivy, Sylvia, and a few others called to say Happy New Year. Sitting in bed I thought this is 2015. For some reason my mind began to reminisce that 35 years ago was the beginning of 1980, the year Herman died. Then five years later in 1985, I had the partial hysterectomy surgery. A few months later Momma died, followed by my incarceration. I prayed that this year would be much better than the previous years. Deep down inside I knew life would remain the same unless I changed my surroundings. Over and over I had tried to make my relationship with Jerome work, but regardless how hard I tried, our relationship and even our marriage ended in turmoil. Now once again our relationship still was not on one accord. How could I live in a home with no communication, understanding and respect? It was at that point I decided to maintain my sanity and survive. I had to finally leave Jerome for good, no ifs, ands, or buts about it. I was done.

Unexpected Blessing. Mrs. Essie was married to Jerome's cousin, Willie Harrison. Over the years, I would see Mr. Willie and Mrs. Essie at family events where we would greet each other followed by small talk. They attended our wedding and reception. Jerome and I attended their 50th Wedding Anniversary Celebration. In July 2014, Jerome, Sheriese, and I went to the funeral service of Aunt Mill who has passed at the blessed age of ninety-two. During the repast Mr. Willie asked if I could answer a few questions he and his wife had about wills and probate matters. I told him of course. I let him know if I could not help them, Jerome's daughter, Jazmyn, who was at the funeral, or my daughter, Ivy, could help them because they both were attorneys.

In September 2014, Mrs. Essie called me to ask for help with administering her brother-in-law's estate. For several months I worked with Mrs. Essie to prepare the paperwork for her to administer the estate. Since her brother-in-law had many various assets it would be time-consuming to prepare the documents for filings with the probate court. It was my routine to stop by her house either on my way to or from work to discuss the case or obtain more information and paperwork or her signature on documents. It was always a pleasure to visit Mrs. Essie and Mr. Willie because they were a beautiful couple that always were very hospitable. By January 2015, the probate case was seventy-five percent administered with only a few more reports that would need to be filed. A few weeks later, I called Mrs. Essie to inform her there were a few documents that she needed to sign. I asked her if it was okay to stop by her house on my way home. She said of course. After talking and obtaining the information from Mrs. Essie, I prepared to walk out the door when she handed me a card. I told her thank you, but that I was not expecting her to give me anything. She said for all my diligent work, she wanted to thank me. I thanked her and said goodnight. When I arrived home and opened the envelope, I almost fainted. I could not believe how she had blessed me financially. Immediately, I called her to say this was too much. Mrs. Essie insisted that was what she wanted to give me to show her appreciation. She went on to say how she was concerned about me over the past few weeks. It was her hope the gift would uplift my spirit. At that point I knew God had directed her to bless me that night. I repeatedly let her know how much I appreciated her generosity. I helped Mrs. Essie for several more months until the court entered an order closing the probate case.

I Am Done. The first week of January, I informed Ivy, Sylvia, and a few close friends that I planned to leave Jerome the next time he went out of town. Sheriese had a cheering competition in Columbus the second weekend of February. With her and I not speaking, either Jerome or Jazmyn would go with her to the competition. Accordingly, I anticipated moving that weekend. Ivy and Sylvia believed I would leave only to go back again as previously. At that point I decided to share with them some of my private battles with depression and several attempts to take my life. I assured them for my sanity this time I really needed to leave and never return. They were stunned by my secrets stating they loved and needed their mother. I told them I appreciated their support. A few days later I disclosed to Nicole my suicidal attempts. Even though Nicole was disappointed that I felt the need to attempt suicide, she spoke words of encouragement and love to me. At that point I had divulged to six of my loved ones my secret attempts to end my life. Each of their acts of love and words of support and encouragement became instilled within my soul. Family support coupled with constantly renewing my trust and faith in Jesus Christ became a vital part of being staying and being alive to this day. Mentally once I began to let my loved ones know that I was contemplating suicide, it helped prevent me from the actual acts to kill myself. This was primarily due to my often hearing that once you let someone know you are attempting suicide, the likelihood that you go through with it decreases. Thankfully even when thoughts to end my life came, and still come today, the actual acts to kill myself have ceased. With much prayer and trusting in my Savior Jesus Christ, I made it through each second of the day.

    I decided to move with Sylvia because it was more practical than leasing an apartment. Mid-January, I started to slowly move my personal items that could not be detected from the house to Sylvia home. Ivy was still on maternity leave from her full-time job until March 2015. It was anticipated that when Ivy returned to work hopefully Eddie would babysit Ivan. Besides working her full-time job, Ivy taught a paralegal class part-time during the evenings at Bryant Stratton. The beginning of January, Bryant Stratton asked Ivy to teach a class on Tuesday and Thursday mornings. Ivy asked me if I could babysit Ivan for ninety minutes while she taught the class, I agreed. Given that it was not busy at the firm, I would take my break during the time Ivy needed me. If there was something necessary while I was away from the office, I could log in and work from her home.

For the first time in a long time, I was mentally happy and excited about my future. Besides Ivy and Sylvia, I shared my intentions to move with my secretary, Nicole, and Trina. By the end of January, I had purchased a new bedroom set which was delivered on February 6th. Elated with happiness I took pictures of the beautiful bedroom set that I texted to Ivy, Sylvia, Nicole, Trina and my secretary with a message, *my new beginnings*. I changed my mailing address in time to get the confirmation notification that would be sent to Jerome's house in order for him not to know where I had moved. A few days later I filed with the Cuyahoga County Probate Court a motion for change of name because I was changing my last name back to my maiden name, Kithcart. I had everything in place, the only uncertainty about the move was if Jerome would go with Sheriese to the competition. The night before the competition Jerome had made no indication he would be going. This made me anxious that I would have to wait until another time to move. Around 2:00 a.m. Jerome came into the bedroom and started packing a small bag. Still woke, I asked him what he was doing. He said, getting ready to go to Columbus for the competition. This made me happy, though thinking to myself as usual Jerome had not even given me the respect to let me know in advance he planned to go. Still refusing my request to communicate with me. Immediately after they left, I started packing the remainder of my things. No movers were needed this time because I had decided not to take any furniture only my personal belongings. By Sunday afternoon I had moved all my things to Sylvia's house.

Chapter Twenty-Two — Reliving a Previous Storms

Once I locked the door to Jerome house and placed the keys in the mail shoot, the heaviness of my heart and mind subsided. It was as if God had given me a fresh new anointing. That weekend I had repeatedly listened to Juanita Bynum song, *Like the Dew in the Morning*. The song was a part of the Holy Spirit uplifting me to a state of glorification and devotion to my Lord and Savior, for I was tremendously thankful for Jesus Christ showing me that He alone has always overseen my destiny. Even when I tried to change how my life story ended with suicide, God said, no you are not in control of your destination.

With a new outlook for my future, I laid comfortable in my new bedroom watching television when my phone rang. Because it was an unidentified caller, I knew Jerome had returned home. I had made a promise when I moved not to answer his phone calls. Following his constantly calling me, I blocked his phone number. Even with blocking his number, Jerome was able to leave voice messages. He then called from different phone numbers. When I realized it was him, I refused to answer. He steadily left numerous messages. Even after listening to a few of the messages, I had no intention on calling him. He left the usual messages of why can't I talk to him? He knew I was going to leave. Was I with another man? Where was I? It was wrong for me to leave that way. I was committed to not let him get to me mentally with these messages. Like always I knew he only left the messages to make me feel bad about leaving. Then the most unexpected message was left. Jerome said, *if I did not answer the phone he was going to call my job and let them know how I killed my first husband, tried to kill my second husband, and probably tried to kill him but he was too smart.* This totally blew my mind away. I felt my heart drop. I was unable to breathe. My hands were shaking. My world stood still. It seemed like I had entered a time machine because my mind had travelled in time and I was sitting in the back seat of the police car. Everything that lead up to the death of Herman and thereafter was swirling all around me. Trying to figure out if what I heard Jerome say was a dream or reality, I closed and opened my eyes several times. Realizing this was reality, I became numb, distraught, and panic-stricken. Why would Jerome say that? Why would he want to do something that devious? Was he that hateful and vindictive to bring up what he knew daily haunted me? He left several additional messages, saying he was trying to give me a chance to call him back before he called my job. Profound panic came when Jerome left a message on my office phone stating, this is the message I am going to leave on the main switchboard, *if you don't know already, I am going to bring it back to your attention. DeBorah killed her husband.* How could he do this? Why was this happening? Why after all these years was he threatening me in this horrible manner? Finally, I texted him requesting that he please leave me alone. That only made him call more and leave additional messages throughout the night into the morning.

In total panic, with my head throbbing, heart aching, stomach in a knot, and my body tensed all over, I was unable to sleep. As the sun arose, I got up and prepared to go to work. My mind in a state of bewilderment, I tried to put on my fake demeanor as I went to wake up Sylvia. This was supposed to be the first day of my new beginning of waking up to prepare for work with my baby girl, yet it had turned into a terribly petrified nightmare. While getting dressed, Jerome kept calling. I thought it was best to find out exactly what he said to my job before arriving at the office. However, not wanting Sylvia to hear me talking to Jerome, I decided to wait until I was in my car. Once in the car, I called Jerome. I asked him to please leave me alone, and why and how could he call my job telling them what happened to Herman. He heartlessly said, *I should have called him back*. He then nonchalantly said, *any way he only wanted to know why I left that way*. Sensing from the tone in his voice, I knew he only was going to intimidate and harass me, I hung up the phone. He repeatedly called, but I would not answer. I thought about Kennedy how he helped us with the incident with Nicole. Before I reached the office, I called Kennedy. When he answered, I briefly told him what occurred over the past few months with Jerome and me. I let Kennedy know about my past and the death of Herman and how Jerome threated to inform my job. I asked him to please talk to Jerome and tell him to stop calling me. Kennedy was very thoughtful and considerate. He agreed to talk to Jerome. He even told me not to worry about my job as there was no way they would fire me after twenty years of service. I told him thanks for the encouragement and willingness to speak with Jerome.

Not knowing if Jerome had left the message on the firm's main phone line, I arrived at the office exhausted with anxiety and frightened beyond measure. Although a few of the people I was close with at the firm were aware about the death of Herman, I knew many were unaware. Considering I had obtained the job without being having to fill out an application or have a background check, I did not want those unaware to be informed about how I shot Herman via a phone message. I went into my office and called my secretary to ask her to come into my office. She came in smiling looking forward to me sharing the wonderful news of my fresh beginning at Sylvia house. Instead in tears I let her know what occurred once Jerome returned home. She could not believe Jerome would stoop this low and encouraged me to be strong. Then I talked to another co-worker who I knew also had a felony. She was supportive, assuring me the firm would understand like they had with her. I really appreciated her encouragement. The unknown was driving me crazy. Thinking back on all those years ago when the mother of my friend said, *did I know one of our classmates killed her husband*. I knew I had to talk to someone at the firm before Jerome told them. Initially I went to the office of the DHR, but she was not in. The chief executive officer (CEO) whose office was next door to hers, was in his office. Knocking on the door I asked to talk to him. He said, of course. Already holding back tears, I sat down and began to tell him of my past, including: the abuse by Herman; filing for a divorce; the day of the shooting and death of Herman; my trial and being found guilty; the appeal; the five years before my incarceration; teaching while incarcerated; my early release; restarting my life; my current martial problems with Jerome; leaving Jerome over the weekend; Jerome's threats to inform the firm about the death of Herman; and because I knew the CEO hadn't been with the firm when I was hired, I even explained how I hadn't completed an application and had never been asked about my past. The CEO listened with a look of horror and disbelief in his blue eyes. Even to this day the way he looked at me, like I was the worst person he had ever seen, is forever embedded in my mind. He stated he would discuss the matter with the DHR. Walking towards the door to leave, he did ask if I had a safe place to stay. I told him, yes, I was staying with my daughter. Returning to my office feeling as if I had walked into the twilight zone, I started crying and praying. My mind took me back to New Year's Eve when the thoughts of 1980 and 1985 suddenly intensely came back to my memory. I prayed to God, please not again. I was not going to let anyone else know how worried and nervous I was except my secretary. She was very thoughtful and consoling. Sadly, I never found out for sure if Jerome left a message on the main phone line.

Jerome was continually calling. I answered and told him that *he might have cost me my job*. He simply replied, *I should have answered the phone*. He then asked me *if I planned to come back home before he changed the locks and alarm*. Angrily I told him, *no, he should do whatever was needed*, then I hung up the phone. I contemplated calling his friend Calvin, who was in our wedding and now the chief of police. At that moment I did not, but later that day I did call him. He did not answer the phone. I left a message, but he never returned my call. Before leaving the office, I e-mailed the CEO to see if he had heard from the DHR. He informed me she would be in the office on Wednesday and we would talk at that time. On my way home, Kennedy called to let me know Jerome had arrived at the station. He asked me if I still needed him to speak to Jerome. I told him, no, as it might not matter now, because I was uncertain what was going to happen with my job. Once more, he like the few others I had talked to, said the firm was not going to fire me after my dedication for twenty years. He then shared how Jerome had always been spiteful and revengeful. I thanked Kennedy for his support and encouragement.

On Wednesday, February 11, 2015, the CEO called me into his office. When I walked into his office both the CEO and DHR were there. The CEO told me to have a seat. After I sat down the CEO said, the firm was firing me effective today. No, my mind was saying, not again. I tried to say something, but it was as if I was in a trance. I heard what was being said, but what was happening was not registering in my mind. It was like they were talking in slow motion, they were saying something about a severance package of one-month salary and benefits was being offered. They said the details were in the termination letter that was handed to me. In shock, I nervously mumbling something to them as I flipped through the pages briefly scanning over them. I was about to sign the document, we thankfully my senses sent a signal to my brain, and I asked them if it was okay to review the document. Both simultaneously said, *yes*. The DHR stated I should review the letter and suggested I get legal advice before signing. The procedure for fired employees was to be escorted out of the building, but I asked the CEO and DHR if they would not escort me out of the building. They agreed.

Never Saw This Coming. Crying, trembling and in a daze, I left the office of the CEO. I went directly to the department head of the bankruptcy section to ask him if he knew about my termination. He did not. In a quick summary I told him what happened in my life with Herman. He appeared earnestly concerned as he expressed words of regret. He then gave me a hug. Leaving his office, I went to my office and begin to pack a few things. When my secretary came into the office, I said they fired me. She was in disbelief and attempted to console me. We then began to pack my things into boxes. Shortly thereafter the CEO came to my office. I foolishly thought it was to check on me. Wrong. It was to tell me to leave the office immediately. He said my personal items would be packed and sent to me later. Saying okay, I put on my coat and got my bags. I headed towards the elevator. The CEO turned in the opposite direction. At the elevator two of the attorneys I worked directly with was waiting for the elevator. Once on the elevator I briefly told them what occurred. The one looked appalled while the other looked concerned. Like the day I was found guilty by a jury of peers for the death of Herman, I was once again found guilty and considered a terrible person in the minds of people I had dedicated twenty years of my life, who now had discarded me without a second thought.

Walking in dismay to my car I felt like a worthlessly awful person. Knowing that after 20 years of stellar service to the firm and over 25 years of dedicated service to the BK attorney, who was now being considered for the position of managing partner of the firm, meant nothing at the end. They believed as the jury did that I was guilty of intentionally killing Herman. I was just another felon. How painful to accept the fact that regardless of striving to prove I never intentionally meant to kill Herman, I would always be considered a murder. Ivy had said for years, Momma you work so hard and sacrifice your family and life for that firm, but they do not genuinely appreciate you. When you die, all they will do is send us a flower. That day I became dead to the firm. Sadly, with this death my family would not even receive a flower.

After Ivy left, I sat mentally trying to absorb what had happened in the past two hours. In a matter of seconds my life once again was forever altered just like thirty-five years ago when I was found guilty, but this time not by a jury of my peers, but people I cared for and respected. No longer was I a devoted, superb, reliable employee, but a felon. None of my good services over all those years made a difference. I was let go without being allowed to give further details of the events that resulted in my incarceration. Simply told I was fired, now leave our office. How could people that had known me for an exceptionally long time and that I believed cared about me not realize that I was a victim forced to become an offender to defend myself from being further abused. Why couldn't they see my crime was different from offenders that victimize the innocent for self-gratification? Thinking about this brought back how several years ago the BK Lawyer told me about one of the secretaries at the other law firm we had worked for was caught stealing thousands of dollars from the firm by using the expense report of the attorney she worked for. This was an intentional criminal act where she made that firm a victim. She was fired, but no criminal charges were filed. In my situation, I had not committed a crime against my employer. Yet my employer did not take into consideration my crime was committed in self-preservation in hopes of preventing injury to my baby and myself. Comparing my crime of self-preservation with the lady from the other firm of a premeditated crime of stealing from the firm, this disparity in my personal opinion confirmed that all is not fair in our world. Thankfully the flicker of light from God was He will forever rescue, strengthen and shield me from those who shun me for committing a crime of self-preservation. How profoundly grateful I am for the Lord being my strength and shield against those that think I am a bad harden criminal. *The Lord is my rock, my fortress, and the One who rescues me; My God, my rock and strength in whom I trust and take refuge; My shield, and the horn of my salvation, my high tower—my stronghold*, Psalm 18:2 (AMP). As I continued to think about losing my job, the Holy Spirit reminded me in the manner God had forgiven me, I too would have to forgive. By forgiving it would allowed me to have a peace of mind with my termination. Instead of regretting those many years with my co-workers and questioning my termination, I would eventually be able to learn how to cherish the fond memories. I work towards turning my gloomiest into joy knowing that God was keeping me not man. The flicker of light was to understand that God kept my heart and mind. *And the peace of God, which passeth all understanding, shall keep your hearts and minds through Christ*

Jesus, Philippians 4:7 (KJV).

Promised Not to Attempt Suicide. The day I was terminated was on the day I had to babysit Ivan while Ivy worked her part-time job. I arrived at Ivy's house so early that she was not ready for work. She looked at me asking, what was wrong. As courageously as I could, I told Ivy what had occurred. She was livid saying, what did you do? With all the strength I could conjure up, I assured her everything would be alright. In the same manner as in the past regardless of what was occurring in my life, I had to reassure my daughters everything would be okay. I could not let them see their mother succumb to how helpless I truly felt. Ivy called Jerome. To this day, I do not know what they said to each other. After Ivy went to work, I merely held onto Ivan while praying and crying out to God for strength. It resembled how I had held onto Ivy 35 years ago after the death of her father. When Ivy returned to the house, I again assured her I was okay. On my way to Sylvia's house, the pain became unbearable. Repeatedly thoughts of being found guilty once more filled my mind. Thirty-five years later, I am still guilty. Where do I go from here? This was supposed to be my new beginning? How could the firm think so little of me? If they, after 20 years, thought I was a horrible guilty person, what would people think that did not even know me? I wanted to just scream out to the entire world, *I am guilty and a bad person*. Then suddenly I began to scream out to God, *why did you let me survive all the suicidal attempts to only face this day*. I then thought how months ago, I made a covenant not to commit suicide. Not only did I make this covenant with God, I promised my daughters and loved ones to not kill myself. How could I honor that promise after again hitting rock bottom in my life? Though sad, in a daze and guilt-ridden, I struggled to get a grip on my life to subdue those thoughts of suicide. I was praying. Crying out to God. Trying desperately to stay sane. If not, I knew it would be impossible to make it through the night. When Sylvia came home I told her what happened. Although upset, she had faith in God that we would survive.

That evening I tried to muster up enough strength to contemplate my future. I needed to figure out how to take care of my well-being, needed to seek legal counsel about the severance letter from the firm and if I was wrongfully fired, and had to contact the firm about withdrawal of my 401k funds and COBRA benefits. The next day I contacted several employment lawyers. Each one I initially spoke to was unable to assist me stating Ohio was an at-will employment state. I even thought of seeking media attention, I decided not to pursue it. Not contacting the media overall was a blessing from God. Jerome was still calling. Finally, when I answered a call, he asked me about paying a bill for his credit cards that I was an authorized user on. With disdain I informed him about my being fired from the job which now made it impossible for me to pay those bills. Then I told him since he had caused me to lose my job, he needed to help me with my bills especially my medical insurance payment. He agreed. Disappointedly he only made the payments towards my medical insurance for three months. After that it became too much of a hassle to beg him for the money each month.

Chapter Twenty-Three – In Need of Prayer and a Lot More Help

Jerome, being one of the loves of my life, was fully aware of the emotional sensitivity and agony the death of Herman had on my life. Still he chose to betray me with threats to inform my employers about the death of Herman. These threats threw my entire world into an uncontrollable downward spiral. He emotionally blindsided me, knocking me into a state of mental disarray. Certainly, Jerome knew those hateful, vengeful, unwarranted, and coldblooded voice messages he left on my cell phone would mar me to the depth of my soul. There was no doubt he fully was aware the messages left on the office phone could adversely affect my employment. His actions resulted in my termination that in-turn caused significant despair and grief both emotionally and financially to my daughters, grandsons, and me. What Jerome did was meant for evil. Glory be to Jesus Christ the flickers of light from God was His strength. Through the strength of God, the evil acts of Jerome were turned into blessings. *Though the fig tree does not blossom And there is no fruit on the vines, Though the yield of the olive fails And the fields produce no food, Though the flock is cut off from the fold And there are no cattle in the stalls, Yet I will [choose to] rejoice in the Lord; I will [choose to] shout in exultation in the [victorious] God of my salvation! The Lord God is my strength [my source of courage, my invincible army]; He has made my feet [steady and sure] like hinds' feet and makes me walk [forward with spiritual confidence] on my high places [of challenge and responsibility]*, Habakkuk 3:17-19 (AMP). From the moment the acts of Jerome traumatically altered my life, God already had everything under control. *Forever will I honor and worship God for He alone is my all and all. Thou hast turned for me my mourning into dancing: thou hast put off my sackcloth and girded me with gladness; To the end that my glory may sing praise to thee, and not be silent. O Lord my God, I will give thanks unto thee for ever*, Psalm 30:10-12 (KJV).

Diagnosed with PTSD. Days after losing my job, silently I became more depressed with continuous suicidal thoughts. The flicker of light from Jesus Christ was do not be dismayed for God will strengthen me. *Fear thou not; for I am with thee: be not dismayed; for I am thy God: I will strengthen thee; yea, I will help thee; yea, I will uphold thee with the right hand of my righteousness*, Isaiah 41:10 (KJV). Mentally in an extremely dark state of mind, the Holy Spirit instilled in me not only would God strengthen and help me through this storm He would bring me forth as pure gold. *"But He knows the way that I take [and He pays attention to it]. When He has tried me, I will come forth as [refined] gold [pure and luminous]*, Job 23:10 (AMP). As in the past, my inter-soul spiritually believed that God would see me through this storm. The problem was during this storm I could not control my outwardly demeanor of faking it. It became necessary for me to acknowledge for the first time in my life that I needed psychological help. Still not wanting Ivy and Sylvia to know the depth of my mental vulnerability, I acted like it was not really serious when I told them I should get some psychological help and suggested they call our family medical doctor, Dr. Kellner to inform her about my depression and what caused it. Ivy called Dr. Kellner, on February 16th. By the time Ivy finished talking with Dr. Kellner, she was insisting Ivy arrange for me to go directly to the hospital. After Ivy, Sylvia and I talked with Dr. Kellner for an hour, she was satisfied that I would be okay once I agreed to talk to the Suicide Hotline. Once Ivy, Sylvia and I talked to the Suicide Hotline counselor, the representative agreed that due to it being after 3:00 a.m. my mental stability and safety was stable enough to wait until the morning to seek psychological help. We assured the counselor that I would contact the mental health crisis center when it opened at 8:00 a.m. to schedule a same day appointment.

The next morning not in the mental state to drive, I called Syl and asked him to take me to the crisis center. Immediately upon speaking with the intake counselor, thirty-five plus years of suppressed mental anguish was finally being released. I had never realized how much was bottled-up inside of me. The tears started and the reality of my life with Herman, Jerome and the BK Lawyer struck me like 100,000 tons of bricks. Within a few minutes into our conversation, the intake counselor told me I needed to go directly to the hospital for further treatment. Still not wanting anyone to know how weak I was, I regrouped as best as possible before returning to the reception area. I informed Syl that I needed to go to University Hospital. When seen by the emergency room nurses and doctors, once more I had an immediate meltdown. It was as if the moment I started to talk about what had occurred from 1977 to present I could not control my tears or mental state. When questioned about committing suicide, I informed the medical staff of my suicidal attempts, and that even though I was thinking about it now, there was no desire to try to kill myself due to my promise to my loved ones. Based on my mental state and previous attempts to commit suicide, the medical staff thought it was in my best interest to be pink slipped. Being pink slipped meant I would be mandatorily detained for a period of 72 hours for emergency mental hospitalization. The medical staff let me know because the hospital mental health unit had no beds available, and I would be transferred by ambulance to Laurelwood Hospital. Upon admission at Laurelwood, the staff gave me a brief admissions orientation, followed by a psychiatric evaluation by Dr. Boyd. By this time my mental state had further deteriorated. My mind was going like a slideshow of all the dark storms of my life. The intensity concerning my stormy life with Herman, Jerome and the BK lawyer were unbearable. Dr. Boyd diagnosed me with posttraumatic stress disorder (PTSD). He prescribed medication to calm me down and enable me to sleep. I explained to him my need to see my daughters, he made special arrangments for them to visit. When they came, I was overly excited to see them. As usual, I pretended like I was good. There was no way I could let my babies know how I was really suffering inwardly. This was a burden I never wanted them to know that I endured.

  Upon my admission, I was classified a suicidal risk which meant every fifteen minutes a staff member would check on me to confirm I had not attempted suicide. Laurelwood required all patients to attend group sessions. This added another layer to my anguish. When attending the sessions, I only listened to the other patients. The thought of the awful dark storms of my life being told to the other patients would make me withdrawn, anxious and despondent. I believed the patients and employees would be saying you are guilty, guilty, guilty like my former co-workers and a lot of other people were already saying. They would stare at me while murmuring amongst themselves, she killed someone, is a horrible person, is a felon, been to jail, keeps marrying the wrong man, and got fired because of the betrayal by her ex-husband. They would think I was stupid to have kept going back to Herman and Jerome. With those thoughts running through my mind, I sat in the meetings quietly listening to the other patients talk. As they talked, I had thoughts of wishing I could take their place in life with only a few storms instead of the load of storms in my life. Beside the mandatory group sessions, there were strict schedules to adhere to for meals, recreation, making phone calls, and watching television. These schedules together with the fifteen minutes suicidal checks, reemerged memories of the rigid routine I had when incarcerated.

That Friday evening, Dr. Boyd met with me again. He encouraged me to attend the various group sessions and adjusted my medication for anxiety attacks. Over the weekend, another doctor checked in on me. On Monday, I met with Dr. Boyd and explained how although there were still thoughts of suicide, I had no intention of turning it into reality. Confident I would not attempt to commit suicide Dr. Boyd, stated I would be discharged with instructions to immediately arrange for out-patient treatment. He offered to prepare a letter to give to potential new employers detailing my felon was a onetime isolated act of self-preservation. I told him how much I appreciated him offering to help me in that way. A few hours later Syl picked me up from the hospital. As Syl drove he told me how good it was to see me doing better and for me not to worry about the future because God would see me through. I told him thanks and how much his support during this challenging time in my life meant more to me than words could ever say. Syl took me to get my prescriptions before dropping me off at Sylvia's house. Before getting out the car I told him again how much I appreciated all he did for me as well as our girls. When Syl drove off, I reflected on how after the shock of my abruptly leaving him, we had developed a thoughtful and supportive friendship, and on that day, I deeply appreciated that we had such a good relationship. The help and support from Syl that day and throughout that storm will forever be cherished for it was truly unconditional love that enabled him to still care for me and vice versa for me.

Once in the house I called the Psychological and Behavioral Center to make my appointments for the next day with a therapist and a nurse practitioner. On February 17, 2015, I began my one-on-one therapy with Nicholette Leanza. From the moment it began, it was evident I should have been in therapy years ago. During the first visit I told her as much about my life as I could mentally endure. Not receiving therapy from as far back as the 1970s when I initially attempted suicide to everything that occurred in my life with Herman and thereafter, caused my mind to be extensively overloaded causing an atrocious mental breakdown. It hindered my ability to discuss the crisis incurred without losing control of my feelings. I was an absolute nervous wreck. Nicholette was very understanding and patient with me. She could not believe I had survived this long without therapy. Immediately she devised a plan to assist me in how to cope and live with PTSD. This would be accomplished through in-depth therapy sessions two to three times a week. A few days after my appointment with Nicholette, I meet Shane Strnad. He would be responsible for prescribing my medicine. Like Nicholette, he was taken back about what provoked my PTSD. Initially he prescribed medications for anxiety, depression, and to assist me with sleeping. Follow-up appointments with Nicholette and Shane helped me with all the issues consuming my mind, from thinking it was only my fault Herman died; the shame and remorsefulness I had for buying the gun instead of running; believing my former employer had found me guilty exactly like the jury had 35 years ago; convinced that I had embarrassed and let down my family members and friends; coming to terms with the hateful betrayal by Jerome; dealing with that fact Jerome wasn't accepting any responsibility for my termination; questioning why God had kept me alive only to again hit rock bottom; feeling ever since my termination I should walk around with a sign on written on my heading saying, *I'm guilty of killing my husband* and shouting out to the entire world, *I went to jail and I'm a felon.* Not only were those thoughts consuming my mind, I was also facing the fact that I was a minority who held an excellent position in a ninety-nine percent Caucasian firm that had been fired because I was a felon. This made me feel guilty and ashamed of not only letting my loved ones down but my African-American race. I felt this way because throughout forty years of working in corporate America, I personally experienced and seen how African-American people are stereotyped as people with immoral characteristics. I believed taking into consideration why I was fired, it would intensify this form of stereotyping at the firm, which in turn could negatively affect the future hiring of minorities. For this reason, I thought my firing had negatively affected regardless of how nominal the progress of my race. With this guilt and stigma how could I expect another firm would hire me when the firm I gave my all to for twenty years did not want me? Coupling the many thoughts consuming my mind and the guilty feelings that my firing would deter the future of minorities at the firm, once more I was daily coping with thoughts of killing myself. Gratefully there was a flicker of light from Jesus Christ of having faith. Daily I meditated on the entire chapter of Psalm 31. Particularly to, *[i]n you, Lord, I have taken refuge; let me never be put to shame; deliver me in your righteousness. Turn your ear to me, come quickly to my rescue; be my rock of refuge, a strong fortress to save me. Since you are my rock and my fortress, for the sake of your name lead and guide me. Keep me free from the trap that is set for me, for you are my refuge. Into your hands I commit my spirit; deliver me, Lord, my faithful God*, Psalm 31:1-5 (NIV). My faith in God together with the promise to my loved ones prevented me from acting on the thoughts of committing suicide. What was oddly perplexing to me during this time was there were two television shows I watched that portrayed suicides. One was an episode of *Being Mary Jane* when the main character's girlfriend committed suicide. The second was a movie that I am unable to recall the title, which showed a man killing himself by taking pills then duct taping a plastic bag over his head. Thankfully I had not seen those episodes before promising God and my loved ones to not commit suicide, because there is no doubt in my mind if I would have seen the man placing the plastic bag over his head after taking the pills, I definitely would have thought to place one over my head after my many failed attempts to die by only taking a lot of pills. Truly this was another flicker of light of the grace and mercy of my Lord and Savior on my life to not allow me to see those episodes before making my promise not to try to kill myself. Although I still have vivid imagines of both of those television shows, thankfully with the grace and strength of God, I stay focused on not bringing the pain of suicide on those that unconditionally love me.

To deal with my emotional state, Nicholette had several goals for me to reach. She wanted me to focus on accepting that I was a victim of domestic violence in the relationships and marriages to Herman and Jerome. For me to work towards understanding that during my marriage to Herman I suffered from domestic violence at a time in society when it was not recognized and treated in the manner it is today. When Herman was abusing me, society did not consider me a victim nor the mental effects his abuse had on me. I needed to also understand that even through Jerome was not physically abusive to the extent Herman was, he was mentally abusive and a controlling person. In addition, she wanted me to accept the behavior of my former employer and the way they handled my situation was absurd.

Additionally, I had to focus on managing to live with PTSD. The goal of Shane was to work on a prescription regimen that would effectively treat my anxiety attacks, depression and sleeping disorder. The flicker of light was knowing that through Jesus Christ my Lord I could be healed with the proper treatment and medication. *Heal me, O Lord, and I shall be healed; save me, and I shall be saved: for thou art my praise*, Jeremiah 17:14 (KJV).

Together with confronting and stabilizing my mental health, I needed to deal with the severance agreement that had to be accepted by March 3rd. One issue was unemployment benefits which I applied for online. The application asked if I had sought employment during certain periods after my termination. I answered, unable to due to being mentally incapable. A representative from the unemployment office called me for clarification regarding my application. She needed further information about the circumstances of my termination. As briefly as possible, I informed the representative of the events leading up to my termination, beginning the domestic violence from Herman through the date of my termination. The representative then said, *are you telling me you never had to complete an employment application and the company never asked you if you had ever committed a crime.* I replied, *yes.* She then asked, *you had worked for the firm for twenty years, and they just let you go after you told them this information about your past.* I answered, *yes.* Then she asked *what reason was given for my termination.* I let her know her, the CEO said, and my letter of termination states, *due to our conversation on Monday.* She told me, I would receive a call back after she spoke with someone at the company to confirm my account of the termination. Within fifteen minutes, the representative called back. She told me, *you will receive the unemployment benefits and a follow-up letter would be forthcoming.* I thanked her and asked *what to do until I was mentally stable to actively seek employment.* She replied, *when I was mentally able to simply re-apply through the normal procedures.* This was another flicker of light during this stormy period that Jesus Christ was blessing me in my direr time of need. *Lord, all my desire is before thee; and my groaning is not hid from thee*, Psalm 38:9 (KJV). Even though at that moment I couldn't receive the unemployment benefits, it was good to know the benefits were available. Since I was unable to receive the unemployment benefits at that time, it was a blessing there were funds in my 401k plan that I could withdraw to financially support me for a brief period of time. More amazing was how God had blessed me with the gift from Mrs. Essie that was exactly the amount I needed to fulfill my financial obligations until the 401k funds were received. Once more a flicker of light from Jesus Christ of unforeseen financial blessings. Never could I imagine being jobless in February 2015 when I was nearing the age of 60. Thankfully God had already made financial provisions for me to endure another mega storm. *And the Lord will continually guide you, and satisfy your soul in scorched and dry places, and give strength to your bones; And you will be like a watered garden, and like a spring of water whose waters do not fail*, Isaiah 58:11 (AMP). The other issue was the severance agreement. I needed to obtain legal advice pertaining to employment matters. After speaking with several lawyers that could not help me, I contacted my long-time lawyer friend, Don Reimer. Don had represented me in two car accidents and represented several family members and friends with legal matters. I informed Don of the unfortunate events that had occurred throughout my life and the termination. He was very compassionate expressing his disappointment with the decision of the firm. Don told me he would ask around for a good employment lawyer.

Spiritual Intervention and Mental Counseling. To enable me to make it through each day, I prayed, read my Bible, and reflected on encouraging scriptures, as well as used the meditation and coping methods being taught in the therapy sessions. The first week of March, Ivy returned to her full-time job. Each morning I would go to their house to babysit Ivan, and Ethan on the days he did not attended preschool. Aiden had begun kindergarten at Hawkins Lower School. Eddie would assist with the boys when I needed to attend psych therapy sessions or other appointments. During the evenings, I would return to Sylvia's house. I would read, play my computer games, and watch television to make it through the long evenings. No matter how I tried to occupy my mind, it became more difficult to accept and deal with the rejection from the firm and the treachery of Jerome. Constantly I was reliving my life with Herman with intense visions of the day Herman died. I was wondering why my lawyer and the judge did not let me know the appeal was denied before I restarted my life with Syl and the months of incarceration. I tried praying to God for strength to endure and understand yet another unexpected storm. Like in the past when too weak to pray, I would cry out to God for help. Yet, no matter how hard I tried, it became more difficult each day to cope with the emotional scars from my entire stormy life.

Don called me several days after we had spoken. He referred me to an employment lawyer, David Young. I called the Law Firm of David A. Young, LLC. I spoke with his assistant, Kate. She was very courteous, patient, and thoughtful while I gave her a summary of my need for legal advice. She let me know Mr. Young would review the summary she prepared from our discussion and either he or she would call be back. The next day Kate called me to schedule an appointment with David. By the time I meet with David, I was feeling severely emotionally shattered. Tearfully I told David the events in my life that led up to my termination. David offered me tissues as he patiently and empathetically listened. When I finished telling him everything, with thoughtfulness he let me know how honestly moved he was by my situation. He then said the words I had heard over the past few week, *Ohio is an at-will State*. David then apologetically let me know *for this reason there was nothing he could do for me*. I thanked him for taking the time to speak with me. Driving home from downtown, I passed the building where I worked for many years and other buildings that I had conducted business in or simply had lunch. I was overcome with emotional pain as I realized never again would I be able to go to work or have lunch in those buildings. At that point I only could think of driving my car off the Ninth Street pier into Lake Erie. Weary with tears pouring down my face, I cried out to God, *please, please help me*. The flicker of light from Jesus Christ was strength to not drive towards the pier. Instead I drove my car towards Mrs. Essie's house to deliver paperwork for the probate case. A few miles from her house, my phone dinged that I had a phone message. My phone had not rung because it was still on vibrate from when I was meeting with the lawyer. I listened to the message, it was the lawyer, David letting me know he was moved by my story and was going to try to see if there was anything he could do for me. He said he was not for sure what could be done legally but was willing to investigate into any potential claims. He told me to call Kate to schedule another appointment. I was overjoyed with praise knowing it was only God that heard my cry for help. God knew without His intervention the darkness of this emotional storm was on the verge of consuming my mind and soul. The flicker of light from Jesus Christ was the mercy and grace of God alone that carried me. From the moment of leaving David's office until receiving his phone message, it was God alone who sustained me. *Cast thy burden upon the Lord, and he shall sustain thee: he shall never suffer the righteous to be moved*, Psalm 55:22 (KJV). From the day I was terminated I had been living in an emotional daze. It was like I was sleepwalking. On the outside I looked okay, but the inside was a complete disaster. Undeniably this was one of those time in my life when my beloved poem *Footprints in the* Sand, by Mary Fishback Powers was crystal clear to me. Because God surely alone was carrying and sustaining me. Pulling into the driveway of Mrs. Essie's home, miraculously my tears of weariness turned to tears of thankfulness, and the weight upon my soul that was draining the life out of me was lifted a little, allowing me to get a much-needed sigh of relief.

Over the next couple of weeks, David met with me a few times to discuss the strategy for the case. He contemplated reaching out to one of the lawyers of the firm he had worked with on previous cases. It was his intention to contact the firm on several occasions and let me know the response. By mid-May, David asked me to come to the office. Upon arriving at the office, David started the meeting by informing me he *was not certain he could represent me in the diligent manner needed for my type of case*. He stated this was due to his relationship with many of the attorneys at the firm. Listening to him say his apologies, my heart dropped, I felt numb, it was like I was a balloon that had been deflated. I had come to the office with lots of hope, only to hear this disappointing news. Then David told me *although he could not represent me, he would like me to talk to a colleague of his who he believed would have the fortitude to fight the case in the correct manner*. He recommended me to Kami Brauer, a sole practice lawyer, who shared the office space with him. I sat there thinking how a second ago I was about to have those negative thoughts of giving up, then instantaneously the flicker of light from the Holy Spirit instilled in my soul that I must trust in the Lord at all times. *Blessed is the man that trusteth in the Lord, and whose hope the Lord is*, Jeremiah 17:7 (KJV). My trust and hope had to be totally in God to defeat the attacks from the adversaries. Astounded by yet another miraculous blessing from God, I worshipped and praised the Lord with submission and thankfulness. The next day Kami called me. I told her the tragedies and misfortunes of my life. She let me know her interest in representing me. After reviewing certain information, Kami agreed to take my case. Immediately she began to formulate the strategy for the case.

Besides the legal blessing, even though the therapy with Nicholette was constructively helping, the problem was the deeper we dug into my life, more emotional scars from my stormy life was revealed that made it challenging for me to make any progress. Confronting one emotional storm, revealed more layers of depression. Addressing the abuse in my life was a major part of my therapy because I was living with mental, physical, and sexual abuse from different people. The abuse from Syl and Jerome was mental abuse, which was extremely destructive for me mentally. This is because the emotional pain from the mental abuse is unseen with the human eye, so, the pain it caused me was invisible to everyone. Since all my emotional scars from the mental abuse was unseen, it caused more mental pain because how could any of my loved ones understand and help me without any visual evidence of abuse? The physical abuse from Herman caused both inwardly mental and outwardly physical emotional scars. The mental inwardly scars caused by Herman affected me the same as the ones from Syl and Jerome. The outwardly scars from Herman's abuse had enabled my loved ones to be aware and try to help me, but in the end, my ignoring their cries for me to leave Herman, put into motion the events that caused Herman to die and me to suffer emotionally for the rest of my life. The one sexual abuse from being raped, was inwardly torment for me that I endured alone for many years. The inwardly emotional scars from the sexual abuse was two-folded from the memories of my body being viciously raped by a man I barely knew and then the aborting of my innocent baby boy. The more I confronted with Nicholette the abuse from my husbands, I began to try to figure out why each of them turned out to have some type of abusive nature? I started to wonder if I had done something wrong. But I honestly knew my only desire in each marriage had been for my dream of the ideal family life as portrayed in the early 1960s television sitcom *Leave It to Beaver* to come true. Sadly, that life never came true.

The aftermath of being fired was that front and center in my mind with the reemerge of the memories from the physical domestic violence from Herman that resulted in my shooting him and his death. For years I had seldom discussed the tragic aspects of my life with Herman. I had only talked about it when necessary to let someone that was becoming close to me know or to encourage a person in an abusive volatile situation. In addition, although I often thought about publicly speaking out about the abuse I suffered and the death of Herman to help other victims of domestic abuse, I never pursued it. But in February 2015, thirty-five years after the death of Herman, my termination from the firm had ignited another powerful storm that had knocked me to back to the ground. This storm forced me to publicly acknowledge to the world what happened in my first marriage, because the *cat was out of the box*. Many people now knew I was a victim of domestic violence and an assaulter who had shot and caused the death of her husband. I had to face my life not only as a victim of domestic violence, but an assaulter, who shot her violent husband.

With the therapy I was beginning to finally acknowledge my surviving the physical abuse from Herman was only by the grace of God, because I could have been the one that died. More importantly, after all these years, I finally realized the flicker of light from God was for me to be a living testimony to other victims and assaulter that God will forgive, bless, and heal. *Pay attention and always be on guard [looking out for one another]! If your brother sins and disregards God's precepts, solemnly warn him; and if he repents and changes, forgive him*, Luke 17:3 (AMP).

Besides working with the emotional scarring from the domestic violence and death of Herman, my termination had taken me from a person of confidence to becoming timid. Once a person who was outgoing to introvert. I went from being energetic to lethargic. My ability to concentrate, focus and multitasking was impeded. Nicholette worked patiently with me to focus on a plan to deal with each emotional crisis I was facing. At one point, she felt I was not mad enough. She wished I could get more upset with Jerome, the firm, and the BK Lawyer. Somehow, I could not get upset. I was truly hurt and felt betrayed, rejected, mistreated, and discarded by those I dearly loved, but even with all the trepidation, I could not get mad. Instead of anger, I felt downhearted by the treacherous acts of Jerome. It was further depressing to know he believed his actions were not what caused me to lose my job. I was in agony from being terminated from my job after many years of loyal, dedicated service. Thoughts of not hearing from at least the BK lawyer I worked with for twenty-five years was hard to accept. How could he discard me without a word? The darkness from this storm made me believe the termination from the job was karma for all my sins. The flicker of light from the Holy Spirit was wait on the Lord. *Wait on the Lord and be of good courage*, Psalm 24:14. Although I was praying, believing, and meditating my days grew tougher to accept. This is when my motto became *make it through one second at a time*. Nicholette and I agreed the therapy sessions, medicine and most importantly babysitting my grandsons enabled me to get through the long days. Holding on and caring for my grandsons calmed me and enabled me to withstand the agony of my life. It reminded me of holding and caring for Ivy when Herman died. I knew my grandsons were solely depending on me to care for them while Aaron and Ivy were at work, just like thirty-five years ago when Ivy was a baby. They were innocent babies that only wanted to be given love, nurturing and attention. I could hold them in my arms without being judged, mistreated and unforgiven for my sins. To them I was simply their Granny. The flicker of light from God was being blessed to have loved ones. I praised God for blessing me with my daughters and grandsons that gave me strength to endure through my stormy life.

As Nicolette worked on ways for me to cope and live with PTSD, Shane watched the effects of my medication, and adjusted the medications as needed to help me with anxiety attacks, depression and sleeping. After several weeks of therapy, adjusting medications and taking into consideration my chronic mental stability, Shane recommended I talk to Dr. Thomas Boyd to see if I met the criteria to take part in the intensive out-patient group therapy. I met with Dr.

Boyd a few days later. After telling him the adversities in my life, he determined the group therapy would be beneficial to my PTSD treatment. In late March 2016, I began the group therapy sessions. The sessions were held for three hours on Mondays, Wednesdays, and Saturdays for sixteen weeks. Dr. Boyd conducted the sessions with three to four other ladies and myself. The therapy sessions focused on recognizing past and present negative thoughts and learning how to prevent them from reoccurring, and working on ways to use my positive thoughts, remedies, and actions to overcome traumatic events. At the beginning of each session we would complete a questionnaire of our current mental status that we would discuss. This was followed by a lesson on mental wellness then a general group discussion about the lesson. Before the end of the session, we would complete a questionnaire detailing our mental status.

Shortly after starting the group therapy sessions, my appointments with Nicholette were reduced to once a week. Shane and I met once to twice a month to discuss if my prescriptions were helping and discuss how the group therapy sessions were easing some of my anxiety. One of the key issues we addressed several times was how to deal with my fear that everyone now thought I intentionally killed Herman and believing I was a bad person who had went to jail and was a felon. This would increase my stress levels to the point I was too frightened to be sociable. I was scared at the thought of seeking employment, because there was no way I would be hired by another company after the firm discarded want me. The thought of applying for employment and being denied would send me into bouts of deep anxiety and severe panic attacks. By mid-May with doubts of when I would be mentally stable enough to apply for workers' compensation, I decided to ask Shane about receiving temporary disability benefits through social security. Shane suggested I apply as soon as possible because it could take time to obtain a response. In June 2015, I applied for social security disability.

The group therapy classes were extremely helpful in assisting me with addressing my mental problems in a more positive manner. Yet as we neared the end of the group sessions, reliving the tragedies and unforeseen circumstances from my past and present persistently caused severe panic attacks and depression. For this reason, after the rigid sixteen-week group sessions, Dr. Boyd referred me for Eye Movement Desensitization and Reprocessing (EMDR) treatment. He explained to me EMDR is a form of treatment for PTSD. It would involve eye movements or other forms of bilateral stimulation to help me in managing the disturbing memories and negative beliefs. Because there were only a selected few therapists licensed to administer EMDR treatment, I needed to select a therapist from the list provided. I selected JoAnna Castrilla. Following my initial meeting with JoAnna, it was determined the treatment would be beneficial for me. We agreed to meet twice a week. Once I began the treatment with JoAnna, I believed it would be too mentally intensive for me to have sessions with Nicholette and JoAnna. For this reason, my therapy with Nicholette was put on hold pending the outcome of my treatment with JoAnna. The treatment with JoAnna was extremely beneficial. With the EMDR treatment and the method acquired during the group therapy classes, I was learning to manage PTSD, the sudden anxiety attacks, and bouts with depression. The problem was daily there were major hurdles that would instantly make me regress into my past. These regressions were prompted when confronting one or more past or current traumatic events such as: a memory that made me think about Herman and his death; discussing the pending legal matter with Kim; dealing with Jerome on not keeping his commitment to assist me financially and refusal to apologize for his hateful act; looking at the hurt and disappointment I had caused many people; knowing how afraid I was about my future; continuing to pretend to be okay when I was in an emotional warfare. Appreciatively, there was a flicker of light from Jesus Christ of miraculous guidance from God to let me know I needed mental health treatment. *O Lord, you are my God; I will exalt You, I will praise and give thanks to Your name; For You have done miraculous things, plans formed long, long ago, [fulfilled] with perfect faithfulness,* Isaiah 25:1 (AMP). In this agonizing mental storm of my life wondrously I received guidance from God to obtain the mental support I really needed. If only I would have listened to my inner spirit crying out for mental help all these years, perhaps a few of my stormy bumps in life could have been avoided. Refusing to seek mental health treatment because of feeling I was not mentally unstable was a mistake. I thought about Momma, Michael and Valerie who depended on mental health providers. Who was I to think I was any better than Momma and my cousins. I needed mental health treatment just as much, if not more, than they did. Whether I had an emotionally challenging or challenge free day, I praised and thanked God for putting me on the dual track of spiritual guidance and mental health treatment.

Nowadays when I look back on when I was diagnosed with the mental disorder of PTSD, I knew little about the disease. I had only recently watched a few television shows that portrayed people suffering from the disease. After my termination, with each passing second, my past consumed my every thought to the point that I was unable to keep it bottled up. Then my bottled busted. All I had kept bottled-up for many years came rushing into my every thought. My past could no longer be held in or managed inwardly. It was uncontrollably overflowing outwardly. With the interceding of the Holy Spirit and the help from my daughters, I finally realized and acknowledged that I needed professional help. The flicker of light from God was acknowledging I needed help. Clinging on the mercy of God, *I am worn out from my groaning. All night long I flood my bed with weeping and drench my couch with tears. My eyes grow weak with sorrow; they fail because of all my foes. Away from me, all you who do evil, for the Lord has heard my weeping. The Lord has heard my cry for mercy; the Lord accepts my prayer*, Psalm 6:6-9 (NIV). Then acknowledging God would use the gifts of my medical professionals to help me. *Each of you should use whatever gift you have received to serve others, as faithful stewards of God's grace in its various forms. If anyone speaks, they should do so as one who speaks the very words of God. If anyone serves, they should do so with the strength God provides, so that in all things God may be praised through Jesus Christ. To him be the glory and the power for ever and ever. Amen.* I Peter 4:10-11 (NLT). I now can say to God be the glory, as I constantly learn to live with the reoccurring thoughts of my past with both spiritual guidance and professional mental health help. To anyone suffering from mental health issues I encourage you to get both spiritual guidance and mental health treatment.

Chapter Twenty-Four – Life Changing Events

In July 2015, Aaron let us know he was informed by his employer, one of the largest pharmacy health care providers in the U.S., the department he managed was being eliminated in August 2015. This would result in Aaron and the employees he managed being laid-off. His employer was offering the employees a severance package. Aaron, Ivy, and family members were in total shock, especially since Aaron had recently returned from a visit to one of the main headquarters of the company in Phoenix, Arizona. During that visit Aaron told us he had met with several upper managers and executives. With us knowing Aaron was exceptionally reliable and hard-working we encouraged him everything would work out. I believed with his experience and excellent work ethics, he would readily secure employment. Aaron had applied for positions with several local hospitals. He had received responses and scheduled several interviews. Prior to any of those interviews, his employer offered him positions at several of the company's other locations in Arizona, Texas, and Pennsylvania. Aaron and Ivy discussed the opportunities and the potential benefits of relocating. They decided Aaron would accept the position in Scottsdale, Arizona. Shortly after Aaron informed his employer he would accept the position, he began commuting to and from Scottsdale with the understanding he had a year to move his family to the Scottsdale area. When Aaron was in Scottsdale, I stayed with Ivy and the boys and would return to Sylvia's house when he returned home.

Although everyone was excited for the Banks' family relocation, one of the major concerns was who would care for the boys. Right away I thought of how before my termination my plan had been when I retired to relocate to Henderson, Nevada. My intentions were to purchase a home where I would reside during the months of November through April. For the other months I intended to return to Cleveland and lease the home. Amazingly those dreams might to some extent come true, as I silently thought okay God, again you are turning my hopelessness into the promises that you would *never leave [me], nor forsake [me]*, Hebrews 13:5. Only God knew before anyone that Aaron and Ivy would relocate and how difficult it would be for them to work comfortable if strangers had to babysit the boys, especially Ivan who wasn't yet one year old. Thinking about all of this, without a second thought, I let Aaron and Ivy know I would go to Scottsdale to babysit my grandsons. The details were discussed with Aaron, Ivy, Eddie, and me. Eddie and I agreed she would come babysit when I was required to be in Cleveland or needed a break. This was a prayer come true. Once more God had blessed each of us.

In August, besides addressing the employment issues of Aaron and other pending matters, I received a call from social security. The representative stated he was calling regarding my disability application. He needed additional information to process my application. A few weeks later in September, the representative again called asking a few more questions. After I answered the questions, he stated a decision would be sent to me. In October as I reviewed my checking account there was a deposit I did not recognize. I called the bank, the representative informed me the deposit was from social security. Saying thank you to the representative, tears of thanksgiving and praise to God rolled down my cheeks thinking, as I thought God you have done it again. Many had told me it would take years or even several applications to get approved. Yet God had blessed me to be approved in less than six months. With an overjoyed thankful heart, I said to God, I praise your name and lift my voice in thanksgiving because with all my faults and sins you endlessly love and forgive me. I had given up on myself many times by trying to take my life and was even still fighting to survive. Yet God alone was carrying me and was always light miles ahead of my thoughts. I only needed to be patient knowing Jesus Christ cared about me. *Humble yourselves therefore under the mighty hand of God, that He may exalt you in due time: Casting all your care upon Him; for He careth for you*, 1 Peter 5:6-7.

By mid-October, Kami had contacted the firm to discuss a potential settlement of my termination. The firm had no intention on discussing any settlement. As a result, Kami drafted and filed a complaint in November. The Court set certain dates for deadlines, status conferences and the trial. The second week of December I received a call from Kami stating the firm had retained counsel. The counsel for the firm requested an extension of time to file a response to the complaint. Knowing this was a customary practice, we agreed to extend the deadline. Meanwhile my EMDR treatment with JoAnna was not proceeding in the manner we had anticipated. This was primarily due to each time I had to confront the complaint, I constantly relived and was reminded of my traumatic past. This caused limited progress with my ability to work on rectifying the traumatic events and impeded my ability to mentally move forward. JoAnne being aware of the reasons for the hindrance in my treatment decided until the legal matter was completed to wait to administer the more rigorous treatment. In the meantime, JoAnne would focus more on ways to lessen my mental anxiety and cope with the PTSD. In conjunction with JoAnne's treatment plan, Shane changed my medication as needed to address the changes in my moods.

Aaron and Ivy had been diligently working on the details for their relocation. Ivy had visited Scottsdale for employment interviews and to meet with their realty brokers to discuss housing and other aspects of the move. In the meantime, Aaron, Ivy, Eddie, Sylvia, and I began us discussing visiting Scottsdale in December to become acquainted with the area and spend the Christmas holiday with family members in California. Everyone thought it was a great idea and we began making plans. By December 2015, Aaron, Ivy, Eddie, Sylvia, and I had our travel arrangements made to visit Scottsdale. Syl had decided not to go with us because Tommy would be visiting Cleveland at the same time. On Saturday, December 19th, Aaron, and Ivy hosted an early Christmas dinner for family members and friends. Ivy had also arranged for Santa Claus to visit the boys at their house. Upon the arrival of Santa, the boys were overjoyed with excitement. Ivy explained to the boys that because they would be out-of-town on Christmas Day, Santa decided to make a special early visit to their house. He brought presents for each of the boys and we took lots of pictures. Santa and the boys had a wonderful time playing together, and he even stayed to enjoy the delicious dinner Ivy had prepared for us. It was a wonderful time filled with recalling happy memories. We also talked about the move going from being happy to sad knowing this would be the Banks last Christmas in that house. Everyone discussed their plans to visit Scottsdale in the future. It was a beautiful family gathering. The next morning, the boys woke up to more gifts under their Christmas tree.

Packing to prepare for two weeks of travel can be a huge undertaking for only one person. When the arrangments are for five adults and three little boys, it required a great deal of planning for airplane reservations, hotel stays, transportation and meals. With lots of detailed organizing, finally on the morning of December 21st we headed for the airport. Upon arriving in Scottsdale, we were really impressed with the beautiful weather, spectacular mountains, and desert atmosphere. Aaron had arranged for us to spend the first few days at a hotel villa. On a few days, we all went with Aaron and Ivy with their realtor to the showing of several lovely homes and to visit potential schools for Aiden and Ethan. Eddie, Sylvia, and I would babysit the boys while Aaron went to work and Ivy on job interviews. In their spare time, Aaron and Ivy took us sightseeing. On the 24th, we loaded both vehicles and headed to Los Angeles. That evening when we arrived in the Los Angeles area, Ivy, Aaron, and the boys spent the night with Vet and his wife, Pia, with their son, Leavitt, and two daughters, Leia, and Lexis. Aiden, who to me looked a lot like Vet and Herman, was excited about seeing his Uncle Vet. While the Banks would be staying with Vet, Sylvia, Eddie, and I had made reservations to stay at a hotel for the evening. On Christmas morning the three of us went to Vet's house for breakfast. The boys, especially Aiden were in awe of their Uncle Vet, Aunt Pia, and cousins. They were also playing with the toys Santa had delivered to the home of their Uncle and Aunt. It was a very sentimental visit for me. Although Ivy and Vet had communicated and seen each other over the years, I had not seen him for years until Ivy's wedding. Because I will forever feel guilty for causing the death of his father, for Vet and Pia to gracious invite me into their home meant more than they could image, which I will always appreciate. Seeing Ivy and Vet together brought happiness to me. I thought this is the way Tim might have felt when he saw Kim and I together.

After breakfast Sylvia and I headed to Pomona to visit with Vicki and her family. Tommie was still in Cleveland visiting Syl and their mother. It was another true blessing spending time with Vicki, who I had been so glad to see at Ivy's wedding, and her family members. Then it was good to see my niece, Courtney; nephew, Christopher; Mrs. Williams; and Vicki's brother, sisters, and other family members who I had not seen in years. Although Syl and I were divorced, it was one of my many blessings the way Tommie and Vicki loved me unconditionally and expressed it by their acts of kindness. Later that evening the Banks family and Eddie arrived. Of course, everyone adored my little grandbabies. This was a loving Christmas that I will forever cherish. The day after Christmas was Ivan's first birthday. We headed to Disneyland to celebrate his and Sylvia's birthdays. The boys had a spectacular time having lunch with the characters, riding the rides, and enjoying the spectacular sights. It was a joy to see the happy faces of my three grandsons eagerly running from one attraction to the next. We returned to our hotels after a wonderful day at Disneyland. The next day Vicki, Courtney, and Rob, Syl's youngest brother, took all of us to the Grauman's Chinese Theater on the historic Hollywood Walk of Fame. We enjoyed the sights and had a nice dinner together. It was good to see everyone spend time bonding together.

Earlier that morning I received a call from Kami letting me know she had received the first set of interrogatories and discovery requests. She let me know the documents needed to be answered by mid-January. I let her know I was out-of-town and would begin working on the interrogatories and discovery request upon my return to Cleveland. Kami said that would be fine and to enjoy the remainder of my vacation. Calls from Kami triggered panic attacks. My anxiety level increased followed by that never-ending slideshow in my mind of life. Of course, I put on my phony temperament to reframe from letting anyone know my mental anguish.

The next day we loaded up and headed back to Scottsdale. For the next several days we had arranged to stay in a condo through AirBNB. Aaron and Ivy resumed their search for a home and schools for the boys. We went on several more sightseeing outings. On the 30th it was back to reality for us as we packed and headed back to Cleveland. With a heavy heart I boarded the plane weary of the thought of facing the legal journey ahead of me. The flicker of light from God was my strength would be renewed. *But they that wait upon the Lord shall renew their strength; they shall mount up with wings as eagles; they shall run, and not be weary; and they shall walk, and not faint*, Isaiah 40.:31 (KJV).

Chapter Twenty-Five -- Favor in the Middle of Thunderstorms

Upon returning home, I began to work on answering the interrogatories and preparing the documentation for the discovery. Trying to complete this heavy task caused me to relive the abuse from Herman and Jerome, coupled with the rejection by the BK Lawyer, and the trauma of losing my job. Reliving these memories caused my anxiety attacks to peak to uncontrollable levels. JoAnne and Shane diligently worked with me to confront the emotional battles in a positive manner and with readjusting my medication. Once the interrogatories and documentation for discovery were completed feelings of bleakness, isolation and guilt filled my days. Once again, praying was replaced with only being able to cry out to God for help. The flicker of light from Jesus Christ was God was my strength and power. Emphasis added. *Why do you complain, [DeBorah] Jacob? Why do you say, Israel my way is hidden from the Lord; my cause is disregarded by my God? Do you not know? Have you not heard? The Lord is the everlasting God, the Creator of the ends of the earth. He will not grow tired or weary, and his understanding no one can fathom. He gives strength to the weary and increases the power of the weak. He giveth power to the faint; and to them that have no might he increaseth strength*, Isaiah 40:27-29 (NIV).

Kami called me later in the month to let me know the depositions had been scheduled for mid-February. Instantly my heart ached, and my mind was in a state of hysteria. Like in the past, it would even become too difficult to pray, so I would simply cry aloud to God for strength. I even began to burst out singing and talking to the Lord. Singing praises and talking to God I would think back on my childhood when I would see Momma spontaneously starting to sing praises to God. Back then when I listened to Momma singing I would wonder what was wrong with her, why was she was acting strange by singing out like that. I would wonder if she was on the verge of another nervous breakdown. But now I understood why Momma was singing. It was because she needed God to give her strength. Exactly like Momma, when I started to sing praises to the Lord it gave me strength and brought me through many seconds of those days when I was unbelievably mentally despondent. All these years later I was very thankful to have witnessed Momma singing praises to God for strength. Thankfully just like it did for Momma, singing and talking to God helped eased the distress and gave me a little peace of mind. During this time the flicker of light was the Holy Spirit imparting into my soul hope and strength. *Now the God of hope fill you with all joy and peace in believing, that ye may abound in hope, through the power of the Holy Ghost*, Romans 15:13.

Joyfulness Intermingled with Heartache. Over the past few years, Kim and I had discussed celebrating her 50th birthday and doing one of our bucket list events by going on the *2015 Tom Joyner Foundation Fantastic Voyage Cruise*. With the loss of my job and Kim unsure if she could financially afford the cruise, it did not seem we would be able to go on the trip. With me facing an uncertain future and challenging legal battle the thought of getting far away from my problems, even if for only temporary, seemed like it would be the perfect antidote. When Kim told me, she could not afford the trip, I discussed with her the possibilities of paying a smaller amount of her cost and I would make up the difference. Unfortunately, she was unable to pay anything towards the cost. I discussed with JoAnne and Shane going on the cruise by myself. They both thought it was a great idea. My primary concern was I never had been anywhere like that alone. This caused me to worry about being lonely and wondering if I would have fun. My anxiety levels intensified with thoughts of doubt, low self-esteem, and if I deserved the cruise. With encouragement from my medical professionals and loved ones, and much prayer to God for guidance, I made plans to go on the cruise in April.

By the end of January, Aaron and Ivy made their final arrangments to move. They had secured a home in Gilbert, Arizona and Ivy had obtained employment. The move would take place the week of February 20th. Aaron and Ivy had decided to have Aiden finish his kindergarten year at Hawkins, so Aiden would stay in Cleveland with Eddie. Syl, Sylvia and Eddie's family members would help Eddie care for Aiden.

By the beginning of February, Kami informed me my deposition was scheduled for February 17th. Concealing from my family members the true emotional hopelessness with a pretend smile, I prepared for my deposition. A few days later Kami met with me to begin preparation for the deposition. On the day of my deposition I met Kami at her office. We walked to the opposing counsel's office. Even before arriving at the office, I was emotionally drained from the thought of being put on trial for a second time and being found guilty by people. Then knowing the need to be coherent for the deposition, the night before I did not take my sleeping or panic medication because both medications made me feel lethargic. As a result, I had a sleepless night full of tossing and turning. Consequently, I was exhausted together with my emotional state being impeded by my inability to concentrate. When we arrived at the opposing counsel office, thoughts filled my mind of how I use to work in this type of atmosphere. This further intensified my anxiety levels. The deposition was comparable to my trial because once again I felt like I had to prove my innocence. During my deposition, many of the events of my adult life and character were viciously attacked while the eyes of the opposing parties judged me with detest and scornfulness. I kept thinking, why am I still alive? I should go jump out of that window right now. I wanted to scream, *I did not mean to kill Herman, so why have you found me guilty all over again*? The flicker of light was knowing that the Lord was keeping me in His perfect peace and everlasting strength. *Thou wilt keep him in perfect peace, whose mind is stayed on thee: because he trusteth in thee. Trust ye in the Lord for ever: for in the Lord Jehovah is everlasting strength*, Isaiah 26:3-4 (KJV). With the peace and strength of God through the Holy Spirit, emotionally I was able to keep my composure and mindset. Then utilizing the methods instructed by my mental health providers to decrease panic attacks, I endured six hours of interrogation. Walking back to Kami's office, we discussed the deposition. When we reached her office, she let me know she would be in contact with me when the depositions of the people from the firm were scheduled. Once I sat in my car, I had a mental melt down. Emotional thoughts of guilt, rejection, shamefulness, and suicide ran rapidly in my mind. It was evident to me the opposing parties believed I was just another harden criminal. After the events of that day, I knew there was no chance anyone would employ me when I was about to be sixty years old, black and a criminal. All of these realizations knocked me to one of my lowest points. Emotionally I felt incapacitated. Here I thought my debt to society had been paid for my crime. Not so. I would always be considered a criminal, a felon. I was not wallowing in self-pity or having a woe is me party. It was simply a truthful reality check. When I arrived home, I went into pretend mood acting like life was great. Trying not to convey to my loved ones the inward mental struggle, I stayed sane by focusing on and preparing for the move to Arizona and the cruise. We were to leave for Arizona on February 20th. However, because of the uncertainty of the deposition dates for the people from my former employer, I was unable to confirm my travel arrangements. In case I was unable to immediately go to Arizona, Eddie made arrangments to go and take care of the boys. A few days later Kami called to inform me of the schedule for the depositions. Thankfully the depositions I needed to attend were prior to February 20th. This enabled me to make arrangements to travel with the family to Arizona.

Attending the depositions of my former co-workers was more difficult mentally than my own deposition. Each of the former co-workers treated me like I was a stranger on the street. Some of them made no to little eye contact with me. At times they were honest, but at other times outright dishonest. Reminiscing on my years of dedicated services to the firm I was known as a hard worker who went beyond the call of duty; considered an integral part of the bankruptcy department; produced superb work products; putting the job first at the sacrifice of my family; well respected by co-workers, court personnel and third parties; and generated significant revenue for the firm. Yet twenty years of this type of service to them meant nothing. My one horrific act of survival outweighed all my good. The truth pierced me to the core of my heart, mind, and soul. I ached from the top of my head to the bottom of my feet. What was the purpose of my life with these types of odds against me? Too weak to do anything on my own, it once more was a period of *Foot Prints in the Sand.* In a trance unable to withstand the emotional storms of my life it was only Jesus Christ the son of God that was carrying me. The flicker of light from Jesus Christ was to listen to God for He would carry me. *Listen to Me [says the Lord], O house of Jacob, and all the remnant of the house of Israel, you who have been borne by Me from your birth, carried from the womb: Even to your old age I am He, and even to hair white with age will I carry you. I have made, and I will bear; yes, I will carry and will save you,* Isaiah 46:3-4 (AMPC). At the end of each deposition I was very distraught. Only meditating on and believing that God was carrying me sustained me. Then God in His omnipotent power gave me a glorious beam of light. Following the deposition of the managing partner of the firm, I stood up to walk towards the door. Suddenly I heard the managing partner called out my name, *Debbie*. I turned with tears forming in my eyes, I solemnly said, his name. Kami and the opposing counsel looked bewildered as they stopped talking and stared at us. With earnest compassion in his eyes, the managing partner reached out to shake my hand. Then he said, *I wish the best for you in the future*. Surprised but very thankful, I replied, *thank you*. He had no idea how much those words meant to me. I knew without a doubt the flicker of light from Jesus Christ was the grace from God. *Let us therefore come boldly unto the throne of grace, that we may obtain mercy, and find grace to help in time of need*, Hebrews 4:16 (KJV). It was the grace of God that caused those unexpected words of kindness to be spoken at that time. Silently I praised and glorified my Lord and Savior Jesus Christ. For it was only God who knew I truly needed a breath of hope to uplift, encourage and bless my soul. Once the other parties had left, Kami asked what the managing partner had said to me. When I told her, she looked at me in awe, saying that was nice. She then said, *I know opposing counsel was wondering what he said*. Following the key people depositions from the firm, Kami scheduled a few additional depositions for late February and early March. We decided the two depositions scheduled in late February did not require my attendance, but the March depositions I would attend.

  Tired and weary I put on my pretend face and attitude for my family members in preparation for the move to Arizona. On February 20th, we headed to Gilbert, Arizona. Several days prior, once the movers had packed and loaded the Banks' household and cars they left for Arizona. They would arrive a few days after our arrival.

Awaiting the arrival of the household, we stayed at a hotel. During the day Aaron went to work while we shopped for items needed for the house. Once he returned from work, we would go to their home to prepare for the move in. It was a huge beautiful thirteen room home with a lovely back yard surrounded with orange and palm trees. We were thrilled to be living in a home with this much space. Within a few days the movers arrived. We thankfully and happily moved into the house. Shortly thereafter it was time for Eddie and Aiden to return to Cleveland. It was difficult to see the sadness on the faces of Ivy and Aaron as Aiden prepared to leave. We encouraged Aiden and each other knowing he would be returning for spring break in several weeks and thereafter it soon would be the end of the school year. Together we prayed for God to strengthen us during this period of separation.

Chapter Twenty-Six – All the Time God Was Working It Out

In early March I returned to Cleveland for the final depositions which were comparable to the previous depositions. At the conclusions of the depositions, Kami and I meet to discuss the first settlement conference scheduled for the first week of April and arranged for me to meet with an expert witness specializing in domestic violence. In between meetings with Kami I spent time with Aiden and Sylvia and attended appointments with JoAnne and Shane. In hopes of selling the house I had bought for Ivy and Aaron, I meet with a broker to arrange to place the house up for sale. On March 6th, I returned to Arizona. It was good mentally to have the responsibility of babysitting Ethan and Ivan. The nice sunny weather was an additional boost to my mindset. It was also time to begin preparing for the cruise. The following week, Aiden was on spring break. Syl had agreed to bring Aiden to Arizona for the week. We were excited to see them. We were very thankful to see Syl because months prior he had battled prostate cancer and had been blessed to a receive a victory report from the doctor that the prostate cancer was in remission. The girls, especially Ivy, never had given up hope Syl and I would get back together, but I knew with everything we had been through remaining friends was more important than being a couple.

Ivy and Aaron were considering purchasing a new car since both of their cars were older. A few days after Syl and Aiden arrived in Gilbert, we went to dinner at one of local favorite restaurant, Lo-Lo's Chicken and Waffles. We were returning home. Aaron, Ivan, and I were in the car together, while Ivy, Syl, Aiden and Ethan were following us. I was listening to a message from Kami regarding the settlement conference. Suddenly Aaron hit the brakes. Looking up to see why he hit the brakes, there was a car making a left turn directly in front of us. Aaron tried to avoid hitting the car, but it was too late. The car hit our car and the air bags deployed. Aaron was able to stop the car without hitting anything by maneuvering it towards the curb. Although momentarily dazed, we were okay. Aaron was asking if I was okay while checking on Ivan. I said, I am okay, while calling the police. Ivy was at the door of the car hysterically trying to make sure Ivan was okay, we let her know he was fine. Upon the arrival of the police, a determination was made that the driver of the car that hit us was turning left heading in the wrong direction towards oncoming traffic onto the off ramp of the highway. The flicker of light from Jesus Christ was the blessing even though the SUV was totaled, we had no major injuries. There were only the minor bruises and scratches I received from the seatbelt and air bags. With the payoff amount Aaron and Ivy were able to obtain two new vehicles and keep Ivy's old car. The accident that could have been a tragedy was a blessing in disguise. The Banks now had two reliable vehicles and I had the older car. It also was not necessary for me to transport my car right away to Gilbert. The remainder of the time with Aiden and Syl was spent enjoying being together and having fun with indoor and outdoor activities. Far too soon the spring break was over, and it was time for Syl and Aiden to return to Cleveland. Tearfully we prepared for them to leave. Aiden was really sad about leaving his family, but we assured him the next few weeks would go by quickly, and that before he knew it, he would be back home for good. When Syl and Aiden left we tried to get use to Aiden not being with us. The blessing was with each passing day we knew it was a day closer to him coming home.

Before the Banks relocated to Arizona, I told Mrs. Essie that I and Eddie would be taking turns going there to babysit the grandbabies. Mrs. Essie told me her daughter lived in Surprise, Arizona, a city located on the outskirts of Phoenix and when she visited her daughter, she would call me. The beginning of March, Mrs. Essie called to let me know she and Mr. Willie were in Surprise visiting her daughter, Elise (Lisa). I was glad to hear from Mrs. Essie and let her know I would love to see her and Mr. Willie as well as meet her daughter. She told me she would talk to her daughter to see if she could bring them to where I lived which was on the opposite side of town. A few days later, Mrs. Essie, her husband and daughter came to visit. We had a pleasant visit, and once Ivy and Aaron came home, I went to dinner with the Harrisons. After dinner, Lisa took us to one of the local casinos and we had a lot of fun. Meeting Lisa was another flicker of light in my life because after her parents went back to Cleveland we stayed in contact. We immediately bonded, calling each other Cuz, since technically I was her cousin-in-law. After I had talked with toddlers all day, I appreciated having a discussion with an adult. When I told Lisa about the Joyner cruise, she told me to make sure I let her know if I went next year, which I promised to do. Lisa also helped me become acquainted with the Phoenix area and invited me to go on outings to the movies, out to eat, and to listen to live bands. One weekend she asked me if I wanted to go with her to Sedona, I said of course. On Friday night I went to her house to spend the night and we had an enjoyable time drinking wine, talking, and laughing. The next day, we headed to Sedona. The beautiful picturesque scenery was awesome. Of course, my only problem was the ride through the mountains, but thank goodness Lisa is a superb driver who drove her Lexus with precision around the curvy roads. On Sunday, I went to church with Lisa. From the moment I walked through the doors of El Bethel where Bishop Gregory Newman is the pastor, I knew I was going to have a hallelujah goodtime. After that Sunday, I continued to visit the church. It is a blessing to know I have a Cuz close by to talk and keep me company in this big city where I do not really know anyone.

Kami called me around the end of March letting me know opposing counsel had requested additional interrogatories and document production. I began working on answering the questions and compiling the documentation. Since I had already planned on being in Cleveland the first weekend in April for the 80th birthday celebration for Olivia, I let Kami know I would meet with her to complete the second request for information. When I arrived in Cleveland the weather was rainy and cold, but I was ecstatic about seeing my baby daughter because we had not seen each other for several weeks. On Saturday evening, Sylvia attended Olivia's birthday party with me. Olivia's daughter, Ja'Netta gave her a spectacular party. It was good to see several of the people that had been with me since my childhood. Before returning to Arizona, I finalized and dropped off to Kami the information requested by the opposing counsel.

When I arrived back in Arizona it was time for me to finish preparing for the cruise. For me to go on the cruise, Aunt Rachel had agreed to come to Arizona to babysit Ethan and Ivan. On April 22nd, I embarked on my first trip by myself. From the moment I boarded the transportation van to the pier, it was the beginning of a dream come true. My fears of being alone, were soon debunked because before we sailed I met several nice people and had talked to and taken pictures with a few celebrities. My cabin was cozy with a balcony. The first evening concert featured Diana Ross. During the concert I began talking to the lady sitting next to me. She told me her name was Veronica, and she had been on the Tom Joyner cruises for the past fourteen years. We bonded right away. After the first concert I attended most of the other concerts and events with Veronica and her sorority sister that was her roommate. A few days later while eating lunch I met a lovely couple, Donna and Johnny. Immediately Donna and I bonded. Over the course of the cruise, I went to a few of the concerts, tours of the islands and ate meals with her and Johnny. When telling Veronica, Donna, Johnny, and others that I came alone on the cruise they could not believe it. Many thought it was courageous, however, others couldn't imagine coming by themselves. The cruise was spectacular with awesome concerts and the seminars and workshops were inspiring and informative. Although I knew there was a workshop on writing a book, I could not bring myself to attend. I worried they might ask what my book would entail, and I would be too embarrassed to say. It did however make me more aware about the *Sybil's Book Club*. Also, surprisingly, the celebrities were very cordial.

The second day of the cruise I received a voice message from Jerome. This was unexpected given I hadn't spoken to him in quite some time. When he called later that day I answered. Instead of saying hello, he made his usual sarcastic comment, *you cannot answer the phone*. I replied, *yes, I can answer my phone*. Before saying anything else the call dropped. I had purchased an international calling plan that enabled outgoing and incoming calls. However, on the days at sea, the calls often dropped. Jerome called back several times and the calls kept dropping. When the calls finally did not drop, he would fuss about why I could not answer the phone. He then went on a rant of his usual questions. What was I doing? Refusing to let him know I was on the cruise, I replied, my daily routine. He had no right to know what I was doing because we were no longer married or a couple. As in the past he accused me of being with another man. I told him, *no, I was not with another man, but it should not matter to him because we are not together*. This line of questioning went on until he finally hung up. Following that call, Jerome called throughout the cruise. I would periodically answer the calls. It would be the same inquiry. He wanted to know why I would not admit to being with another man. My response persistently was the truth, I am not with another man. Then I asked him why it would matter to him, reminding him we are not a couple and that we were both going on with our own lives. He would tell me he just wanted to know. I would let him know if he believed I was with someone else to just leave me alone. He would agree, and we would hang up. Then a few moments later he would call again asking the same questions. Then he started telling me he still cared about me and only wanted to know the truth about what I was doing. I began to think how I was miles away from him., yet he was still driving me crazy. Why was he calling now when I was on the cruise? We had not spoken in weeks. Too exhausted to debate with him, I would listen to his accusations. Once I became tired of his tirade, I would lose it asking him why he was being so insensitive when he betrayed me. I let him know despite his hateful act I did not hate him. Telling him exactly like I told Nicolette, I was not mad at him, I was only extremely disappointed and hurt he caused me to lose my job, and I did not understand him contacting me when he never loved me in the manner I deserved and needed. I let him know that regardless of how awful he had treated me, he would always have a special place in my heart because truth be told I still loved him. However, I was learning to accept the fact that we did not have a healthy relationship and that would always prevent us from being together in a harmonious relationship. Expressing my honest feelings, Jerome remained in complete denial of the part he played in us not being together and even more disturbing not acknowledging that he caused me to lose my job. In his narcissistic attitude he believed I planned to get fired. No matter how much I told him what happened, nothing could convenience him there was no way I would bring this mayhem upon myself and loved ones. The calls became mentally exhausting and caused me to become very tired of defending myself against his negative accusations. It came to a point I would have to hang up on him or ignore the calls. Then on top of dealing with his calls of all the people to run into on the cruise was George, a police officer that was Jerome's co-worker and friend, who had been one of the groomsmen in our wedding. George who called his mother, said, hey and introduced me to the lady he was talking to as his mother. We briefly talked, and I let him know Jerome and I were no longer together and I was on the cruise by myself. I asked him not to let Jerome know I was on the cruise. He agreed to not say a word to Jerome. Throughout the cruise we would see each other and have short conversations.

Although I was dealing with calls from Jerome, the cruise was miles away in a different world far from my troubles. Even though it was a temporary fantasy world that had to end, I relished in the chance to not think about the emotional scarring from my stormy life. When I was alone there were a few times negative thoughts would surface. I wondered how the people I met would think of me if they knew about my entire life. How would they judge me? Would they continue to communicate with me? My other negative thought was dealing with randomly contemplating suicide. Remembering the instructions during my mental health treatment, thoughts were different from acting of my thoughts. The flicker of light from God was strength to keep my mind sound. *For God hath not given us the spirit of fear; but of power, and of love, and of a sound mind*, 2 Timothy 1:7. I was committed not to try to kill myself. Thinking back when boarding the cruise, I did not know how it would end. Would I return to the port to go home or jump off the ship in the darkness of the night? Once more in my life Jesus Christ intervened and the joy of the Lord outshined the darkness. I was surrounded by beautiful friendly people, especially Donna and Veronica, who I prayed would remain my friends when they learned about my stormy life. Even after the cruise Veronica and I spoke sporadically, and Donna and I talked several times a week. The cruise was a blessing by strengthening me to know I could go places alone and meet nice people.

With the cruise ending, the thought of facing my real world became front and center in my mind. In a few days I would be confronting the opposing parties at the initial settlement conference. Even though having fun on the cruise, I had been in sincere prayer and meditation for guidance from God on what path to take with the complaint. Do I seek a settlement or prepare for trial? When I arrived in Cleveland, I looked forward to spending time with Sylvia and Aiden. The next day Kami and I met at her office to discuss potential settlement terms before walking to the courthouse. The entire time I was silently praying for spiritual strength to make the correct decision. The flicker of light from the Holy Spirit was for me to trust in the Lord and He would show me the way. *Answer me quickly, Lord; my spirit fails. Do not hide your face from me or I will be like those who go down to the pit. Let the morning bring me word of your unfailing love, for I have put my trust in you. Show me the way I should go, for to you I entrust my life. Rescue me from my enemies, Lord, for I hide myself in you*, Psalm 143:7-9 (NIV). Approaching the courthouse, I was extremely nervous and anxious. As we entered the building, many memories resurfaced about my trial and being found guilty. When we arrived at the courtroom, a trial was in session. Initially I was told to wait in the front lobby. A few moments later it was agreed by the parties for me to sit in the waiting area of the Judge's chamber.

The negotiations began very hostile and negative. I sat there silently praying to God for peace, guidance and understanding. Looking at all the men and women working diligently, my emotions were engulfed with hurt, shame and even resentment that I would never again enjoy this type of work environment. I had to accept the fact because of committing a crime I would be paying for self-inflicted storm the rest of my life. My chances were one in a million that I would ever be successful employed in corporate America. Steadily looking at the people working around me made me feel defeated and rejected. I sat on the bench persistently asking the Lord, why must I continue to live in this world? The negotiations went on for hours. All the time my mind going from *the Lord is my strength and my shield; my heart trusts in Him*, Psalm 28:7 (KJV). To *my God why have you forsaken me?* Psalm 22:1 (KJV). I was in a mental whirlwind. Then the flicker of light from Jesus Christ were little acts of kindness from strangers. First, the clerk for the Judge was truly kind. He asked me several times if I was okay. He even offered me something to drink. Secondly during a break in her trial, the Judge introduced herself to me. She was extremely kind stating I looked familiar from when she was in private practice. These two acts of kindness eased my anxiety. In turn it enabled me to remain coherent instead of on the verge of losing my mind. After more than six hours of negotiations, an amicable settlement was reached. My negative thoughts were telling me, no do not agree to this settlement, because taking it to trial it will be much better for you. On the other hand, my logical thoughts told me being found guilty again by a jury would be daunting to my emotional well-being. More importantly I was at peace with my decision because of the revelation from the Holy Spirit that God instilled in my soul. This time in my life I was obedient to the Holy Spirit. I placed all my trust in the Lord to guide my path instead of doing it my way. *But if from there you will seek (inquire for and require as necessity) the Lord your God, you will find Him if you [truly] seek Him with all your heart [and mind] and soul and life. When you are in tribulation and all these things come upon you, in the latter days you will turn to the Lord your God and be obedient to His voice. For the Lord your God is a merciful God; He will not fail you or destroy you or forget the covenant of your fathers, which He swore to them*, Deuteronomy 4:29-31 (AMPC). Praise be to God my complaint against the firm was over. Astonishingly when everyone was preparing to leave, the opposing parties were courteous to me. The attorney from the firm who attended each deposition finally acknowledged me with a hand shake and a smile. Emotionally I stated to him, *I was so sorry for everything*. Further blessings from God was the opposing counsel offered helpful suggestions to the agreement that were beneficial for me. On that day spiritually and mentally I acknowledged regardless of whether it was from the first day I knew right from wrong until that moment I was *sorry* for all my known and unknown sins against others. This became and is still my sentiment to anyone I ever hurt, disappointed, misunderstood, deceived, or offended, that I am sorry and seek forgiveness. Meditating on Matthew 4:17 (AMP). *From that time Jesus began to preach and say, "Repent [change your inner self—your old way of thinking, regret past sins, live your life in a way that proves repentance; seek God's purpose for your life], for the kingdom of heaven is at hand."*

Subsequently to the settlement hearing, I returned to Gilbert to babysit my grandbabies. I often returned to Cleveland to visit Sylvia and attend special celebrations. Periodically I would return to receive mental health therapy until January 2017 when my healthcare benefits became financially unfeasible because the cost for the premium was several hundred dollars a month with an astronomical deductible amount of several thousands of dollars. My intention was to pay out of pocket for therapy until August 2017 when I would become eligible for Medicare. Gratefully the flicker of light was blessings from God. Although I would not have the level of professional mental therapy, I was blessed to have my grandsons to babysit which was a major part of my therapy. Caring for my grandsons kept my mind occupied and holding them in my arms calmed me when my stormy life caused floods of anxiety. Then I began the other suggested therapy. I began to write this book. Deciding to write this book was difficult because I wondered what help it could be to anyone when I had such a stormy life. How could I encourage anyone when I had: relentlessly tried to make an abusive marriage normal; hit rock bottom after unintentionally causing the death of my first husband; was found guilty of manslaughter; reestablished a successful life with my second husband only to once more hit rock bottom when I was abruptly incarcerated to pay my debt to society; upon being released, tried to reestablish a successful life; was unfaithful to my second husband that lead to a divorce; married my third husband who became mentally abusive; have attempted suicide numerous times; finally left my third husband for good only to be viciously betrayed; and hit rock bottom for the third time when my third husband's actions initiated my being terminated from my job. So, with all these self-inflicted and unforeseen storms in my life, how could I encourage anyone with my story? The flicker of light was the Holy Spirit encouraging me to exalt the Lord my God for the many miraculous things He had done for me in the midst of my stormy life. To tell everyone I am still standing only because of the strength of God, grace and mercy of the Lord Jesus Christ and the anointing of the Holy Spirit. Satan of course tried to discourage me by filling my mind with negative thoughts of how I had broken the majority of the Ten Commandments and was habitual a sinner. Glory be to God the flicker of light from the Holy Spirit revealed to my soul there is no condemnation for those who are in Jesus Christ. *Therefore, there is now no condemnation for those who are in Christ Jesus, because through Christ Jesus the law of the Spirit who gives life has set you free from the law of sin and death. For what the law was powerless to do because it was weakened by the flesh, God did by sending His own Son in the likeness of sinful flesh to be a sin offering. And so He condemned sin in the flesh, in order that the righteous requirement of the law might be fully met in us, who do not live according to the flesh but according to the Spirit*, Romans 8:1-4 (NIV). The Holy Spirit further reminded me once I had confessed my sins Jesus Christ had forgiven and cleansed me. *If we say that we have fellowship with him, and walk in darkness, we lie, and do not the truth: But if we walk in the light, as He is in the light, we have fellowship one with another, and the blood of Jesus Christ His Son cleanseth us from all sin. If we say that we have no sin, we deceive ourselves, and the truth is not in us. If we confess our sins, He is faithful and just to forgive us our sins, and to cleanse us from all unrighteousness. If we say that we have not sinned, we make Him a liar, and His word is not in us*, 1 John 1:6-10 (KJV). Meditating on the faithfulness and forgiveness of Jesus Christ through my stormy life I knew without a doubt the presence of the grace and mercy of God had abound. When others had not forgiven me, I knew Jesus Christ had forgiven me. Then even at times when I would confess my sins but would constantly think about them and I could not forgive myself. *For I know my transgressions, and my sin is always before me*, 51:3 (NIV). That is when the Holy Spirit thankfully intervened enabling me to pray to God to give me a pure heart and to renew, restore and sustain me. *Create in me a pure heart, O God, and renew a steadfast spirit within me. Do not cast me from your presence or take your Holy Spirit from me. Restore to me the joy of your salvation and grant me a willing spirit, to sustain me. Then I will teach transgressors your ways, so that sinners will turn back to you*, Psalm 51:10-13 (NIV). This is one of the many verses that sustained me for three years of writing this book to bear witness of what God could do and had done for me and could do for others. All the time Jesus Christ patiently kept hold of me waiting to help me. *"For I the Lord your God keep hold of your right hand; [I am the Lord], Who says to you, 'Do not fear, I will help* you", Isaiah 41:13 (AMP).

Throughout the tribulations of my stormy life the favor of God was present. The love of God enabled me to love Tim even after knowing I was conceived by him raping Momma and abandoning me. The power of God enabled me to endure molestation and rape as well as overcome being promiscuous and an adulterer without contracting any sexual diseases. By the grace of Jesus Christ, I survived physical and mental domestic violence. The forgiveness of God gave me the ability to accept causing the death of Herman and aborting my unborn baby. The mercy of God kept me alive after many attempts of suicide. While incarcerated my Lord and Savior blessed me to be assigned a job of teaching other inmates. Upon being released from prison Christ Jesus enabled me to reestablish a successful life for many years. With faith in God I was able to withstand the betrayal by Jerome that precipitated the termination of my employment. It was the goodness of my Lord God that my mental breakdown set in motion the mental health treatment necessary for my emotional stability. Then the blessings of God from being ostracized by the firm resulted my ability to care for my grandbabies and write this book. Overwhelmed with appreciation for all the blessing bestowed upon me from my Lord and Savior Jesus Christ, I graciously yield to the Holy Spirit inspiring me to write this book. A testament of how my ordinary life filled with many heartbreaking storms that God constantly gave me flickers of light to encourage me to be strong and steadfast until the storms subsided.

Nearing the end of this book, knowing all the favor in my life, I cannot be untrue by saying I wake up to a marvelously beautiful filled day with nothing but hallelujahs and praise the Lord. Some days and sometimes each second of the day is a struggle to keep my sanity. At times I feel extremely guilty for many things that happened in my life, particularly the death of Herman and the unborn baby boy, as well as the emotional and physical damage to my daughters, especially how Ivy has suffered as of result of the death of her father. As mentioned before, following my termination from the firm, I believed my forehead should have been engraved with all my sins to prevent me from any further hurt and rejection from others. Since branding my forehead was unrealistic, writing this book would allow everyone to know my transparent life story. By being transparent about the many horrendous storms in my life that resulted in several permanent emotional scars to not only me but others, this book will allow people to judge and decide if they should continue to be or become a part of my life.

Even after coming to the end of this book where I have revealed to the world the permanent emotional scars from my stormy life, I am still haunted by many insecurities and *why* questions. Why did my daughters had to suffer? Why Herman died instead of me? Why my marriages did not work? Why I did not die after many suicidal attempts? Why I lost my job after two decades of dedication? The difference is before writing the book and now that I have completed it, I am learning daily to depend more on the flickers of light from God to get me through each second of the day. I also now often recall what the Holy Spirit imparted to me that my stormy life was similar at times to the children of Israel wondering in the wilderness for years. This is because when I was disobedient it caused me to needlessly wonder in the wildness for a period of time before realizing the actual favor God had upon my life. During those times, I could not see the flickers of light God was bestowing upon me. In addition, the Holy Spirit imparted into my soul to accept the forgiveness from my Lord and Savior Jesus Christ. In receiving forgiveness, the Holy Spirit revealed to me how I must forgive those that have negatively affected my life.

Yes, my stormy life resulted in many permanent emotional scars. Throughout many of those storms I doubted, had disbelief, and questioned if God loved me. It took that most recent major storm of my life of betrayal, termination, and mental breakdown to truly recognize the many flickers of light from Jesus Christ. Praise be to God, He never left me alone. Jesus Christ had always been there knocking on the door of my heart. *Behold, I stand at the door, and knock: if any man hear my voice, and open the door, I will come in to him, and will sup with him, and he with me*, Revelation 3:20 (KJV). I now know that until God calls me to my final resting place, I will have other heavy storms with emotional scarring to endure. The difference now is I know through any storm in my life to look for a flicker of light knowing Jesus Christ will keep me in His perfect peace. *Peace I leave with you; My [perfect] peace I give to you; not as the world gives do I give to you. Do not let your heart be troubled, nor let it be afraid. [Let My perfect peace calm you in every circumstance and give you courage and strength for every challenge.]*, John 14:27 (AMP). Because God is my hope and strength for tomorrow. *For You are my hope; O Lord God, You are my trust and the source of my confidence from my youth. Upon You have I relied and been sustained from my birth; You are He who took me from my mother's womb and You have been my benefactor from that day. My praise is continually of You. I am as a wonder to many, For You are my strong refuge. My mouth is filled with Your praise And with Your glory all day long,* Psalm 71:5-8 (AMP).

Conclusion

Many years before my termination from the firm, the Holy Spirit had encouraged me to be a witness to others by sharing the grace, mercy, and forgiveness from God I received in the midst of my stormy life. Instead of working with organizations that helped people with many of the storms of my life or writing a book, I chose to help others by serving in churches; aiding and supporting those in need and less fortune than me; speaking words of inspiration to the disheartened; and sharing with some people how the Lord blessed me during certain times of my stormy life. However, I procrastinated in yielding to the Holy Spirit to bear witness to the world how God had brought me through my entire stormy life. Many days I would think about contacting organizations that assisted victims of domestic violence and rape victims, as well as writing a book. Unfortunately, I never did act on these compulsions. I heard and felt God knocking on my door waiting for me to answer, *[God] stand[s] at the door and knock*, Revelation 3:20 (KJV). Still I refused to listen. Afraid that some people would consider me too immoral instead of being a blessed person. Then came the unexpected termination from the firm initiating another awful life changing storm. Finally, I yielded totally to the will of God. With Chapter 116 (AMP) of Psalm, with emphasis on verses 12-14 *What will I give to the Lord [in return] For all His benefits toward me? [How can I repay Him for His precious blessings?] I will lift up the cup of salvation And call on the name of the Lord. I will pay my vows to the Lord, Yes, in the presence of all*

His people. Shortly thereafter I received further confirmation of what the Holy Spirit had been inspiring me to do for years when my legal and medical professionals, strangers, family members and friends were encouraging me to write this book. It was time for me to be obedient.

As I began to write this book revealing to the world the most intimate situations of my life, negative thoughts attacked my mind. Had I waited too long to write the book. My life had hit rock bottom again with the termination from my job. How could my life story now still be inspiring? At sixty years old, I was no longer successfully employed. There was no way anyone would see my story as inspiring. Then the flicker of light through the Holy Spirit was knowing that the Lord was my light, salvation encouragement. I leaned on Psalm Chapter 27 (AMP) to strengthen me. Focusing on verses 1 and 14. *The Lord is my light and my salvation—Whom shall I fear? The Lord is the refuge and fortress of my life—Whom shall I dread?....Wait on the Lord: be of good courage, and He shall strengthen thine heart.* Only by the spiritual intervention of God was I able to begin writing this book. Without inspiration from God it would have been impossible for me to reveal to the world my stormy life.

Another concern was how often people only remember the negative aspects of your life while forgetting the many positives. Gratefully, the Holy Spirit revealed everyone would not accept or approve of the book. God lead me to Mark 6:11 (NIV) *if a place will not welcome you or listen to you, leave that place.* There were other prevalent concerns. Would there be any negative effects for my daughters and grandsons. Would people be forgiving or unforgiving towards me? Who no longer would associate with me? Would I be regarded as a horrible person guilty of so many sins? I had to consider the potential for unforeseen negative consequences. Taking each of my concerns to heart, I put all my trust and faith in God and with guidance from the Holy Spirit, I stepped out with complete faith in Jesus Christ, fully relying on God to guide me through all aspects of not only publishing this book, but with my entire life. Because there is no doubt in my mind that unless God is in control of my life it will be unbearable for me. I now sing *I've Learned How to Lean and Depend on Jesus* by Isaac Haney when negative doubt attacks my mind.

My prayer is this book will be an encouragement for those who have faced storms in their lives whether lighter or heavier than I experienced. That each person that reads it will hopefully use it as a learning tool to help prevent or navigate through their stormy life. That it will encourage people to not only depend on their spiritualty for strength, but mental health treatment from specific non-profit organizations or mental health facilities. Finally, and most importantly that through trials and tribulations, to know you will know that your spiritual ideology will always give flickers of light. Each flicker, no matter how tiny, will give hope to make it from second to second until the next breakthrough of sunshine.

Please note that even with the mercy and grace of God directing my life, storms still come. There are days were I still only make it second by second. Nonetheless, praise be to God for the amazing glory that I am able weather the storms. Utilizing the constant renewing of my mind with the anointing of the Holy Spirit, I am able to make it through the day. There are nights when I go to sleep praying to enter my eternal sleep. Then miraculously the light of the new day cracks through the blinds of my window. I then say, good morning Jesus thank you for giving me another day of life. Yes, many days I still hurt to the core of my soul resulting in my heart crying out. Then a flicker of light calms my soul. I even continue to privately suppress within my soul the heavy storms of my life that causes inner turmoil. Yet the peace of God renews my strength, as I sing praises to His name. My insecurities bring back the thoughts that guilty should be engraved on my forehead. Then I realize once this book is published, no longer will I have to hide in darkness.

In closing, know even being in the never-ending love, salvation, mercy, and grace of Jesus Christ, we will constantly be confronted with some type of adversity. The glory and peace are knowing how to equip our minds, hearts, bodies, and souls to endure and survive the storms. To endure I plan to constantly rejoice in our true Redeemer. Be patient in tribulations. Pray without ceasing. Study the word of God. For Roman 12:12 (NKJV) says, *Rejoicing in hope, patient in tribulation, continuing steadfastly in prayer.* Followed by remembering what God has already done, I attest to Lamentations Chapter 3 (ESV). Imbedding in my mind verses 21-25, *Remember my affliction and my wanderings, the wormwood and the gall! My soul continually remembers it and is bowed down within me. But this I call to mind, and therefore I have hope: The steadfast love of the Lord never ceases; his mercies never come to an end; they are new every morning; great is your faithfulness. "The Lord is my portion," says my soul, "therefore I will hope in him." The Lord is good to those who wait for him, to the soul who seeks him.* Together with singing that renowned song *My Hope Is Built on Nothing Less Than Jesus' Blood and Righteousness* written by Edward Mote, I wait on the Lord. Confident that no matter the intensity of my storms, they are bearable through our Lord and Savior Jesus Christ. Forever witnessing to everyone, *I can do all things through Christ who strengths me*, Philippians 4:13 (NKJV).